THE WALLFLOWER

YAMATONADESHIKO SHICHIHENGE

5

Tomoko Hayakawa

TRANSLATED AND ADAPTED BY
David Ury

LETTERED BY
Dana Hayward

DEL REY

BALLANTINE BOOKS • NEW YORK

The Wallflower 5 is a work of fiction. Names, characters, places, and incidents are the products of the author's imagination or are used fictitiously. Any resemblance to actual events, locales, or persons, living or dead, is entirely coincidental.

2005 Del Rey® Trade Paperback Edition

Published in the United States by Del Rey® Books, an imprint of Random House Publishing Group, a division of Random House Inc., New York.

Del Rey is a registered trademark and the Del Rey colophon is a trademark of Random House, Inc.

Originally published in Japan in 2002 by Kodansha Ltd., Tokyo as *Yamatonadeshiko Shichihenge*. This publication—rights arranged through Kodansha Ltd.

Library of Congress Control Number: 2004095918

ISBN 0-345-48094-5

Printed in the United States of America

www.delreymanga.com

9 8 7 6 5 4 3 2 1

First Edition

Translator and adapter—David Ury

Lettering—Dana Hayward

Cover design—David Stevenson

Contents

A Note from the Author

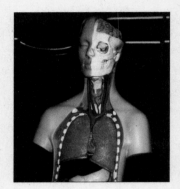

AKIRA-
KUN...

...IN THE
FLESH
♥

♥ I'm really happy because I'm surrounded by such fantastic people. Human kindness truly is wonderful. I'm gonna quit complaining and really start hanging in there. From now on, my new motto is "be nice to people." I love you all! ♥

—Tomoko Hayakawa

THE **wallflower**
YAMATONADESHIKO SHICHIHENGE

ヤマトナデシコ七変化♡

CONTENTS

Once upon a time,
there was a very
scary little girl.

The girl's mother
sent her to visit her
sick grandmother.

Bonus Story...
Sunako Goes to Grandma's

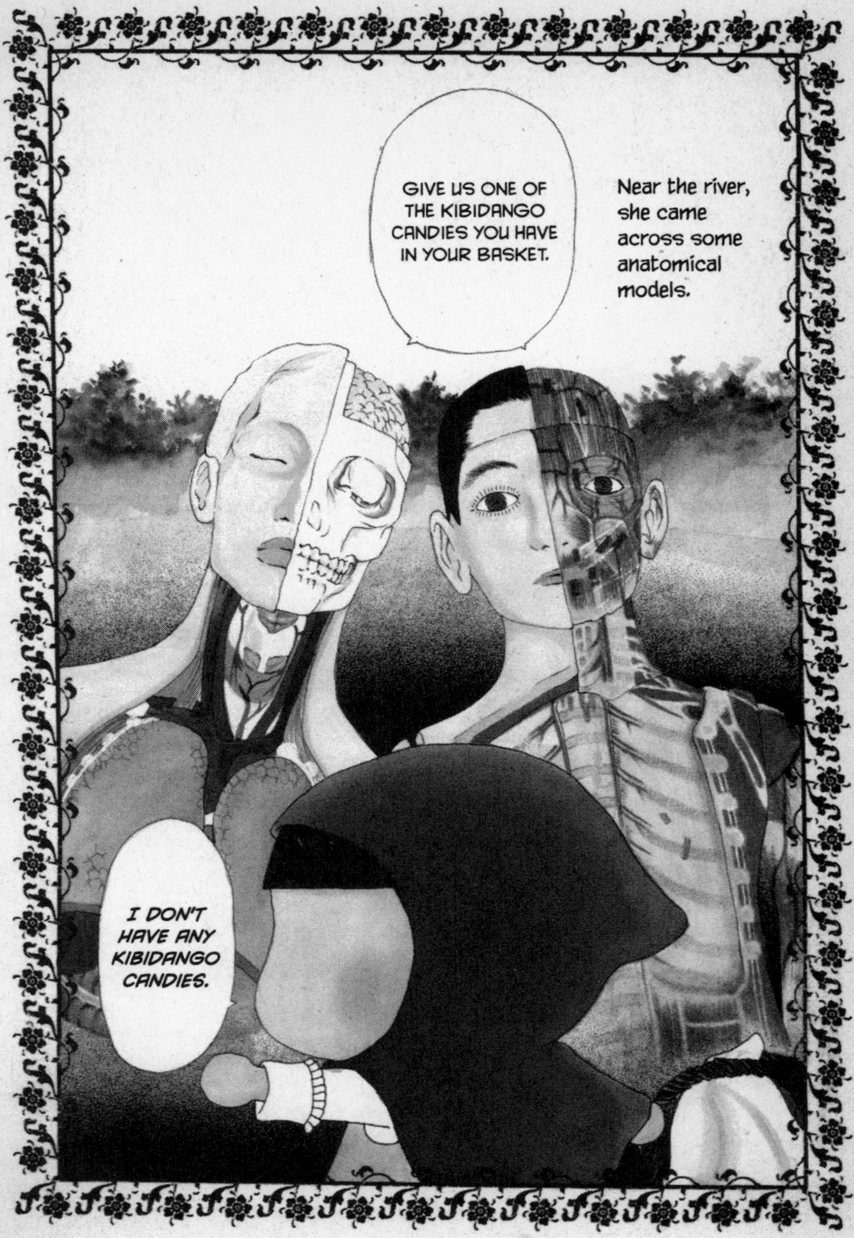
Near the river, she came across some anatomical models.
GIVE US ONE OF THE KIBIDANGO CANDIES YOU HAVE IN YOUR BASKET.
I DON'T HAVE ANY KIBIDANGO CANDIES.

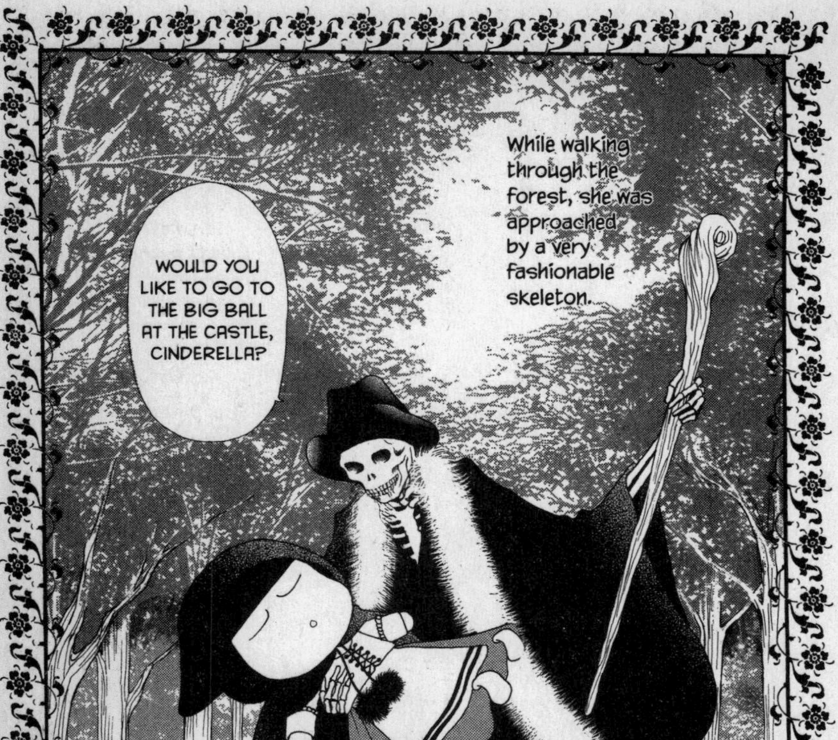
While walking through the forest, she was approached by a very fashionable skeleton.
WOULD YOU LIKE TO GO TO THE BIG BALL AT THE CASTLE, CINDERELLA?
NO FREAKING WAY.

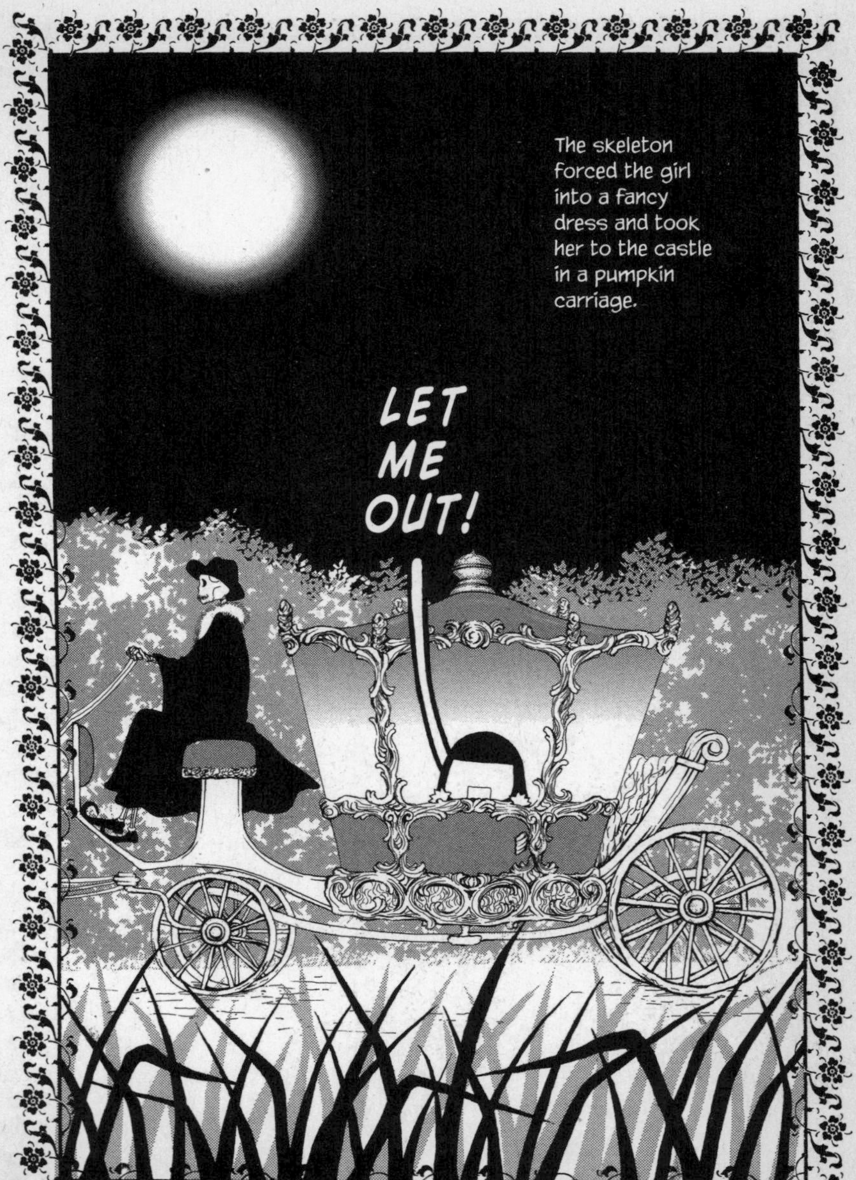
The skeleton forced the girl into a fancy dress and took her to the castle in a pumpkin carriage.
LET ME OUT!

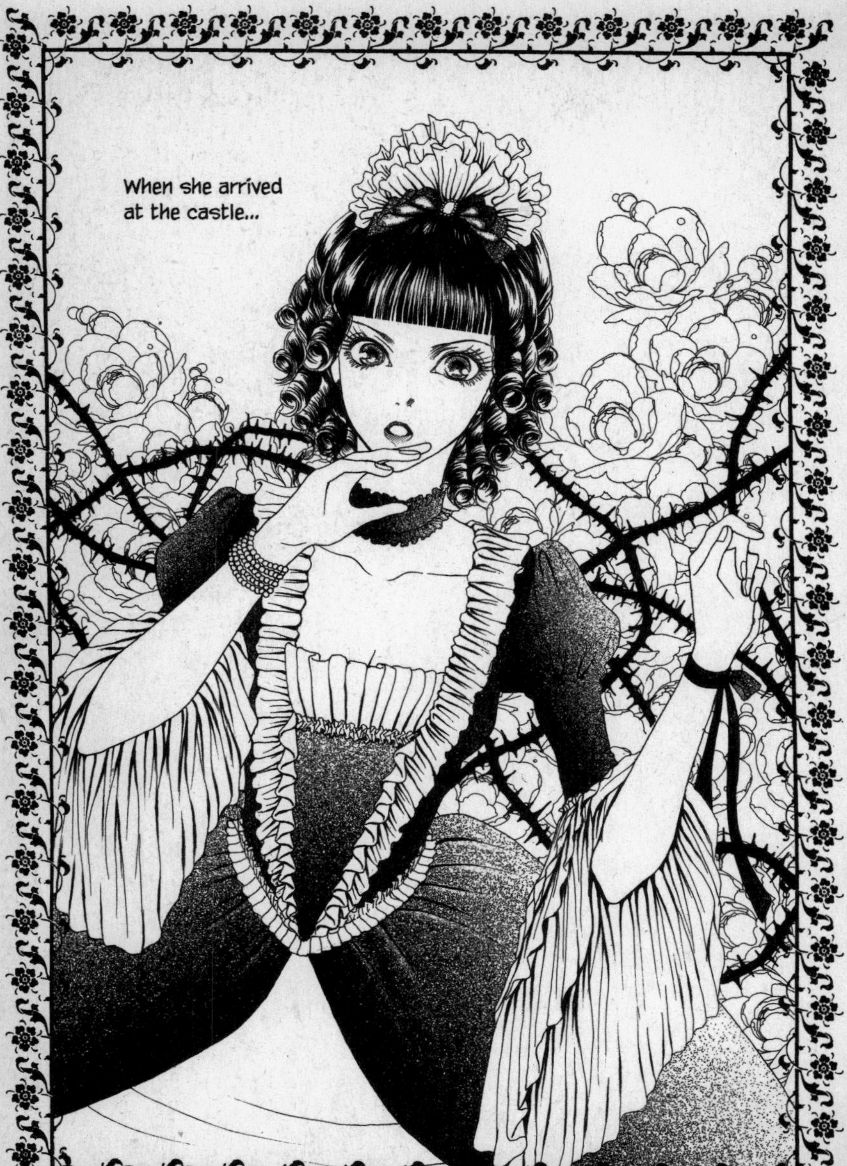
When she arrived at the castle...

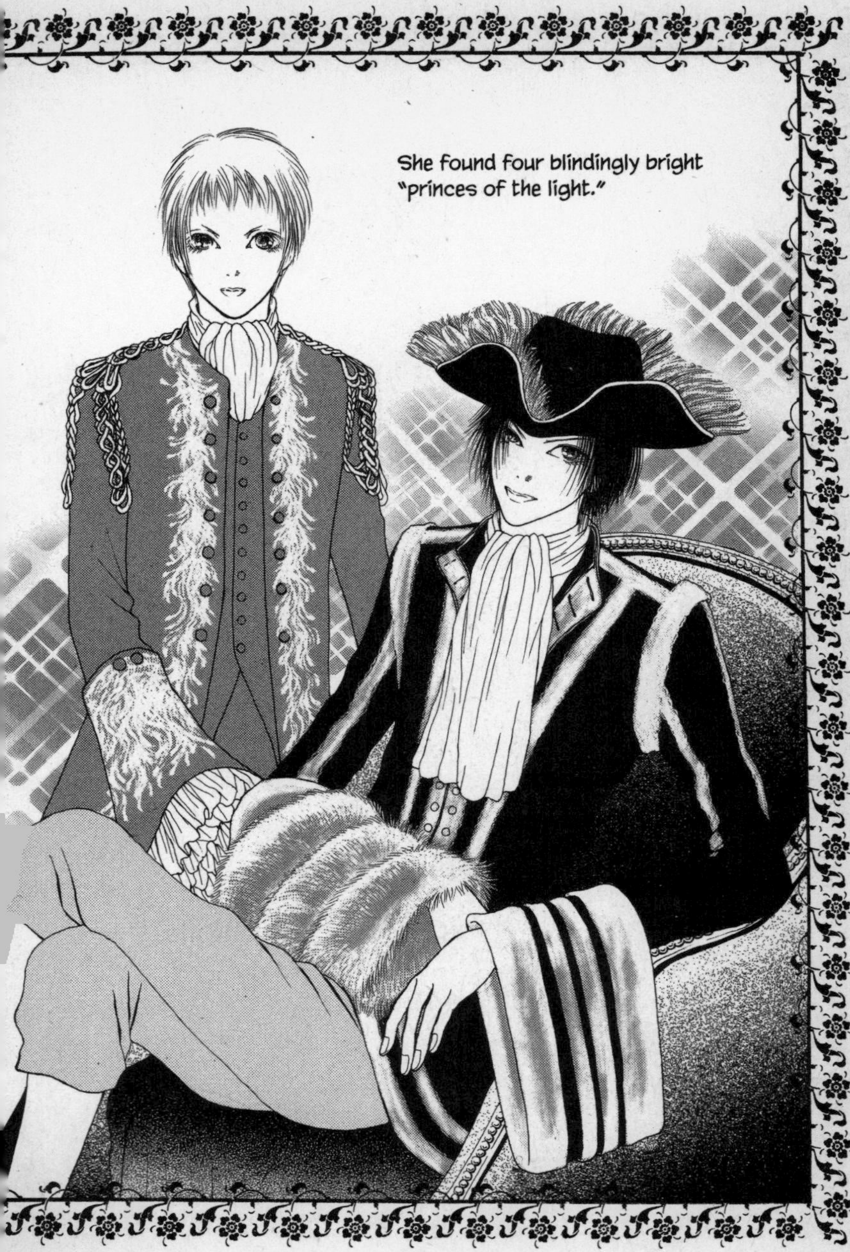
She found four blindingly bright "princes of the light."

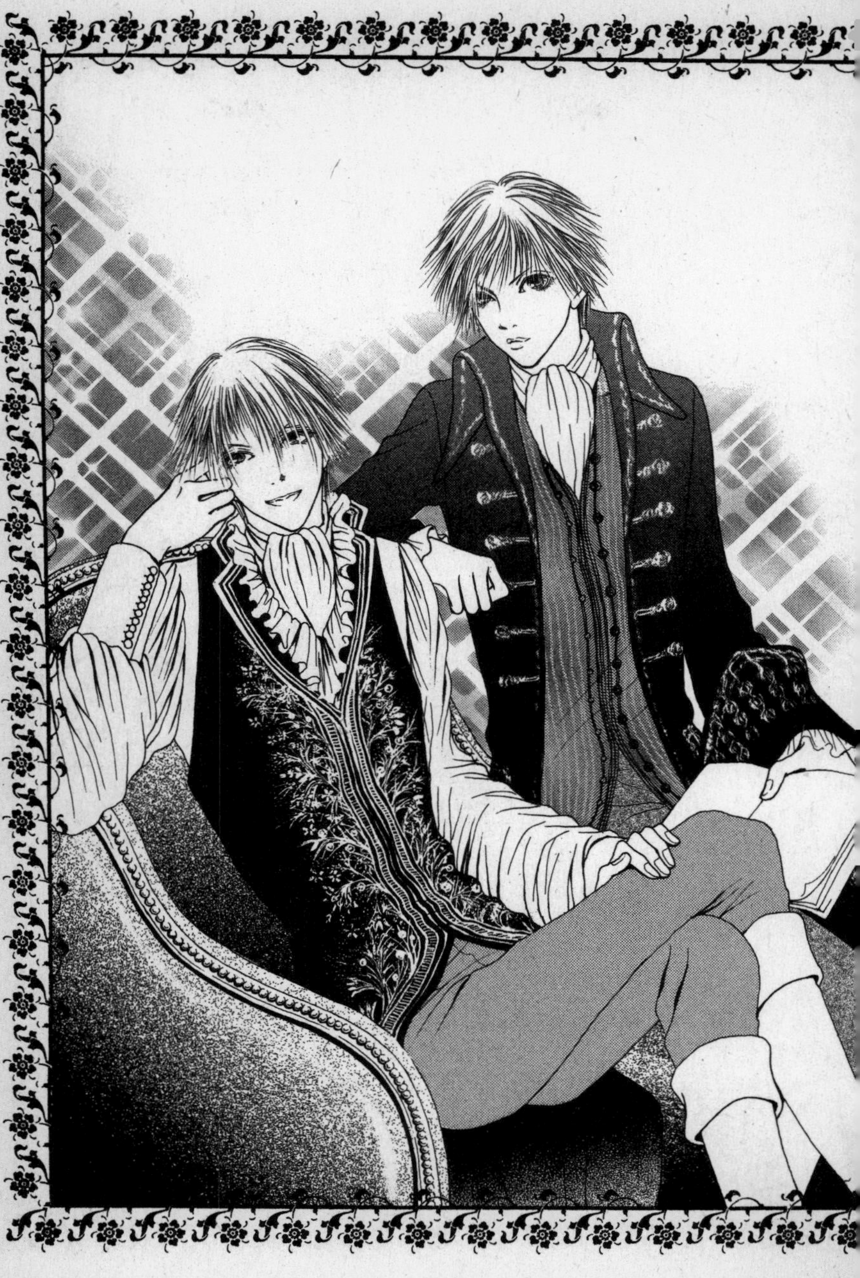

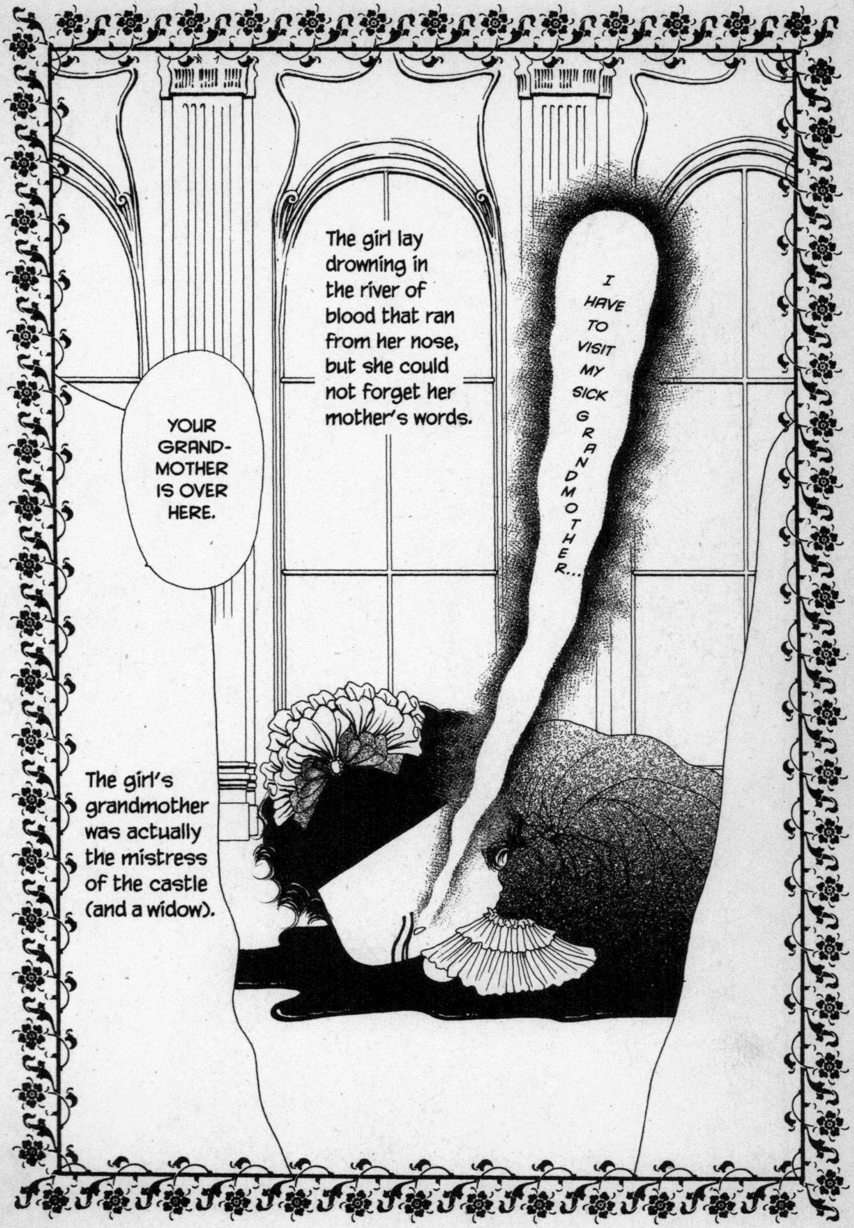
I HAVE TO VISIT MY SICK GRANDMOTHER...
The girl lay drowning in the river of blood that ran from her nose, but she could not forget her mother's words.
YOUR GRANDMOTHER IS OVER HERE.
The girl's grandmother was actually the mistress of the castle (and a widow).

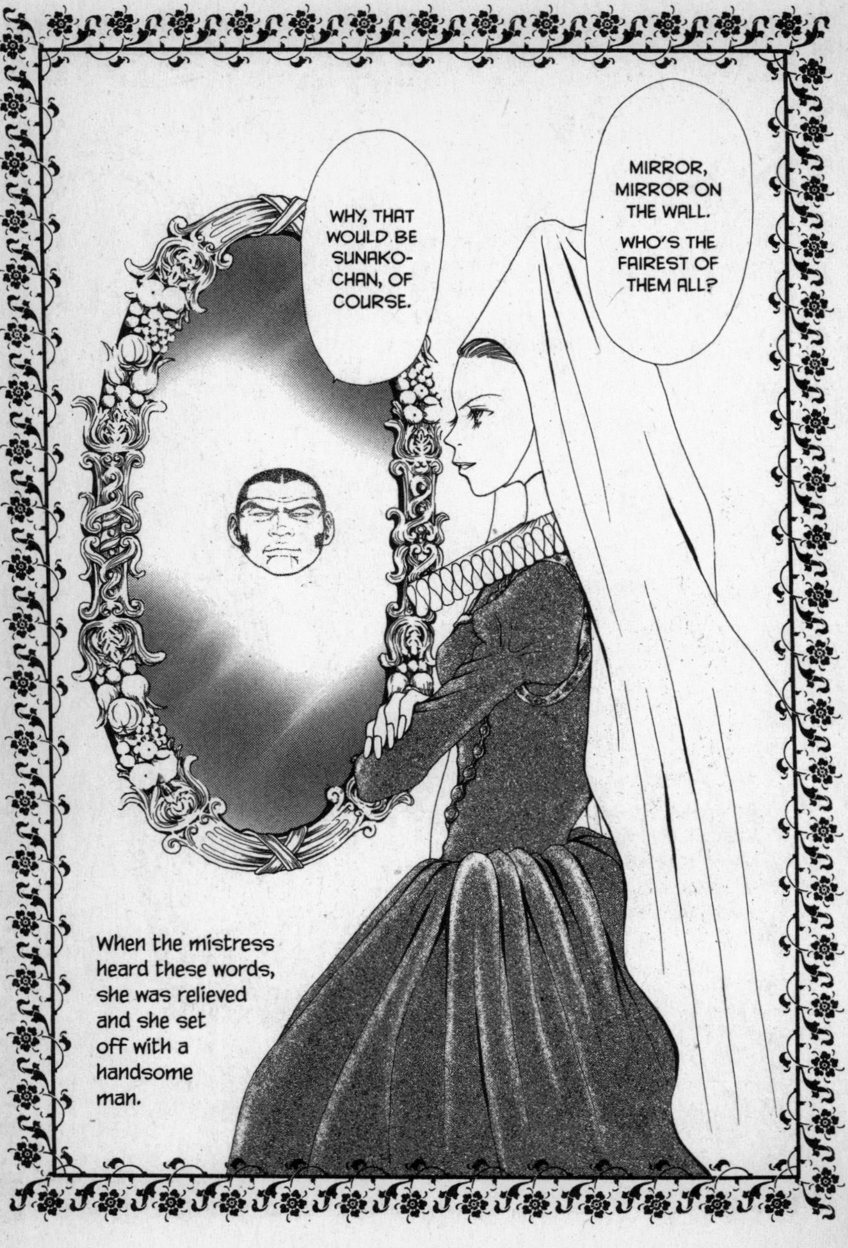
MIRROR, MIRROR ON THE WALL. WHO'S THE FAIREST OF THEM ALL?
WHY, THAT WOULD BE SUNAKO-CHAN, OF COURSE.
When the mistress heard these words, she was relieved and she set off with a handsome man.

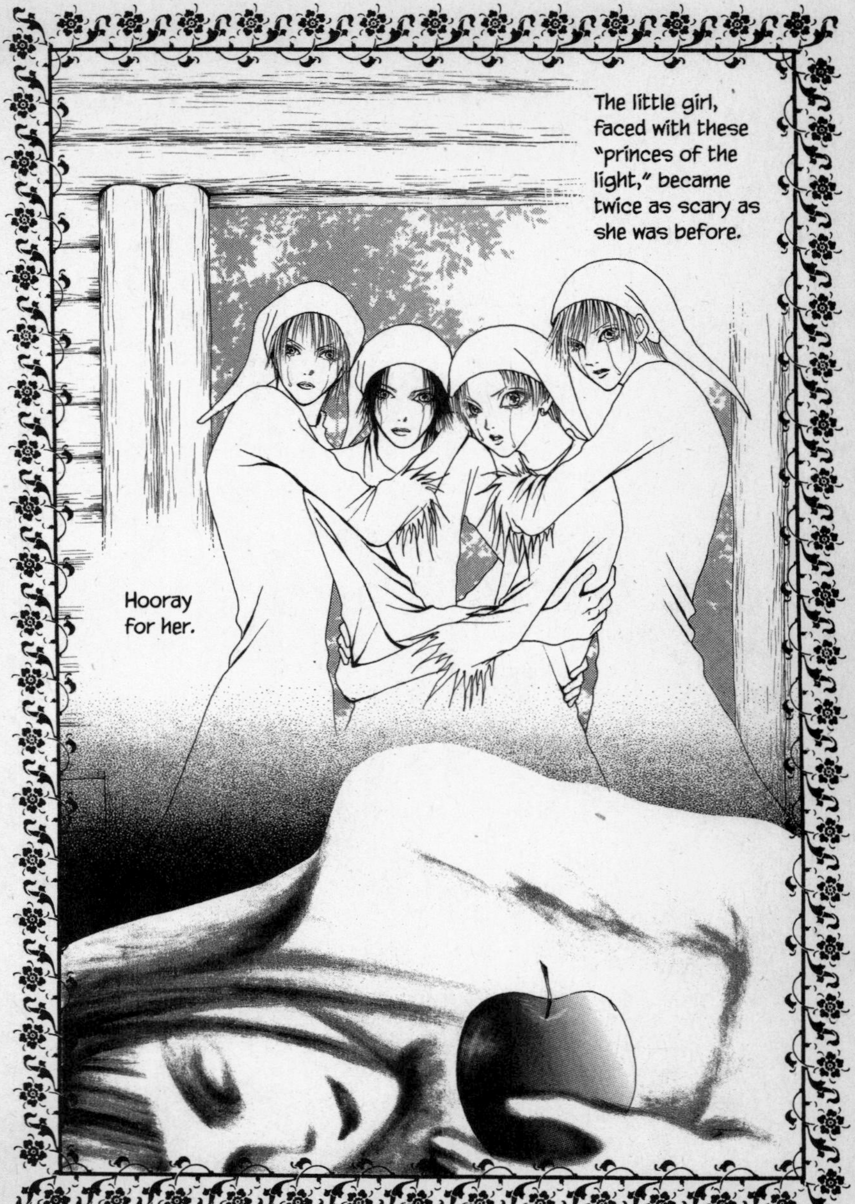
The little girl, faced with these "princes of the light," became twice as scary as she was before.
Hooray for her.

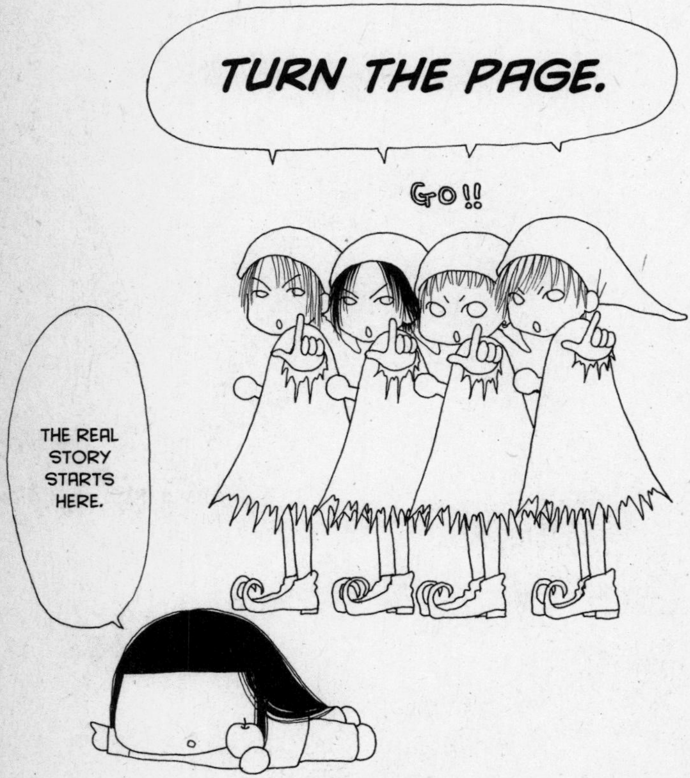
TURN THE PAGE.
GO!!
THE REAL STORY STARTS HERE.

Wallflower's Beautiful Cast of Characters (?)

SUNAKO IS A DARK LONER WHO LOVES HORROR MOVIES. WHEN HER AUNT, THE LANDLADY OF A BOARDING HOUSE, LEAVES TOWN WITH HER BOYFRIEND, SUNAKO IS FORCED TO LIVE WITH FOUR HANDSOME GUYS. SUNAKO'S AUNT MAKES A DEAL WITH THE BOYS, WHICH CAUSES NOTHING BUT HEADACHES FOR SUNAKO. "MAKE SUNAKO INTO A LADY, AND YOU CAN LIVE RENT-FREE." SUNAKO IS HAPPIEST WHEN SHE'S IN HER ROOM, SURROUNDED BY HER "BEST FRIENDS" (SOME ANATOMICAL MODELS AND A HUMAN SKULL). "PLEASE JUST LEAVE ME ALONE."

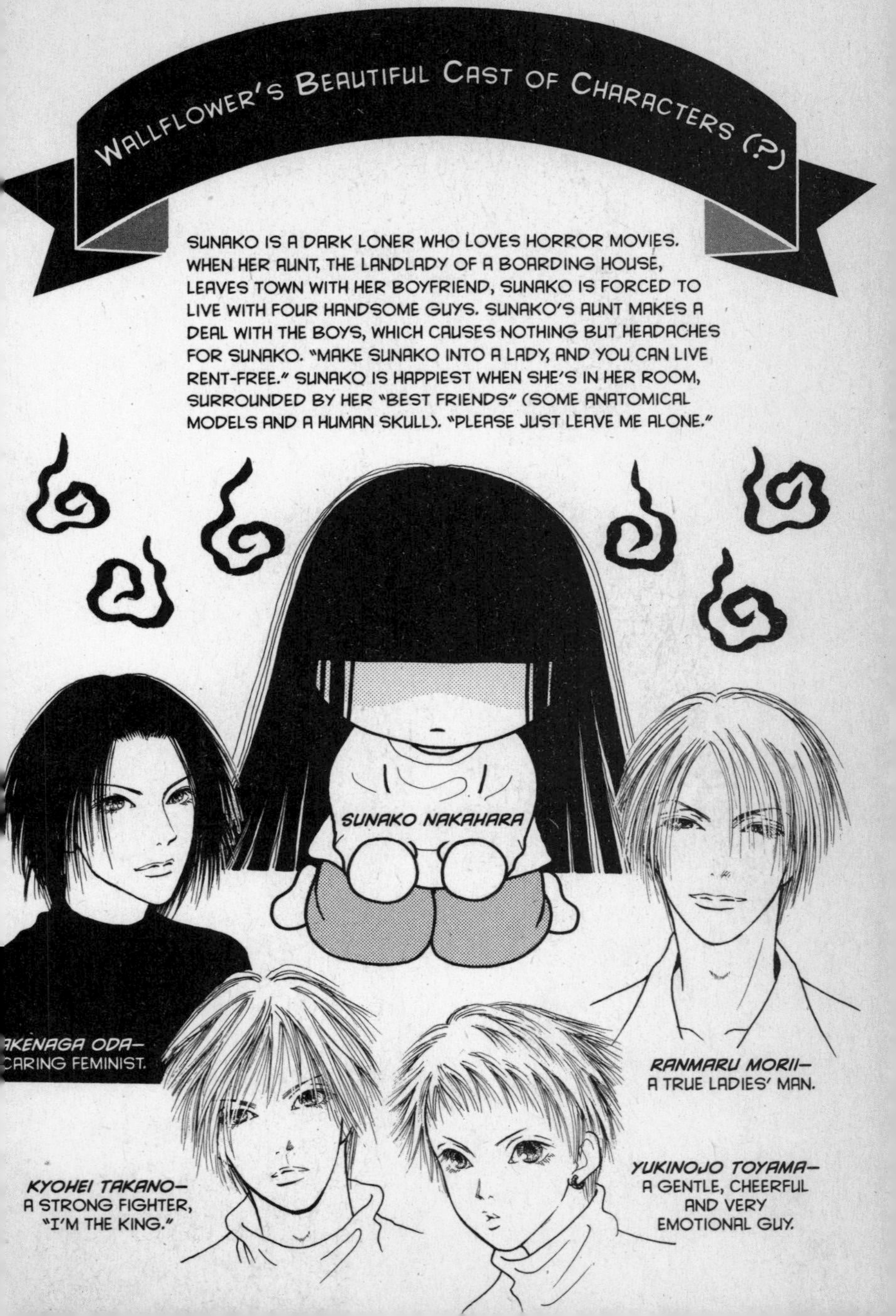
SUNAKO NAKAHARA
RANMARU MORII—
A TRUE LADIES' MAN.
AKENAGA ODA—
CARING FEMINIST.
YUKINOJO TOYAMA—
A GENTLE, CHEERFUL
AND VERY
EMOTIONAL GUY.
KYOHEI TAKANO—
A STRONG FIGHTER,
"I'M THE KING."

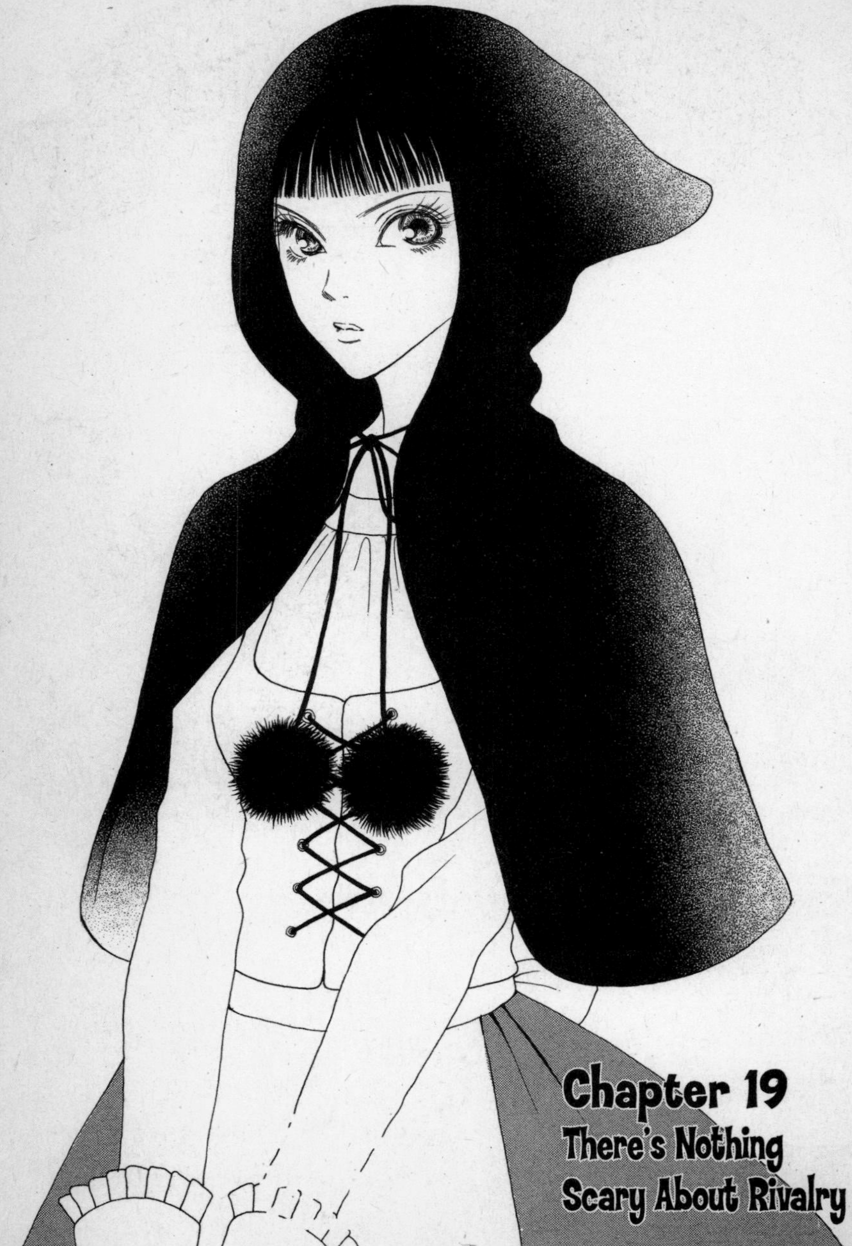

Chapter 19

There's Nothing Scary About Rivalry

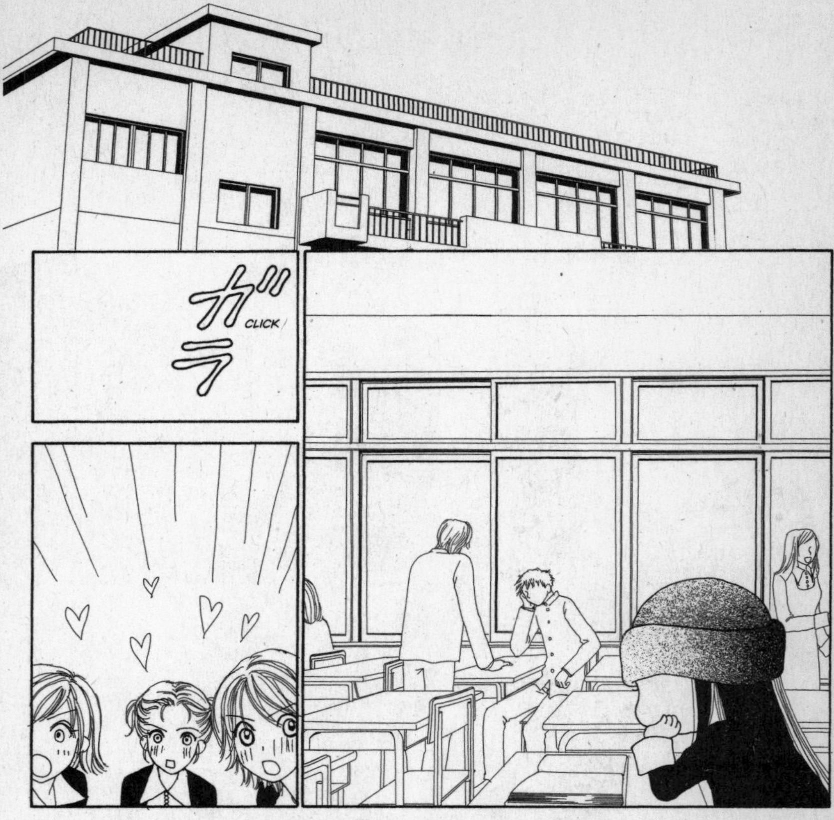
ガラ
CLICK!

BEHIND THE SCENES

WHEN THIS STORY FIRST CAME OUT IN THE MAGAZINE, IT APPEARED AS A TWO-PART STORY. IT WAS A RUTHLESS SCHEDULE.

AS ALWAYS, I GOT A LOT OF HELP FROM THE OTHER *BEKKAN FRIEND* MANGA ARTISTS. ♥ SHO HIROSE-SAMA AND AYUAYU WATANABE ... THANK YOU SO MUCH. ♥ ALSO THANKS TO IYU KOZAKURA AND AKIRA YUUKI-SAN. ♥

I WROTE ABOUT THIS WHEN THE COMIC ORIGINALLY APPEARED TOO, BUT... I LOVE "LOLITA"-STYLE GIRLS. BONNETS AND RIBBONS ARE SO CUTE. WHENEVER I SEE A CUTE LOLITA GIRL, I CAN'T HELP BUT STARE, EVEN THOUGH I KNOW IT'S RUDE.

I LOVE GOTH GIRLS AND GOTH LOLITA GIRLS TOO. ♥

WHILE I WAS WORKING ON THIS, I GOT SO STRESSED OUT I THOUGHT MY HEAD WOULD EXPLODE. SO I WENT TO A "MEET THE BAND" EVENT THAT THE INDIE BAND BAROKKU PUT ON... ♥

WHAT THE HELL ARE YOU DOING? AREN'T YOU A LITTLE TOO OLD FOR THAT?

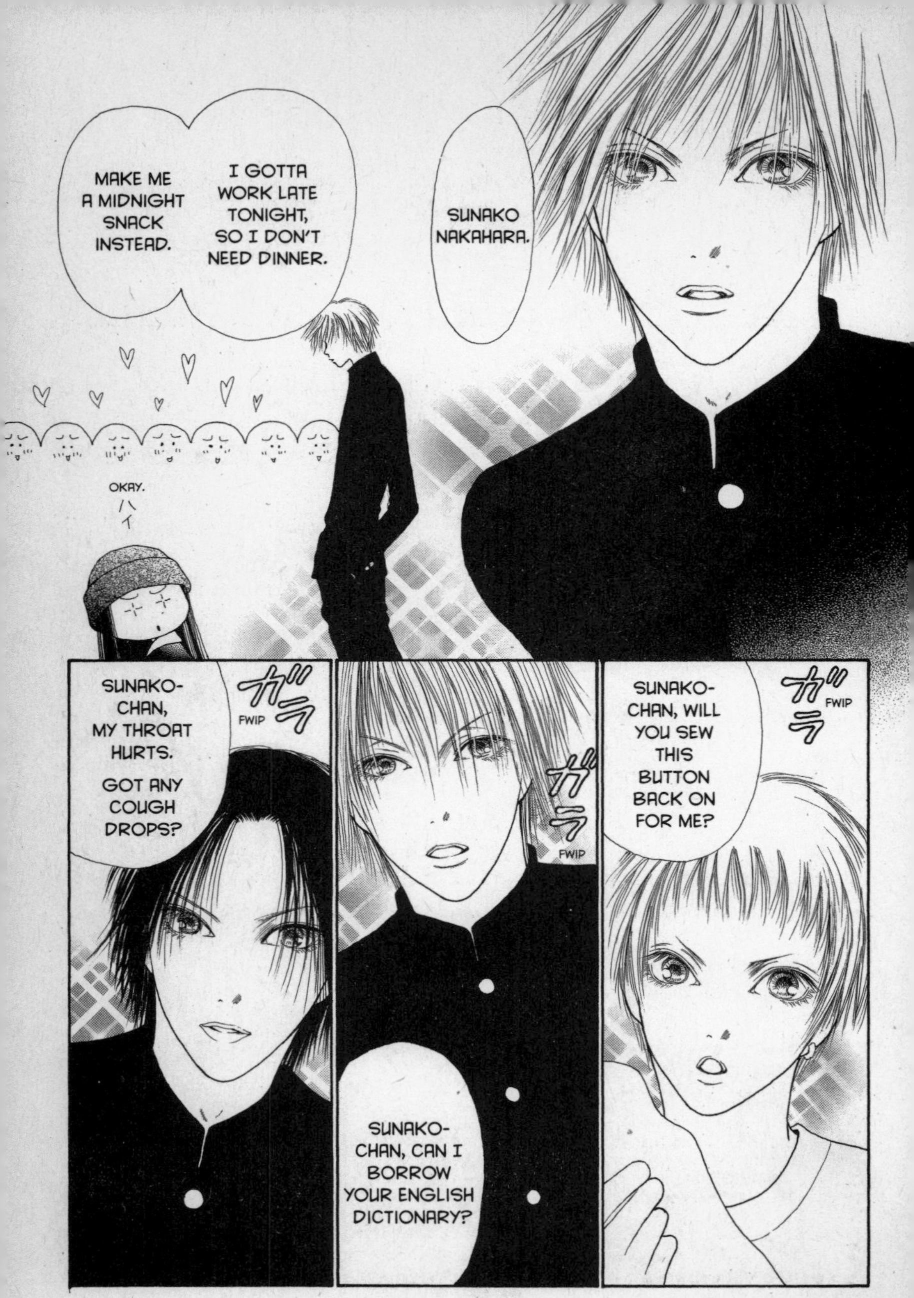
SUNAKO NAKAHARA.
I GOTTA WORK LATE TONIGHT, SO I DON'T NEED DINNER.
MAKE ME A MIDNIGHT SNACK INSTEAD.
OKAY.
ハイ
ガラ
FWIP
SUNAKO-CHAN, WILL YOU SEW THIS BUTTON BACK ON FOR ME?
ガラ
FWIP
SUNAKO-CHAN, CAN I BORROW YOUR ENGLISH DICTIONARY?
ガラ
FWIP
SUNAKO-CHAN, MY THROAT HURTS.
GOT ANY COUGH DROPS?

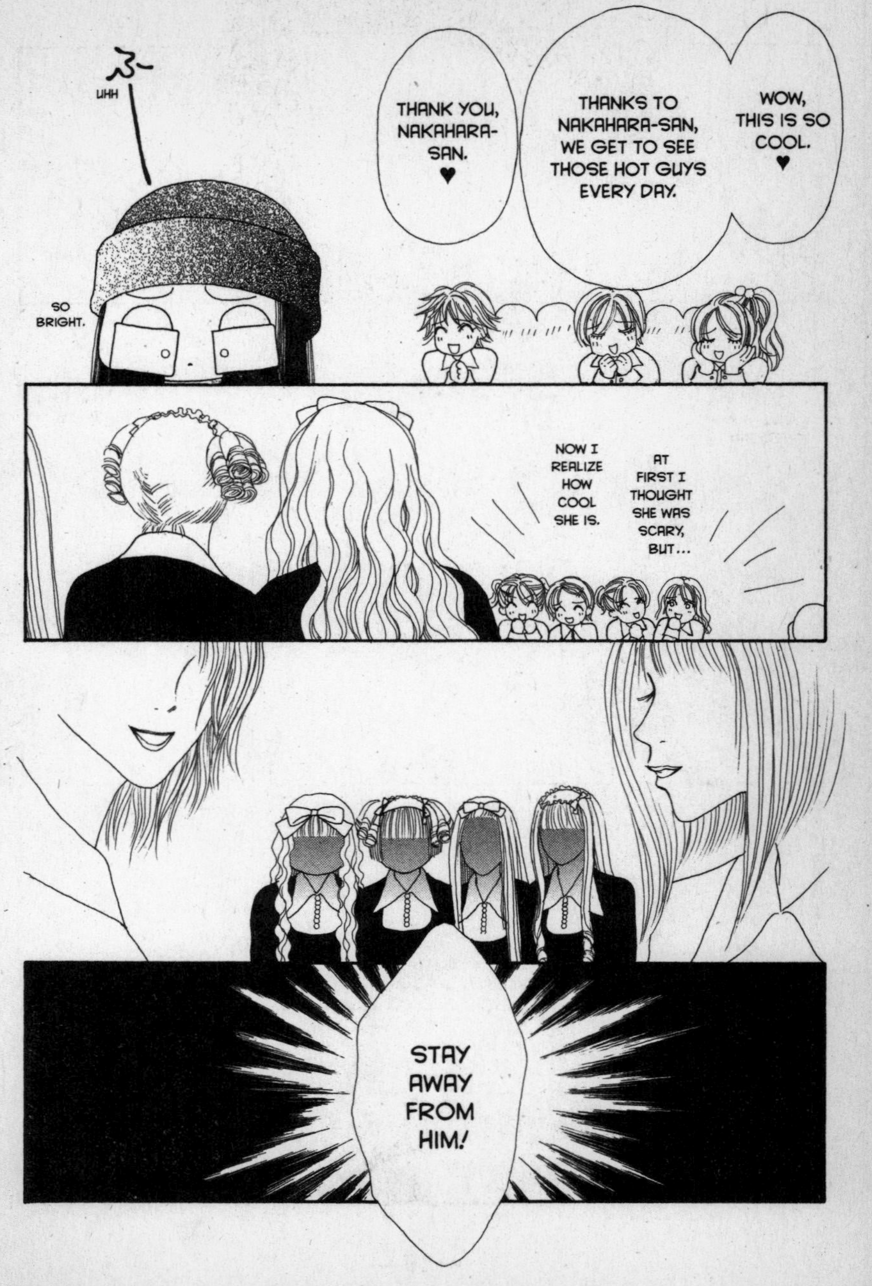

WOW, THIS IS SO COOL. ♥
THANKS TO NAKAHARA-SAN, WE GET TO SEE THOSE HOT GUYS EVERY DAY.
THANK YOU, NAKAHARA-SAN. ♥
ふー
UHH
SO BRIGHT.
AT FIRST I THOUGHT SHE WAS SCARY, BUT...
NOW I REALIZE HOW COOL SHE IS.
STAY AWAY FROM HIM!

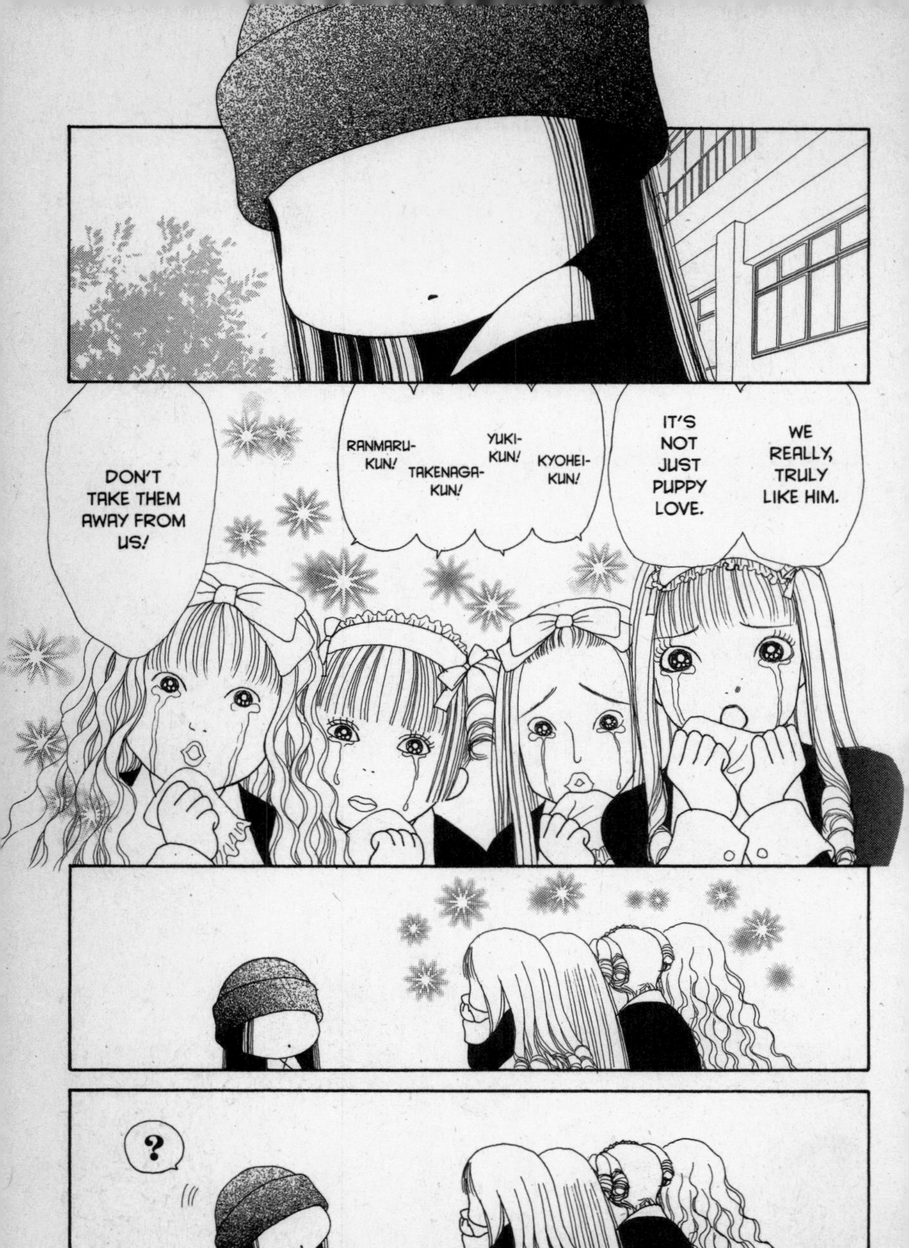
WE REALLY, TRULY LIKE HIM.
IT'S NOT JUST PUPPY LOVE.
KYOHEI-KUN!
YUKI-KUN!
TAKENAGA-KUN!
RANMARU-KUN!
DON'T TAKE THEM AWAY FROM US!
?

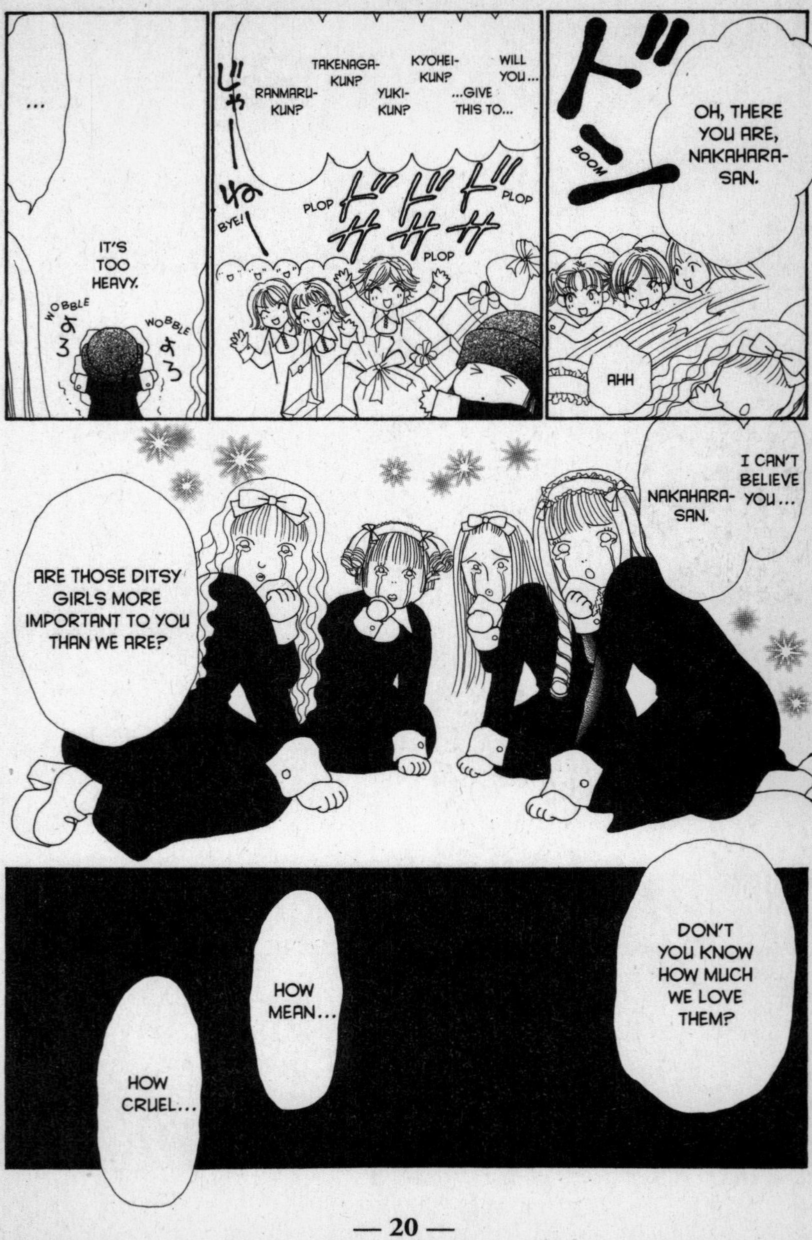

ドーン
BOOM
OH, THERE YOU ARE, NAKAHARA-SAN.
AHH
WILL YOU...
...GIVE THIS TO...
KYOHEI-KUN?
YUKI-KUN?
TAKENAGA-KUN?
RANMARU-KUN?
じゃーね
BYE!
PLOP
ドドド
ザザザ
PLOP
PLOP
...
IT'S TOO HEAVY.
WOBBLE
よろ
WOBBLE
よろ
I CAN'T BELIEVE YOU...
NAKAHARA-SAN.
ARE THOSE DITSY GIRLS MORE IMPORTANT TO YOU THAN WE ARE?
DON'T YOU KNOW HOW MUCH WE LOVE THEM?
HOW MEAN...
HOW CRUEL...

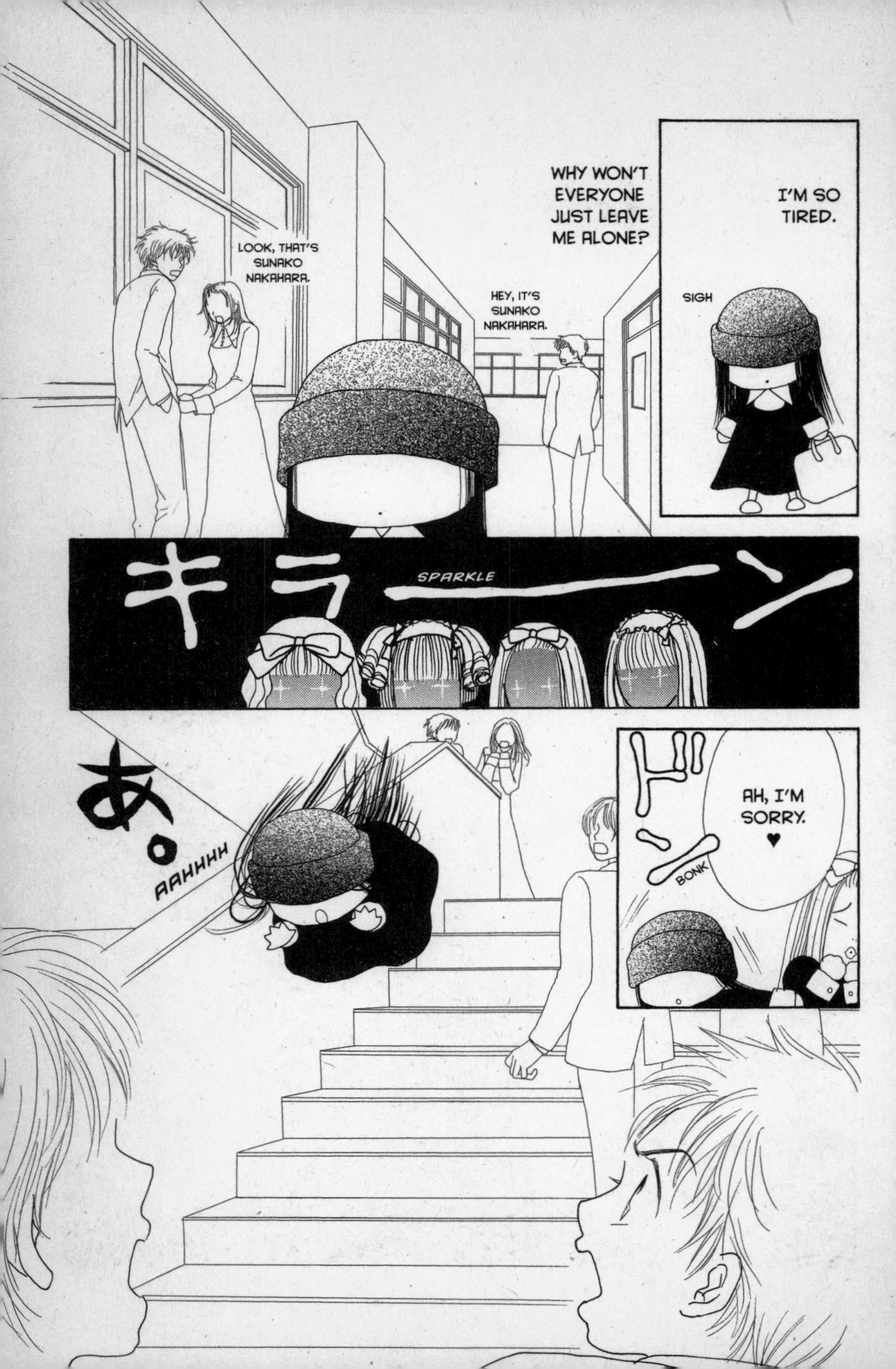
I'M SO TIRED.
SIGH
WHY WON'T EVERYONE JUST LEAVE ME ALONE?
HEY, IT'S SUNAKO NAKAHARA.
LOOK, THAT'S SUNAKO NAKAHARA.
キラーン
SPARKLE
ドン
BONK
AH, I'M SORRY. ♥
あ。
AAHHHH

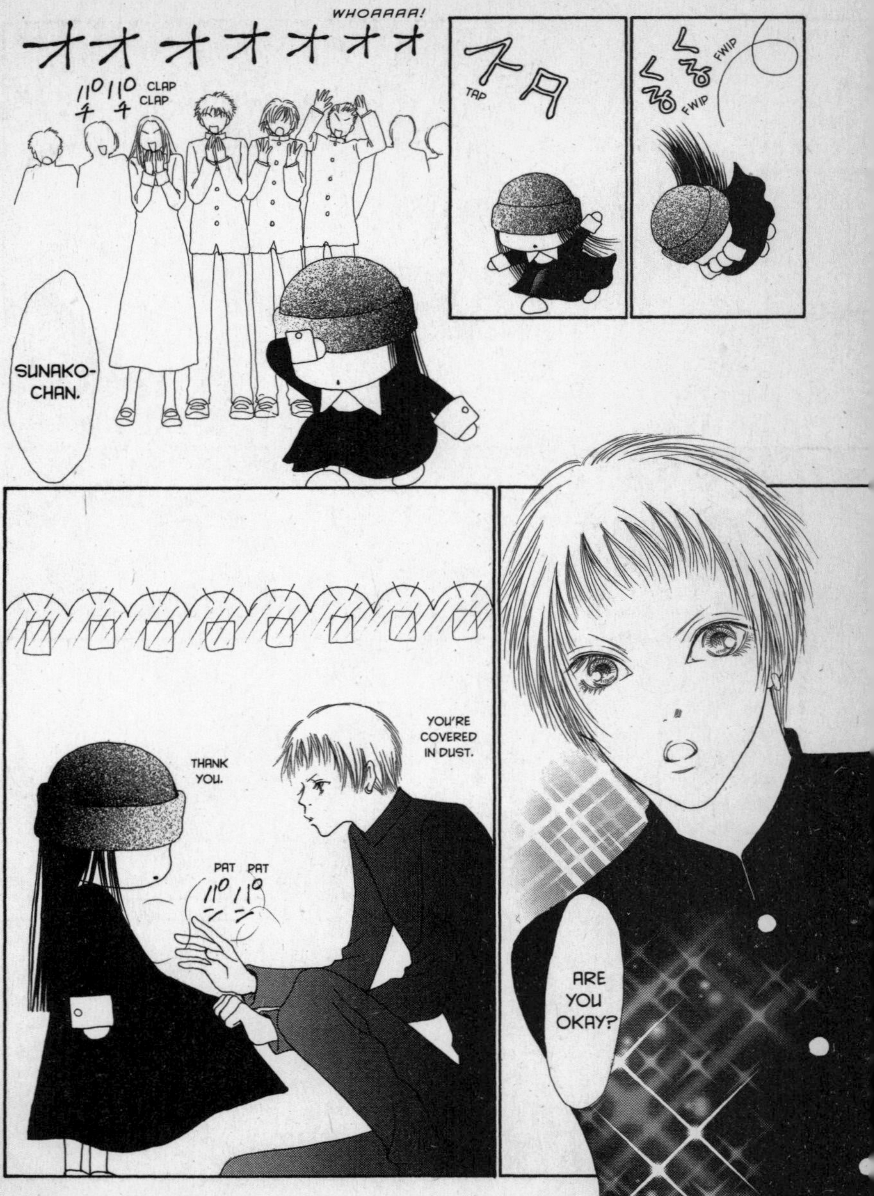
くるくる
FWIP
FWIP
スタ
TAP
オオオオオオオ
WHOAAAAA!
パチパチ
CLAP CLAP
SUNAKO-CHAN.
ARE YOU OKAY?
YOU'RE COVERED IN DUST.
THANK YOU.
パパ
PAT PAT

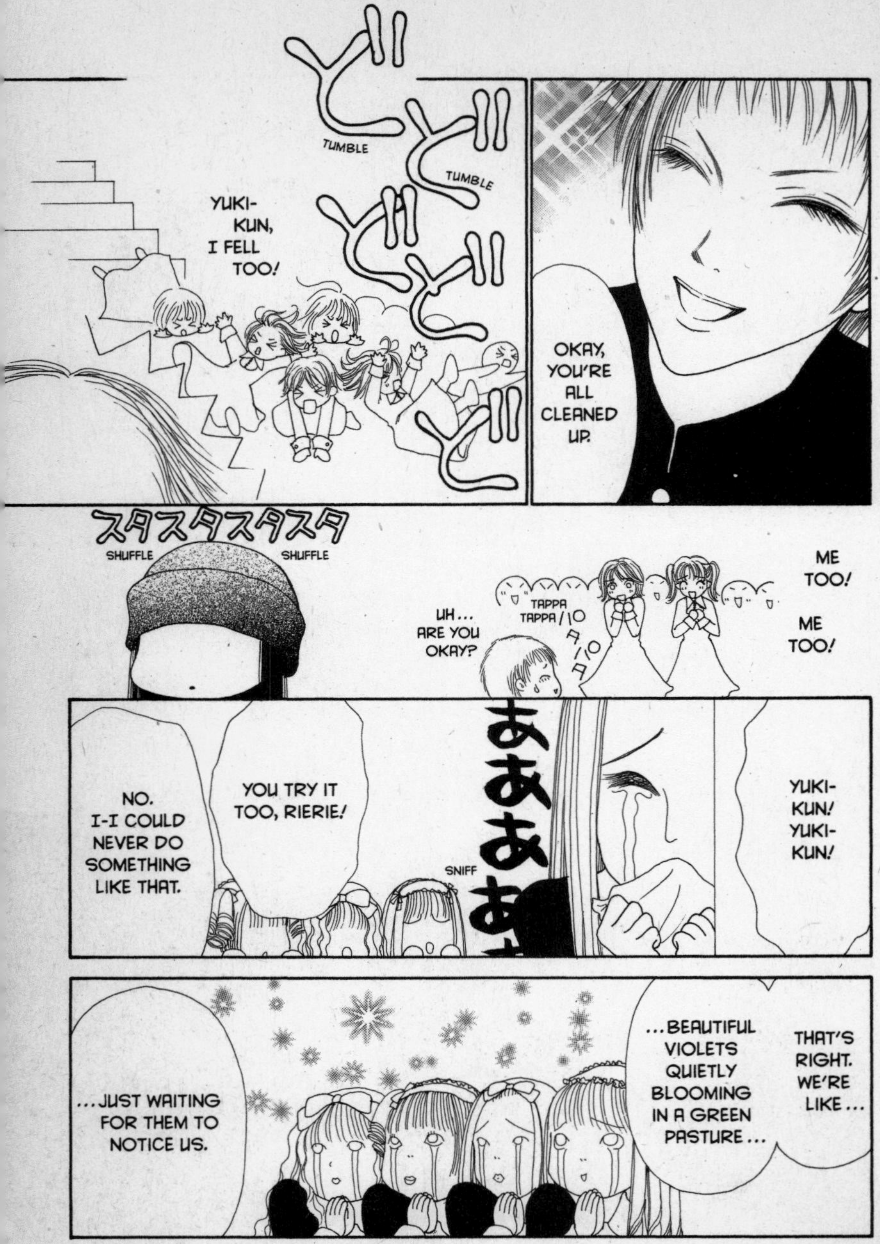
OKAY, YOU'RE ALL CLEANED UP.
どどどどど
TUMBLE
TUMBLE
YUKI-KUN, I FELL TOO!
ME TOO!
ME TOO!
パタパタ
TAPPA TAPPA
UH... ARE YOU OKAY?
スタスタスタスタ
SHUFFLE
SHUFFLE
YUKI-KUN! YUKI-KUN!
あああ
SNIFF
YOU TRY IT TOO, RIERIE!
NO. I-I COULD NEVER DO SOMETHING LIKE THAT.
THAT'S RIGHT. WE'RE LIKE...
...BEAUTIFUL VIOLETS QUIETLY BLOOMING IN A GREEN PASTURE...
...JUST WAITING FOR THEM TO NOTICE US.

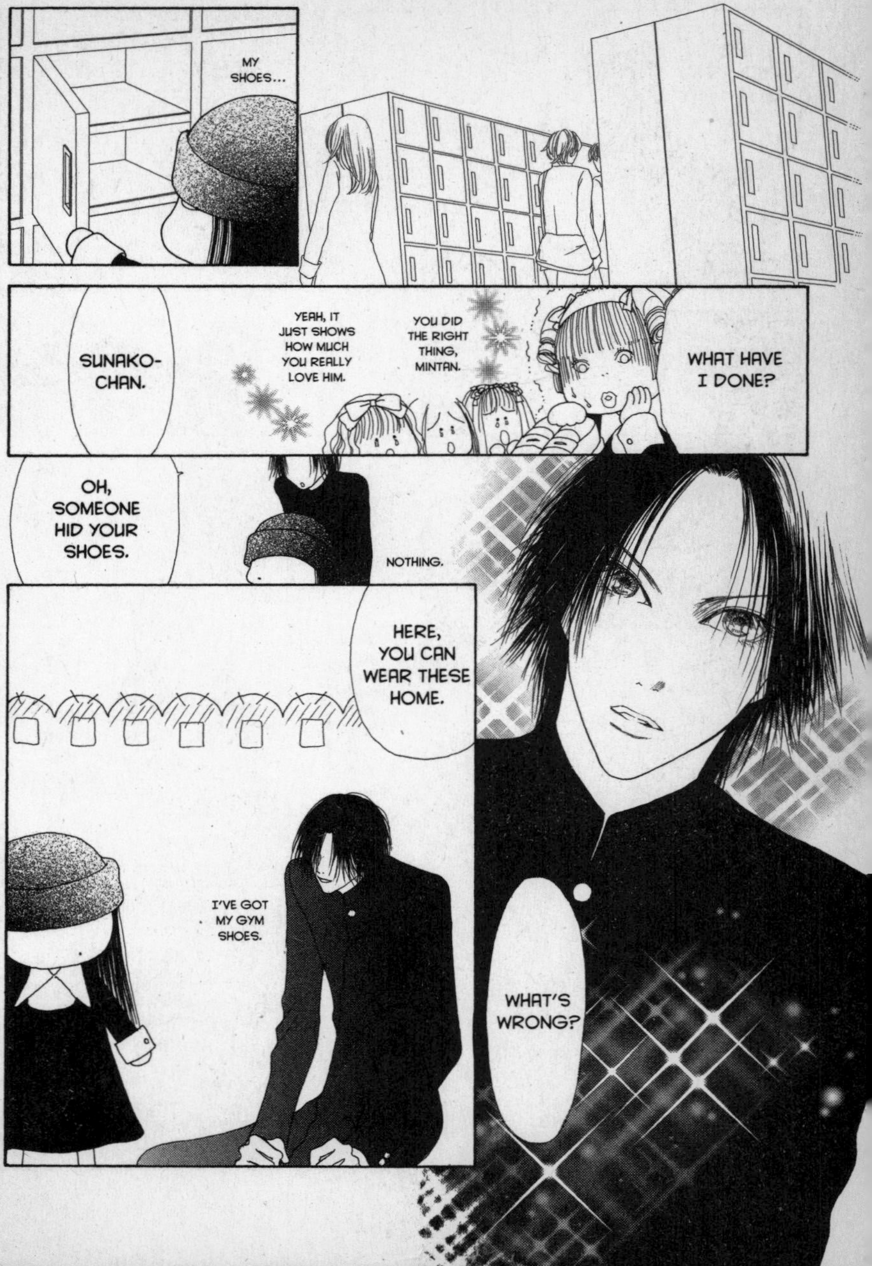
MY SHOES...
WHAT HAVE I DONE?
YOU DID THE RIGHT THING, MINTAN.
YEAH, IT JUST SHOWS HOW MUCH YOU REALLY LOVE HIM.
SUNAKO-CHAN.
WHAT'S WRONG?
NOTHING.
OH, SOMEONE HID YOUR SHOES.
HERE, YOU CAN WEAR THESE HOME.
I'VE GOT MY GYM SHOES.

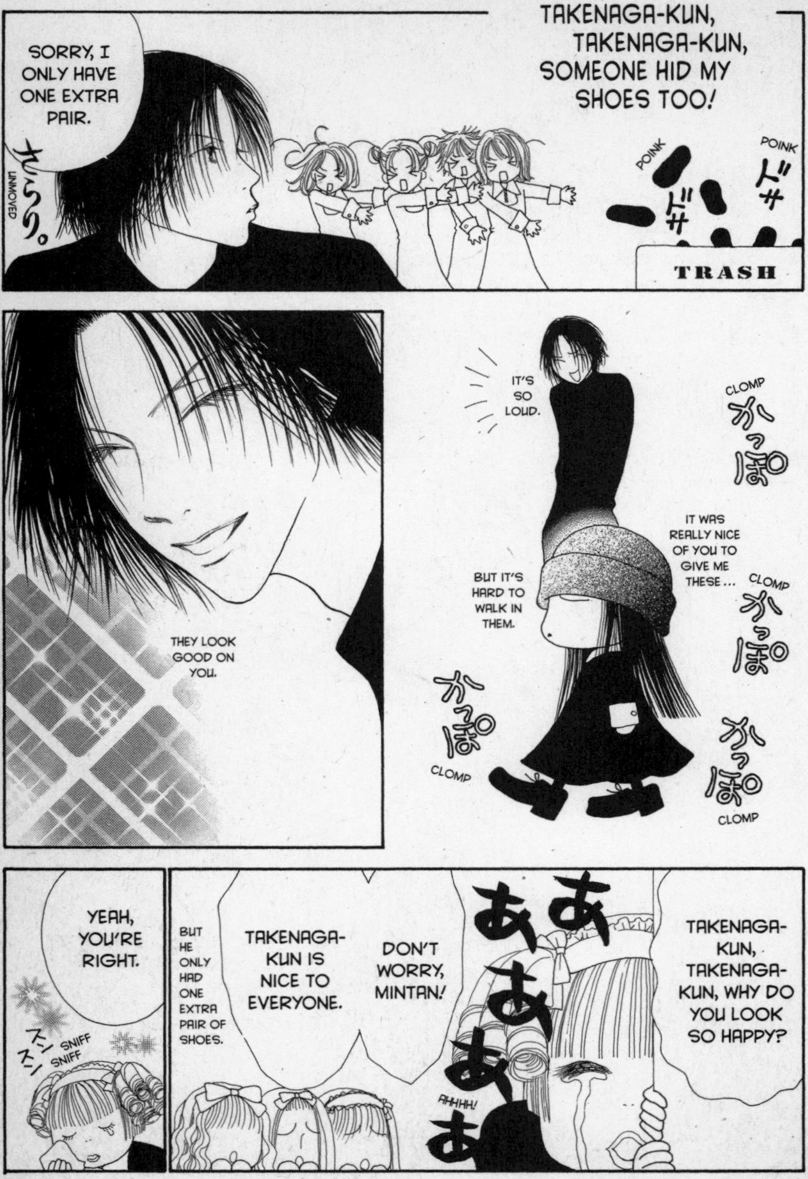

TAKENAGA-KUN, TAKENAGA-KUN, SOMEONE HID MY SHOES TOO!
POINK
POINK
TRASH
SORRY, I ONLY HAVE ONE EXTRA PAIR.
UNMOVED
IT'S SO LOUD.
CLOMP
IT WAS REALLY NICE OF YOU TO GIVE ME THESE...
CLOMP
CLOMP
BUT IT'S HARD TO WALK IN THEM.
CLOMP
THEY LOOK GOOD ON YOU.
TAKENAGA-KUN, TAKENAGA-KUN, WHY DO YOU LOOK SO HAPPY?
AHHHH!
DON'T WORRY, MINTAN!
TAKENAGA-KUN IS NICE TO EVERYONE.
BUT HE ONLY HAD ONE EXTRA PAIR OF SHOES.
YEAH, YOU'RE RIGHT.
SNIFF
SNIFF

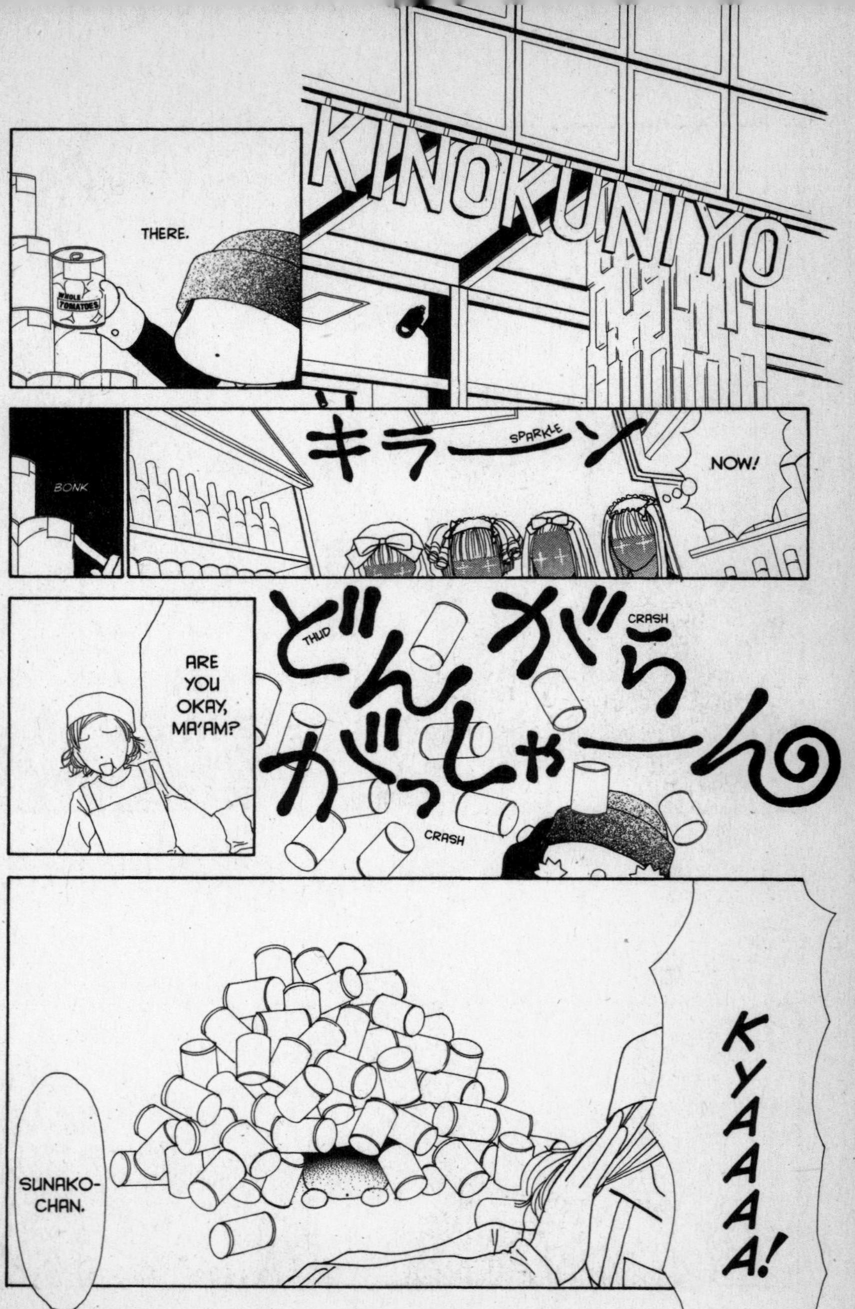
KINOKUNIYO
THERE.
WHOLE TOMATOES
キラーン
SPARKLE
NOW!
BONK
どんがらがっしゃーん
THUD
CRASH
CRASH
ARE YOU OKAY, MA'AM?
KYAAAAA!
SUNAKO-CHAN.

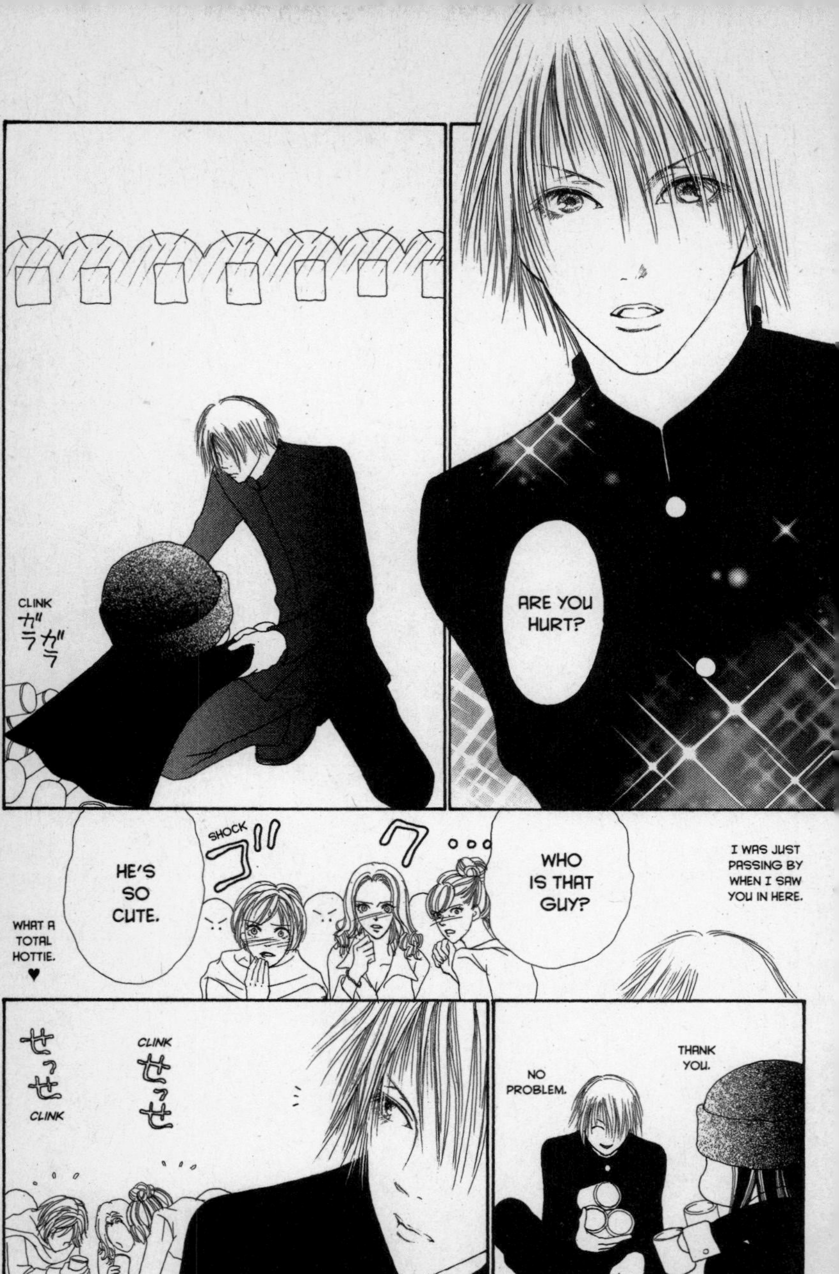
ARE YOU HURT?
CLINK
ガラガラ
I WAS JUST PASSING BY WHEN I SAW YOU IN HERE.
WHO IS THAT GUY?
...
SHOCK
ゴク
HE'S SO CUTE.
WHAT A TOTAL HOTTIE. ♥
THANK YOU.
NO PROBLEM.
CLINK
せっせ
せっせ
CLINK

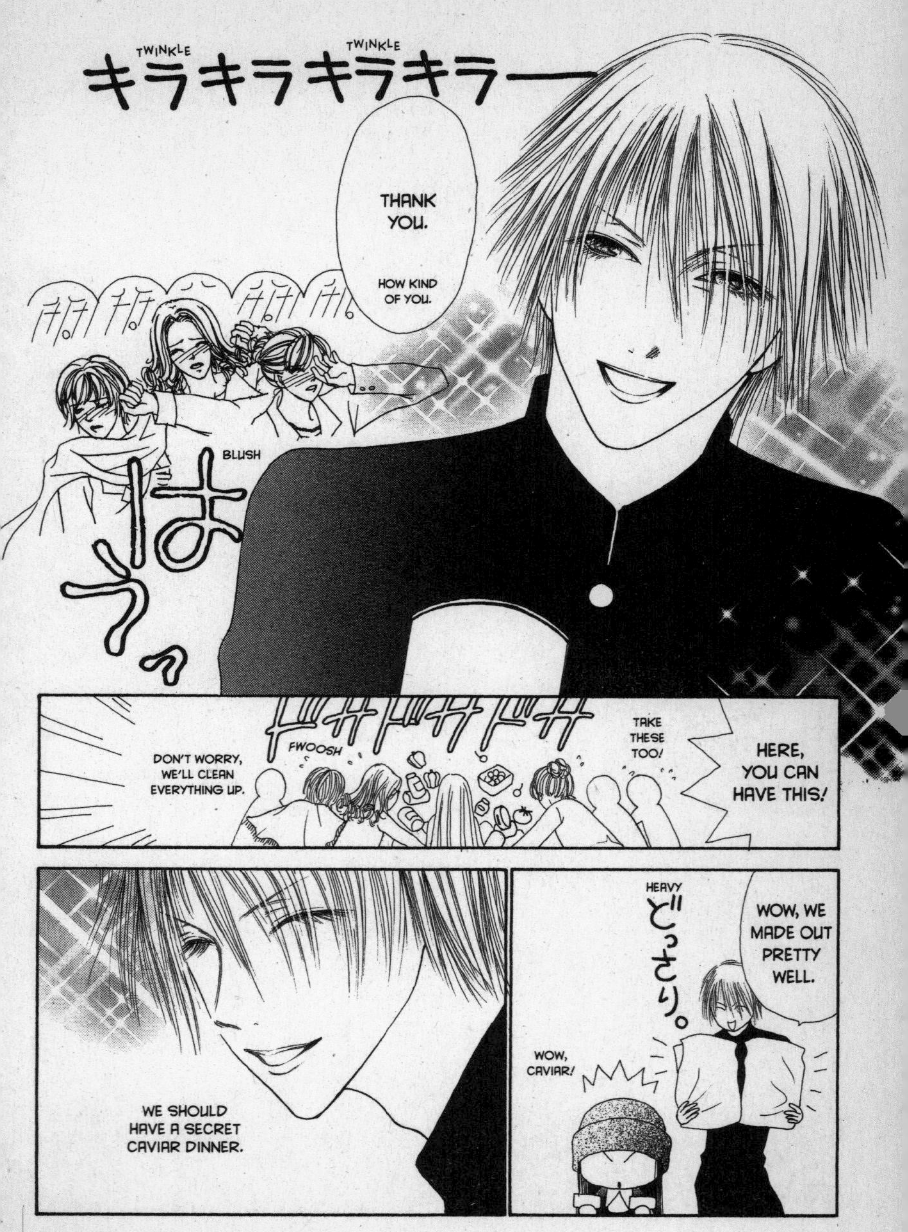
TWINKLE TWINKLE
キラキラキラキラー
THANK YOU.
HOW KIND OF YOU.
BLUSH
はうっ
HERE, YOU CAN HAVE THIS!
TAKE THESE TOO!
FWOOSH
ドサドサドサ
DON'T WORRY, WE'LL CLEAN EVERYTHING UP.
HEAVY
どっさり。
WOW, WE MADE OUT PRETTY WELL.
WOW, CAVIAR!
WE SHOULD HAVE A SECRET CAVIAR DINNER.

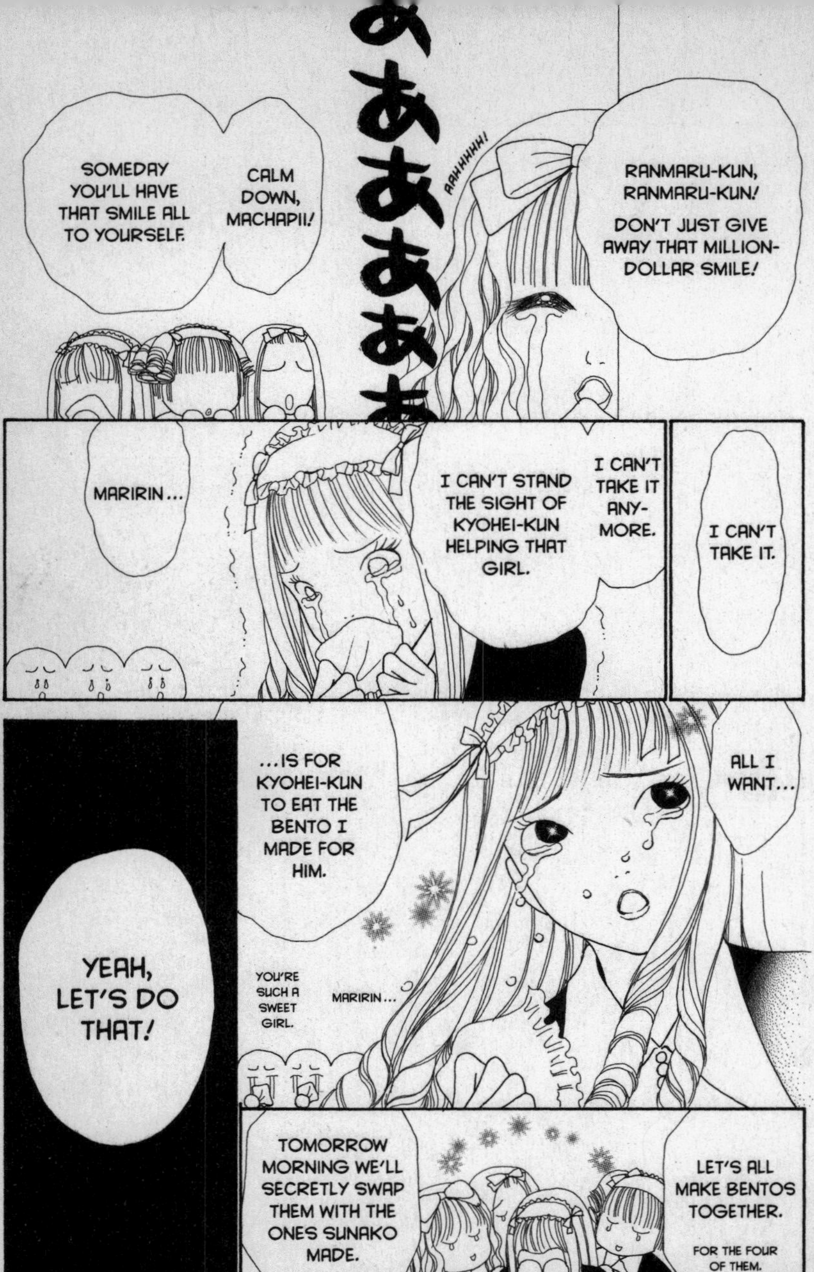
RANMARU-KUN, RANMARU-KUN!
DON'T JUST GIVE AWAY THAT MILLION-DOLLAR SMILE!
ああああ
AHHHHH!
CALM DOWN, MACHAPII!
SOMEDAY YOU'LL HAVE THAT SMILE ALL TO YOURSELF.
I CAN'T TAKE IT.
I CAN'T TAKE IT ANY-MORE.
I CAN'T STAND THE SIGHT OF KYOHEI-KUN HELPING THAT GIRL.
MARIRIN...
ALL I WANT...
...IS FOR KYOHEI-KUN TO EAT THE BENTO I MADE FOR HIM.
MARIRIN...
YOU'RE SUCH A SWEET GIRL.
LET'S ALL MAKE BENTOS TOGETHER.
FOR THE FOUR OF THEM.
TOMORROW MORNING WE'LL SECRETLY SWAP THEM WITH THE ONES SUNAKO MADE.
YEAH, LET'S DO THAT!

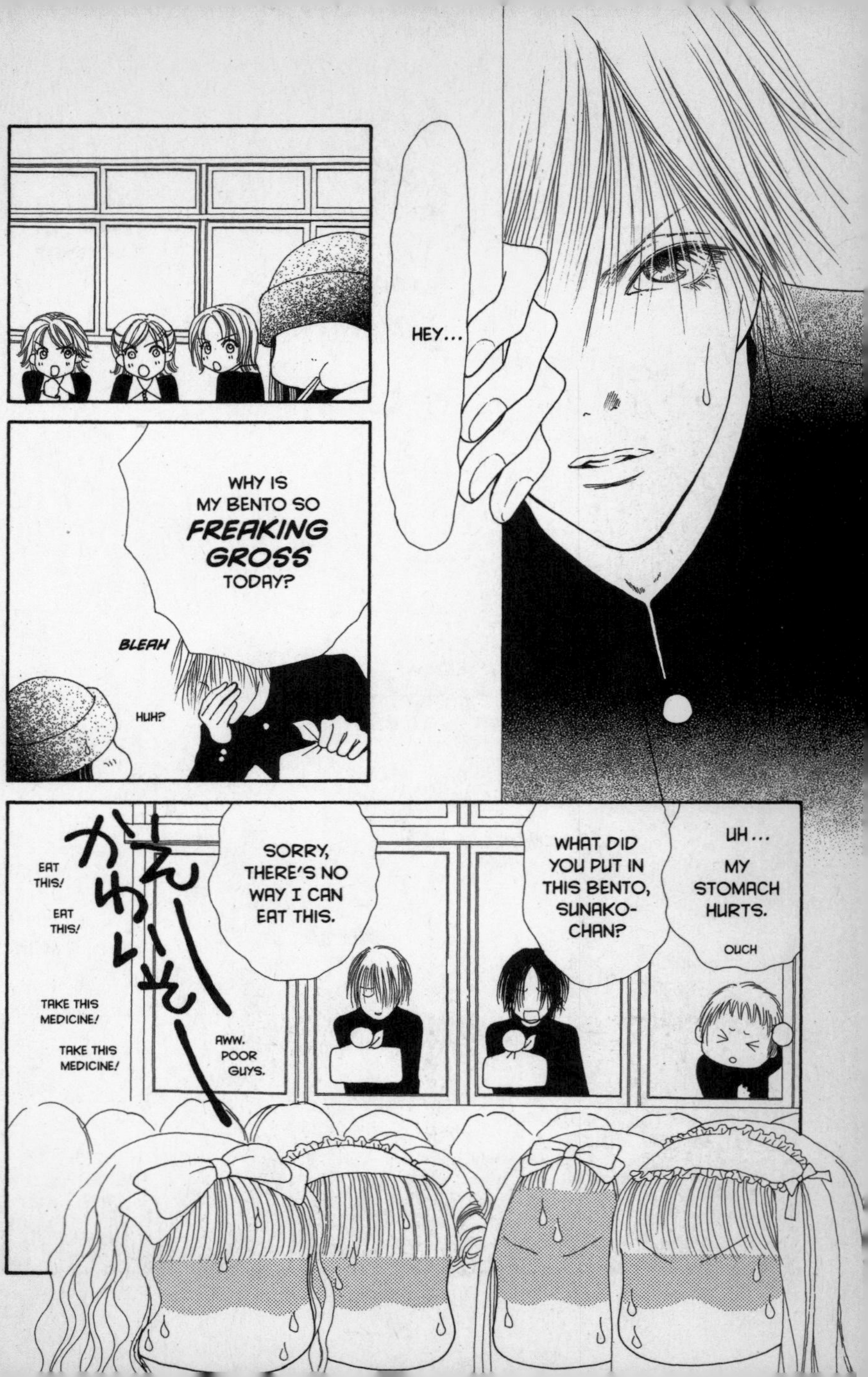
HEY...
WHY IS MY BENTO SO FREAKING GROSS TODAY?
BLEAH
HUH?
UH... MY STOMACH HURTS.
OUCH
WHAT DID YOU PUT IN THIS BENTO, SUNAKO-CHAN?
SORRY, THERE'S NO WAY I CAN EAT THIS.
EAT THIS!
EAT THIS!
TAKE THIS MEDICINE!
TAKE THIS MEDICINE!
AWW. POOR GUYS.

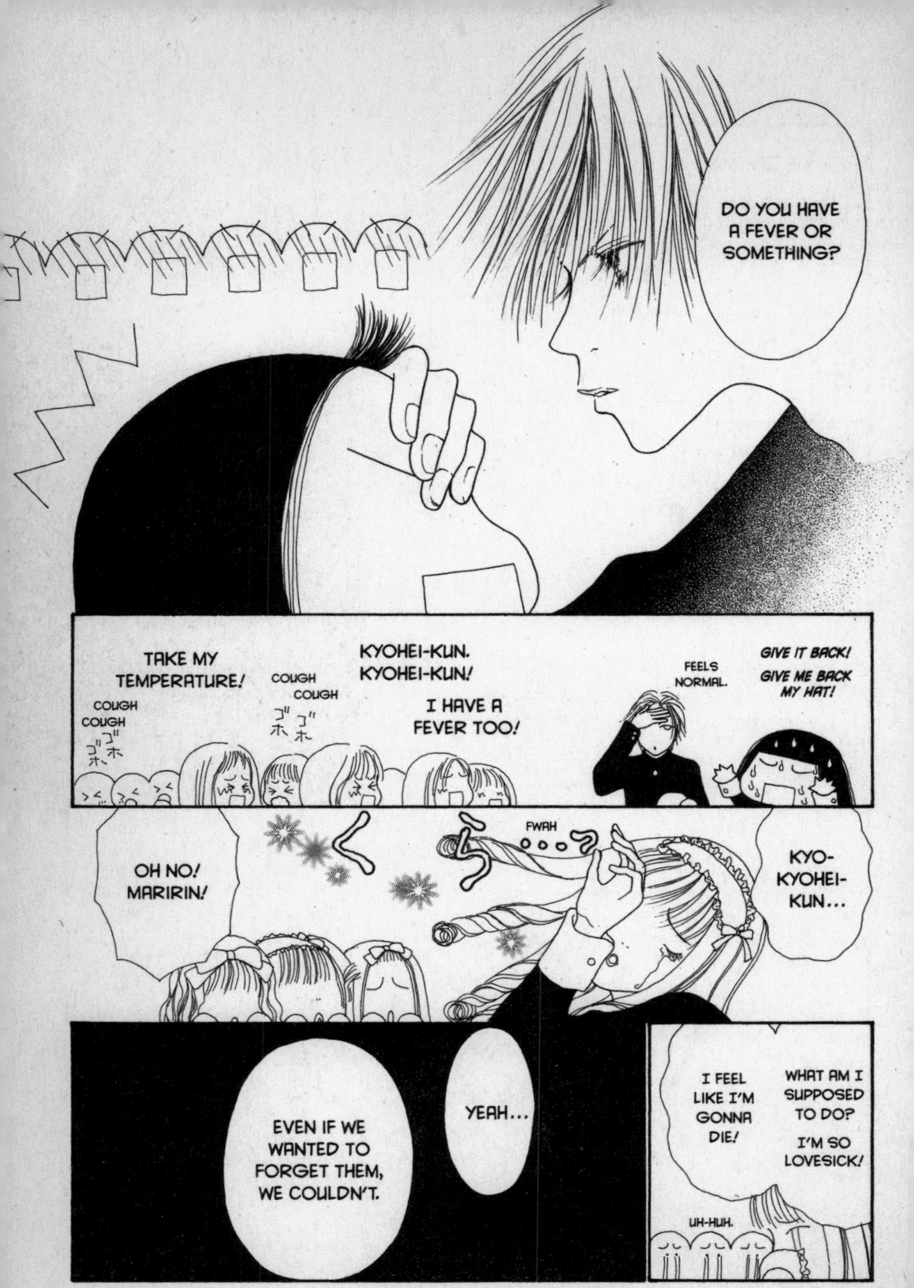
DO YOU HAVE A FEVER OR SOMETHING?
GIVE IT BACK! GIVE ME BACK MY HAT!
FEELS NORMAL.
KYOHEI-KUN. KYOHEI-KUN!
I HAVE A FEVER TOO!
COUGH COUGH
TAKE MY TEMPERATURE!
COUGH COUGH
KYO-KYOHEI-KUN...
FWAH
OH NO! MARIRIN!
WHAT AM I SUPPOSED TO DO?
I'M SO LOVESICK!
I FEEL LIKE I'M GONNA DIE!
UH-HUH.
YEAH...
EVEN IF WE WANTED TO FORGET THEM, WE COULDN'T.

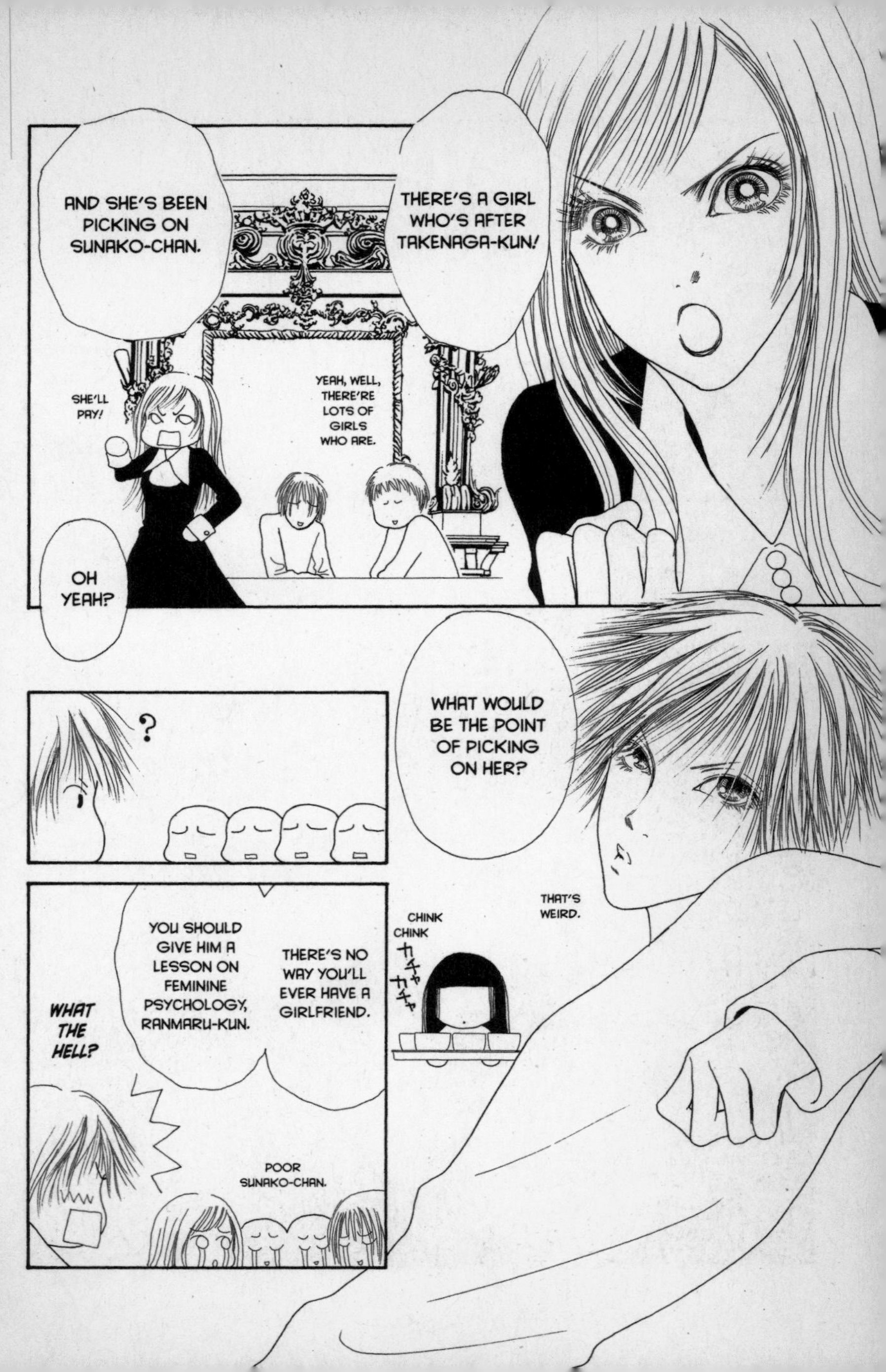
THERE'S A GIRL WHO'S AFTER TAKENAGA-KUN!
AND SHE'S BEEN PICKING ON SUNAKO-CHAN.
SHE'LL PAY!
YEAH, WELL, THERE'RE LOTS OF GIRLS WHO ARE.
OH YEAH?
WHAT WOULD BE THE POINT OF PICKING ON HER?
THAT'S WEIRD.
CHINK CHINK
カチャ カチャ
?
THERE'S NO WAY YOU'LL EVER HAVE A GIRLFRIEND.
YOU SHOULD GIVE HIM A LESSON ON FEMININE PSYCHOLOGY, RANMARU-KUN.
WHAT THE HELL?
POOR SUNAKO-CHAN.

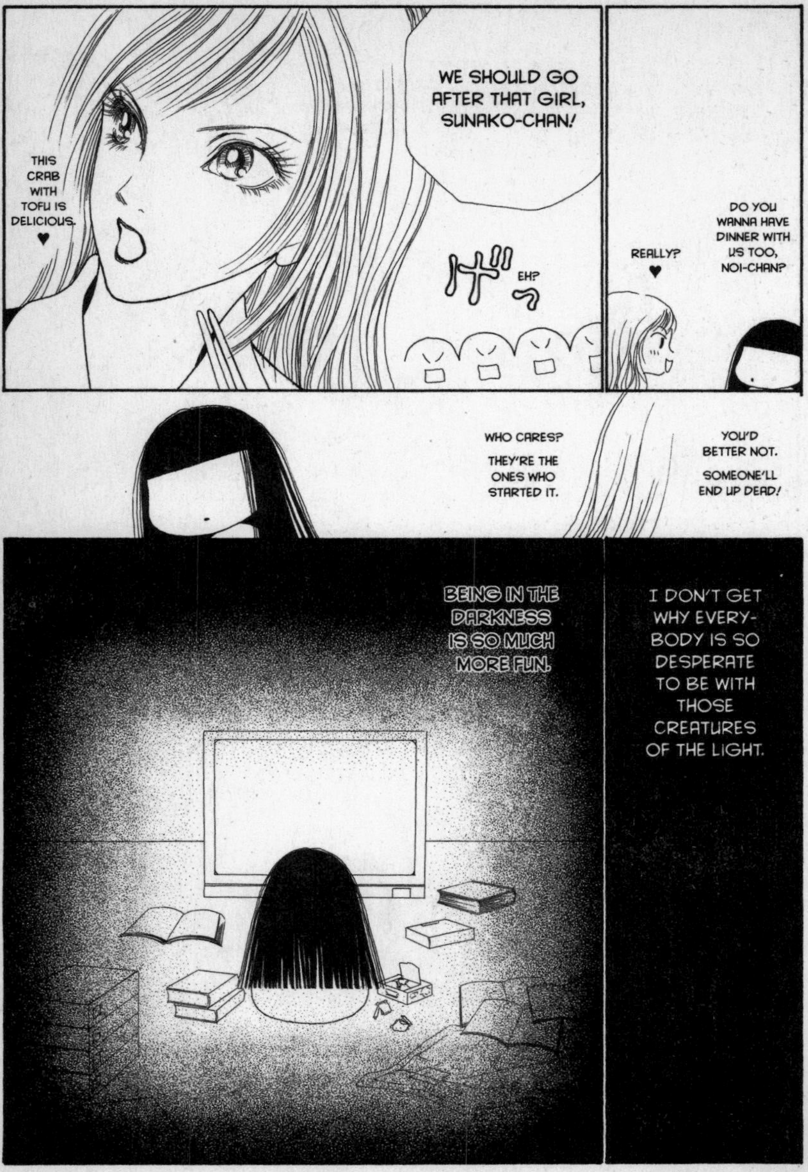

DO YOU WANNA HAVE DINNER WITH US TOO, NOI-CHAN?
REALLY? ♥
WE SHOULD GO AFTER THAT GIRL, SUNAKO-CHAN!
ゲッ
EH?
THIS CRAB WITH TOFU IS DELICIOUS. ♥
YOU'D BETTER NOT.
SOMEONE'LL END UP DEAD!
WHO CARES?
THEY'RE THE ONES WHO STARTED IT.
I DON'T GET WHY EVERY-BODY IS SO DESPERATE TO BE WITH THOSE CREATURES OF THE LIGHT.
BEING IN THE DARKNESS IS SO MUCH MORE FUN.

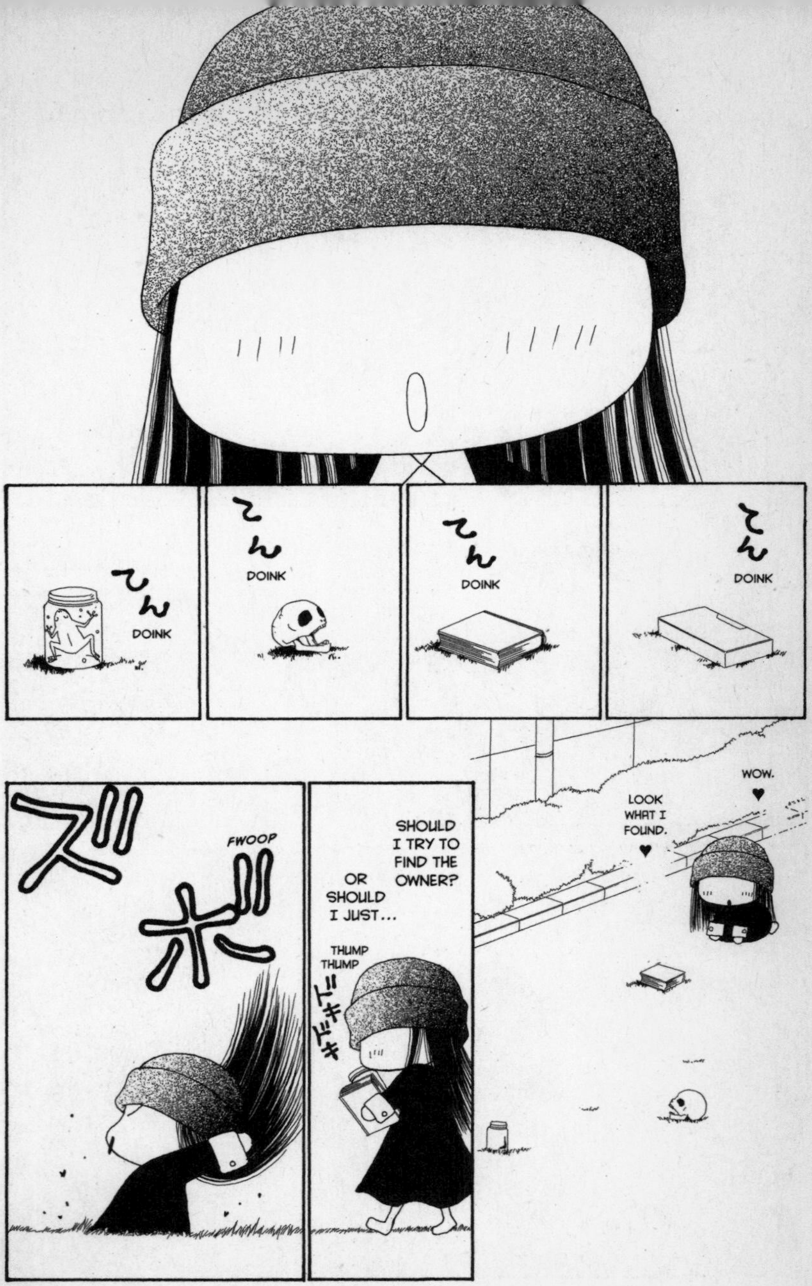

てん
DOINK
てん
DOINK
てん
DOINK
てん
DOINK
WOW. ♥
LOOK WHAT I FOUND. ♥
SHOULD I TRY TO FIND THE OWNER?
OR SHOULD I JUST...
ドキドキ
THUMP THUMP
ズボー
FWOOP

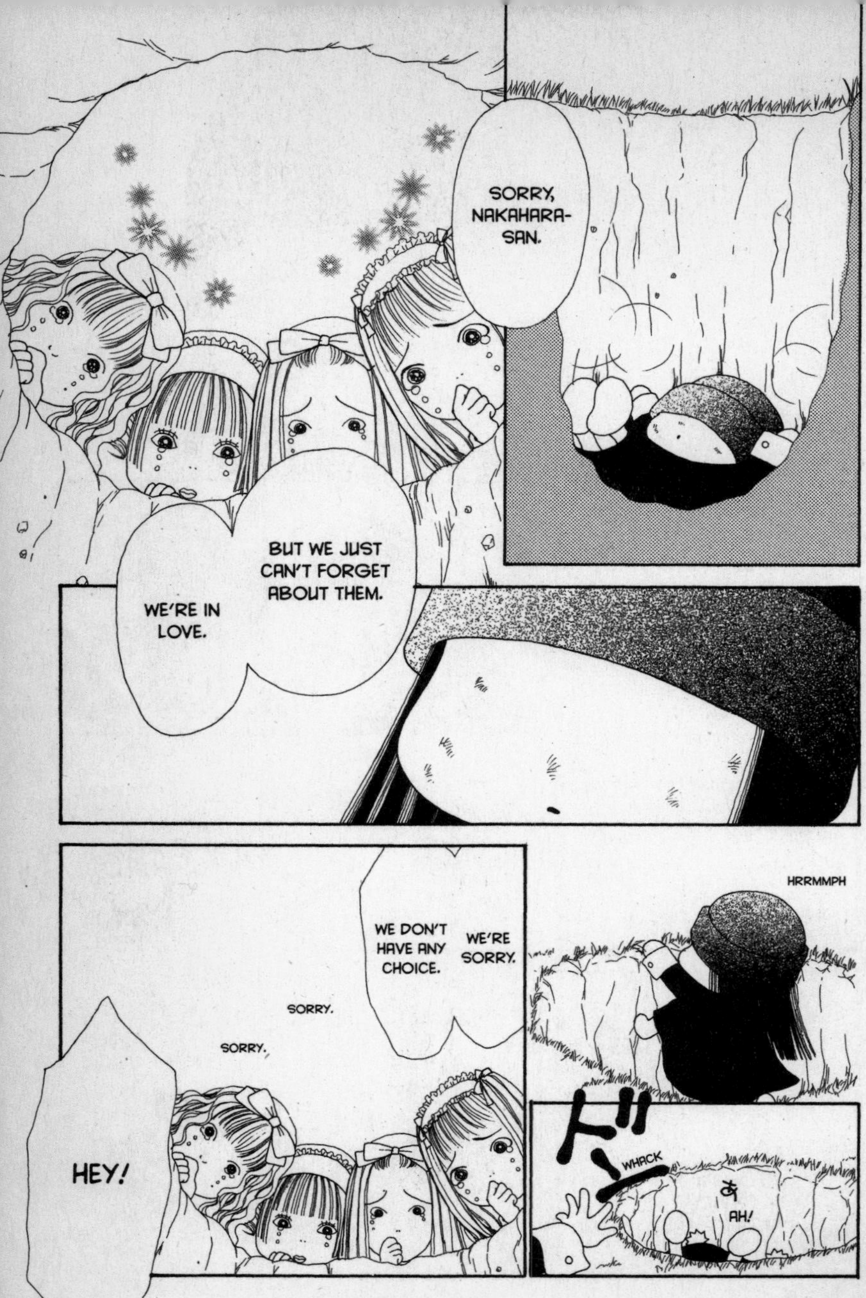
SORRY, NAKAHARA-SAN.
WE'RE IN LOVE.
BUT WE JUST CAN'T FORGET ABOUT THEM.
HRRMMPH
WHACK
AH!
WE'RE SORRY.
WE DON'T HAVE ANY CHOICE.
SORRY.
SORRY.
HEY!

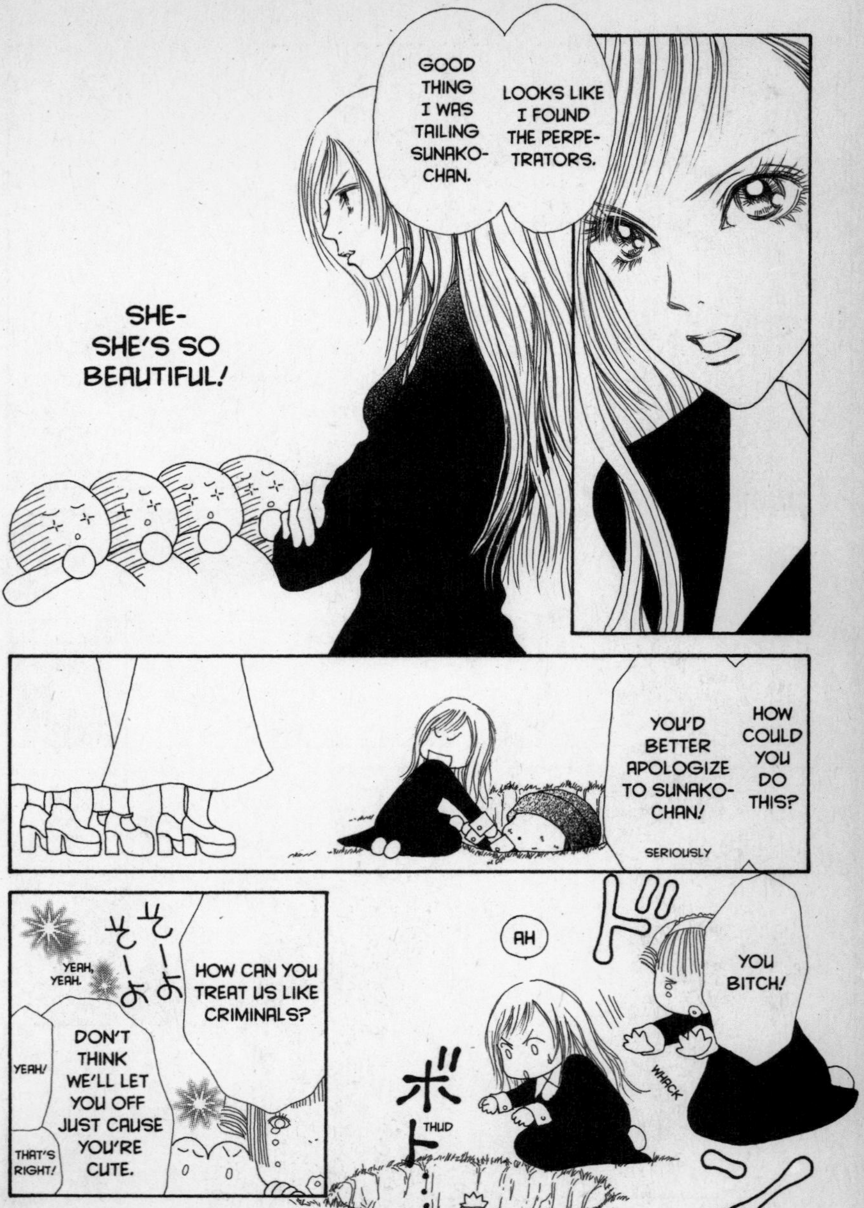
LOOKS LIKE I FOUND THE PERPETRATORS.
GOOD THING I WAS TAILING SUNAKO-CHAN.
SHE-SHE'S SO BEAUTIFUL!
HOW COULD YOU DO THIS?
YOU'D BETTER APOLOGIZE TO SUNAKO-CHAN!
SERIOUSLY
ド
YOU BITCH!
AH
WHACK
ボト
THUD
HOW CAN YOU TREAT US LIKE CRIMINALS?
そーよそーよ
YEAH, YEAH.
DON'T THINK WE'LL LET YOU OFF JUST CAUSE YOU'RE CUTE.
YEAH!
THAT'S RIGHT!

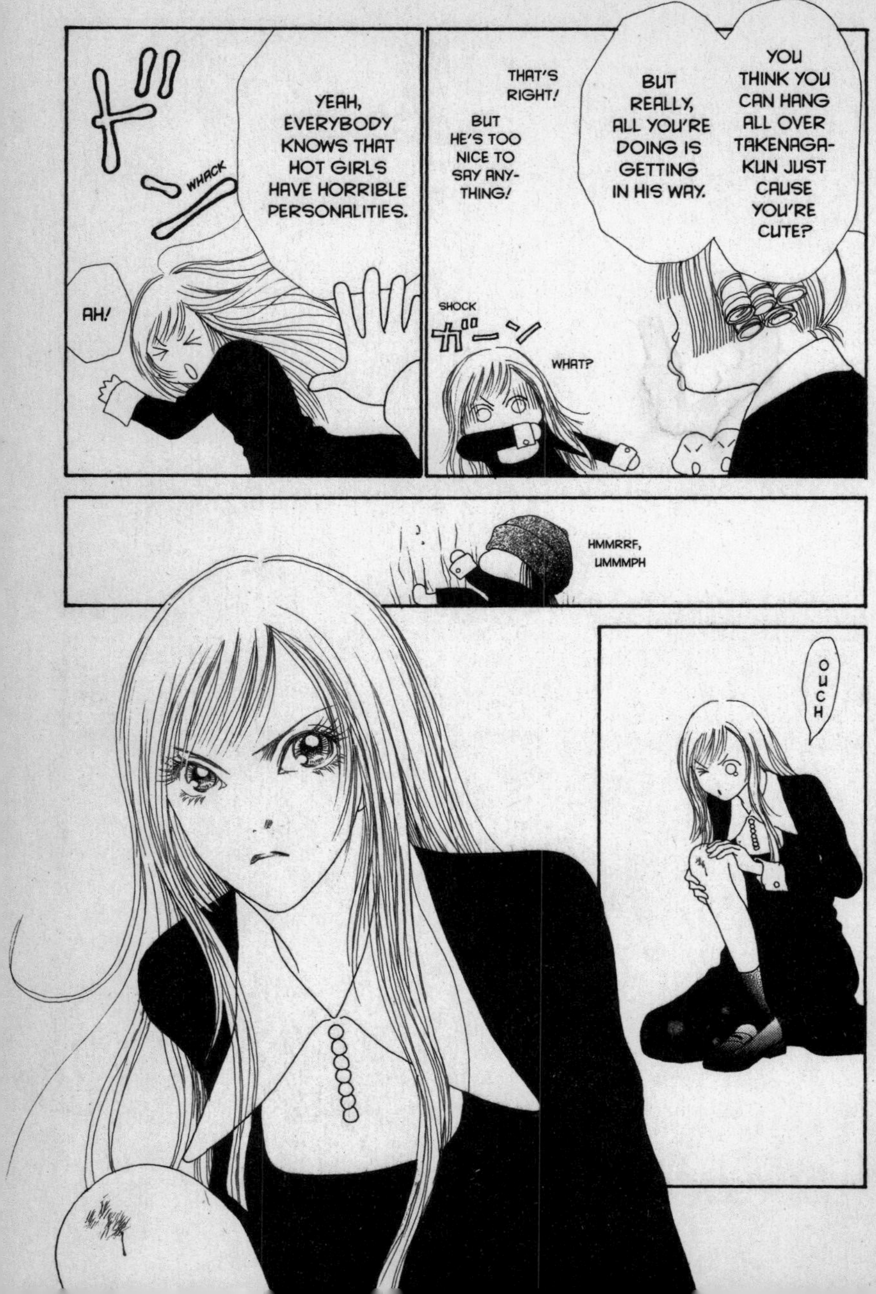
YOU THINK YOU CAN HANG ALL OVER TAKENAGA-KUN JUST CAUSE YOU'RE CUTE?
BUT REALLY, ALL YOU'RE DOING IS GETTING IN HIS WAY.
THAT'S RIGHT!
BUT HE'S TOO NICE TO SAY ANY-THING!
SHOCK
WHAT?
YEAH, EVERYBODY KNOWS THAT HOT GIRLS HAVE HORRIBLE PERSONALITIES.
WHACK
AH!
HMMRRF, UMMMPH
OUCH

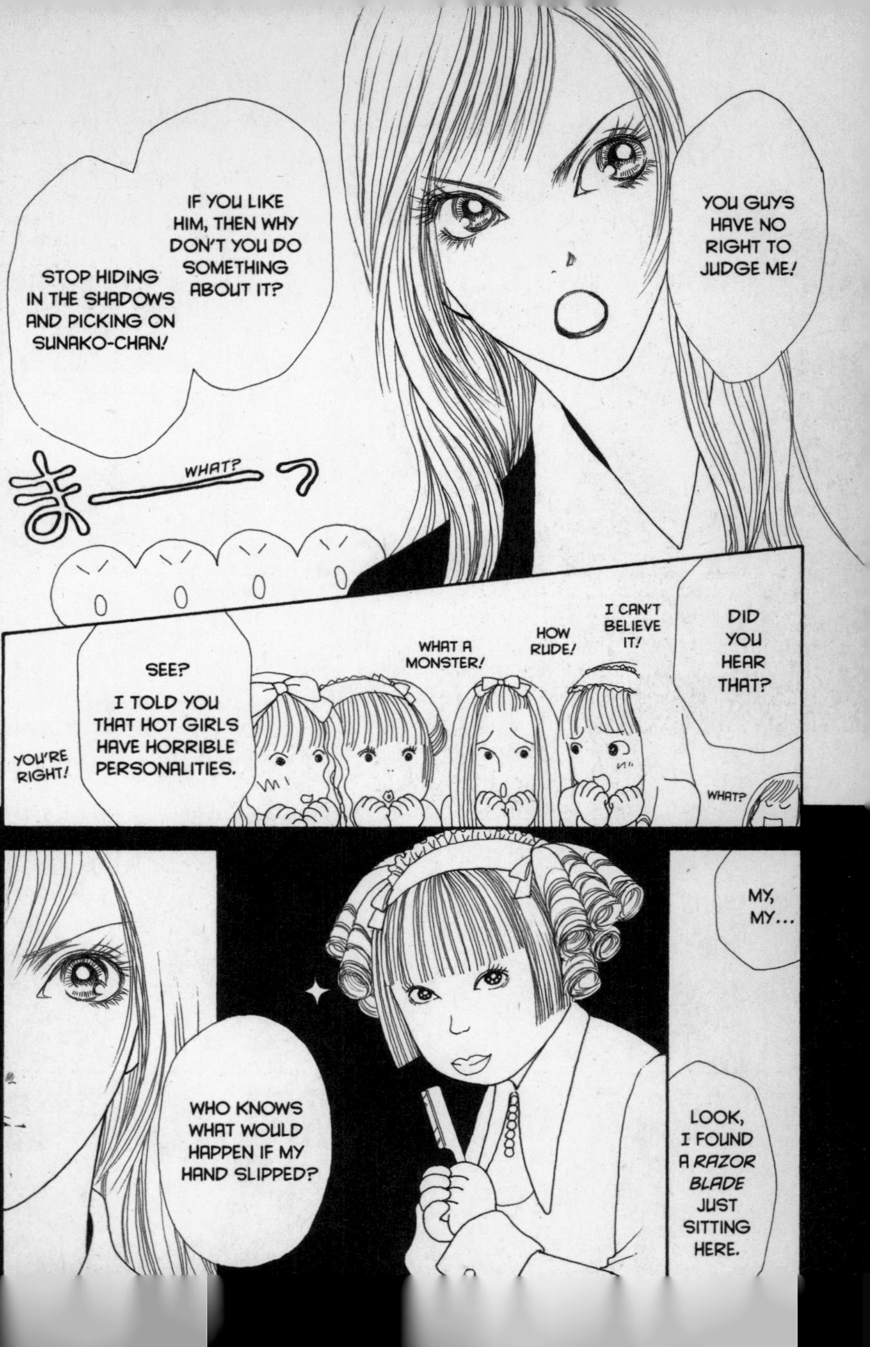
YOU GUYS HAVE NO RIGHT TO JUDGE ME!
IF YOU LIKE HIM, THEN WHY DON'T YOU DO SOMETHING ABOUT IT?
STOP HIDING IN THE SHADOWS AND PICKING ON SUNAKO-CHAN!
WHAT?
DID YOU HEAR THAT?
WHAT?
I CAN'T BELIEVE IT!
HOW RUDE!
WHAT A MONSTER!
SEE?
I TOLD YOU THAT HOT GIRLS HAVE HORRIBLE PERSONALITIES.
YOU'RE RIGHT!
MY, MY...
LOOK, I FOUND A *RAZOR BLADE* JUST SITTING HERE.
WHO KNOWS WHAT WOULD HAPPEN IF MY HAND SLIPPED?

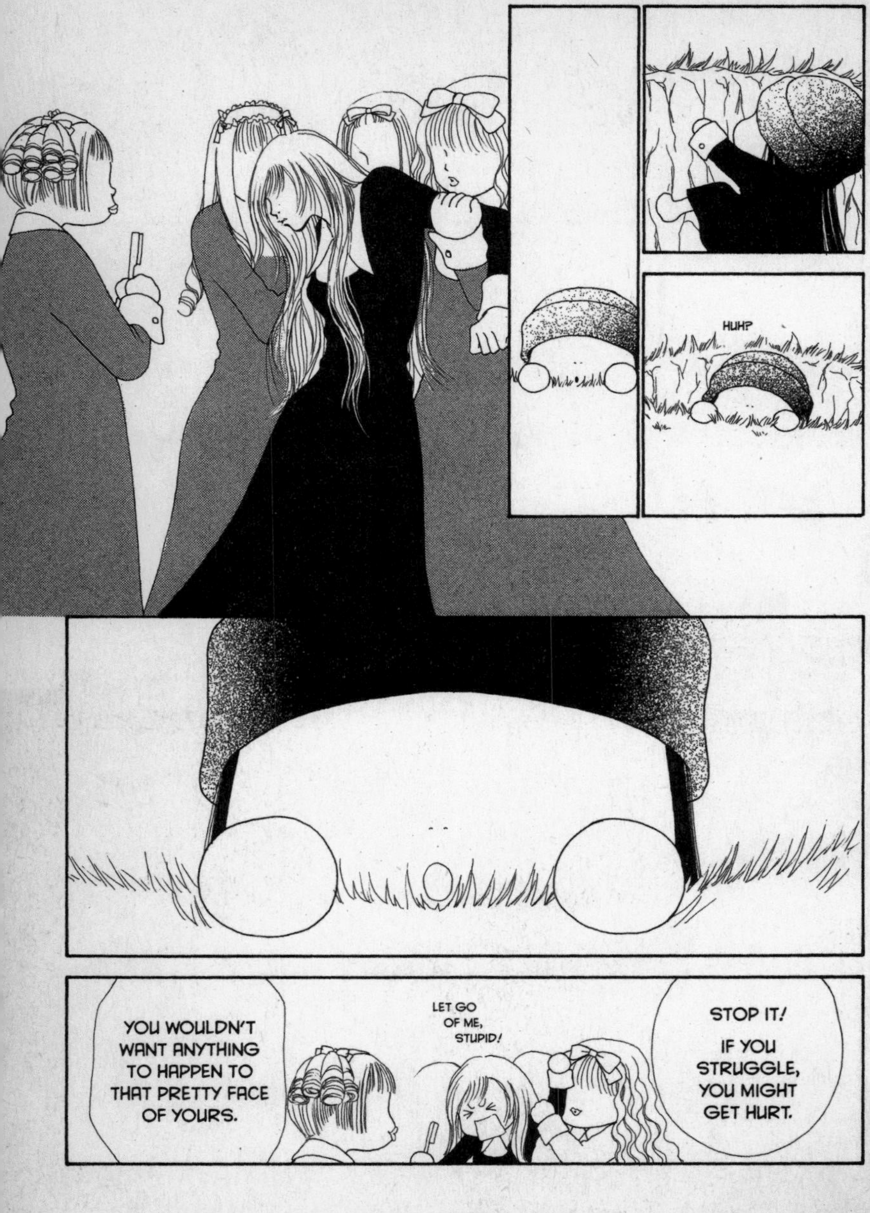
HUH?
STOP IT! IF YOU STRUGGLE, YOU MIGHT GET HURT.
LET GO OF ME, STUPID!
YOU WOULDN'T WANT ANYTHING TO HAPPEN TO THAT PRETTY FACE OF YOURS.

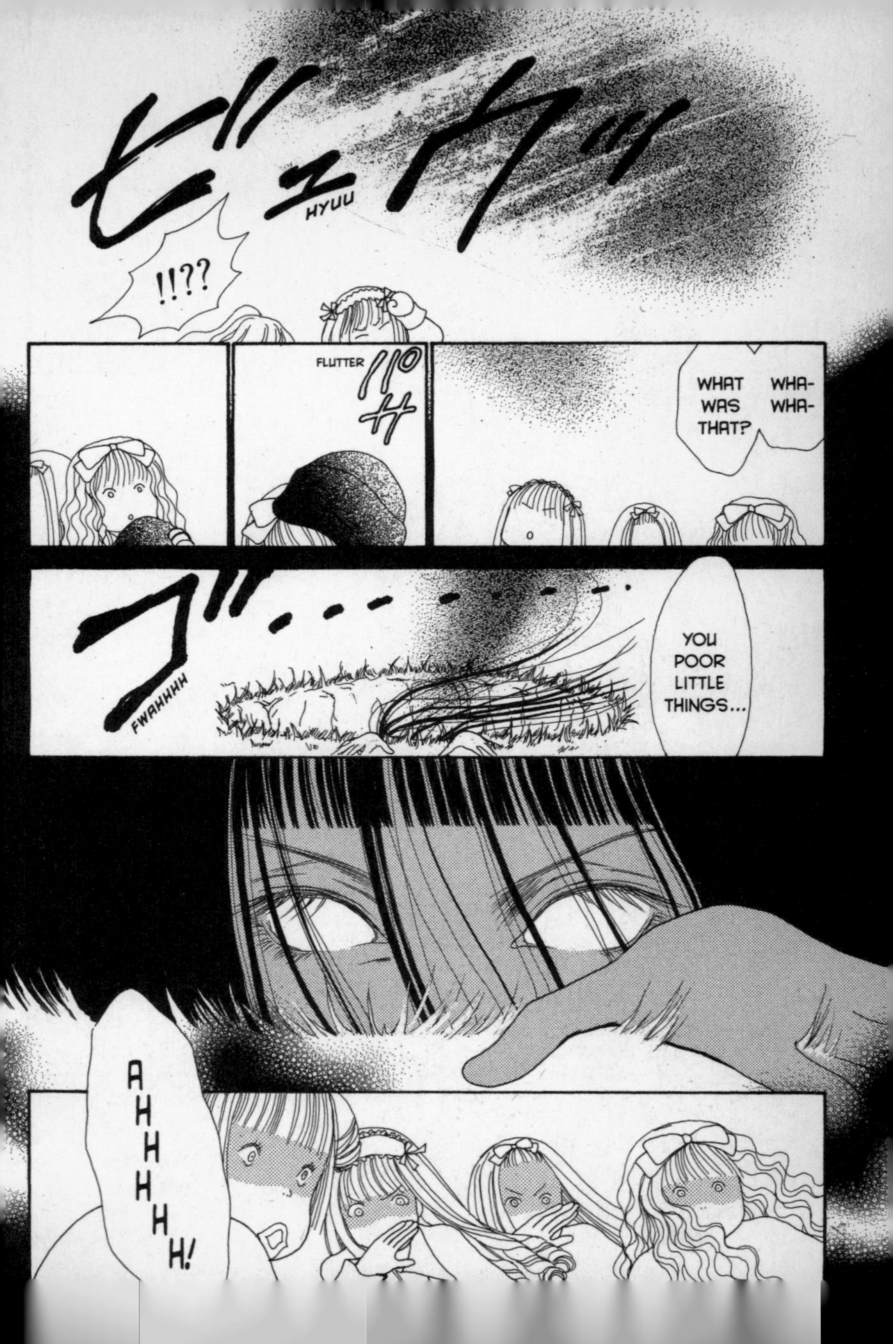
HYUU
!!??
WHA- WHA-
WHAT WAS THAT?
FLUTTER
YOU POOR LITTLE THINGS...
FWAHHHH
AHHHHHH!

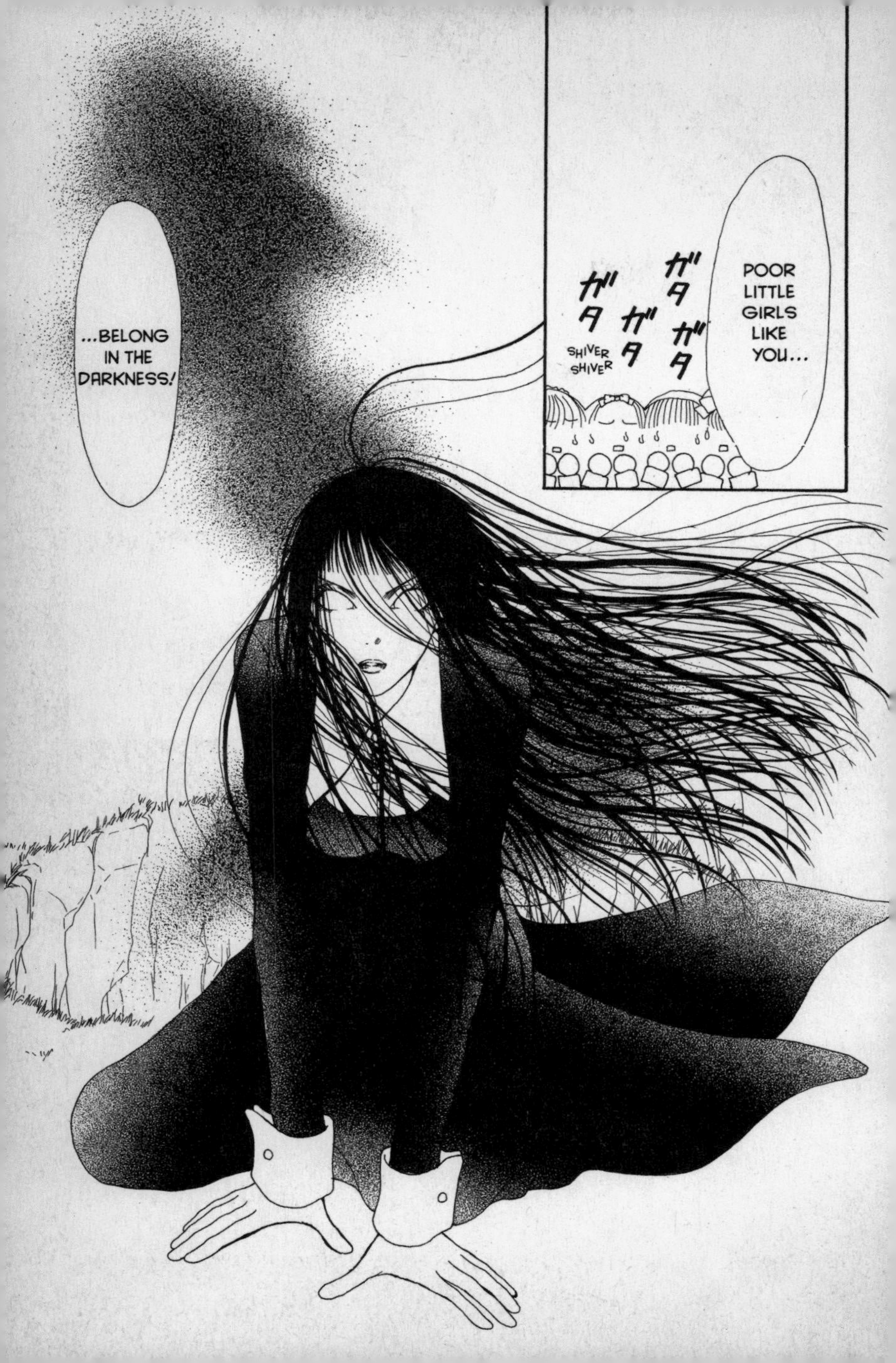
POOR LITTLE GIRLS LIKE YOU...
ガタガタ
ガタ
ガタ
SHIVER SHIVER
...BELONG IN THE DARKNESS!

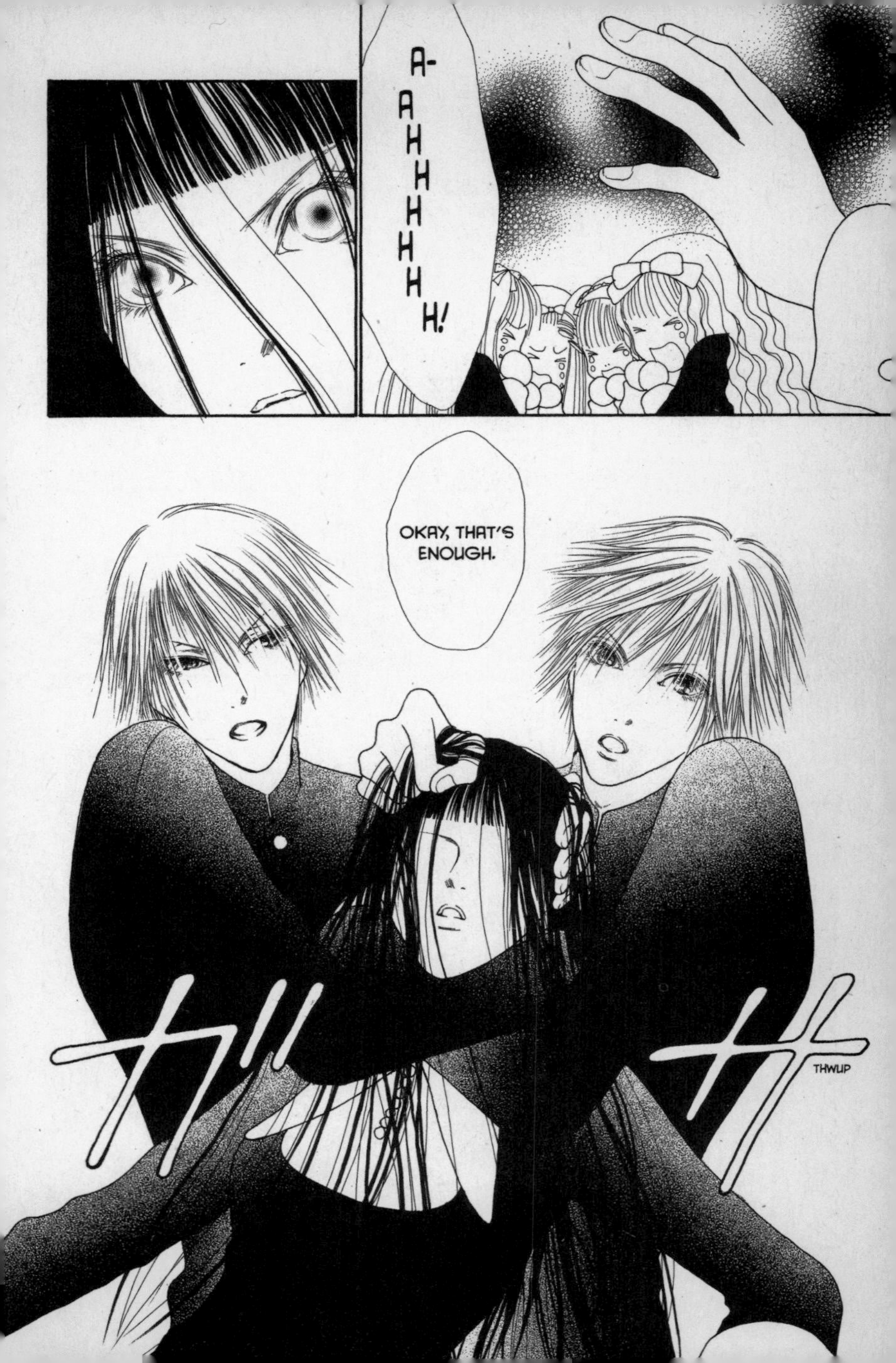
A-AHHHHHH!
OKAY, THAT'S ENOUGH.
カッ
THWUP

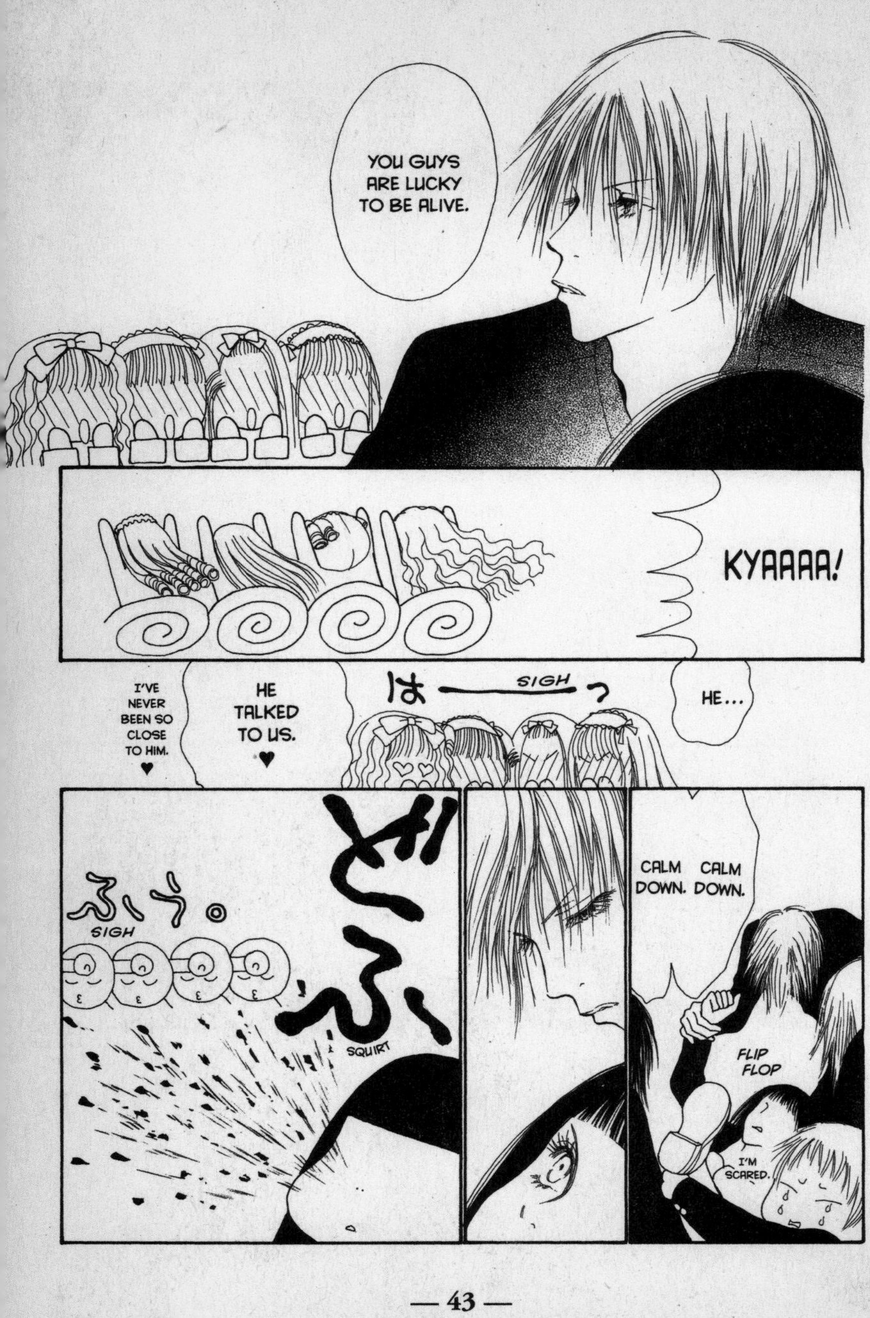
YOU GUYS ARE LUCKY TO BE ALIVE.
KYAAAA!
HE...
は——っ
SIGH
HE TALKED TO US. ♥
I'VE NEVER BEEN SO CLOSE TO HIM. ♥
CALM DOWN. CALM DOWN.
FLIP FLOP
I'M SCARED.
どふ
SQUIRT
ふぅ。
SIGH

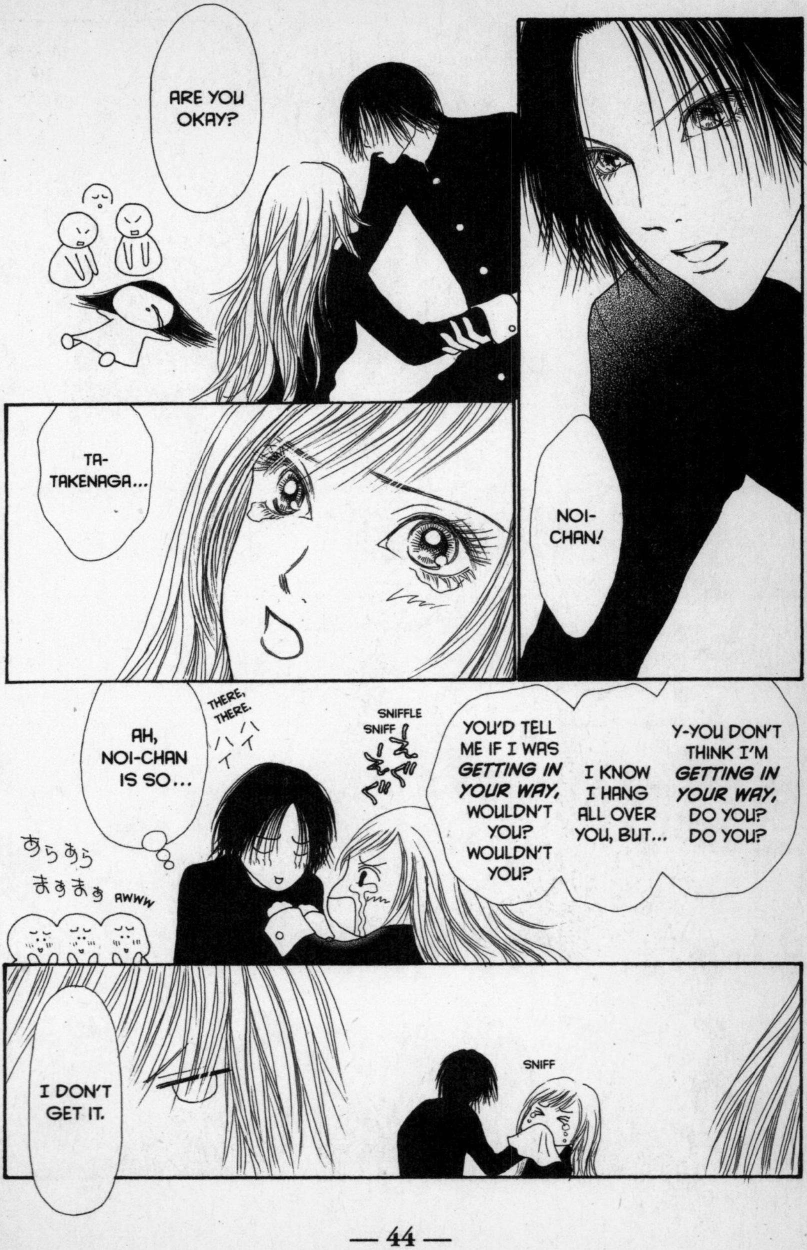
NOI-CHAN!
ARE YOU OKAY?
TA-TAKENAGA...
Y-YOU DON'T THINK I'M *GETTING IN YOUR WAY,* DO YOU? DO YOU?
I KNOW I HANG ALL OVER YOU, BUT...
YOU'D TELL ME IF I WAS *GETTING IN YOUR WAY,* WOULDN'T YOU? WOULDN'T YOU?
SNIFFLE
SNIFF
THERE, THERE.
ハイハイ
AH, NOI-CHAN IS SO...
あらあら
まぁまぁ
AWWW
SNIFF
I DON'T GET IT.

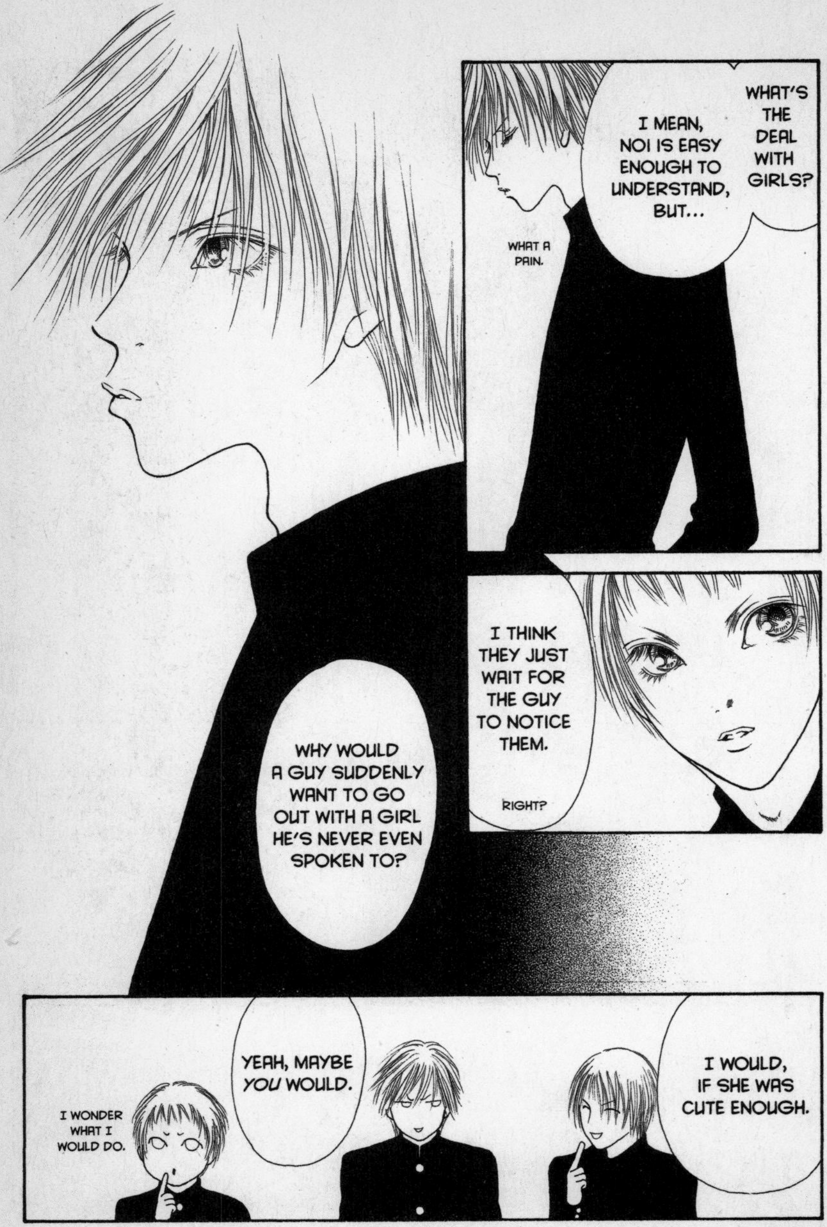
WHAT'S THE DEAL WITH GIRLS?
I MEAN, NOI IS EASY ENOUGH TO UNDERSTAND, BUT...
WHAT A PAIN.
I THINK THEY JUST WAIT FOR THE GUY TO NOTICE THEM.
RIGHT?
WHY WOULD A GUY SUDDENLY WANT TO GO OUT WITH A GIRL HE'S NEVER EVEN SPOKEN TO?
I WOULD, IF SHE WAS CUTE ENOUGH.
YEAH, MAYBE *YOU* WOULD.
I WONDER WHAT I WOULD DO.

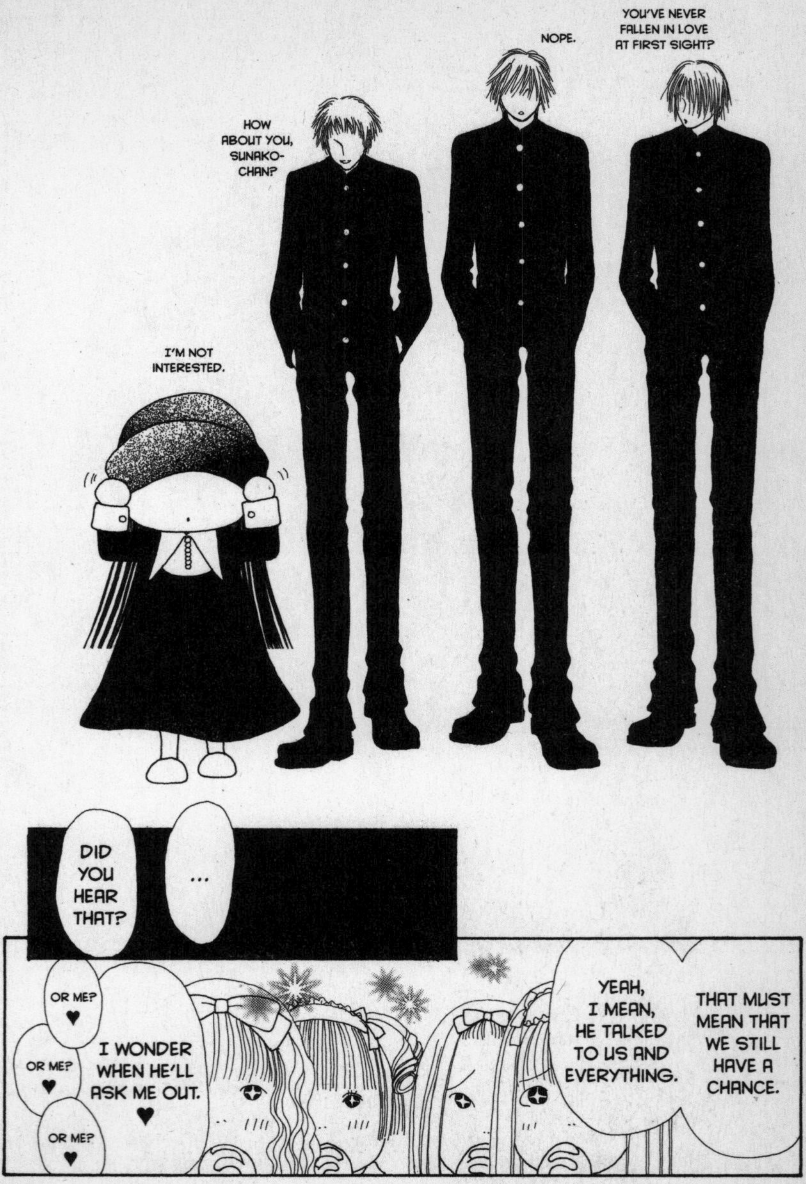
YOU'VE NEVER FALLEN IN LOVE AT FIRST SIGHT?
NOPE.
HOW ABOUT YOU, SUNAKO-CHAN?
I'M NOT INTERESTED.
...
DID YOU HEAR THAT?
YEAH, I MEAN, HE TALKED TO US AND EVERYTHING.
THAT MUST MEAN THAT WE STILL HAVE A CHANCE.
I WONDER WHEN HE'LL ASK ME OUT. ♥
OR ME? ♥
OR ME? ♥
OR ME? ♥

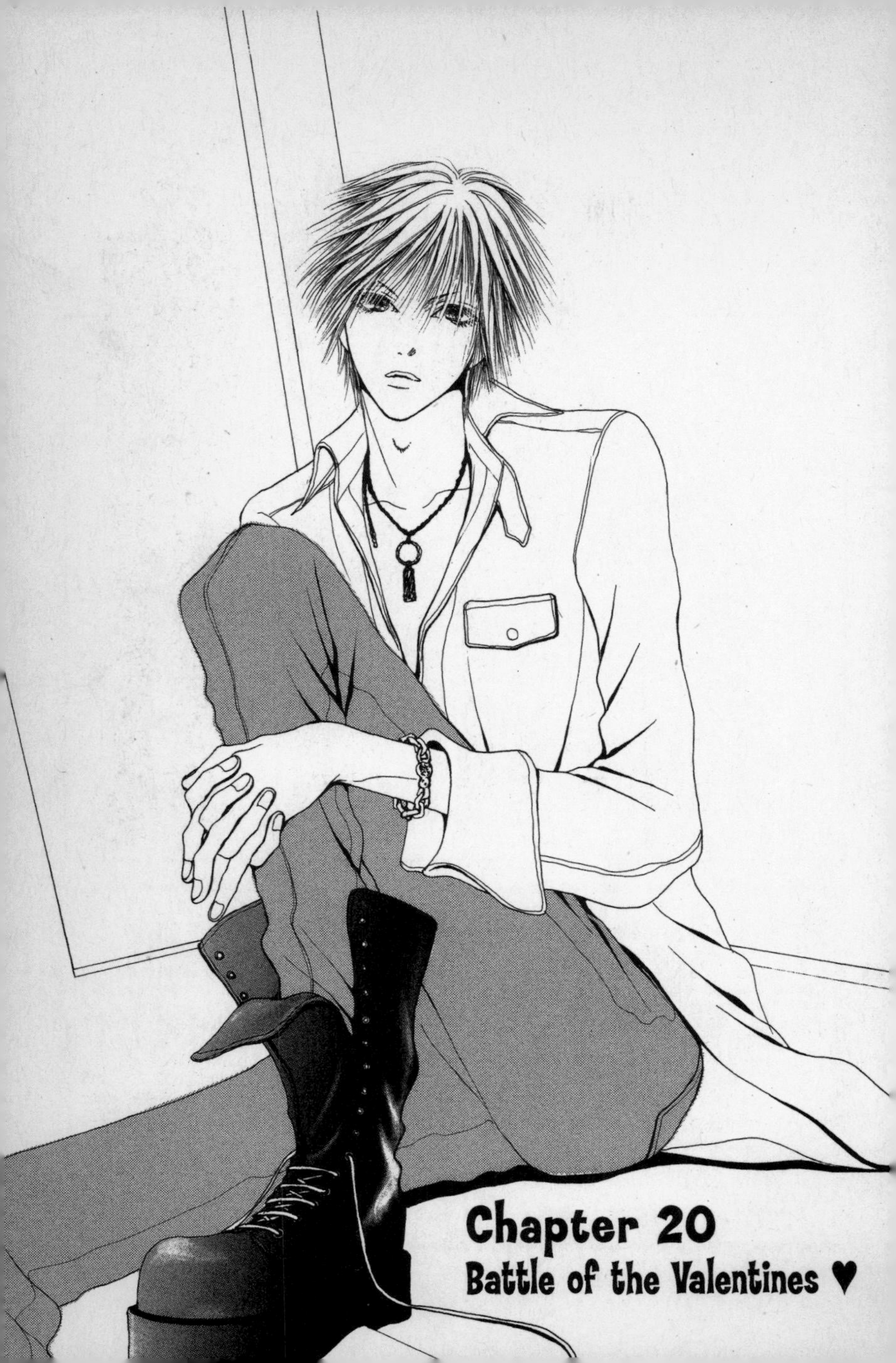

Chapter 20

Battle of the Valentines ♥

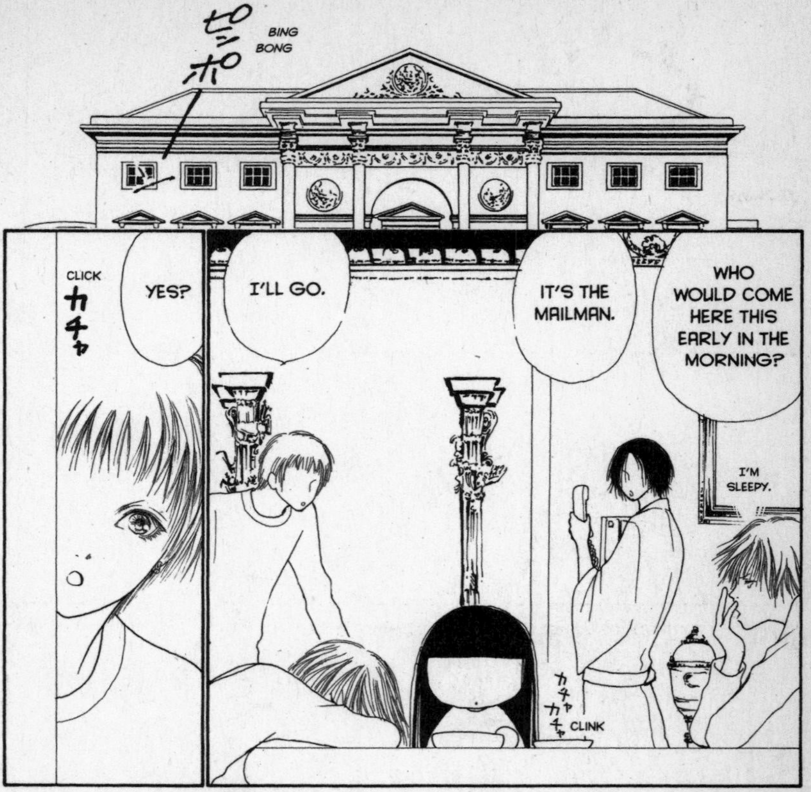
BING BONG
WHO WOULD COME HERE THIS EARLY IN THE MORNING?
IT'S THE MAILMAN.
I'LL GO.
I'M SLEEPY.
CLINK
YES?
CLICK

BEHIND THE SCENES

WELL, THIS STORY IS JUST JAM-PACKED WITH *SPECIAL GUESTS*. HANA-CHAN CAME BACK, AYUAYU WATANABE IS HERE... AND EVEN YUKI SUETSUGU-SENSEI IS HERE! HOW CAN THEY BE SO DIFFERENT FROM ME EVEN THOUGH THEY WRITE FOR THE SAME MAGAZINE? I GUESS IT'S JUST THE DIFFERENCE BETWEEN THE FOOLISH AND THE WISE. HMMPH. MACHIKO SAKURAI CAME TO VISIT AN HOUR BEFORE MY DEADLINE.

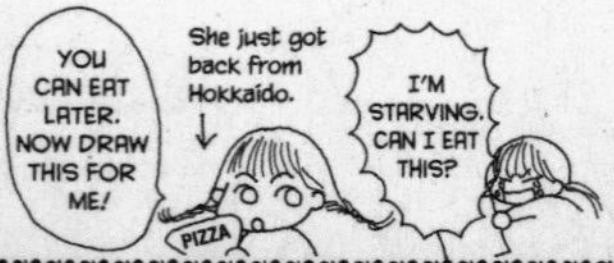
I'M STARVING. CAN I EAT THIS?
She just got back from Hokkaido.
PIZZA
YOU CAN EAT LATER. NOW DRAW THIS FOR ME!

I PUT HER TO WORK RIGHT AWAY. SORRY.

IT WAS DURING MY DECEMBER DEADLINE. AFTER THE DEADLINE, SAKURAI AND I PARTIED LIKE CRAZY. AS SOON AS SAKURAI WENT BACK HOME, I HEADED FOR NAGOYA. (APPARENTLY, I WAS REALLY EXCITED.)

RIGHT WHEN I GOT BACK TO TOKYO, I CAUGHT A TERRIBLE COLD. I WAS IN BED MORNING DURING THE NEW YEAR'S COUNTDOWN... WHEN YOU'RE TIRED, IT'S IMPORTANT TO REST. OKAY, EVERYBODY?

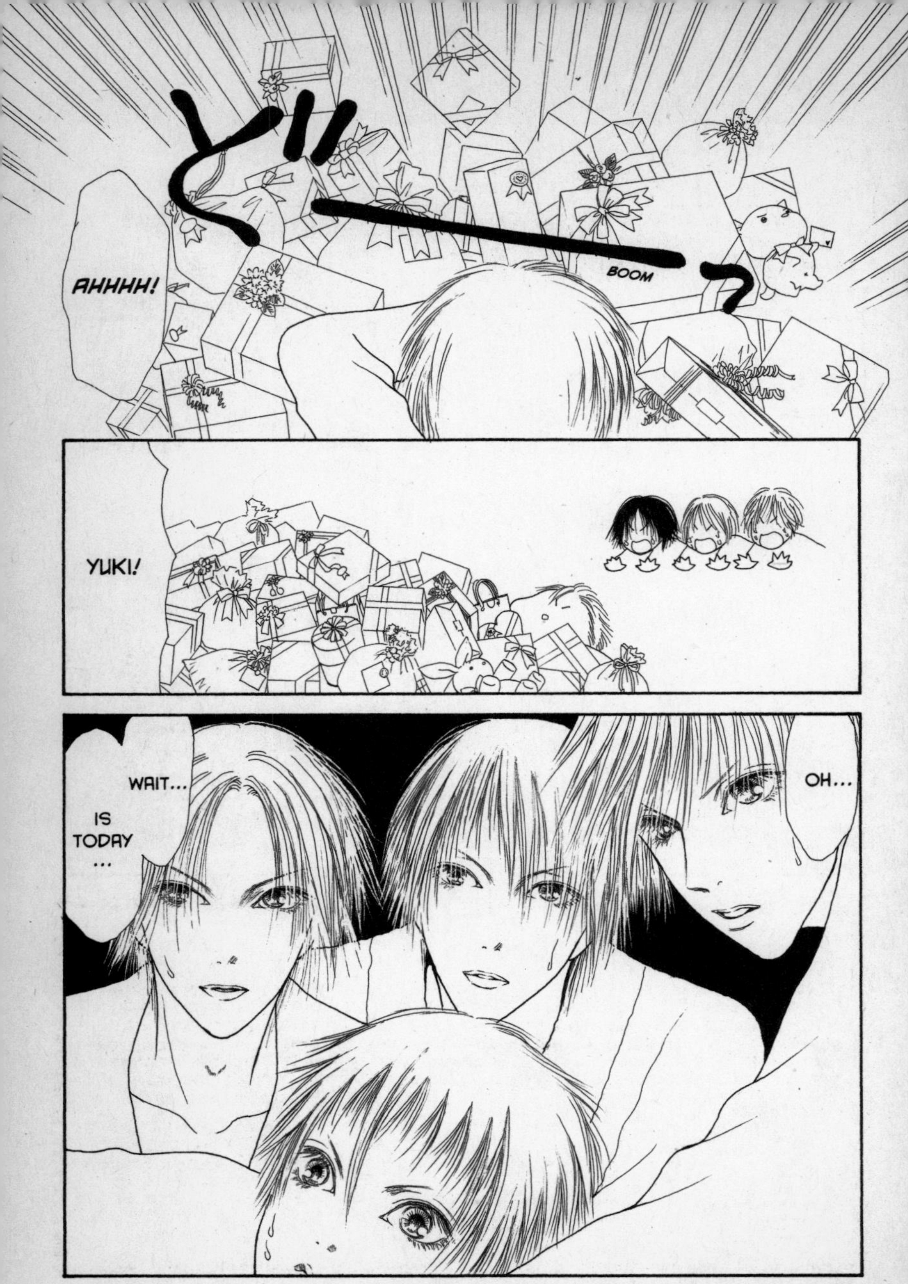
BOOM
AHHHH!
YUKI!
OH...
WAIT...
IS TODAY ...

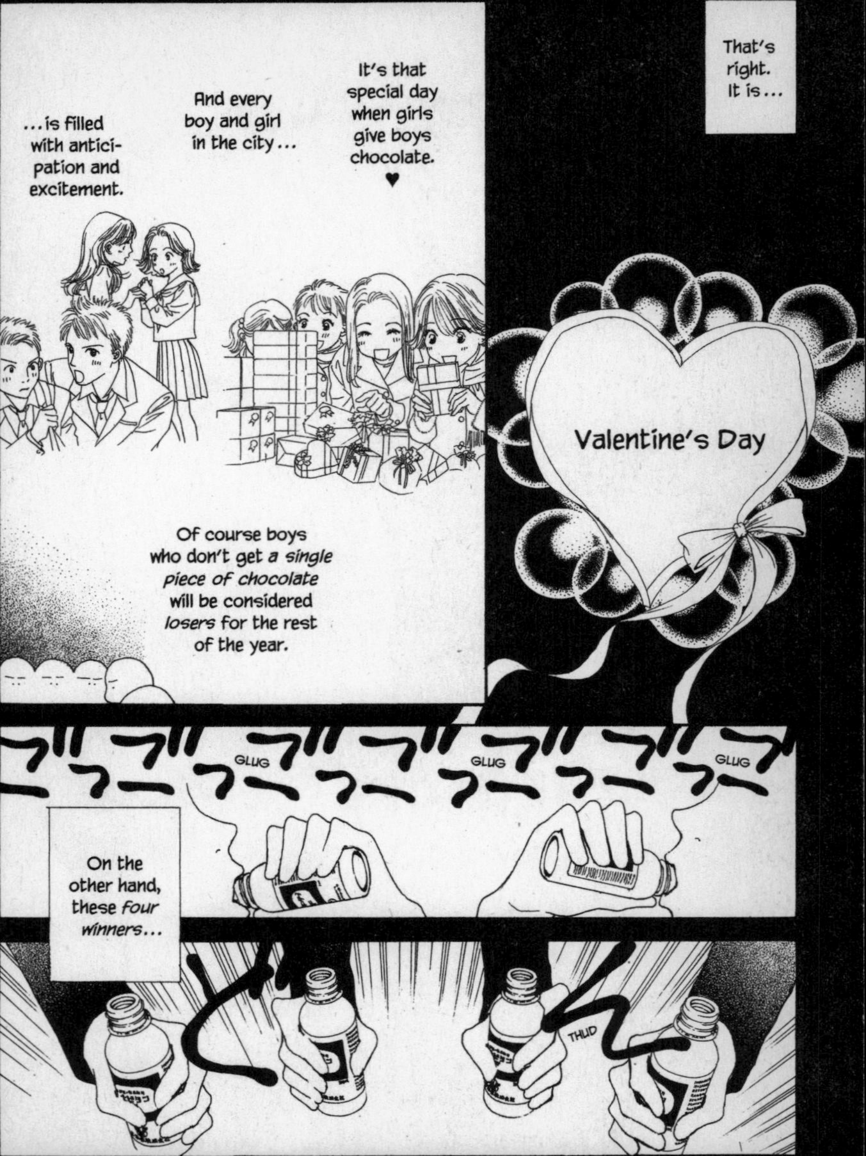
That's right. It is...
Valentine's Day
It's that special day when girls give boys chocolate. ♥
And every boy and girl in the city...
...is filled with antici-pation and excitement.
Of course boys who don't get *a single piece of chocolate* will be considered *losers* for the rest of the year.
GLUG
GLUG
GLUG
On the other hand, these *four winners*...
THUD

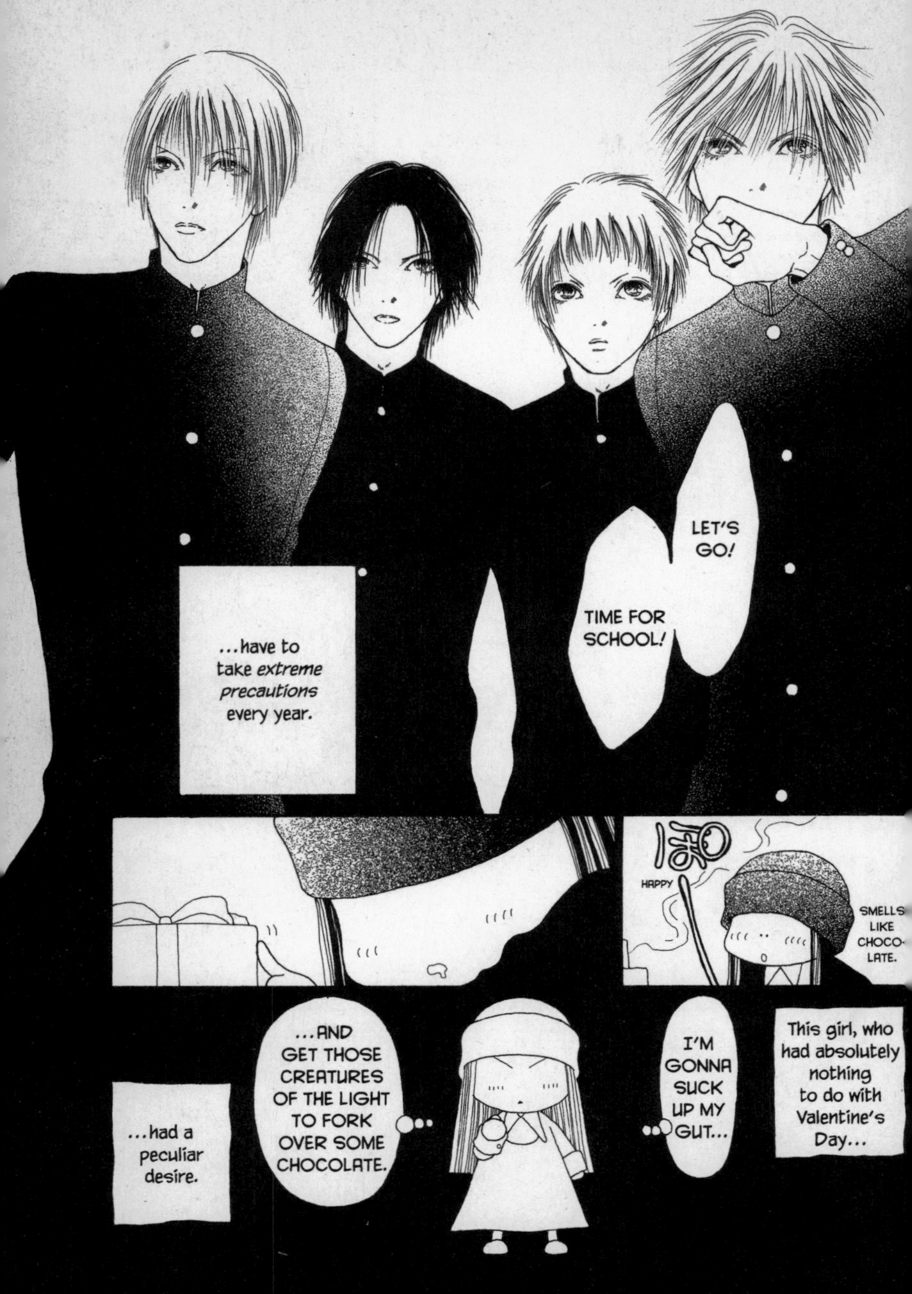
LET'S GO!
TIME FOR SCHOOL!
...have to take *extreme precautions* every year.
HAPPY
SMELLS LIKE CHOCO-LATE.
This girl, who had absolutely nothing to do with Valentine's Day...
I'M GONNA SUCK UP MY GUT...
...AND GET THOSE CREATURES OF THE LIGHT TO FORK OVER SOME CHOCOLATE.
...had a peculiar desire.

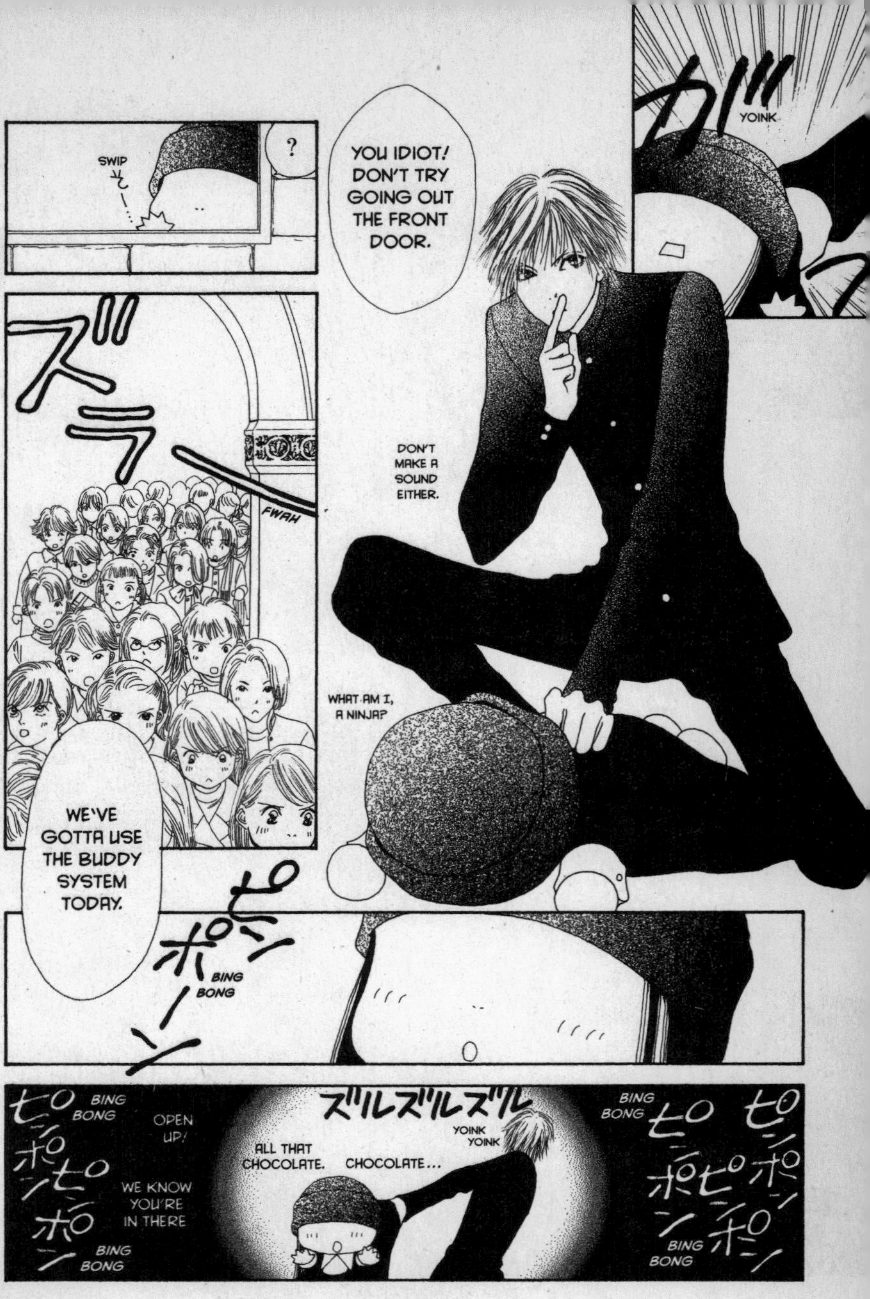

ガッ
YOINK
YOU IDIOT! DON'T TRY GOING OUT THE FRONT DOOR.
DON'T MAKE A SOUND EITHER.
WHAT AM I, A NINJA?
?
SWIP
ズラ
FWAH
WE'VE GOTTA USE THE BUDDY SYSTEM TODAY.
ピンポーン
BING BONG
ピンポンピンポン
BING BONG
BING BONG
ズルズルズル
YOINK YOINK
ALL THAT CHOCOLATE.
CHOCOLATE...
OPEN UP!
WE KNOW YOU'RE IN THERE
ピンポンピンポン
BING BONG
BING BONG

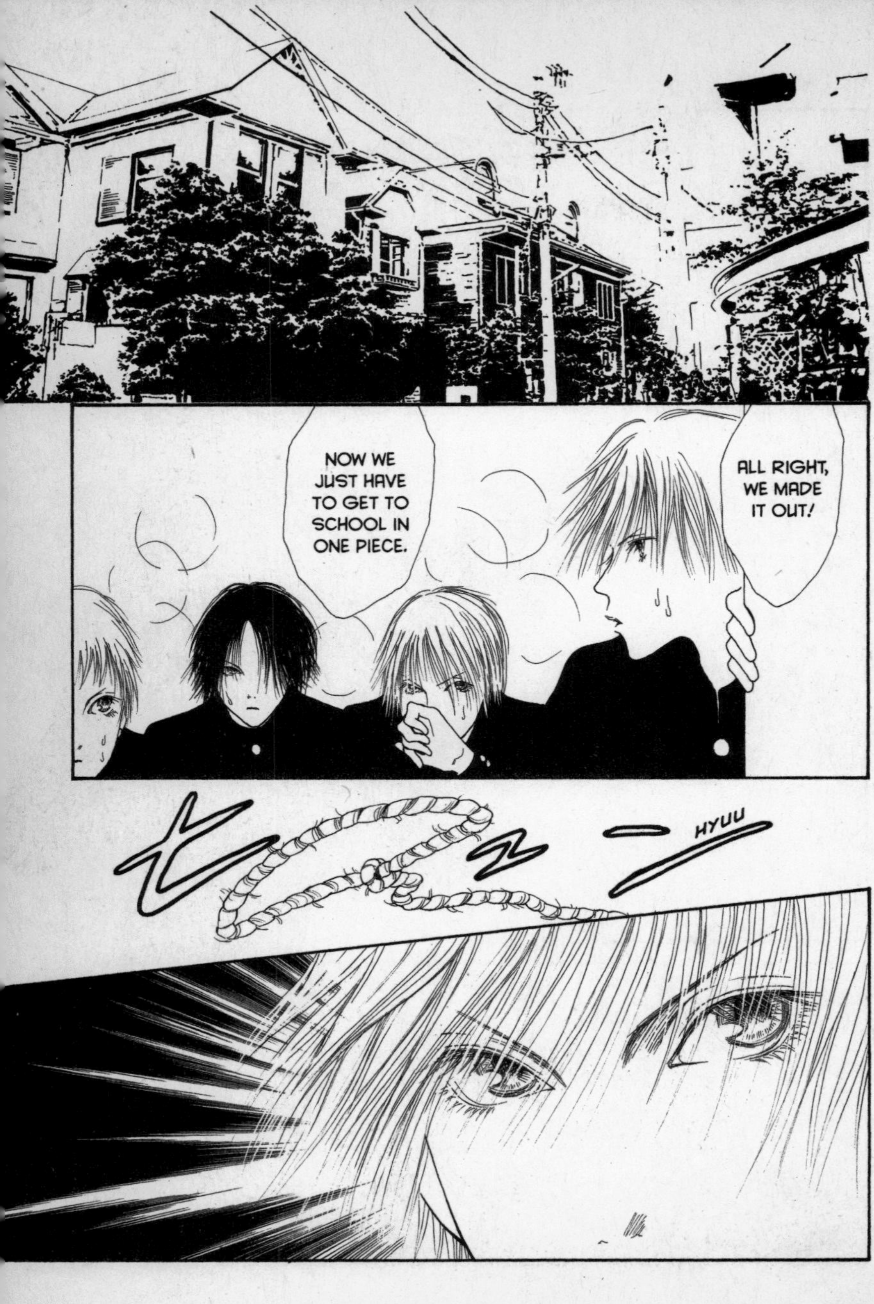
ALL RIGHT, WE MADE IT OUT!
NOW WE JUST HAVE TO GET TO SCHOOL IN ONE PIECE.
HYUU

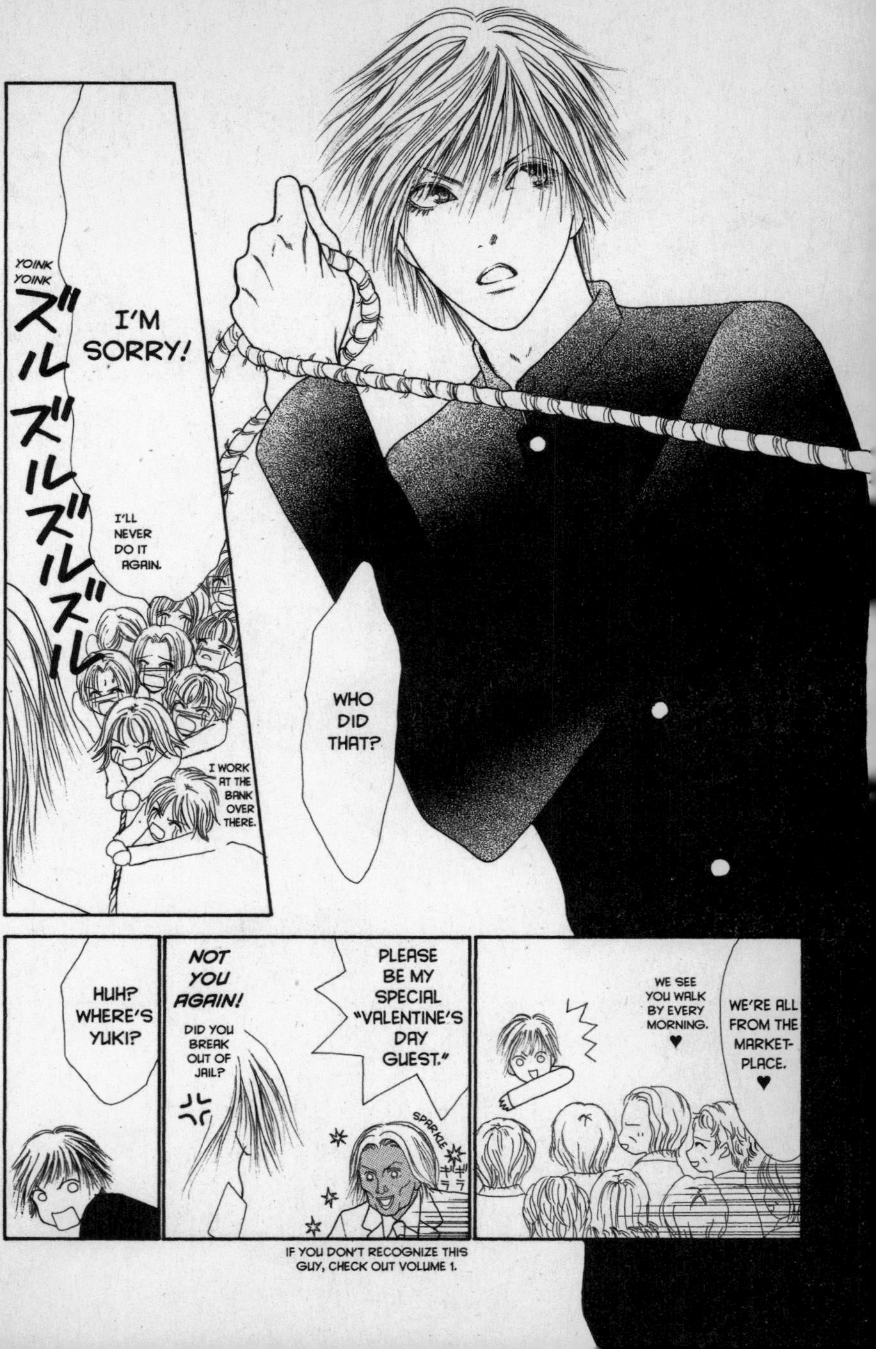
WHO DID THAT?
YOINK YOINK
ズルズルズルズル
I'M SORRY!
I'LL NEVER DO IT AGAIN.
I WORK AT THE BANK OVER THERE.
WE'RE ALL FROM THE MARKET-PLACE. ♥
WE SEE YOU WALK BY EVERY MORNING. ♥
PLEASE BE MY SPECIAL "VALENTINE'S DAY GUEST."
SPARKLE
キラ キラ
NOT YOU AGAIN!
DID YOU BREAK OUT OF JAIL?
HUH? WHERE'S YUKI?

IF YOU DON'T RECOGNIZE THIS GUY, CHECK OUT VOLUME 1.

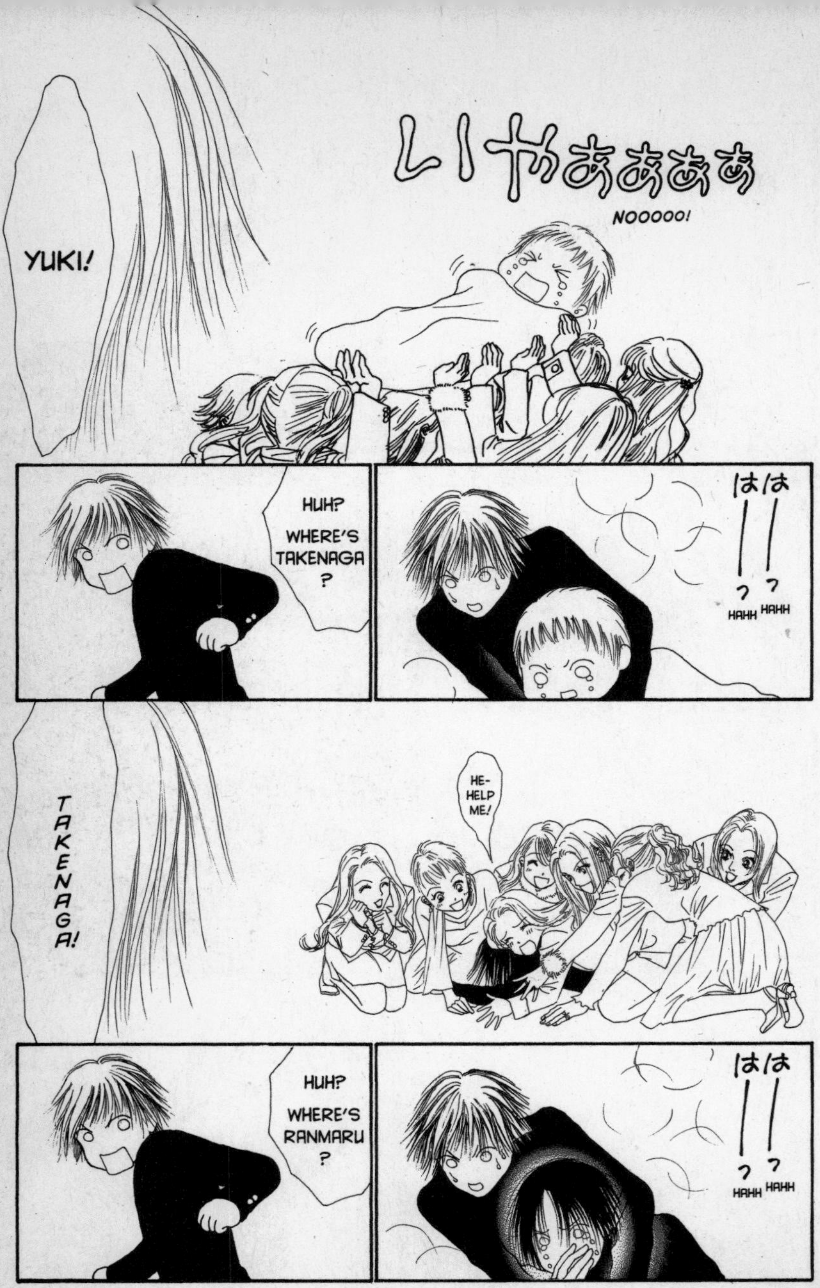
いやああああ
NOOOOO!
YUKI!
はーっ はーっ
HAHH HAHH
HUH? WHERE'S TAKENAGA?
HE-HELP ME!
TAKENAGA!
はーっ はーっ
HAHH HAHH
HUH? WHERE'S RANMARU?

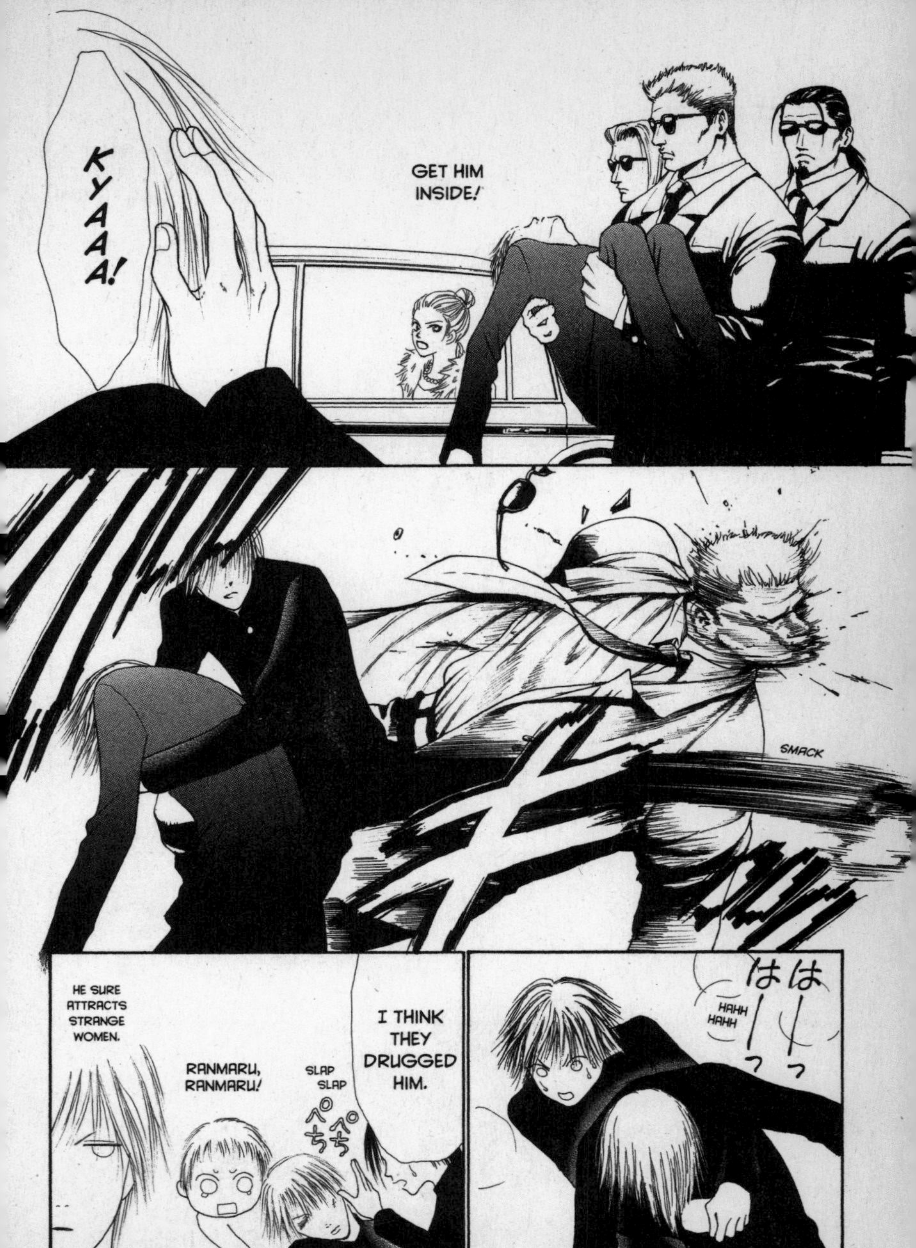
GET HIM INSIDE!
KYAAA!
SMACK
HAHH HAHH
はーっ はーっ
I THINK THEY DRUGGED HIM.
SLAP SLAP
ぺちぺち
RANMARU, RANMARU!
HE SURE ATTRACTS STRANGE WOMEN.

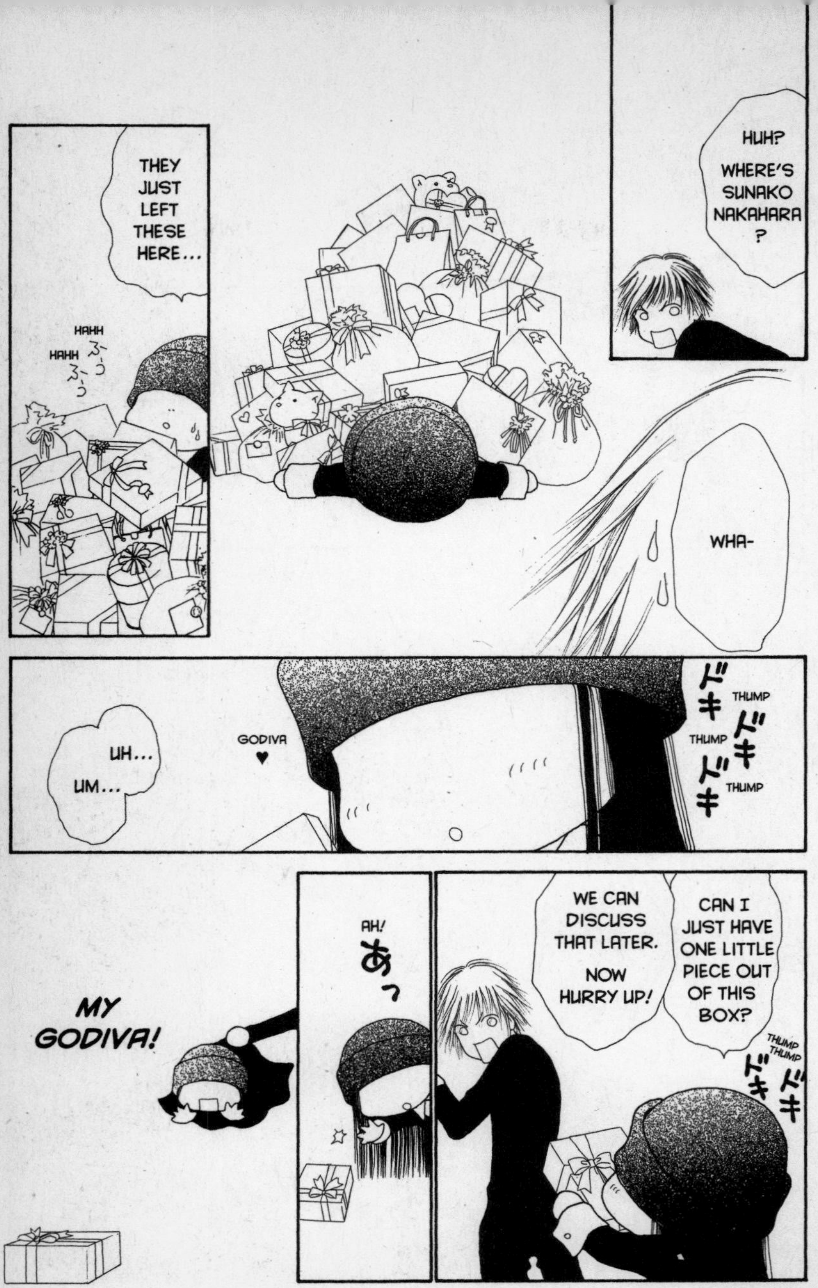
HUH?
WHERE'S SUNAKO NAKAHARA?
WHA-
THEY JUST LEFT THESE HERE...
ふーふー HAHH HAHH
ドキドキドキ THUMP THUMP THUMP
GODIVA ♥
UH... UM...
CAN I JUST HAVE ONE LITTLE PIECE OUT OF THIS BOX?
WE CAN DISCUSS THAT LATER.
NOW HURRY UP!
ドキドキ THUMP THUMP
あっ AH!
MY GODIVA!

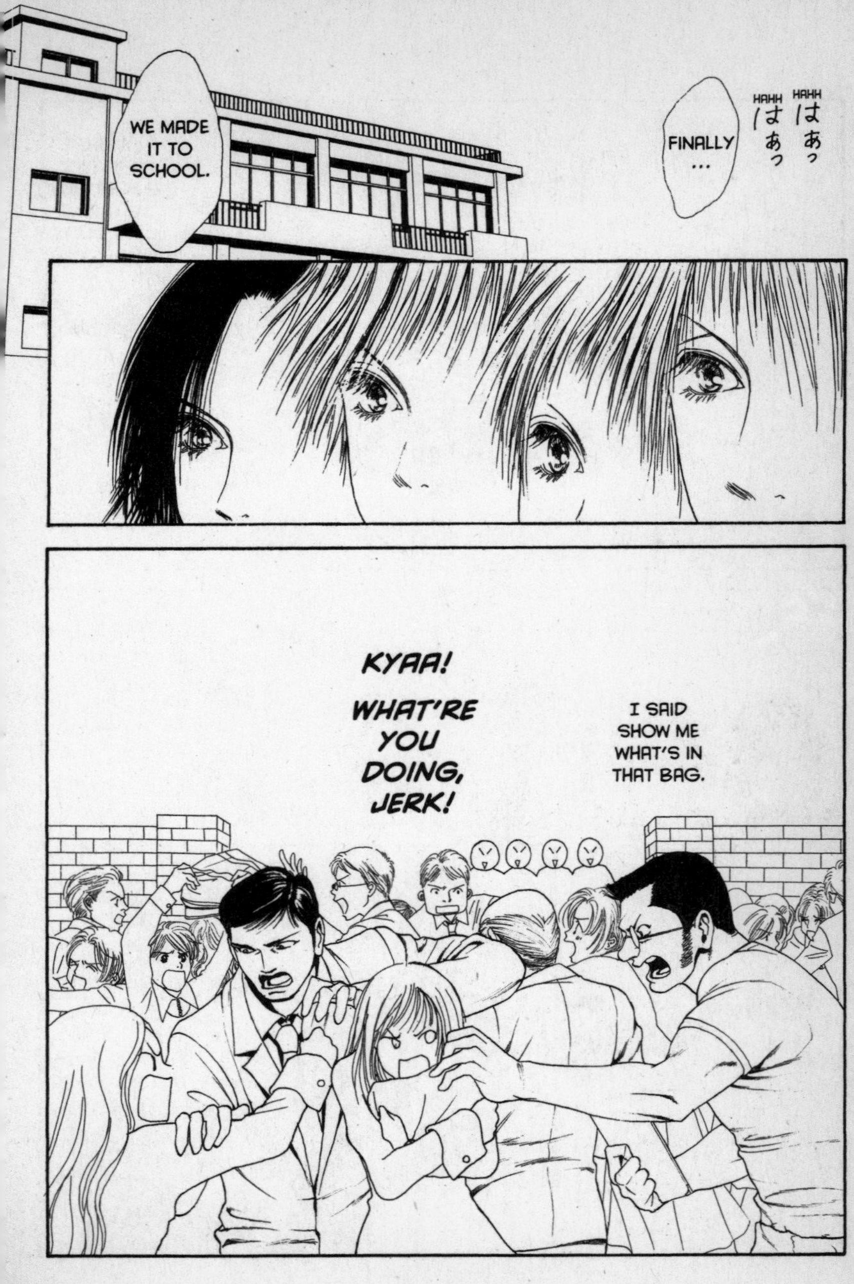
HAHH はぁっ
HAHH はぁっ
FINALLY …
WE MADE IT TO SCHOOL.
I SAID SHOW ME WHAT'S IN THAT BAG.
KYAA!
WHAT'RE YOU DOING, JERK!

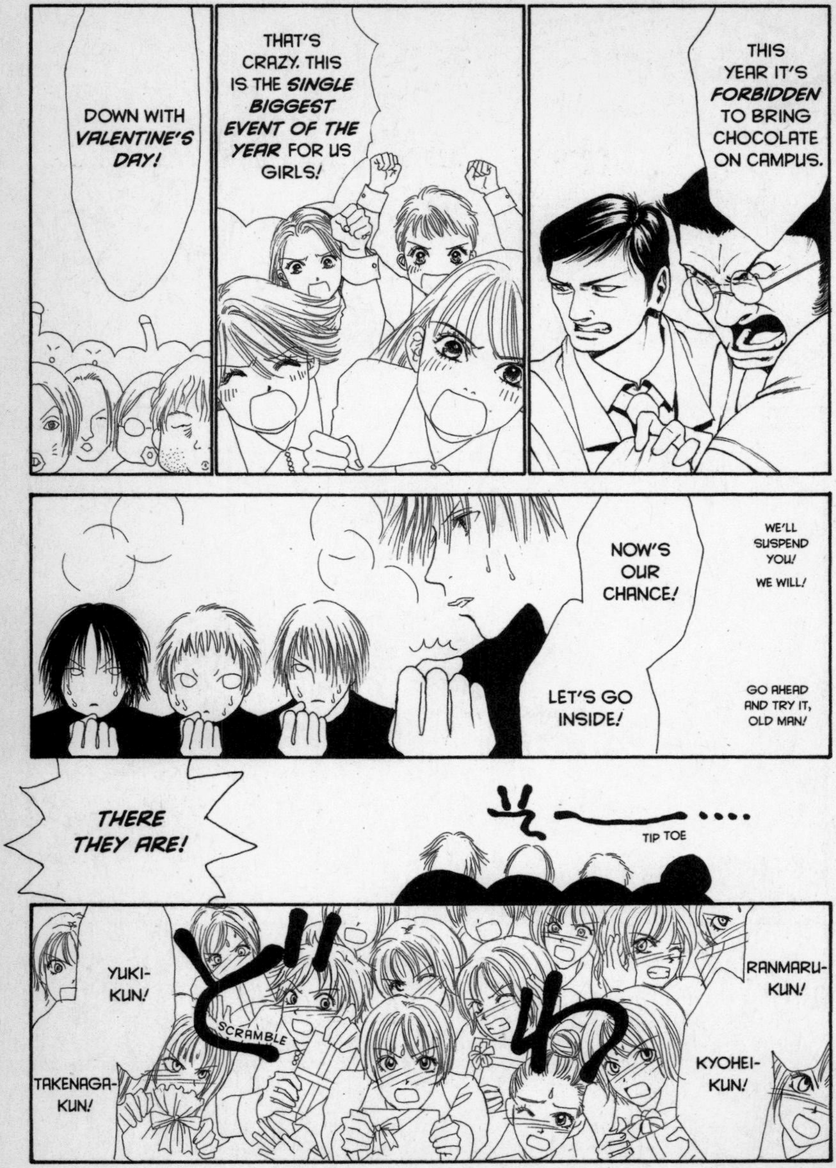
THIS YEAR IT'S FORBIDDEN TO BRING CHOCOLATE ON CAMPUS.
THAT'S CRAZY. THIS IS THE SINGLE BIGGEST EVENT OF THE YEAR FOR US GIRLS!
DOWN WITH VALENTINE'S DAY!
WE'LL SUSPEND YOU!
WE WILL!
GO AHEAD AND TRY IT, OLD MAN!
NOW'S OUR CHANCE!
LET'S GO INSIDE!
TIP TOE
THERE THEY ARE!
RANMARU-KUN!
KYOHEI-KUN!
SCRAMBLE
YUKI-KUN!
TAKENAGA-KUN!

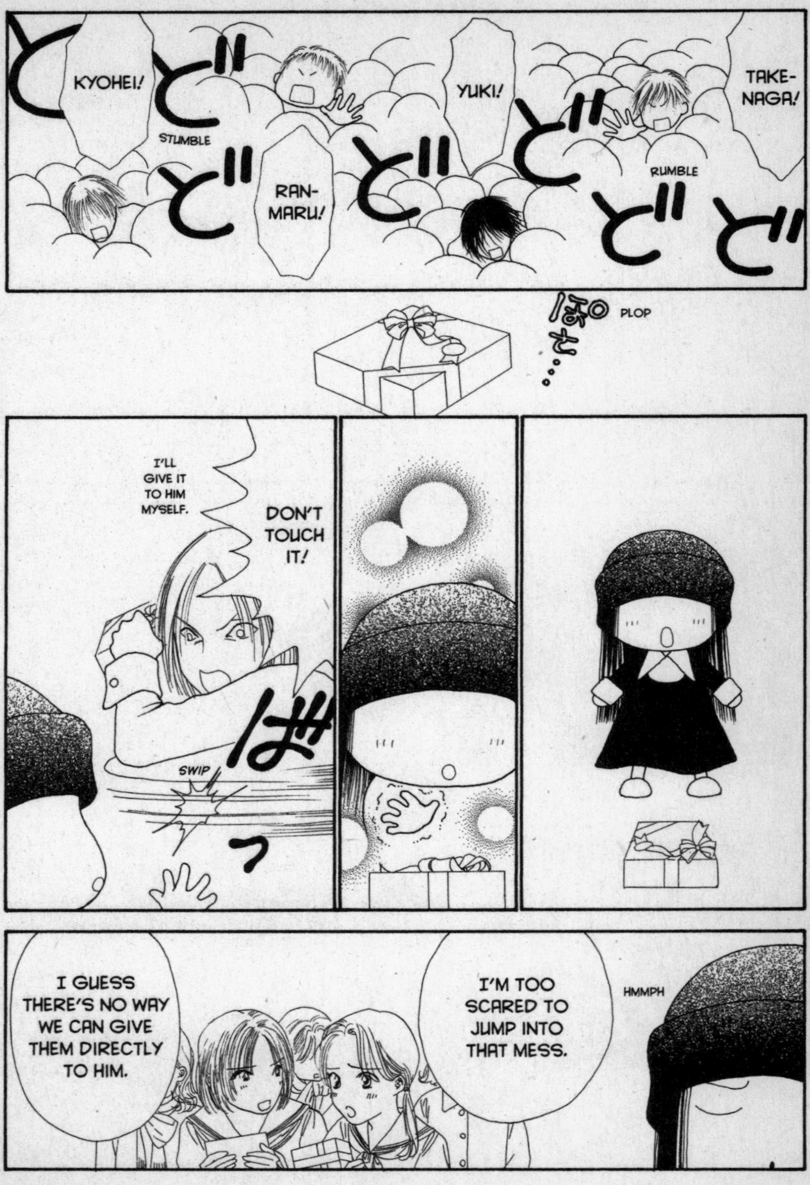
TAKE-NAGA!
RUMBLE
どどどど
YUKI!
RAN-MARU!
STUMBLE
どどど
KYOHEI!
ぽと…
PLOP
DON'T TOUCH IT!
I'LL GIVE IT TO HIM MYSELF.
ぱっ
SWIP
HMMPH
I'M TOO SCARED TO JUMP INTO THAT MESS.
I GUESS THERE'S NO WAY WE CAN GIVE THEM DIRECTLY TO HIM.

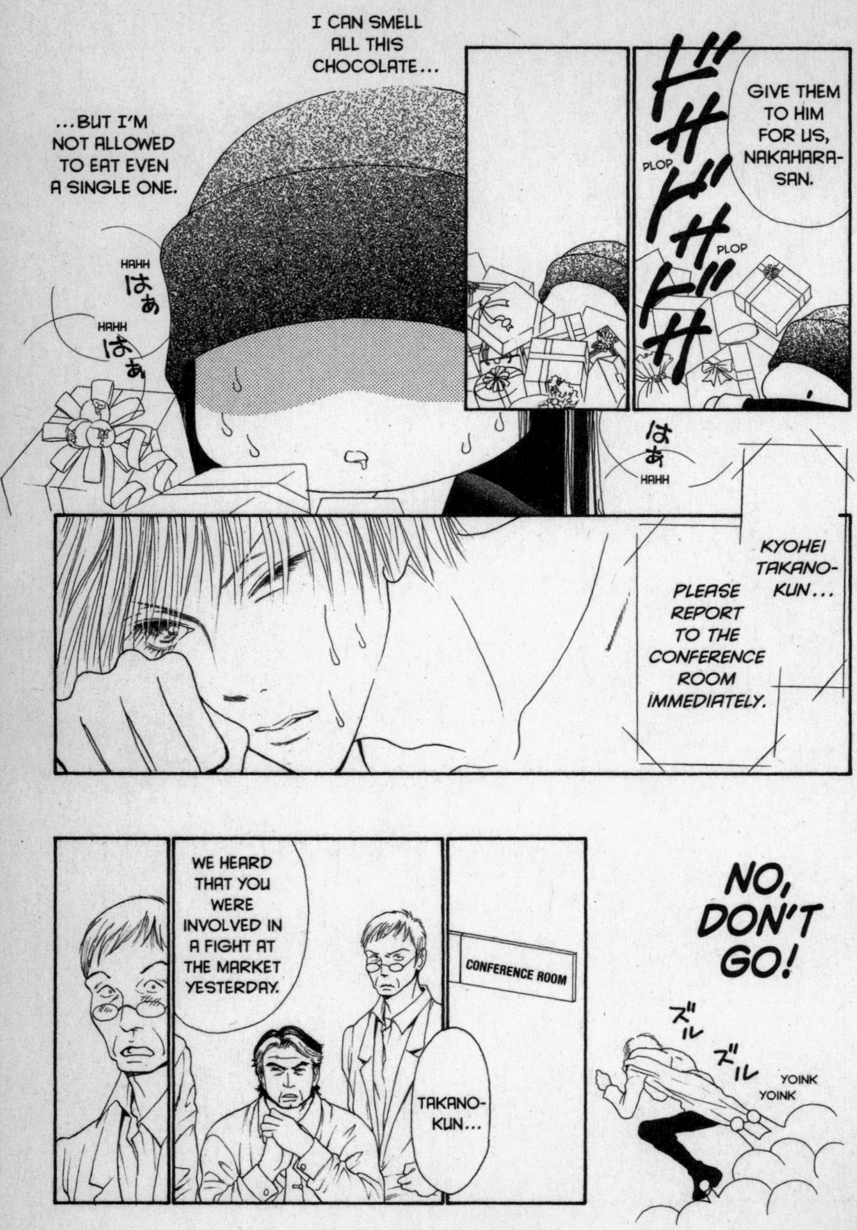
ドサドサドサ
PLOP
PLOP
GIVE THEM TO HIM FOR US, NAKAHARA-SAN.
I CAN SMELL ALL THIS CHOCOLATE...
...BUT I'M NOT ALLOWED TO EAT EVEN A SINGLE ONE.
はぁ
HAHH
はぁ
HAHH
はぁ
HAHH
KYOHEI TAKANO-KUN...
PLEASE REPORT TO THE CONFERENCE ROOM IMMEDIATELY.
NO, DON'T GO!
ズル
ズル
YOINK
YOINK
TAKANO-KUN...
WE HEARD THAT YOU WERE INVOLVED IN A FIGHT AT THE MARKET YESTERDAY.
CONFERENCE ROOM

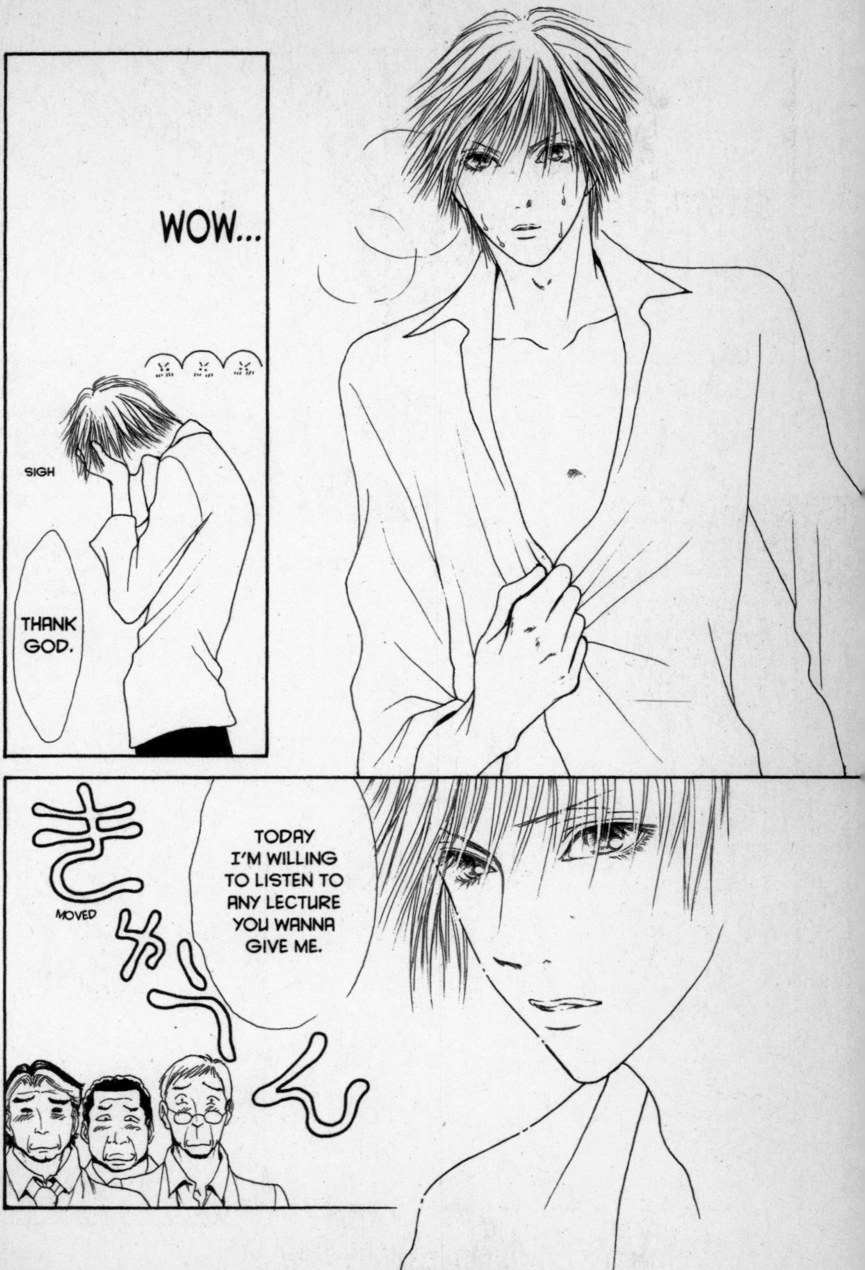
WOW...
SIGH
THANK GOD.
TODAY I'M WILLING TO LISTEN TO ANY LECTURE YOU WANNA GIVE ME.
きゅ〜ん
MOVED

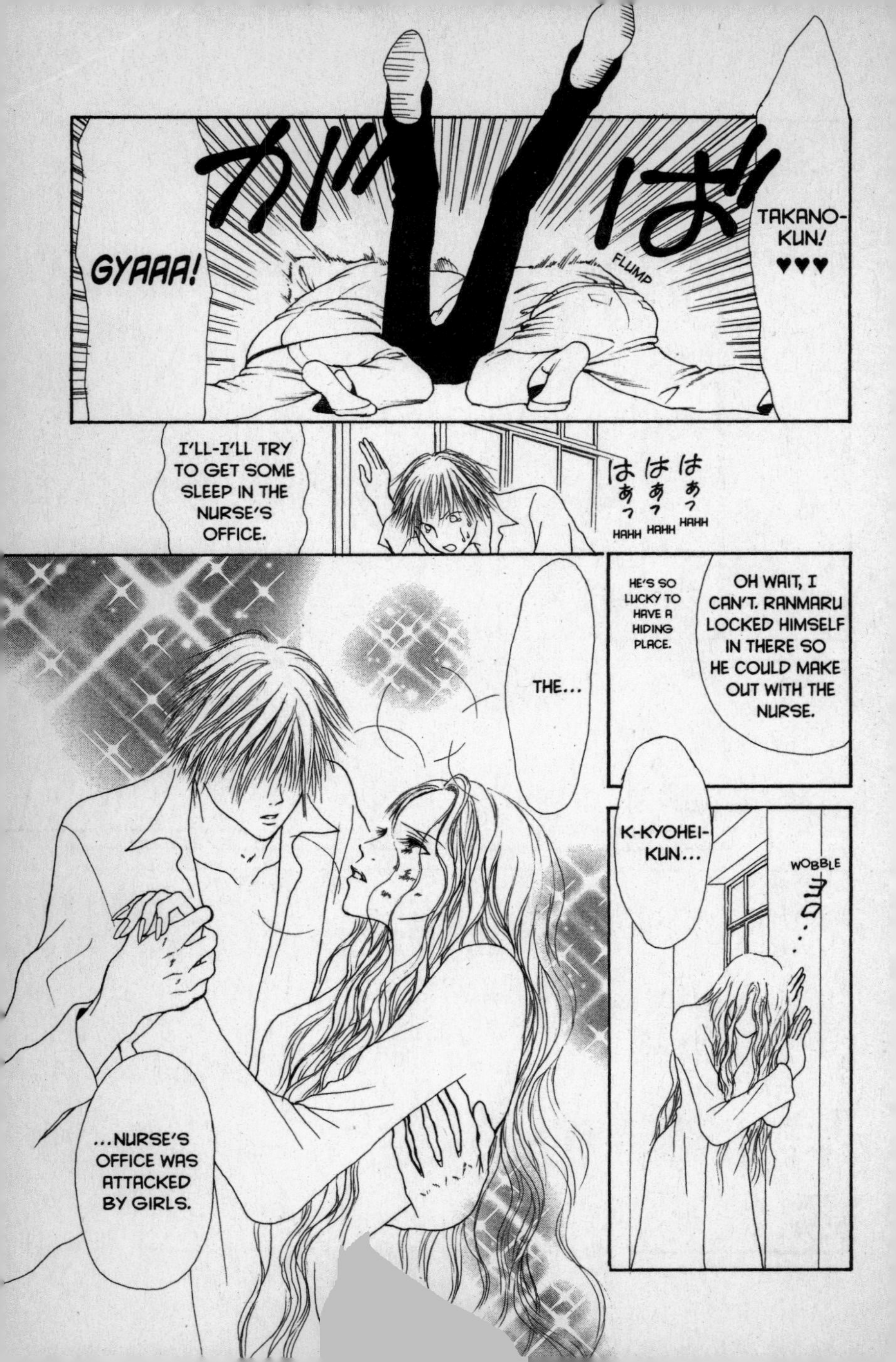
TAKANO-KUN! ♥♥♥
がッばッ
FLUMP
GYAAA!
はあっ はあっ はあっ
HAHH HAHH HAHH
I'LL-I'LL TRY TO GET SOME SLEEP IN THE NURSE'S OFFICE.
OH WAIT, I CAN'T. RANMARU LOCKED HIMSELF IN THERE SO HE COULD MAKE OUT WITH THE NURSE.
HE'S SO LUCKY TO HAVE A HIDING PLACE.
WOBBLE
ヨロ...
K-KYOHEI-KUN...
THE...
...NURSE'S OFFICE WAS ATTACKED BY GIRLS.

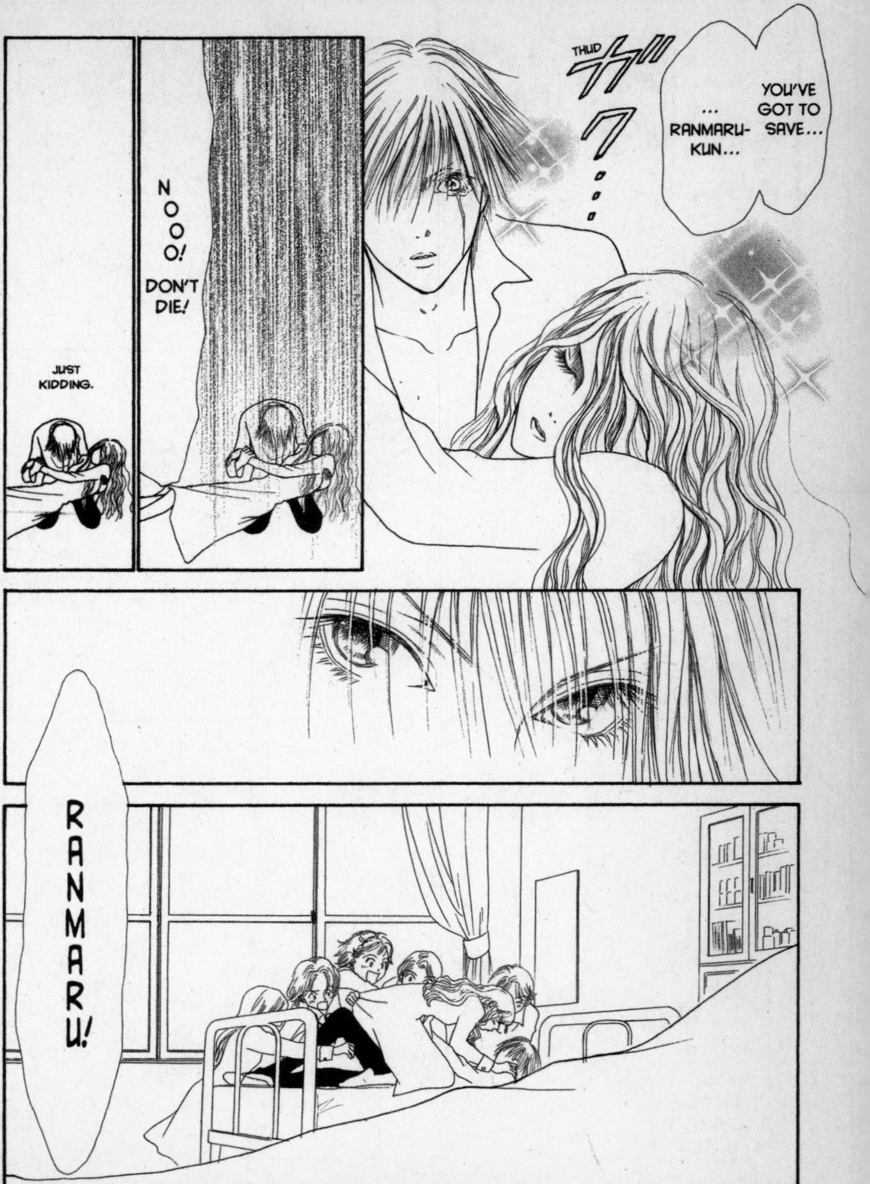
THUD
... RANMARU-KUN... YOU'VE GOT TO SAVE...
NOOO! DON'T DIE!
JUST KIDDING.
RANMARU!

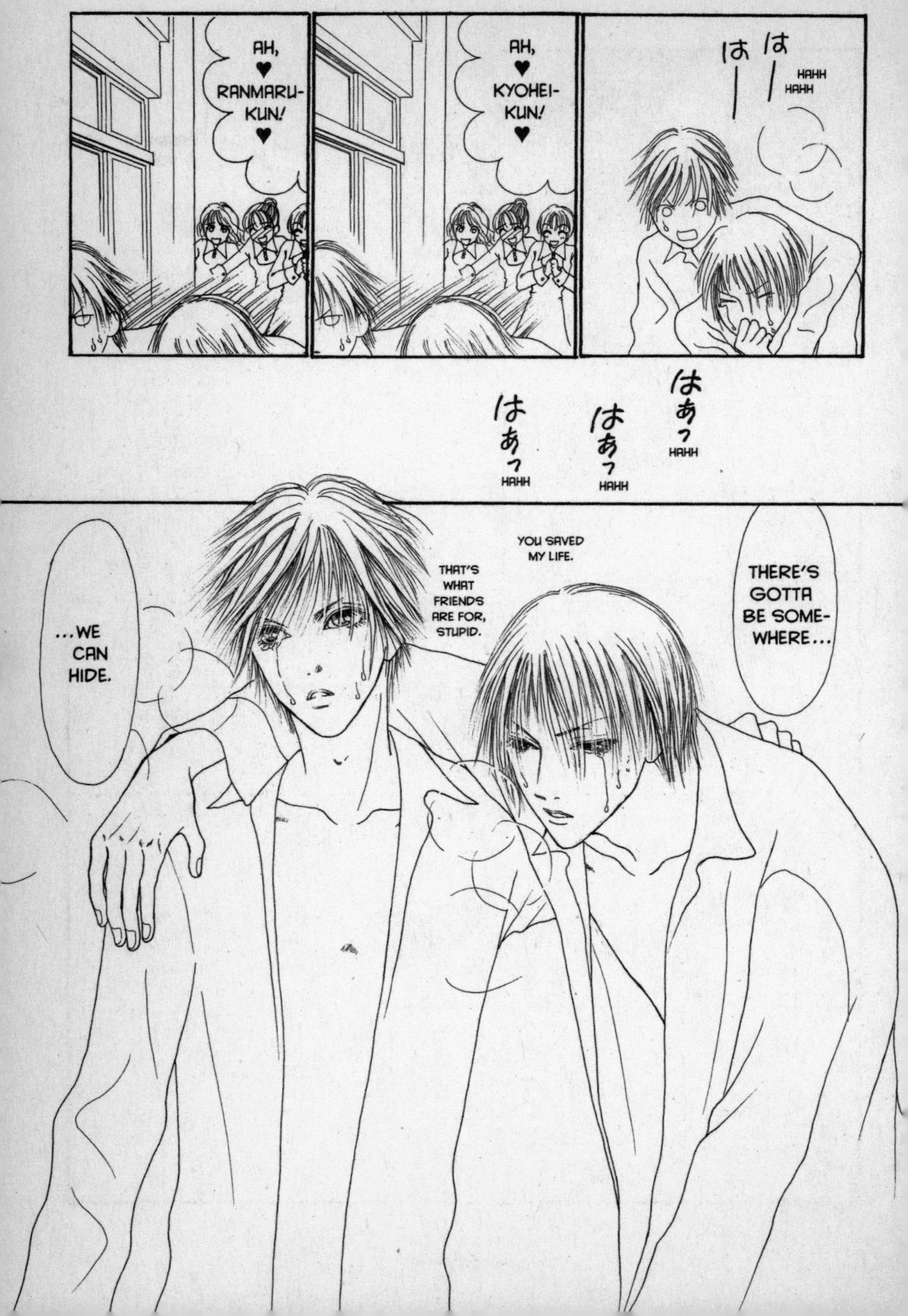
はーはー
HAHH HAHH
AH, ♥ KYOHEI-KUN! ♥
AH, ♥ RANMARU-KUN! ♥
はあっ
HAHH
はあっ
HAHH
はあっ
HAHH
THERE'S GOTTA BE SOMEWHERE...
YOU SAVED MY LIFE.
THAT'S WHAT FRIENDS ARE FOR, STUPID.
...WE CAN HIDE.

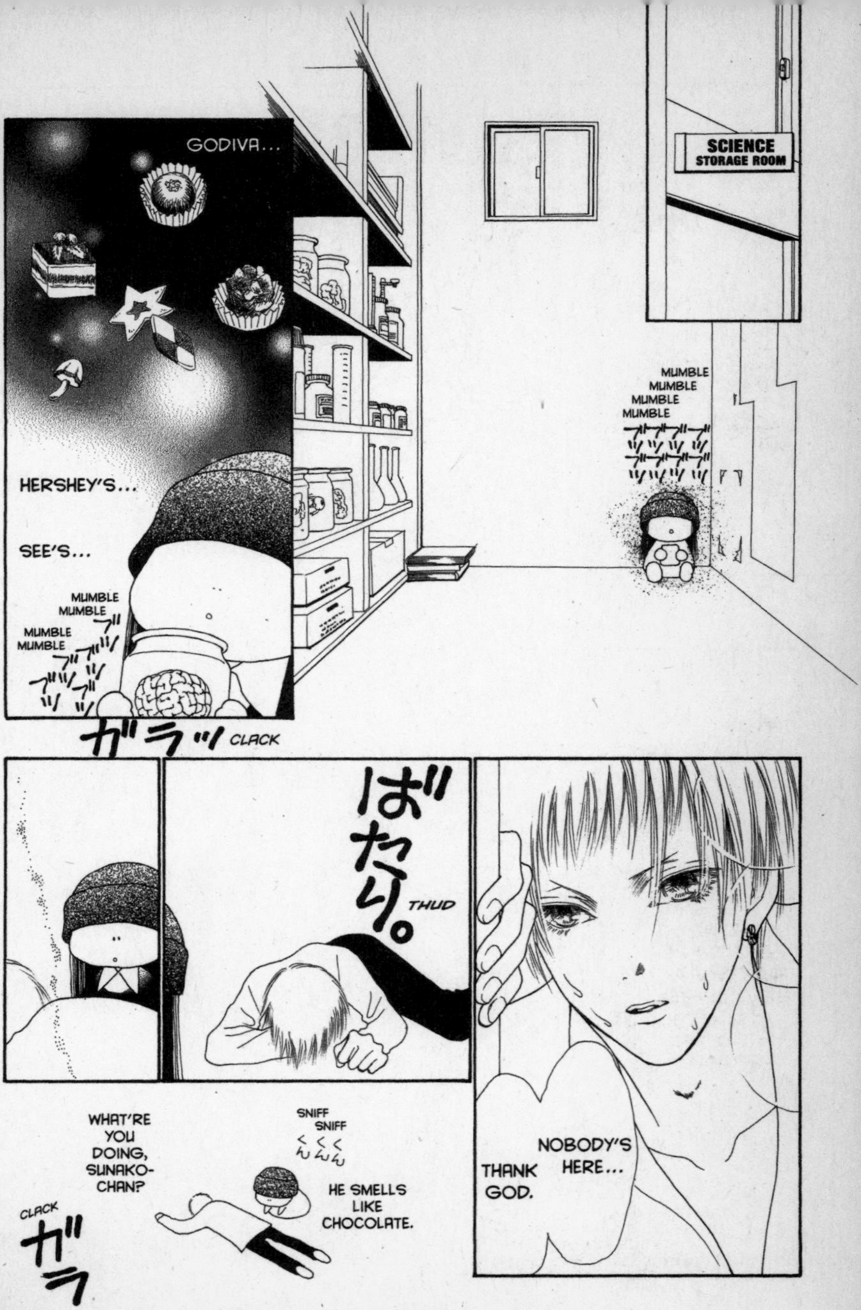
SCIENCE
STORAGE ROOM
MUMBLE
MUMBLE
MUMBLE
MUMBLE
ブツブツブツブツ
ブツブツブツブツ
GODIVA...
HERSHEY'S...
SEE'S...
MUMBLE
MUMBLE
MUMBLE
MUMBLE
ブツブツブツブツ
ガラッ CLACK
NOBODY'S HERE...
THANK GOD.
ばたり。 THUD
SNIFF
SNIFF
くんくんくん
HE SMELLS LIKE CHOCOLATE.
WHAT'RE YOU DOING, SUNAKO-CHAN?
CLACK
ガラ

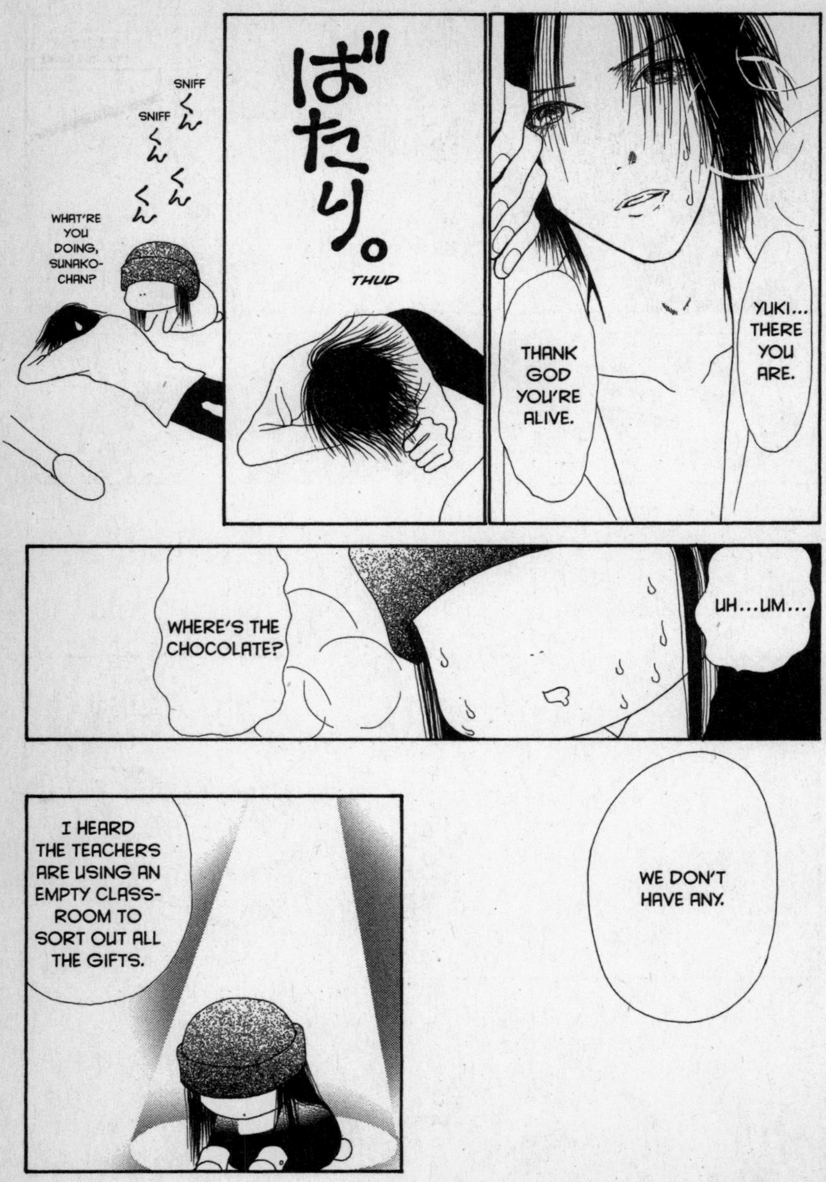
YUKI... THERE YOU ARE.
THANK GOD YOU'RE ALIVE.
ばたり。
THUD
SNIFF
SNIFF
くんくんくんくん
WHAT'RE YOU DOING, SUNAKO-CHAN?
UH...UM...
WHERE'S THE CHOCOLATE?
WE DON'T HAVE ANY.
I HEARD THE TEACHERS ARE USING AN EMPTY CLASS-ROOM TO SORT OUT ALL THE GIFTS.

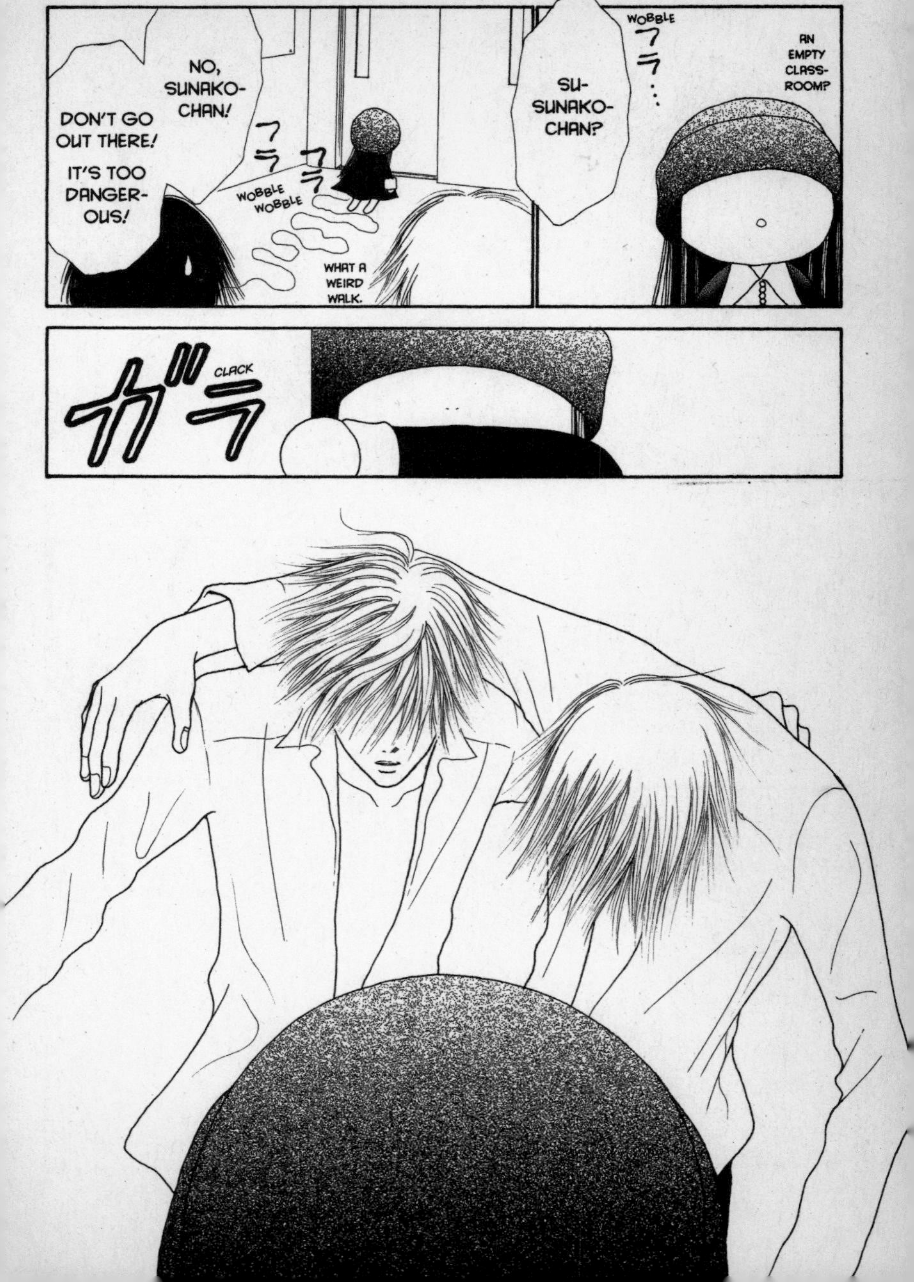
AN EMPTY CLASSROOM?
WOBBLE
フラ…
SU-SUNAKO-CHAN?
NO, SUNAKO-CHAN!
DON'T GO OUT THERE!
IT'S TOO DANGEROUS!
フラ フラ
WOBBLE WOBBLE
WHAT A WEIRD WALK.
ガラ
CLACK

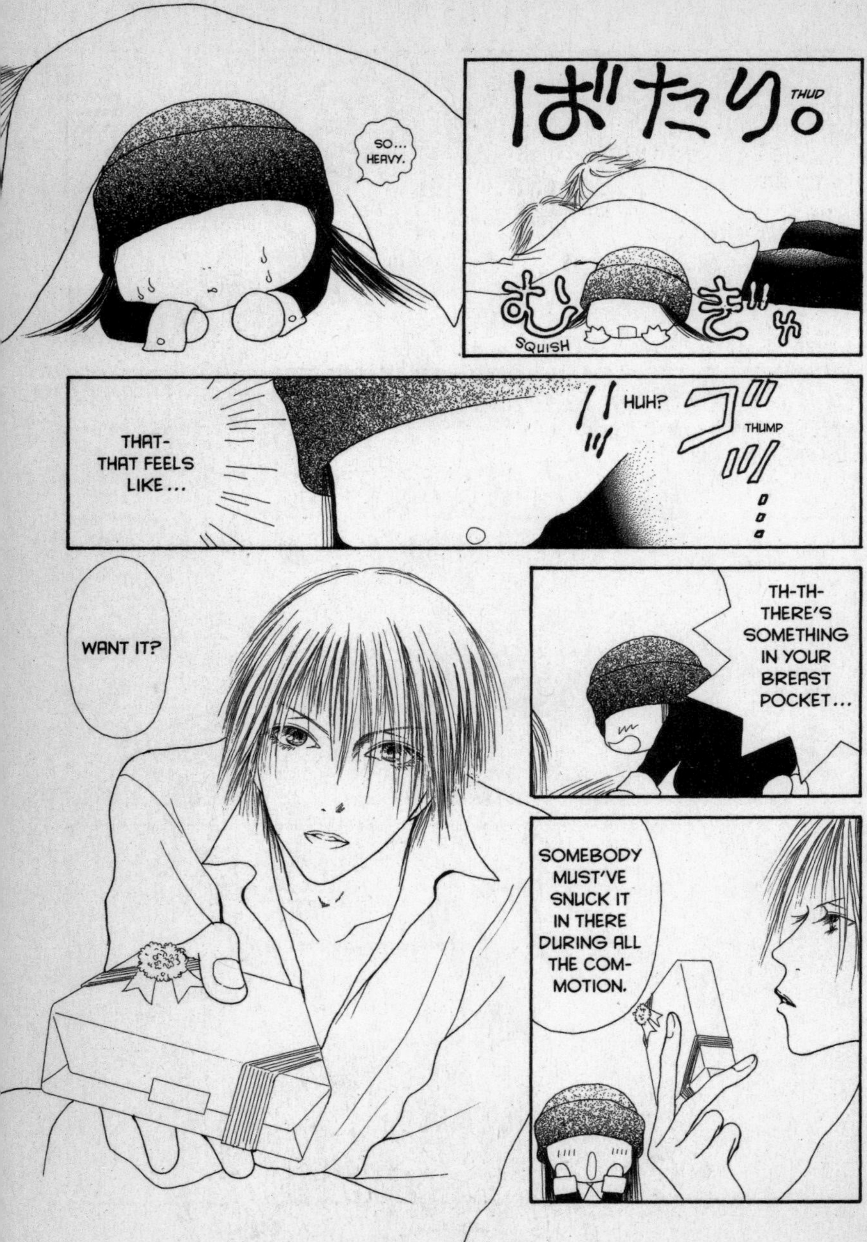
ばたり。
THUD
むぎゅ
SQUISH
SO... HEAVY.
ゴッ
THUMP
HUH?
THAT-THAT FEELS LIKE...
TH-TH-THERE'S SOMETHING IN YOUR BREAST POCKET...
SOMEBODY MUST'VE SNUCK IT IN THERE DURING ALL THE COM-MOTION.
WANT IT?

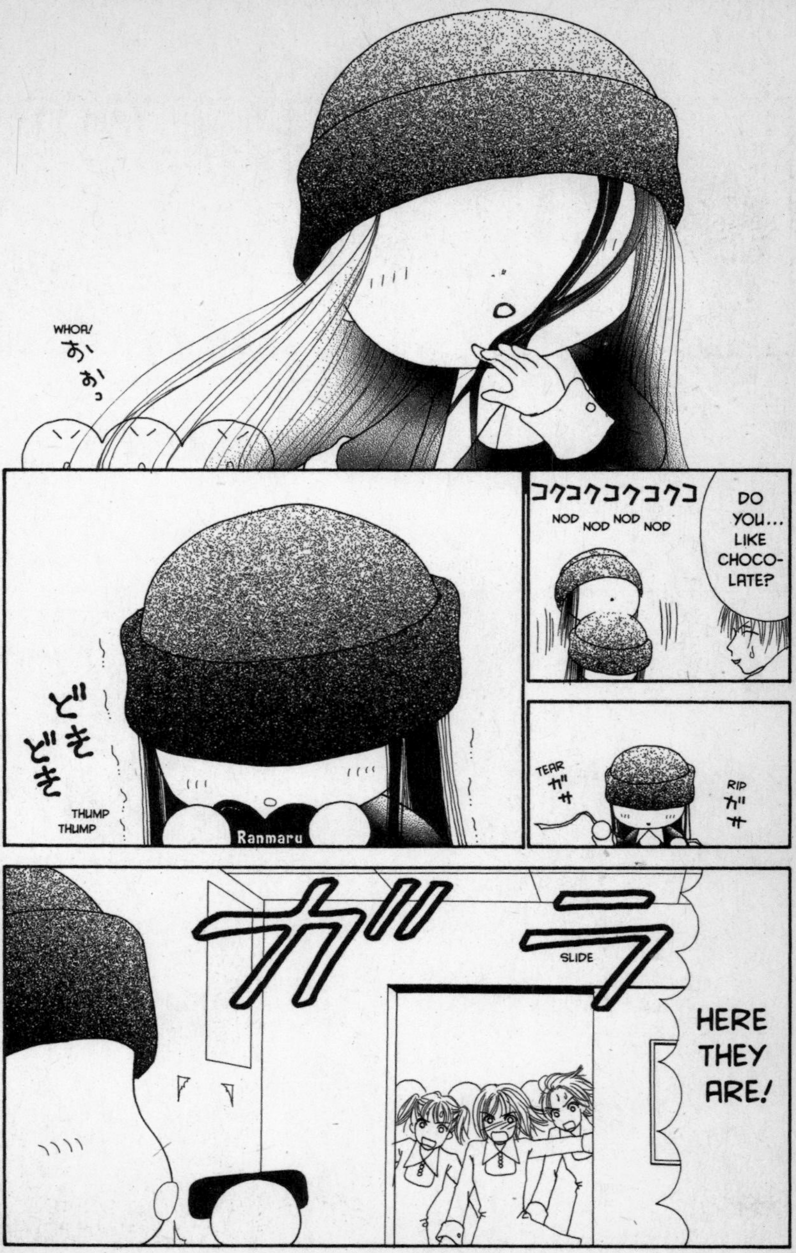
WHOA!
おおっ
DO YOU... LIKE CHOCOLATE?
コクコクコクコクコ
NOD NOD NOD NOD
RIP
ガサ
TEAR
ガサ
どきどき
THUMP THUMP
Ranmaru
ガラ
SLIDE
HERE THEY ARE!

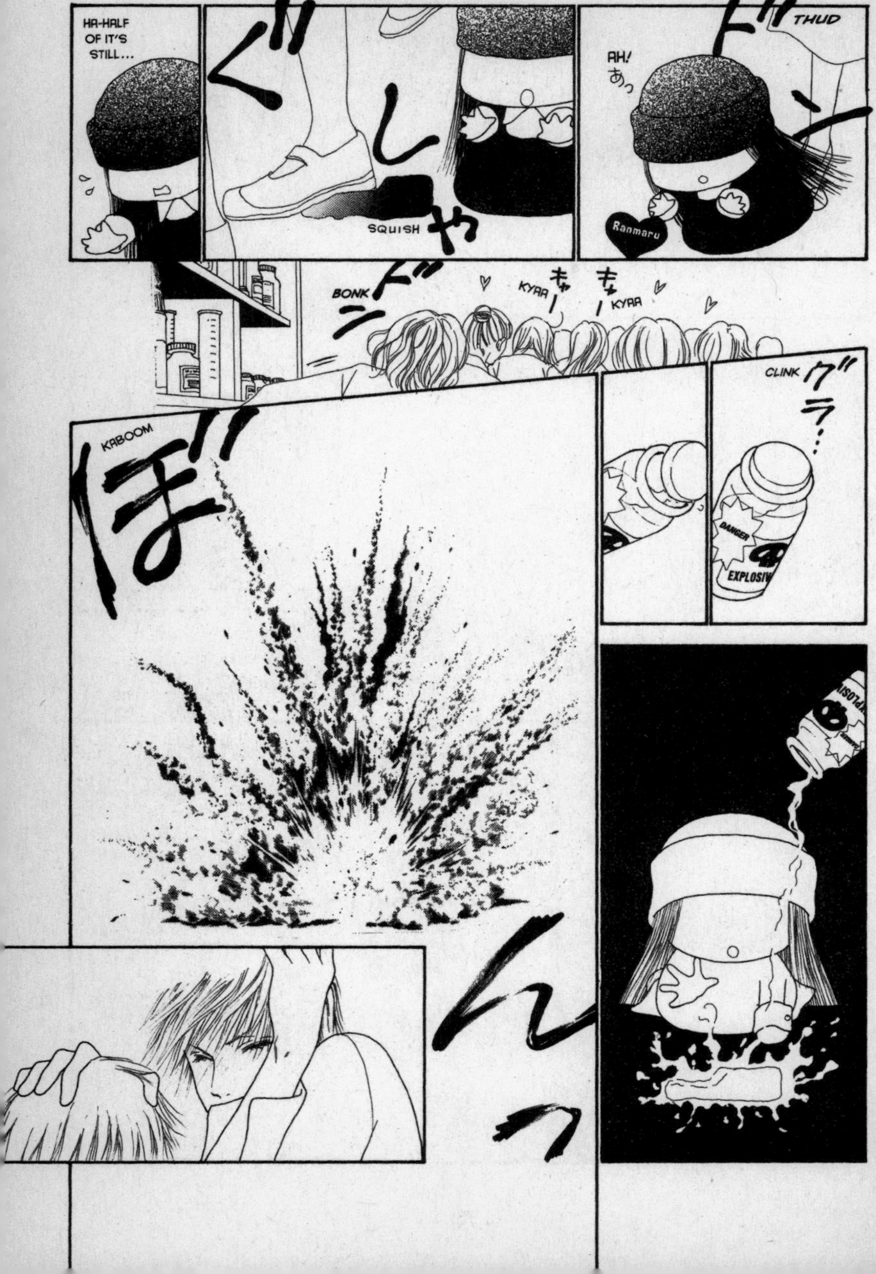
THUD
ドッ
ン
AH!
あっ
Ranmaru
ぐしゃ
SQUISH
HA-HALF OF IT'S STILL...
ドッ
ン
BONK
きゃー
KYAA
きゃー
KYAA
グラ...
CLINK
DANGER
EXPLOSIV
KABOOM
ぼん
っ

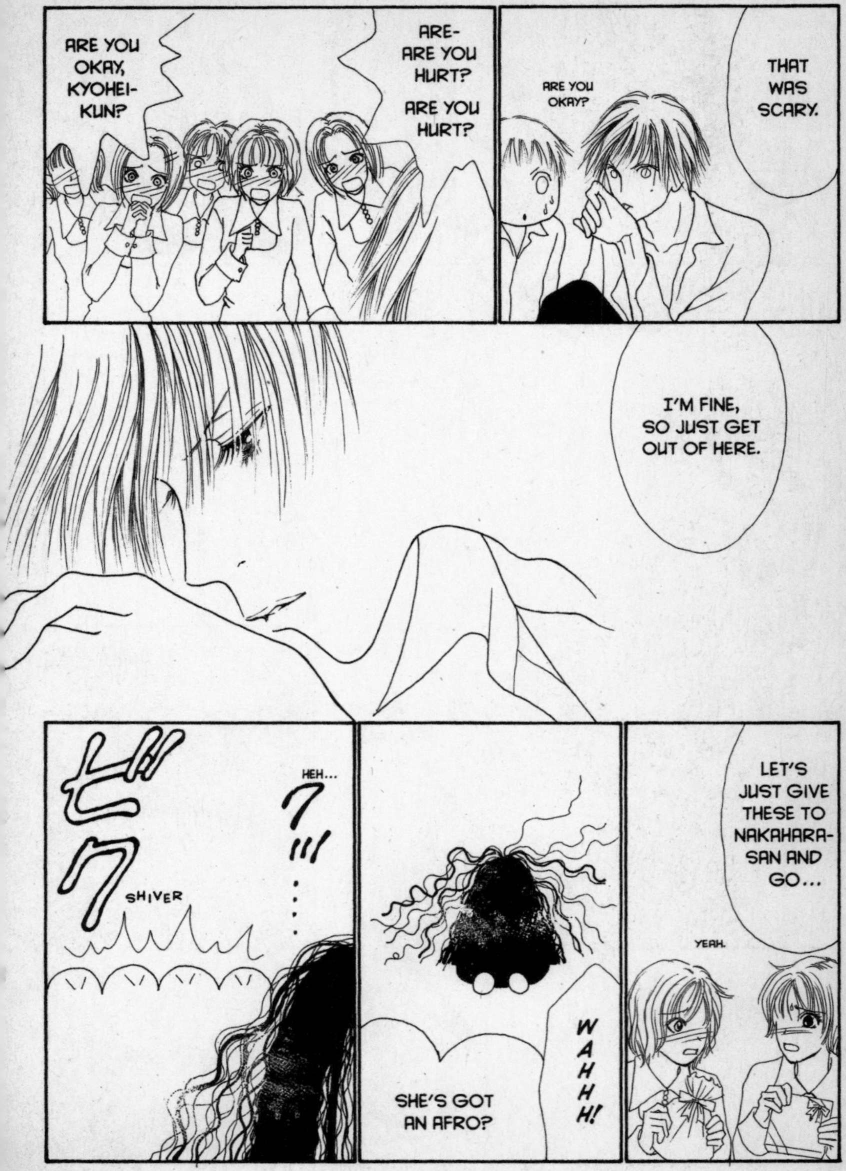
THAT WAS SCARY.
ARE YOU OKAY?
ARE- ARE YOU HURT?
ARE YOU HURT?
ARE YOU OKAY, KYOHEI-KUN?
I'M FINE, SO JUST GET OUT OF HERE.
LET'S JUST GIVE THESE TO NAKAHARA-SAN AND GO...
YEAH.
WAHHH!
SHE'S GOT AN AFRO?
HEH...
クッ...
ビク
SHIVER

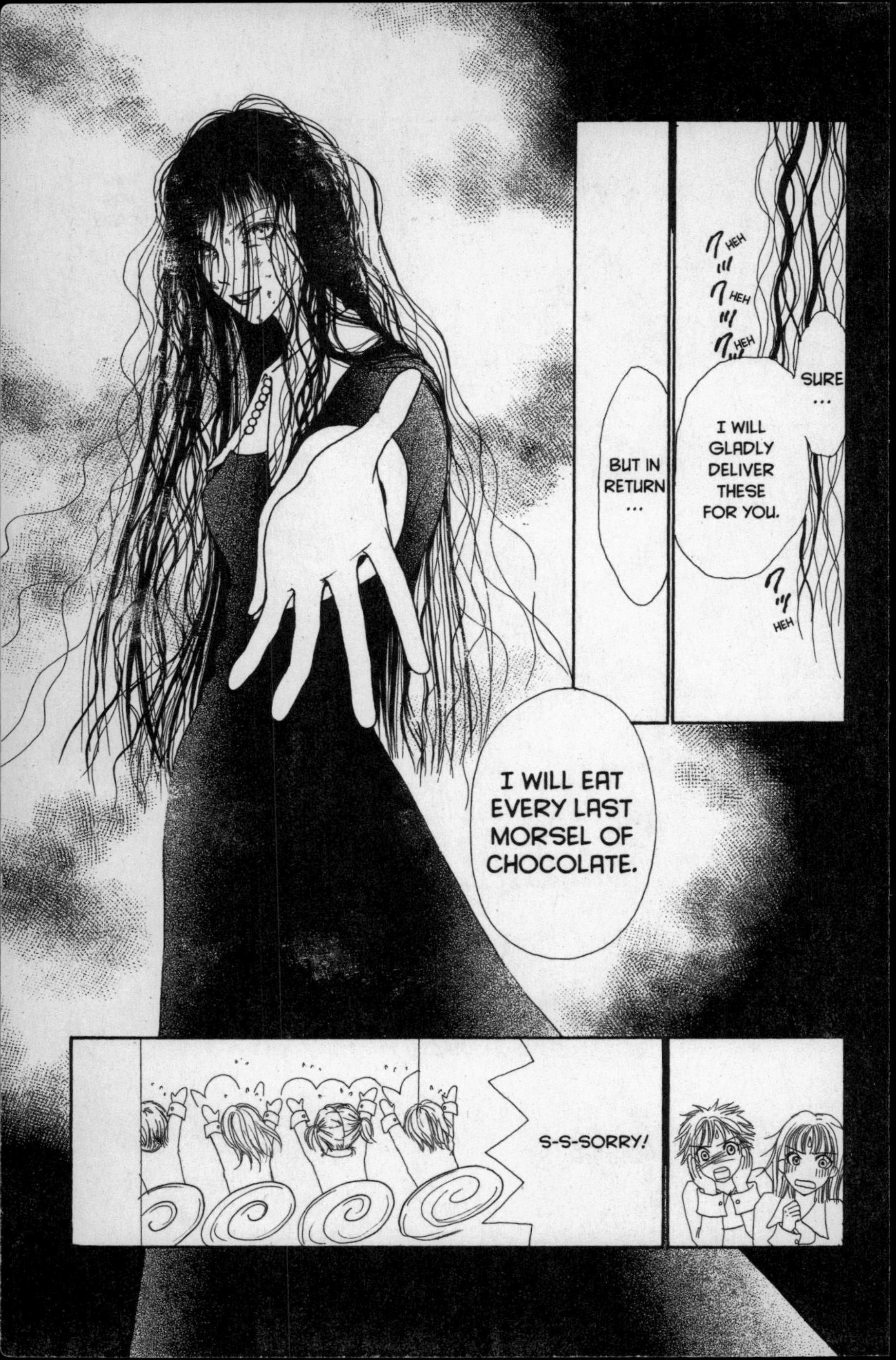
HEH
HEH
HEH
SURE...
I WILL GLADLY DELIVER THESE FOR YOU.
HEH
BUT IN RETURN...
I WILL EAT EVERY LAST MORSEL OF CHOCOLATE.
S-S-SORRY!

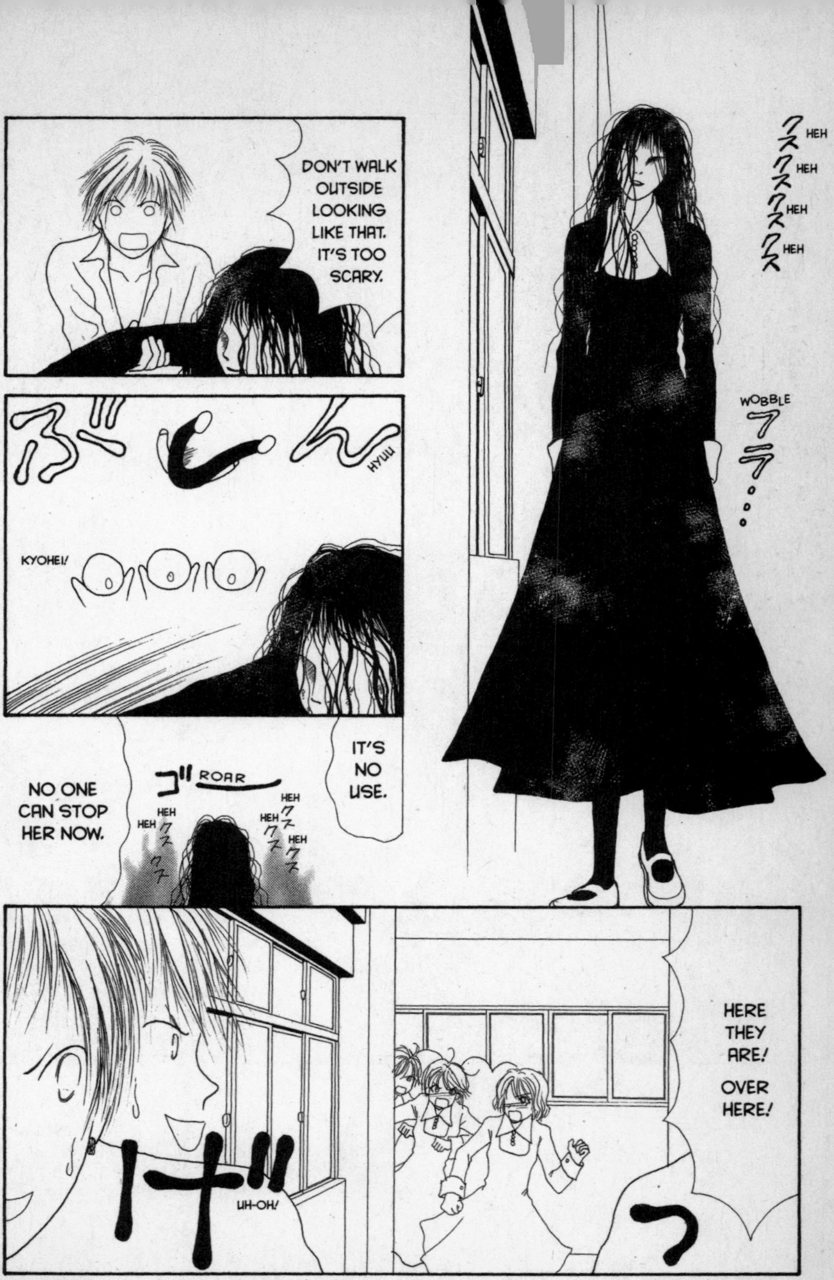

HEH HEH HEH HEH
WOBBLE
DON'T WALK OUTSIDE LOOKING LIKE THAT. IT'S TOO SCARY.
HYUU
KYOHEI!
IT'S NO USE.
ROAR
HEH HEH HEH HEH
NO ONE CAN STOP HER NOW.
HERE THEY ARE!
OVER HERE!
UH-OH!

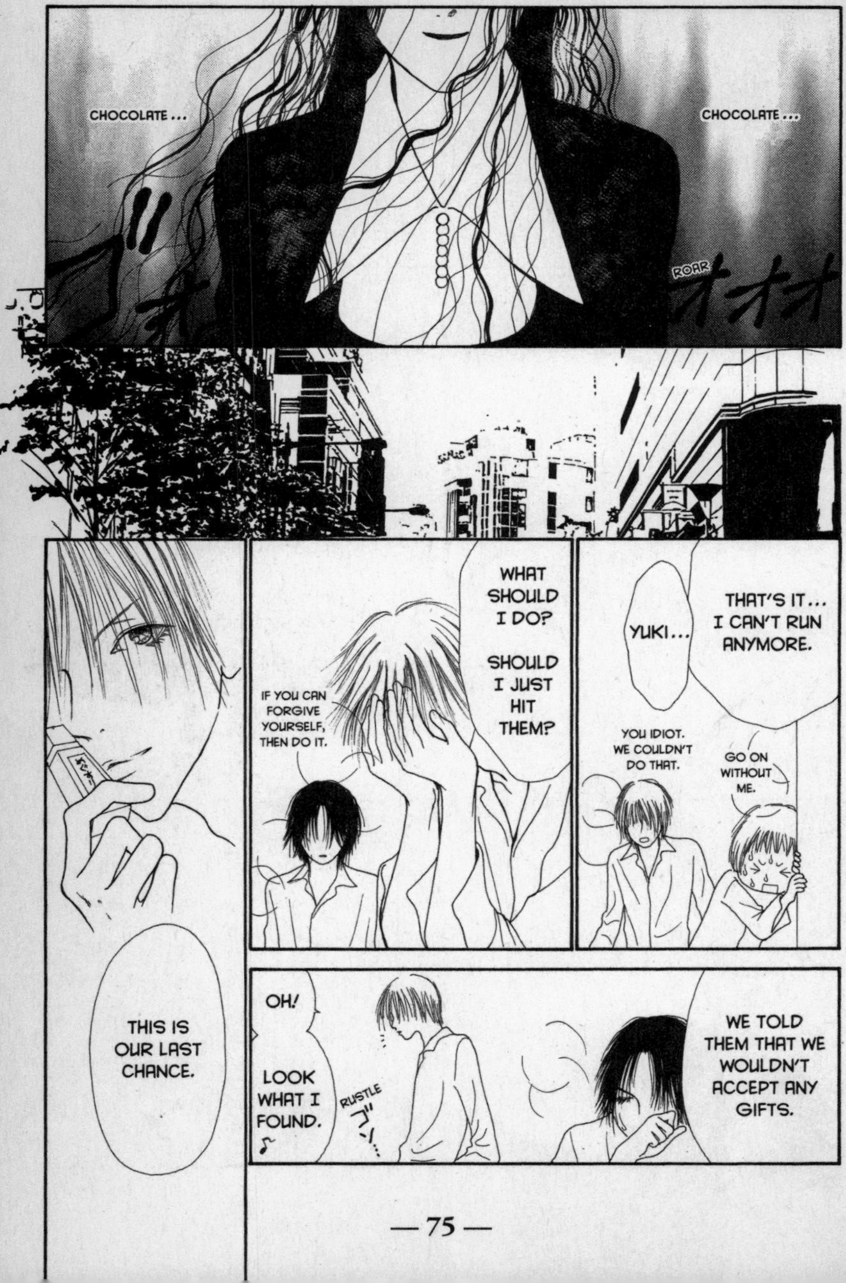
CHOCOLATE...
CHOCOLATE...
ROAR
THAT'S IT... I CAN'T RUN ANYMORE.
YUKI...
GO ON WITHOUT ME.
YOU IDIOT. WE COULDN'T DO THAT.
WHAT SHOULD I DO?
SHOULD I JUST HIT THEM?
IF YOU CAN FORGIVE YOURSELF, THEN DO IT.
WE TOLD THEM THAT WE WOULDN'T ACCEPT ANY GIFTS.
RUSTLE
OH!
LOOK WHAT I FOUND. ♪
THIS IS OUR LAST CHANCE.

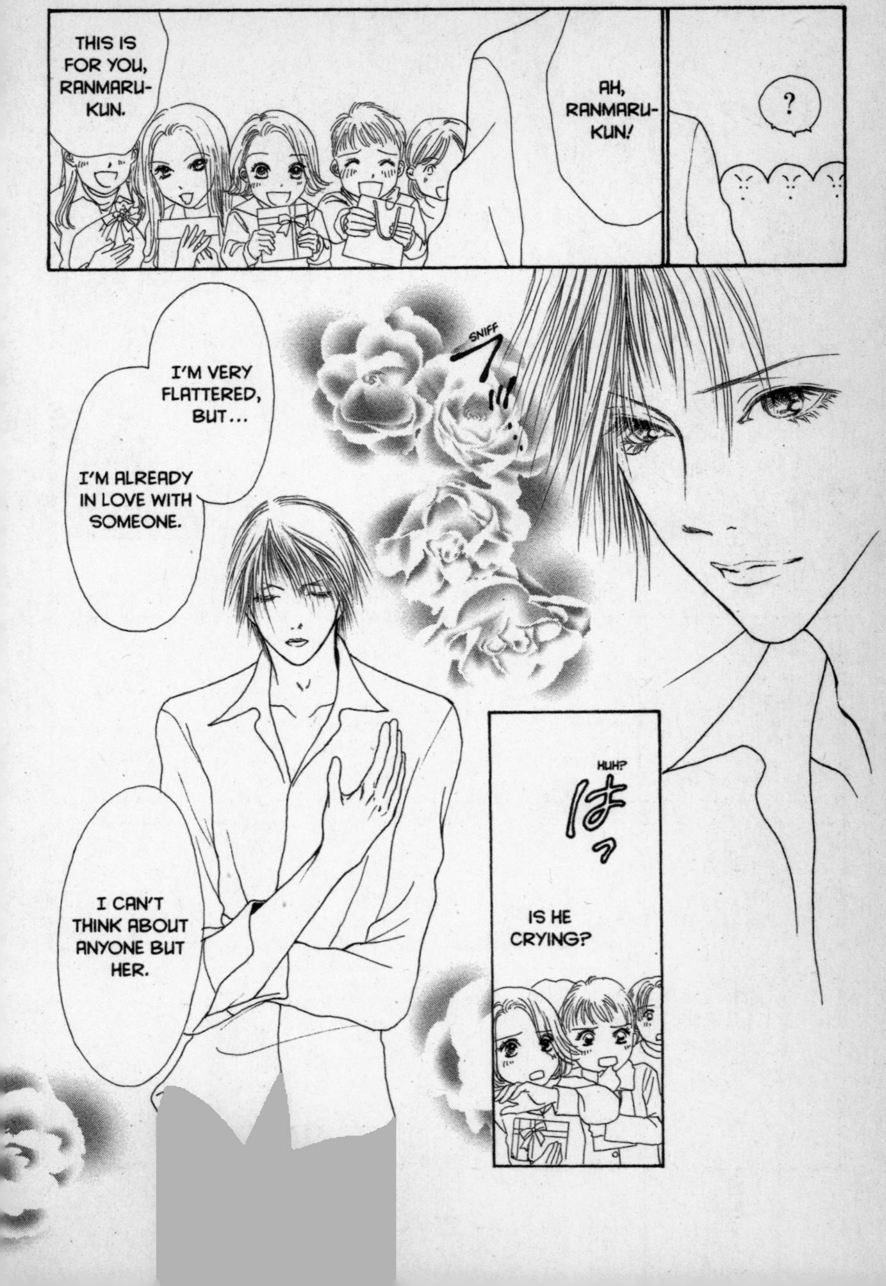
?
AH, RANMARU-KUN!
THIS IS FOR YOU, RANMARU-KUN.
SNIFF
I'M VERY FLATTERED, BUT...
I'M ALREADY IN LOVE WITH SOMEONE.
I CAN'T THINK ABOUT ANYONE BUT HER.
HUH?
はっ
IS HE CRYING?

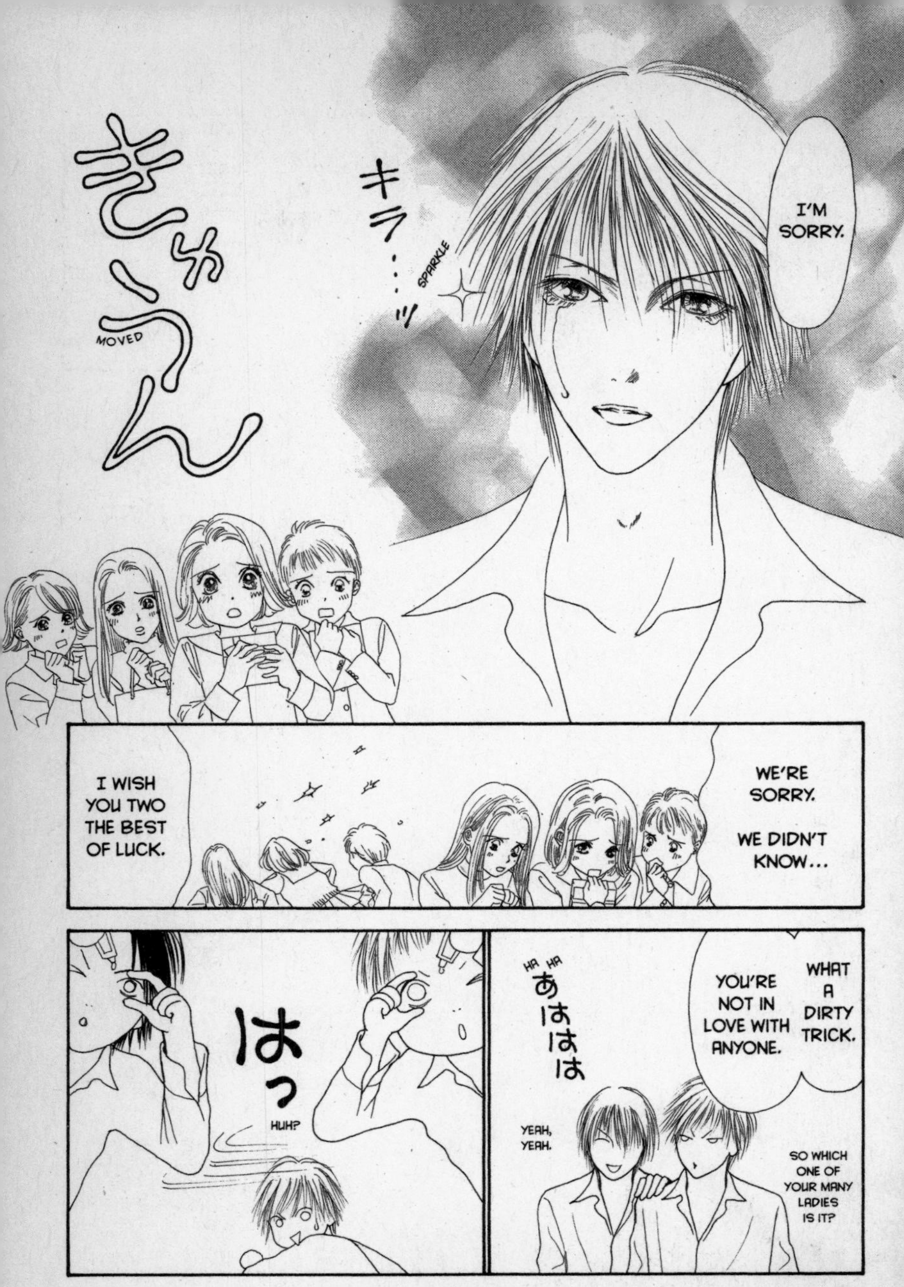
I'M SORRY.
キラ…ッ
SPARKLE
きゅうん
MOVED
WE'RE SORRY.
WE DIDN'T KNOW…
I WISH YOU TWO THE BEST OF LUCK.
WHAT A DIRTY TRICK.
YOU'RE NOT IN LOVE WITH ANYONE.
あははは
HA HA
SO WHICH ONE OF YOUR MANY LADIES IS IT?
YEAH, YEAH.
はっ
HUH?

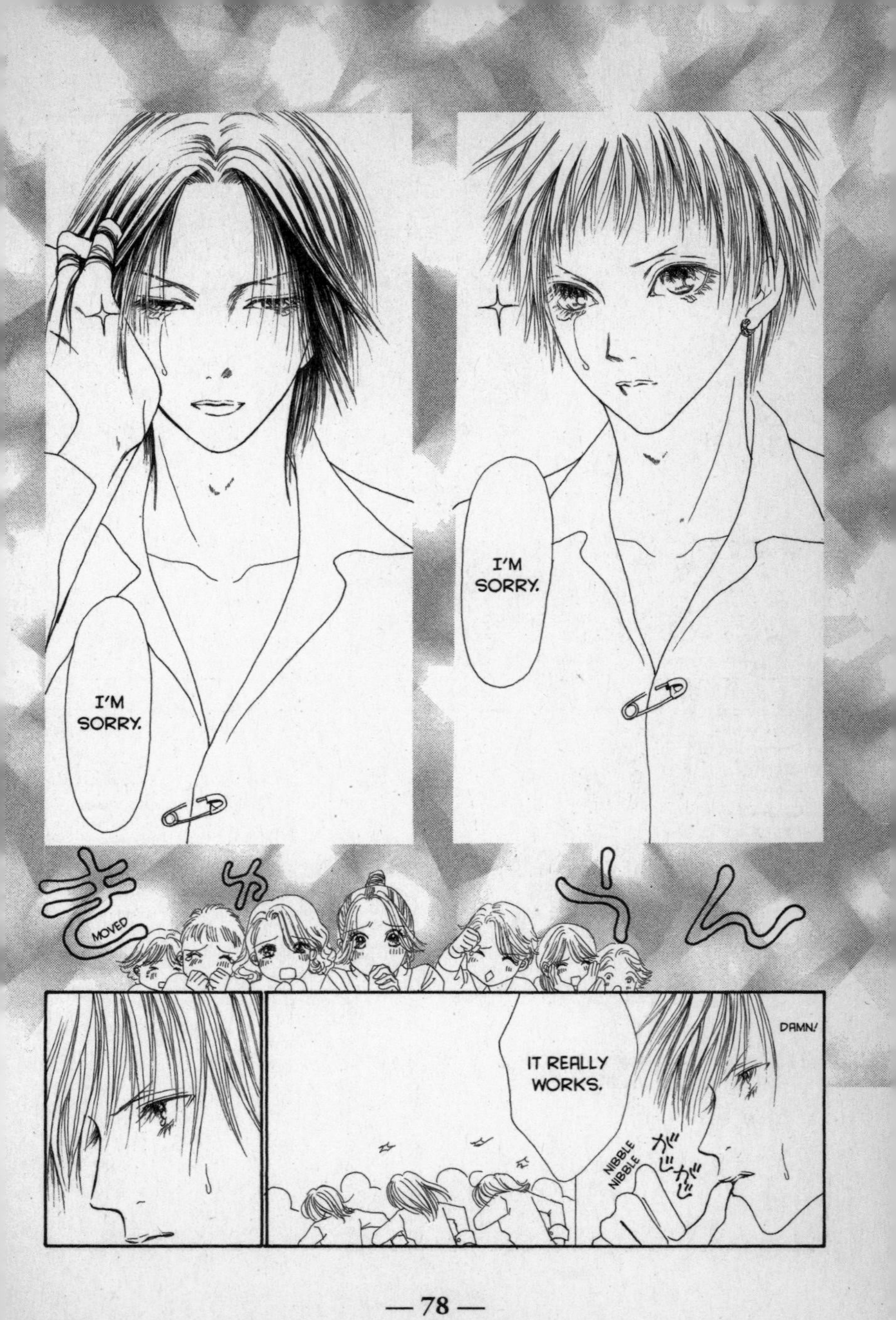
I'M SORRY.
I'M SORRY.
きゃーん
MOVED
DAMN!
がじがじ
NIBBLE NIBBLE
IT REALLY WORKS.

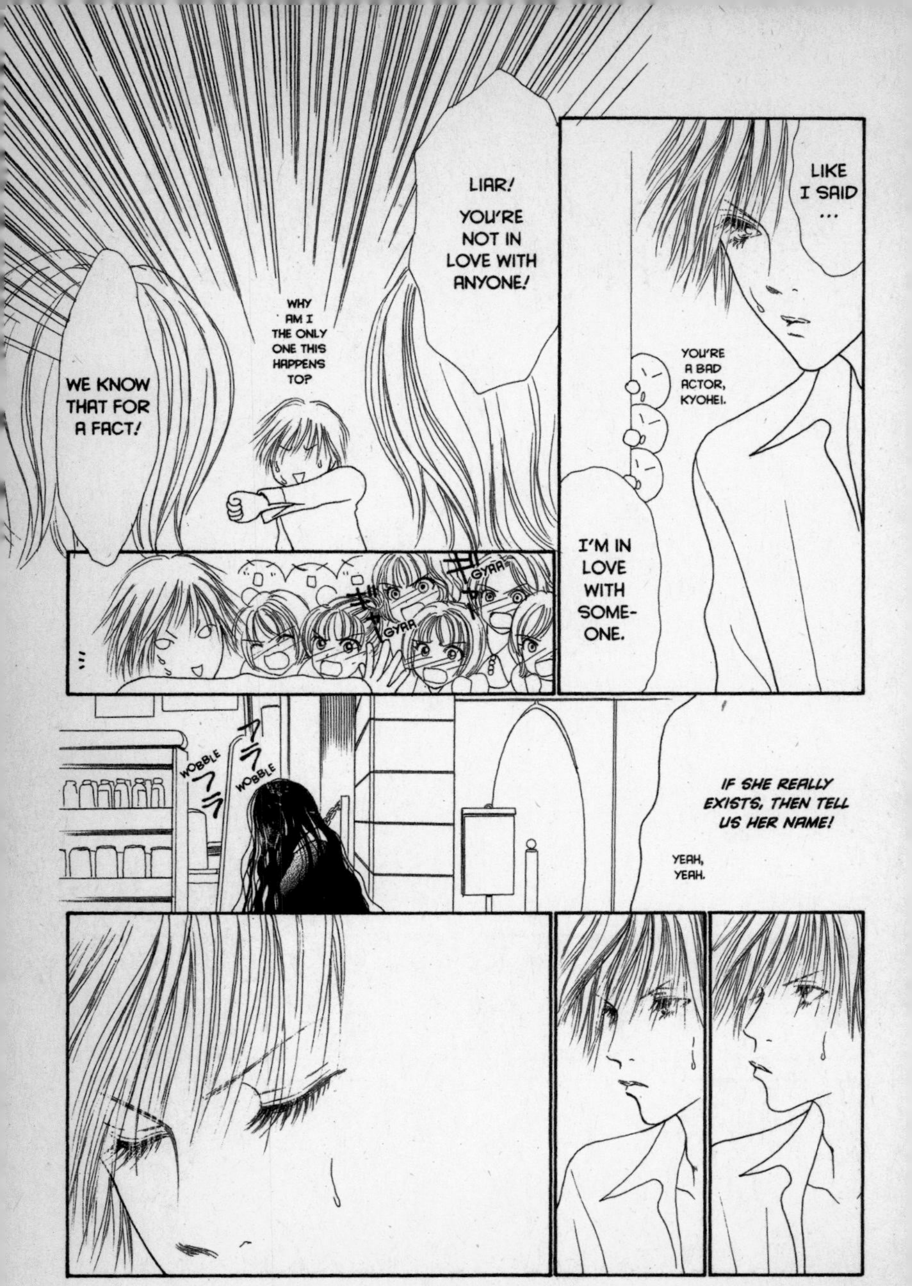
LIKE I SAID ...
YOU'RE A BAD ACTOR, KYOHEI.
I'M IN LOVE WITH SOMEONE.
LIAR!
YOU'RE NOT IN LOVE WITH ANYONE!
WHY AM I THE ONLY ONE THIS HAPPENS TO?
WE KNOW THAT FOR A FACT!
GYAA
GYAA
IF SHE REALLY EXISTS, THEN TELL US HER NAME!
YEAH, YEAH.
WOBBLE
WOBBLE

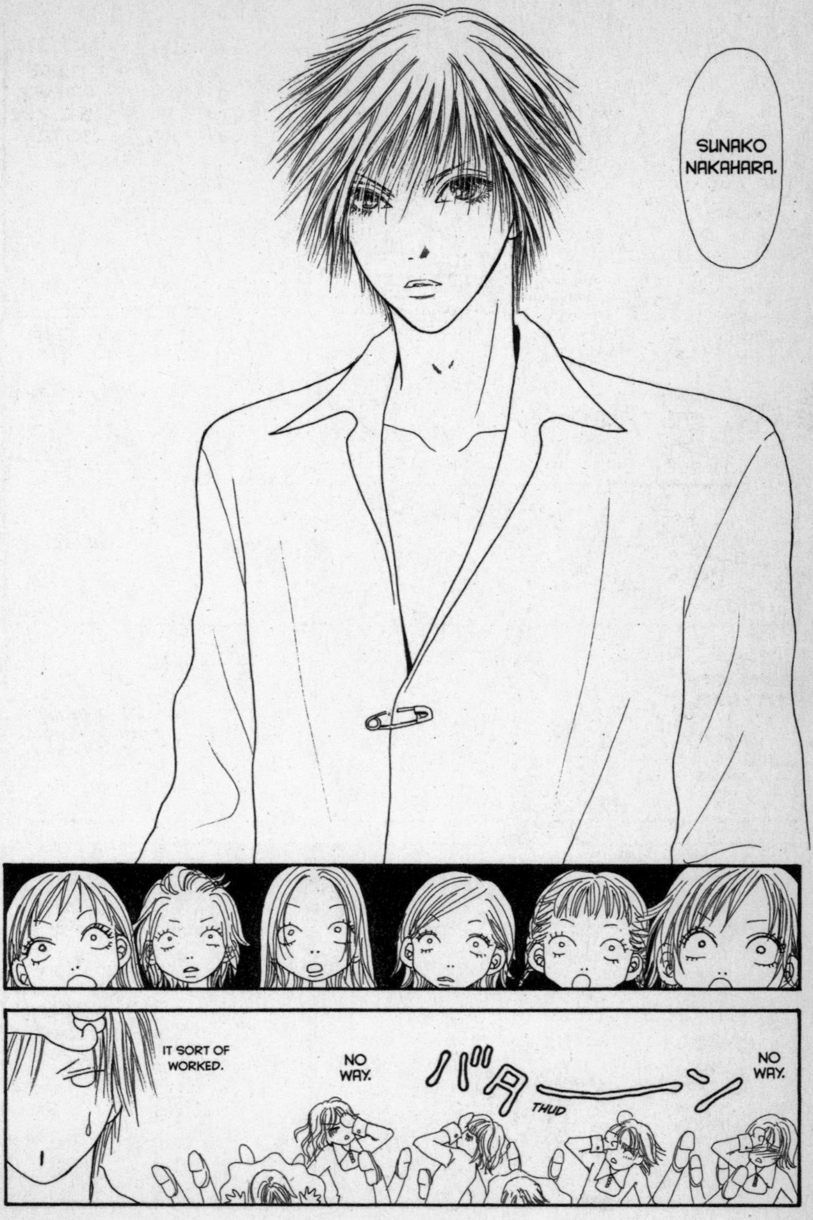
SUNAKO NAKAHARA.
NO WAY.
THUD
NO WAY.
IT SORT OF WORKED.

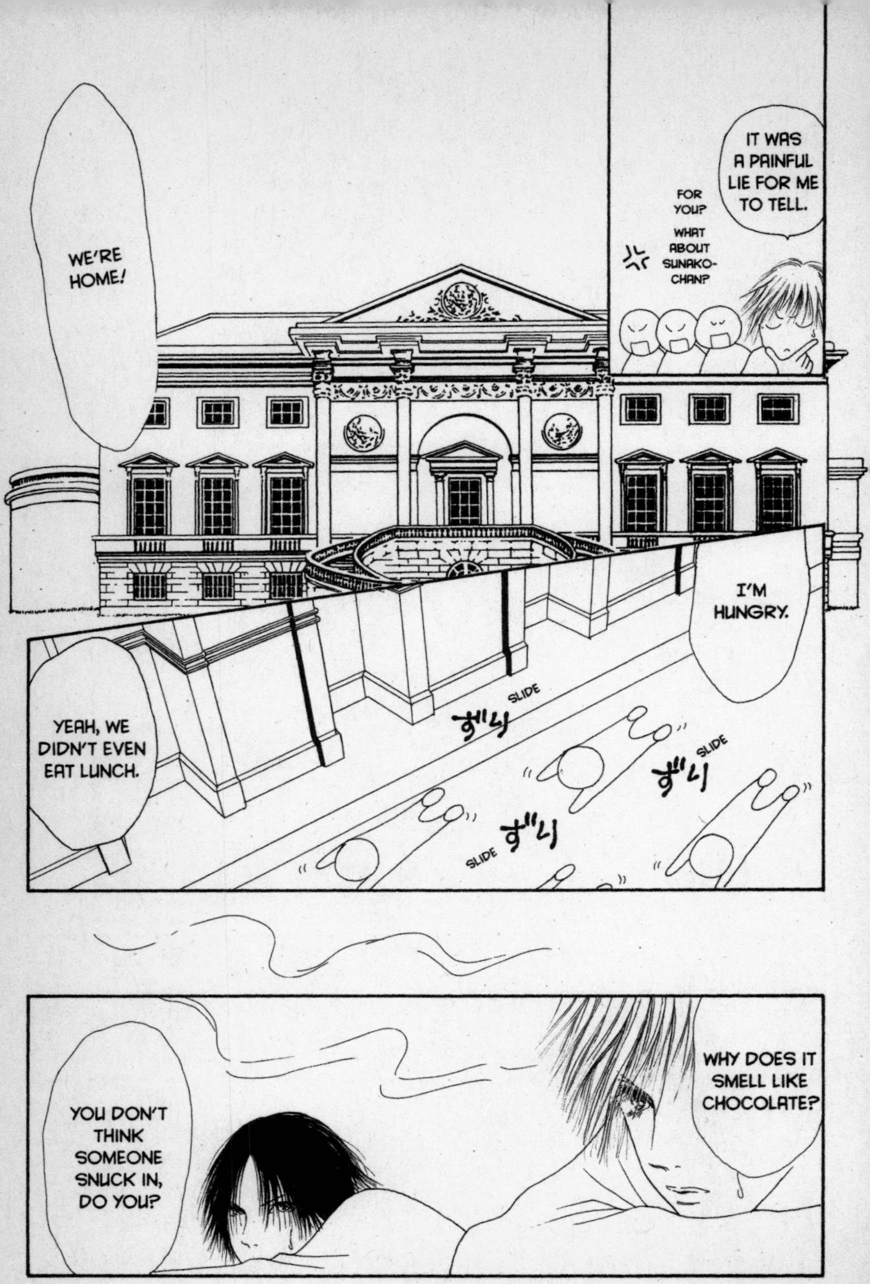
IT WAS A PAINFUL LIE FOR ME TO TELL.
FOR YOU? WHAT ABOUT SUNAKO-CHAN?
WE'RE HOME!
I'M HUNGRY.
SLIDE ずりり
SLIDE ずりり
SLIDE ずりり
YEAH, WE DIDN'T EVEN EAT LUNCH.
WHY DOES IT SMELL LIKE CHOCOLATE?
YOU DON'T THINK SOMEONE SNUCK IN, DO YOU?

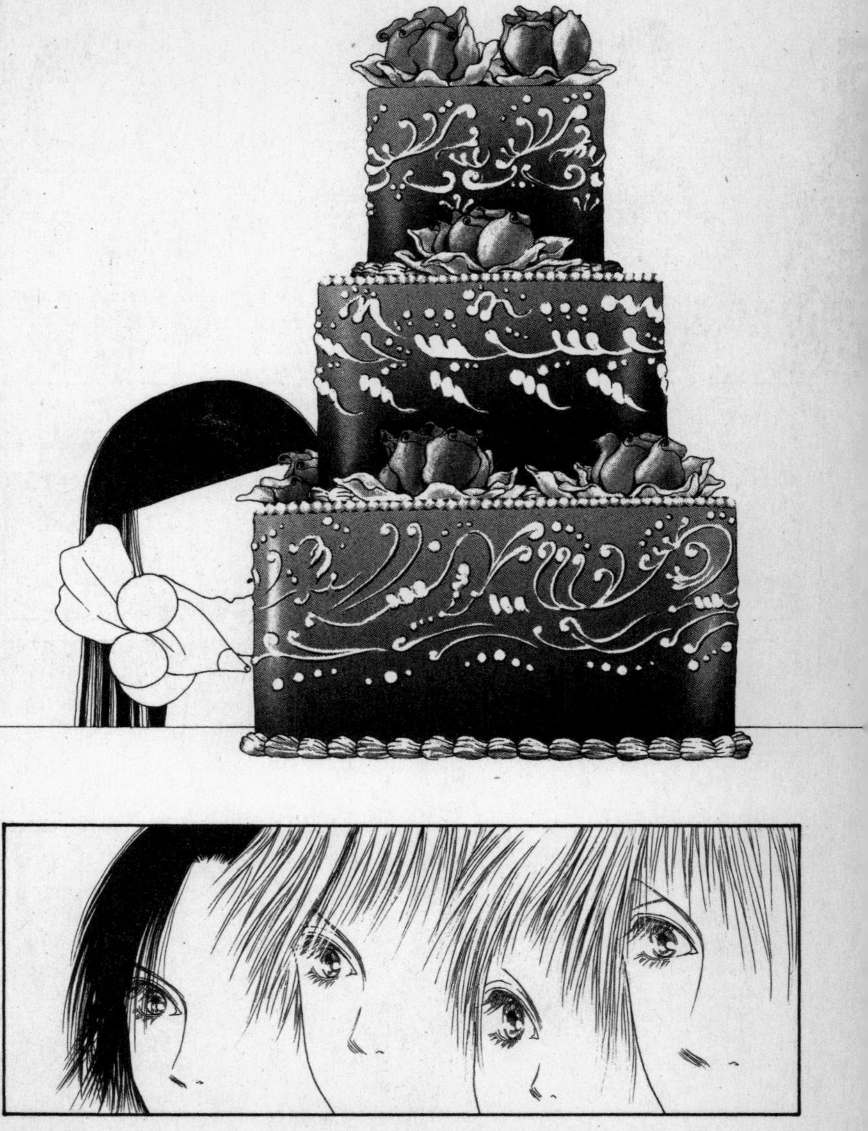

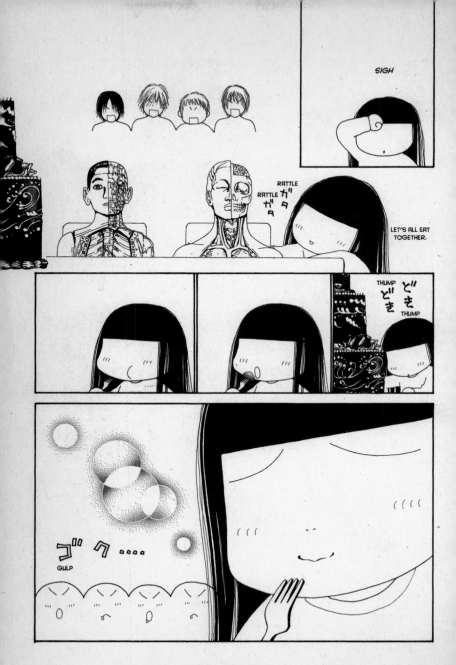

SIGH

RATTLE
RATTLE ガタ

ガタ

LET'S ALL EAT
TOGETHER.

THUMP どき
どき
THUMP

ゴ ク ‥‥
GULP

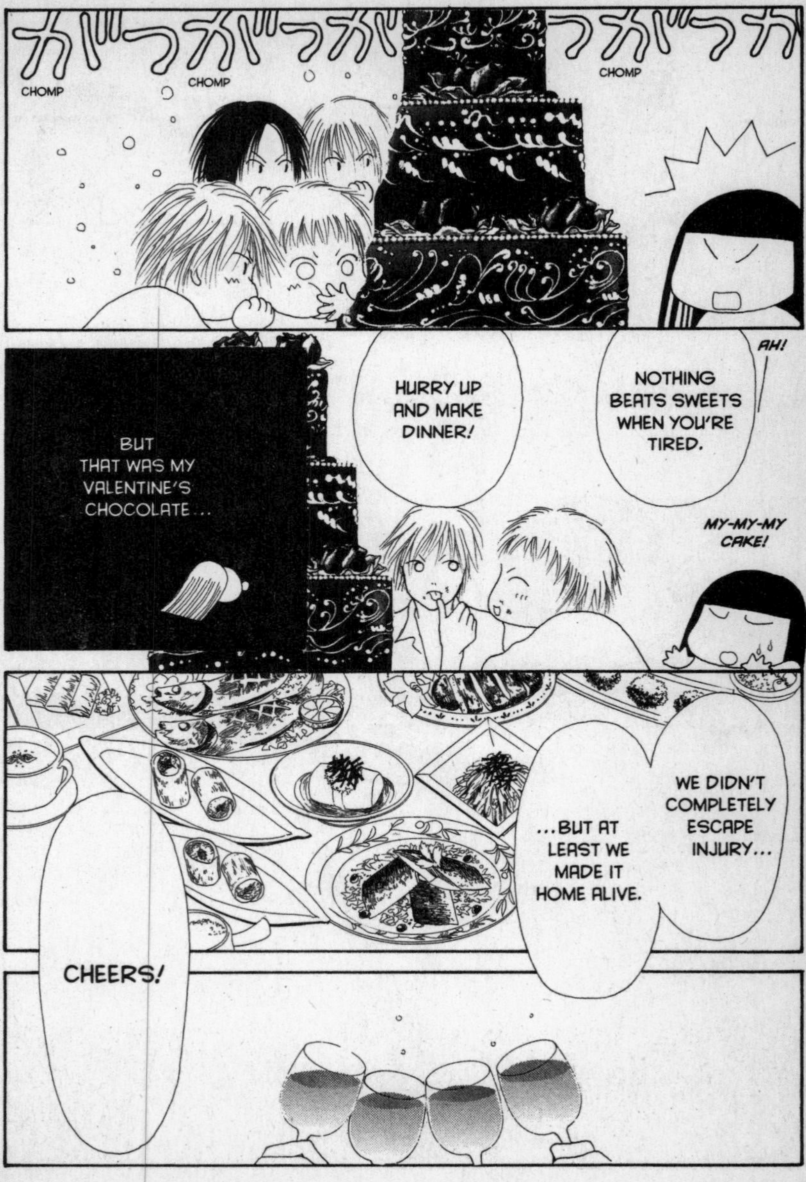
CHOMP
CHOMP
CHOMP
AH!
NOTHING BEATS SWEETS WHEN YOU'RE TIRED.
HURRY UP AND MAKE DINNER!
MY-MY-MY CAKE!
BUT THAT WAS MY VALENTINE'S CHOCOLATE...
WE DIDN'T COMPLETELY ESCAPE INJURY...
...BUT AT LEAST WE MADE IT HOME ALIVE.
CHEERS!

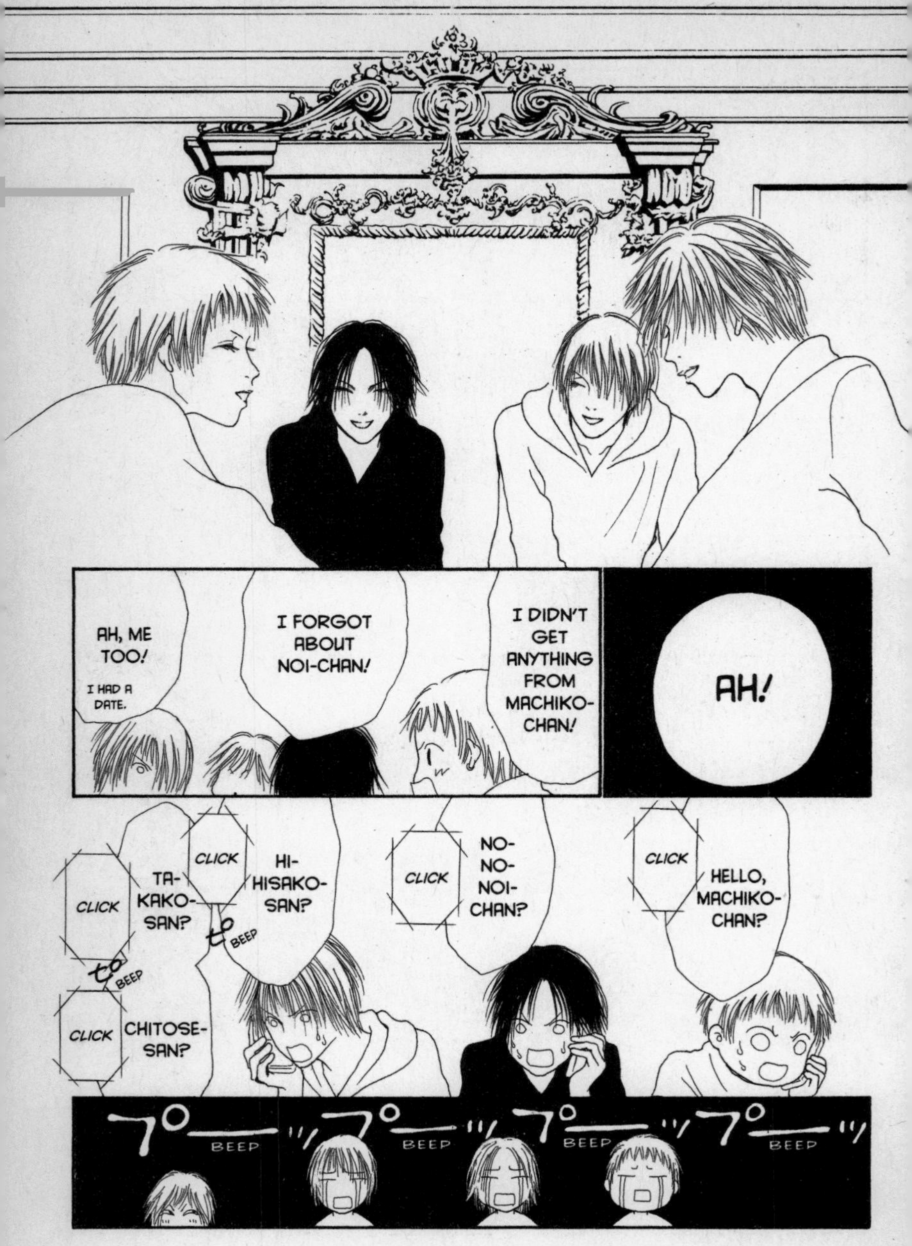
AH!
I DIDN'T GET ANYTHING FROM MACHIKO-CHAN!
I FORGOT ABOUT NOI-CHAN!
AH, ME TOO!
I HAD A DATE.
CLICK
HELLO, MACHIKO-CHAN?
CLICK
NO-NO-NOI-CHAN?
CLICK
HI-HISAKO-SAN?
BEEP
CLICK
TA-KAKO-SAN?
BEEP
CLICK
CHITOSE-SAN?
プーーッ
BEEP
プーーッ
BEEP
プーーッ
BEEP
プーーッ
BEEP

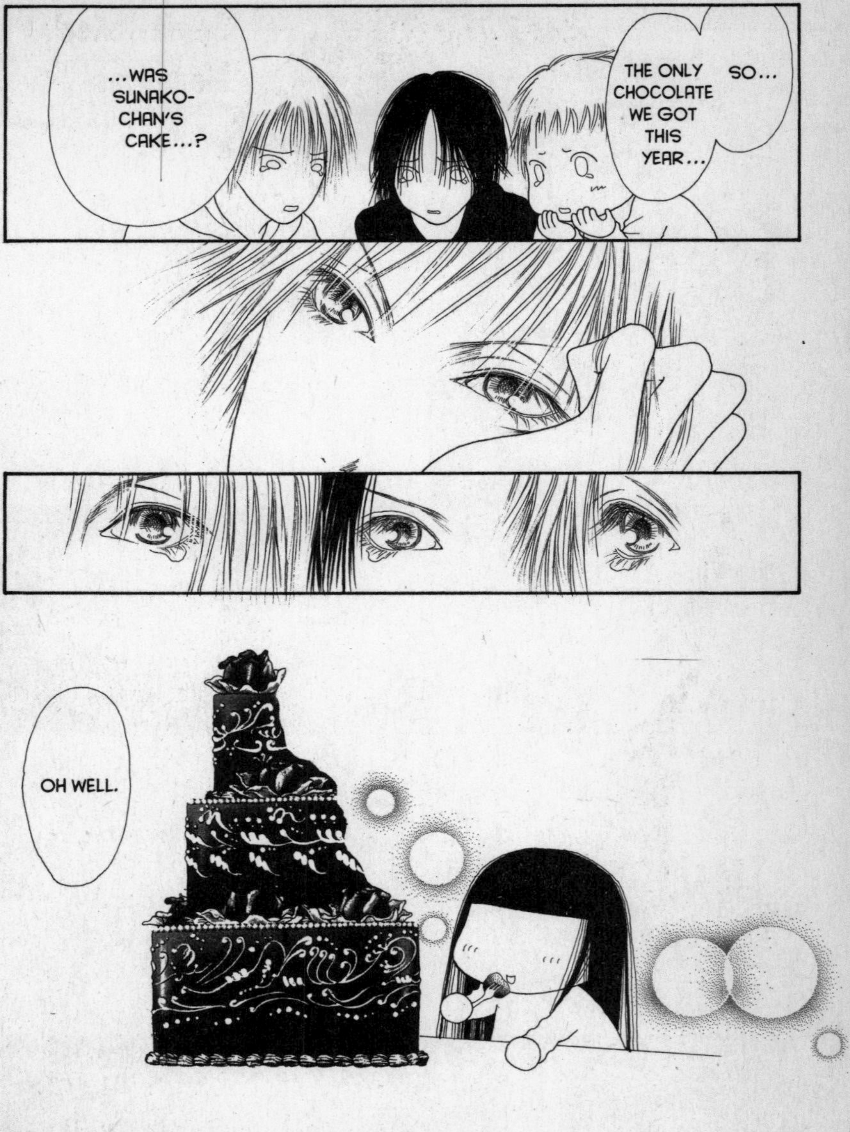
SO... THE ONLY CHOCOLATE WE GOT THIS YEAR...
...WAS SUNAKO-CHAN'S CAKE...?
OH WELL.

Chapter 21
Sepia-Toned Memories

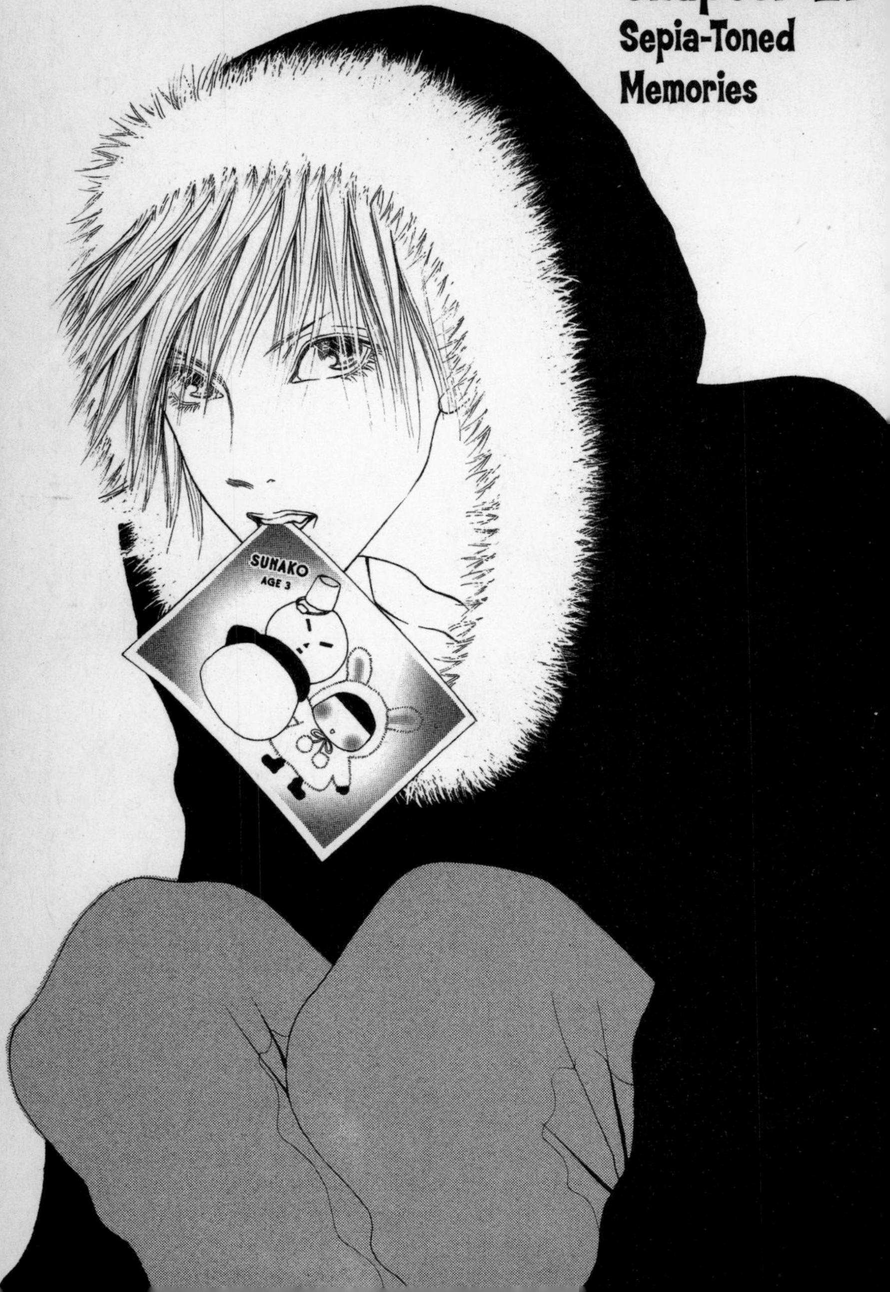
SUNAKO
AGE 3

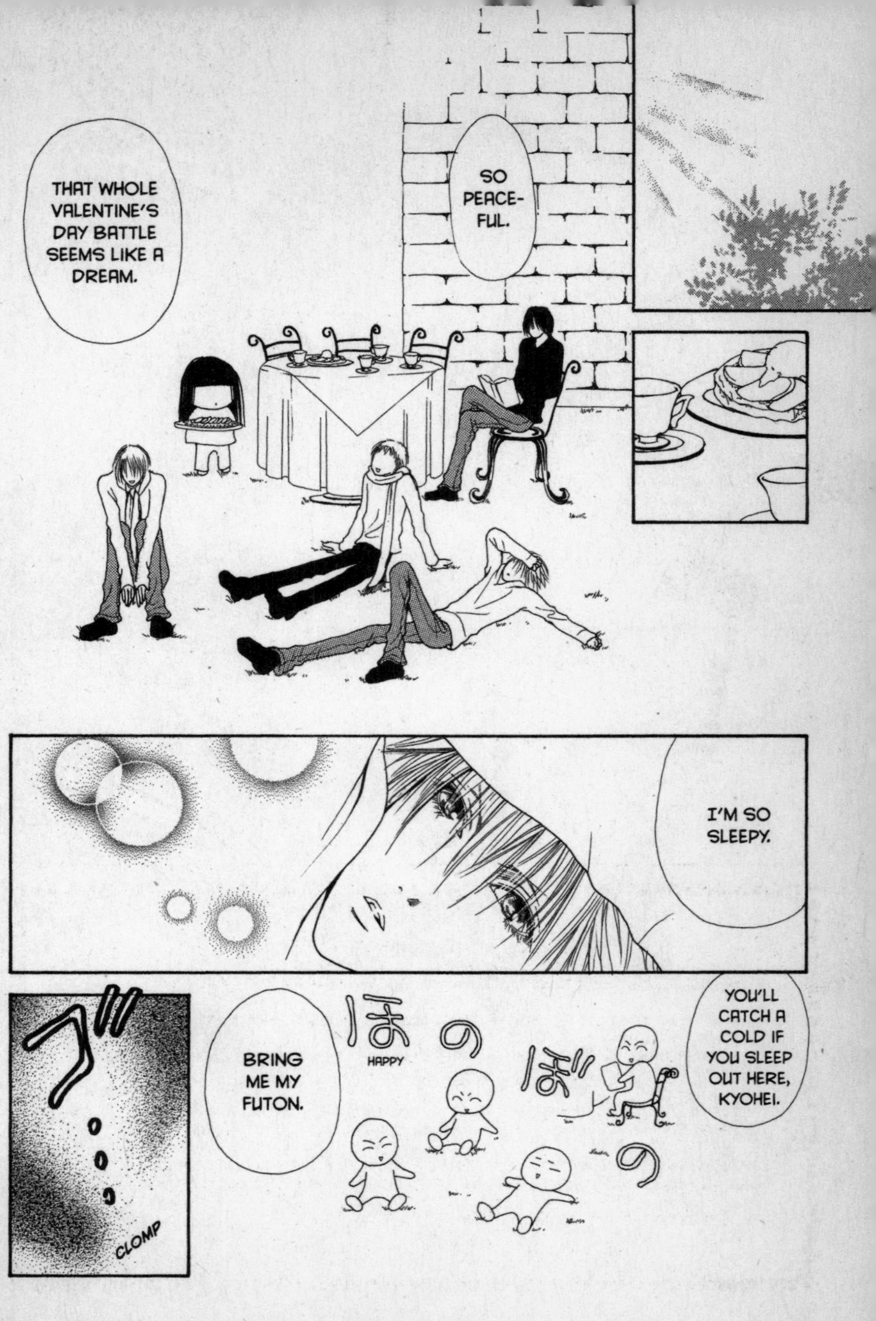
SO PEACE-FUL.
THAT WHOLE VALENTINE'S DAY BATTLE SEEMS LIKE A DREAM.
I'M SO SLEEPY.
YOU'LL CATCH A COLD IF YOU SLEEP OUT HERE, KYOHEI.
ほのぼの
HAPPY
BRING ME MY FUTON.
CLOMP

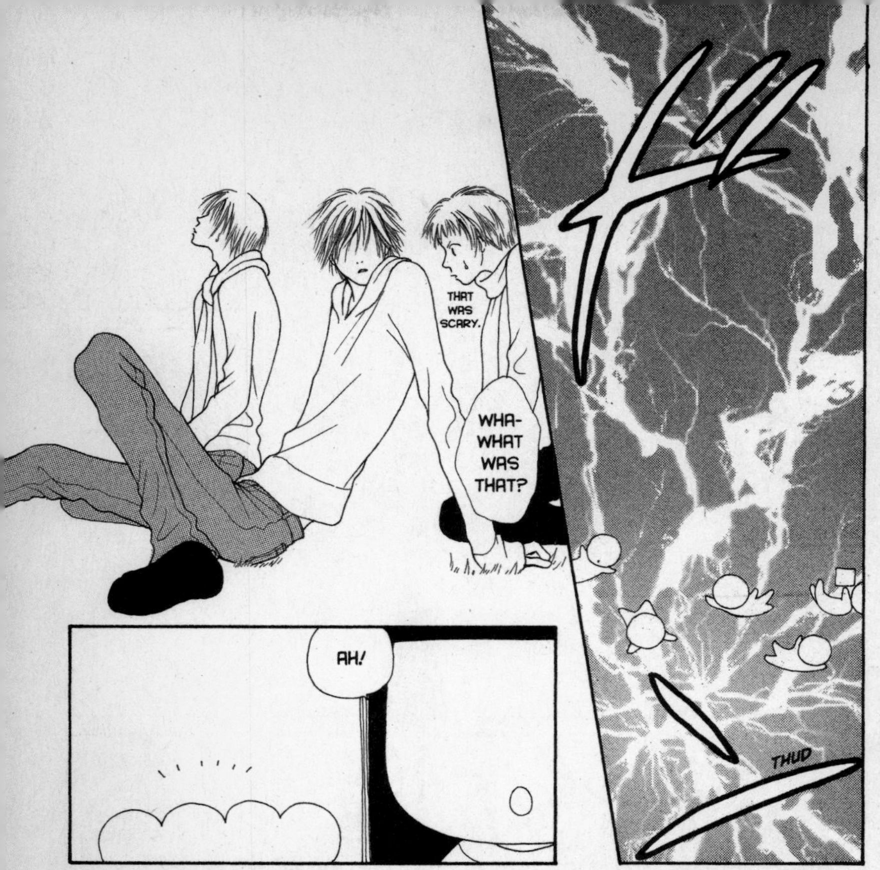
THUD
THAT WAS SCARY.
WHA- WHAT WAS THAT?
AH!

BEHIND THE SCENES

I WOULD LIKE TO THANK SOME MORE SPECIAL GUESTS ⟵ NOT AGAIN...

THANK YOU SO MUCH, ATSUKO NAMBA-CHAN AND YUKIO IKEDA-CHAN. ♥♥♥

IT'S ALREADY JANUARY. EVER SINCE NEW YEAR'S DAY, I'VE BEEN REALLY DEPRESSED, AND I HAVEN'T BEEN ABLE TO GET MUCH WORK DONE... SIGH.

YOU REALLY CAN'T MIX BUSINESS WITH PLEASURE. I REALLY WAS DEPRESSED. RELATIONSHIPS ARE SO DIFFICULT. LUCKILY, MY FRIENDS WERE THERE TO CHEER ME UP.

AROUND THAT TIME, I WAS GOING OUT TO EAT WITH IKEDA-SAN AND IYU KOZAKURA, AND WE WALKED RIGHT BY THE FAMOUS *"MIWA-SAMA."*... ♥♥♥ HOW COOL. ♥♥♥

SOMETIMES IT'S GOOD TO BE ALIVE. LA-LA-LA ♪

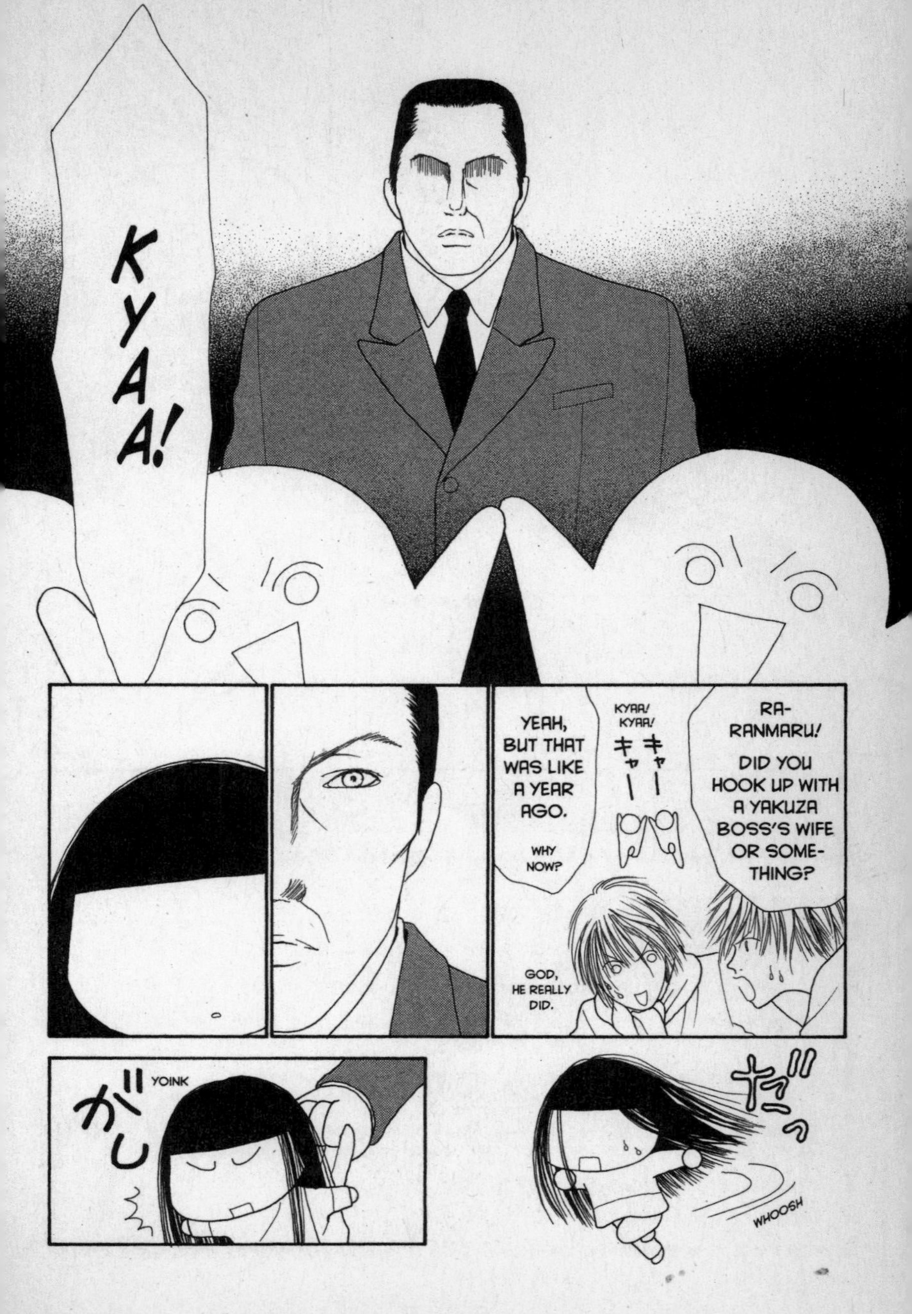
KYAA!
RA-RANMARU!
DID YOU HOOK UP WITH A YAKUZA BOSS'S WIFE OR SOMETHING?
KYAA! KYAA!
キャーキャー
YEAH, BUT THAT WAS LIKE A YEAR AGO.
WHY NOW?
GOD, HE REALLY DID.
WHOOSH
がし
YOINK

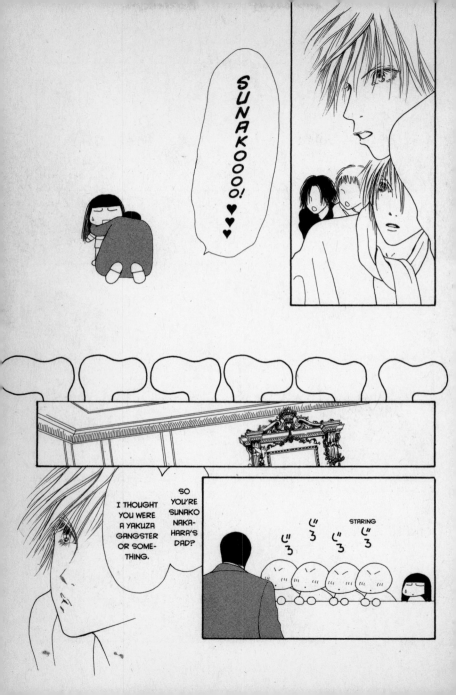

SUNAKOOO! ♥♥♥♥

SO YOU'RE SUNAKO NAKAHARA'S DAD?

I THOUGHT YOU WERE A YAKUZA GANGSTER OR SOMETHING.

STARING

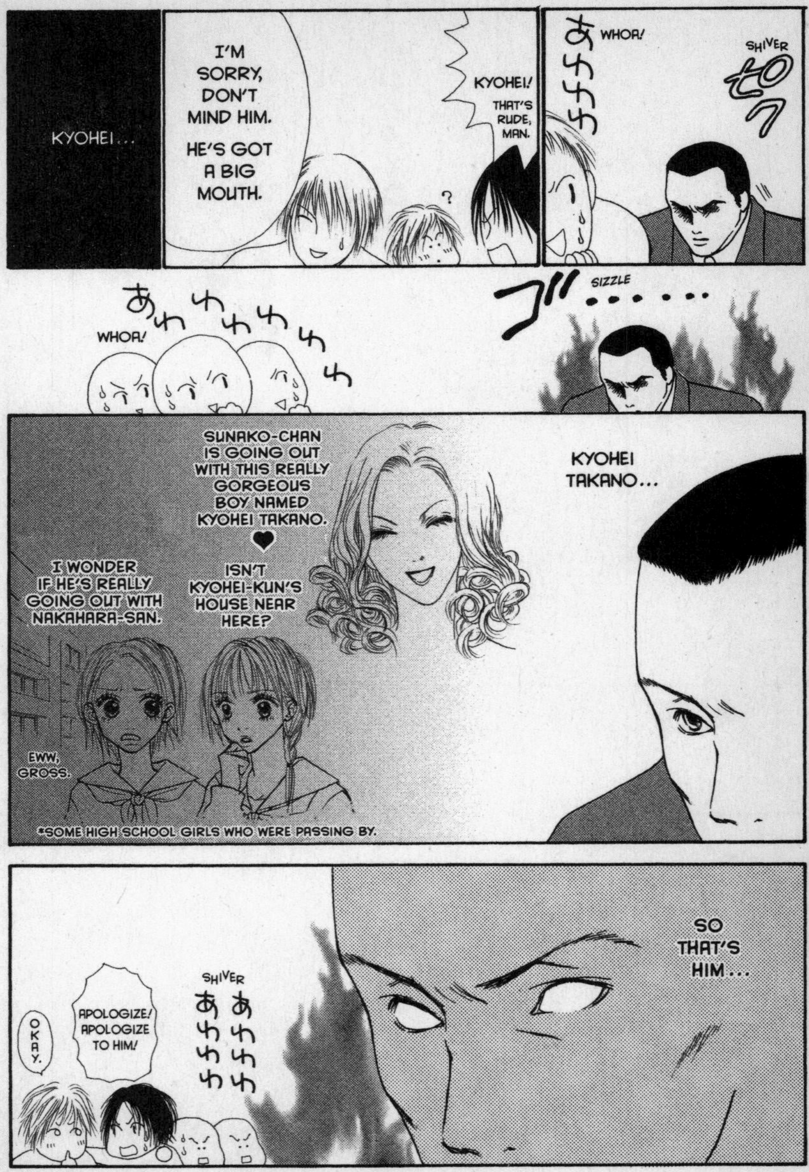
あわわわ
WHOA!
ぞく
SHIVER
KYOHEI!
THAT'S RUDE, MAN.
I'M SORRY, DON'T MIND HIM.
HE'S GOT A BIG MOUTH.
?
KYOHEI...
ゴ……
SIZZLE
あわわわわわ
WHOA!
KYOHEI TAKANO...
SUNAKO-CHAN IS GOING OUT WITH THIS REALLY GORGEOUS BOY NAMED KYOHEI TAKANO. ♥
ISN'T KYOHEI-KUN'S HOUSE NEAR HERE?
I WONDER IF HE'S REALLY GOING OUT WITH NAKAHARA-SAN.
EWW, GROSS.
*SOME HIGH SCHOOL GIRLS WHO WERE PASSING BY.
SO THAT'S HIM...
あわわわ
あわわわ
SHIVER
APOLOGIZE! APOLOGIZE TO HIM!
OKAY.

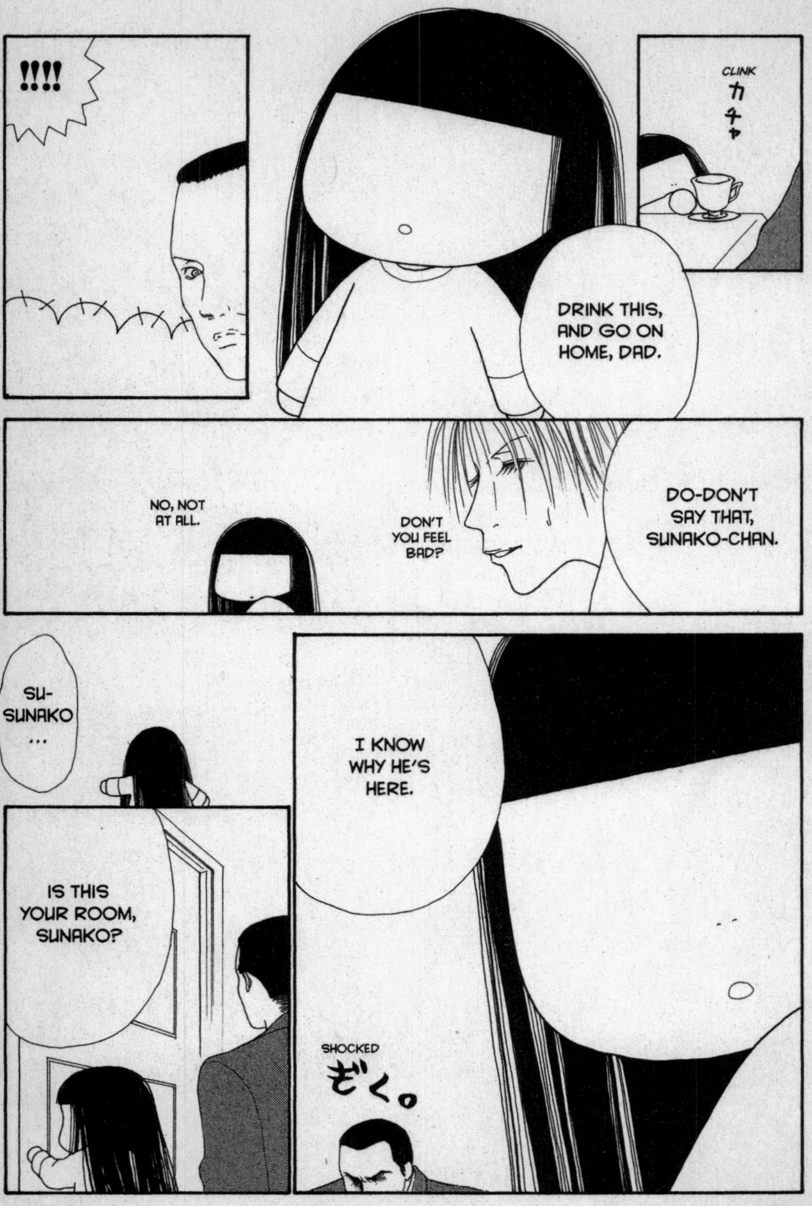
CLINK
カチャ
DRINK THIS, AND GO ON HOME, DAD.
!!!!
DO-DON'T SAY THAT, SUNAKO-CHAN.
DON'T YOU FEEL BAD?
NO, NOT AT ALL.
I KNOW WHY HE'S HERE.
SHOCKED
ぞく。
SU-SUNAKO ...
IS THIS YOUR ROOM, SUNAKO?

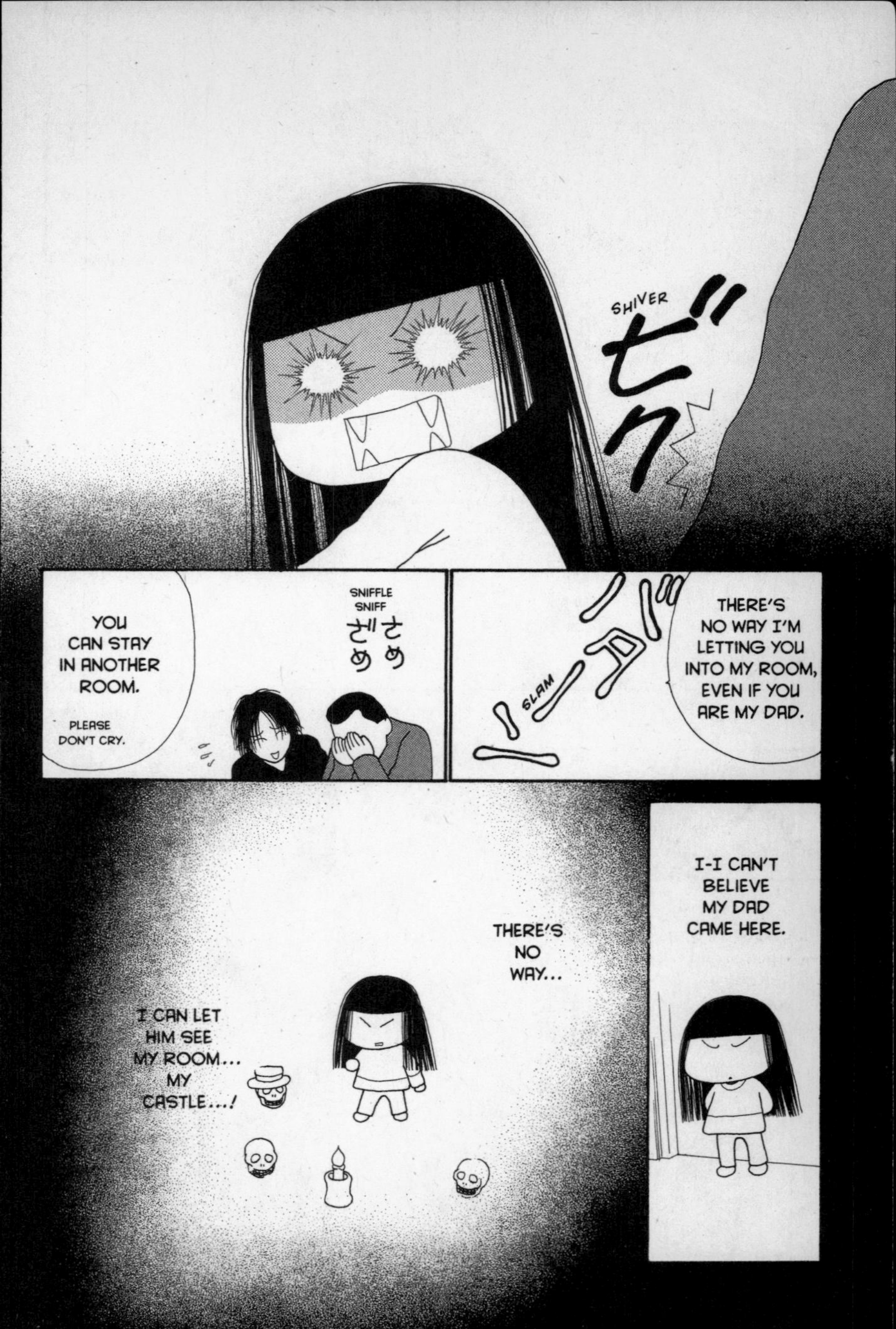
SHIVER
ビク
THERE'S NO WAY I'M LETTING YOU INTO MY ROOM, EVEN IF YOU ARE MY DAD.
SLAM
SNIFFLE SNIFF
さめざめ
YOU CAN STAY IN ANOTHER ROOM.
PLEASE DON'T CRY.
I-I CAN'T BELIEVE MY DAD CAME HERE.
THERE'S NO WAY...
I CAN LET HIM SEE MY ROOM... MY CASTLE...!

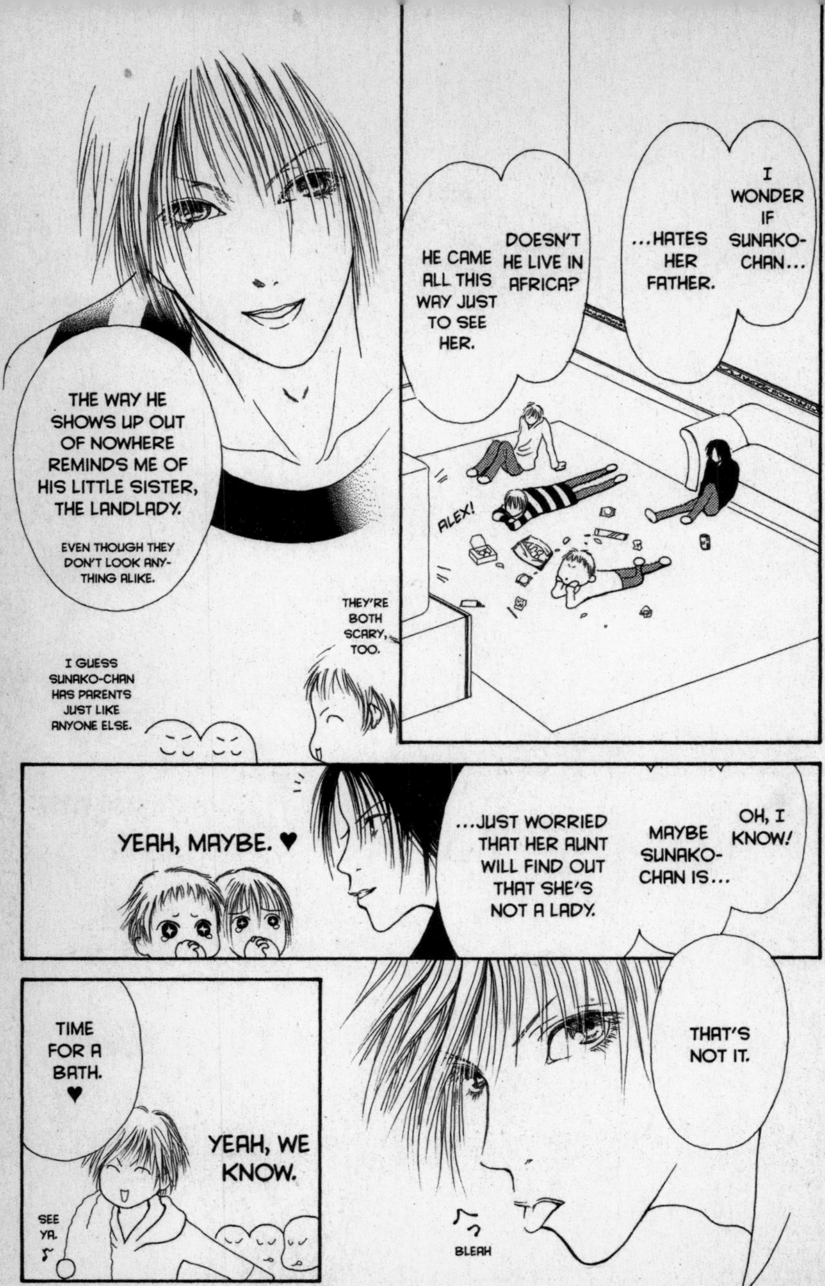
I WONDER IF SUNAKO-CHAN...
...HATES HER FATHER.
DOESN'T HE LIVE IN AFRICA?
HE CAME ALL THIS WAY JUST TO SEE HER.
ALEX!
THE WAY HE SHOWS UP OUT OF NOWHERE REMINDS ME OF HIS LITTLE SISTER, THE LANDLADY.
EVEN THOUGH THEY DON'T LOOK ANYTHING ALIKE.
THEY'RE BOTH SCARY, TOO.
I GUESS SUNAKO-CHAN HAS PARENTS JUST LIKE ANYONE ELSE.
OH, I KNOW!
MAYBE SUNAKO-CHAN IS...
...JUST WORRIED THAT HER AUNT WILL FIND OUT THAT SHE'S NOT A LADY.
YEAH, MAYBE. ♥
THAT'S NOT IT.
BLEAH
TIME FOR A BATH. ♥
YEAH, WE KNOW.
SEE YA.

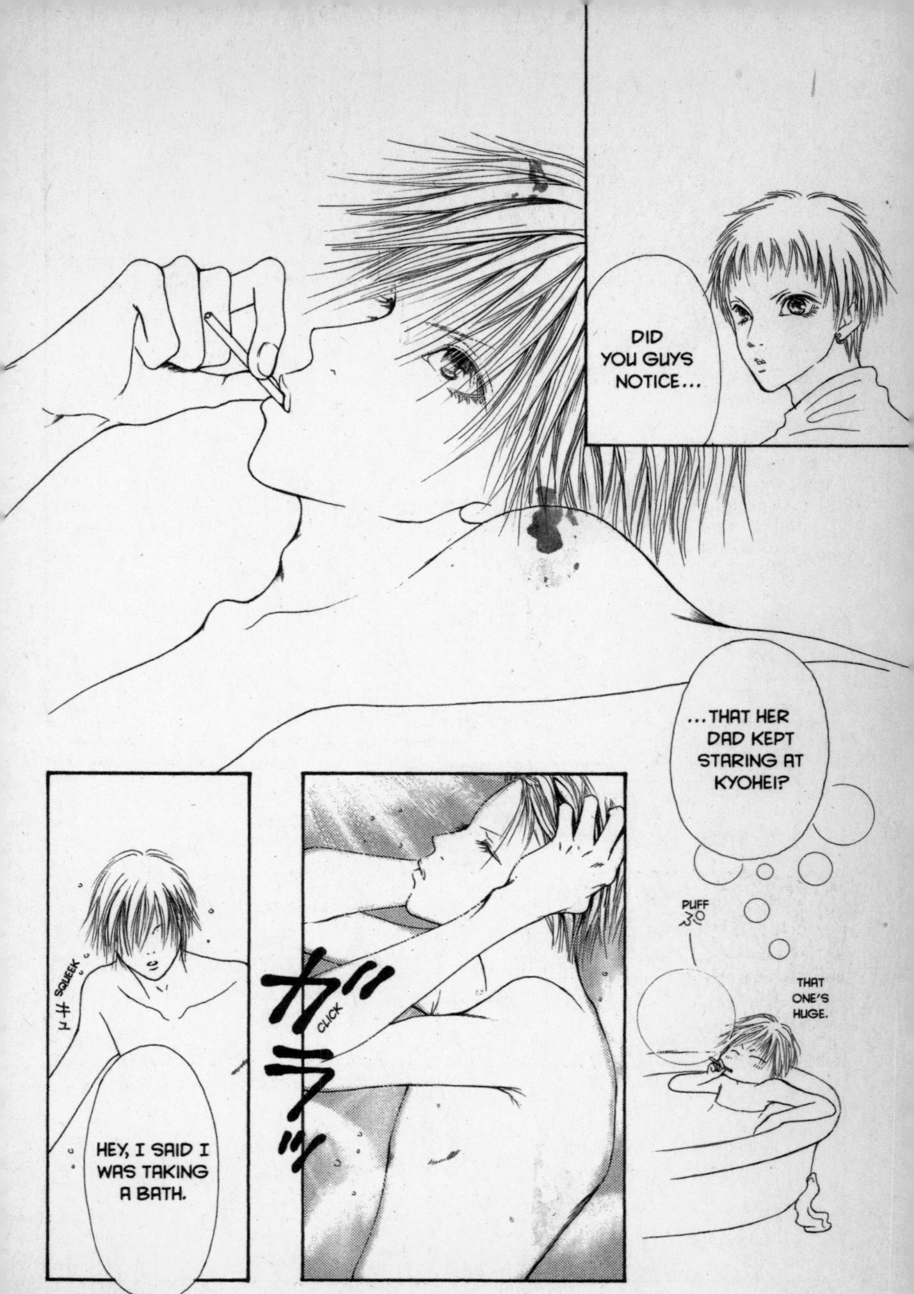
DID YOU GUYS NOTICE...
...THAT HER DAD KEPT STARING AT KYOHEI?
PUFF
THAT ONE'S HUGE.
ガラッ
CLICK
SQUEEK
HEY, I SAID I WAS TAKING A BATH.

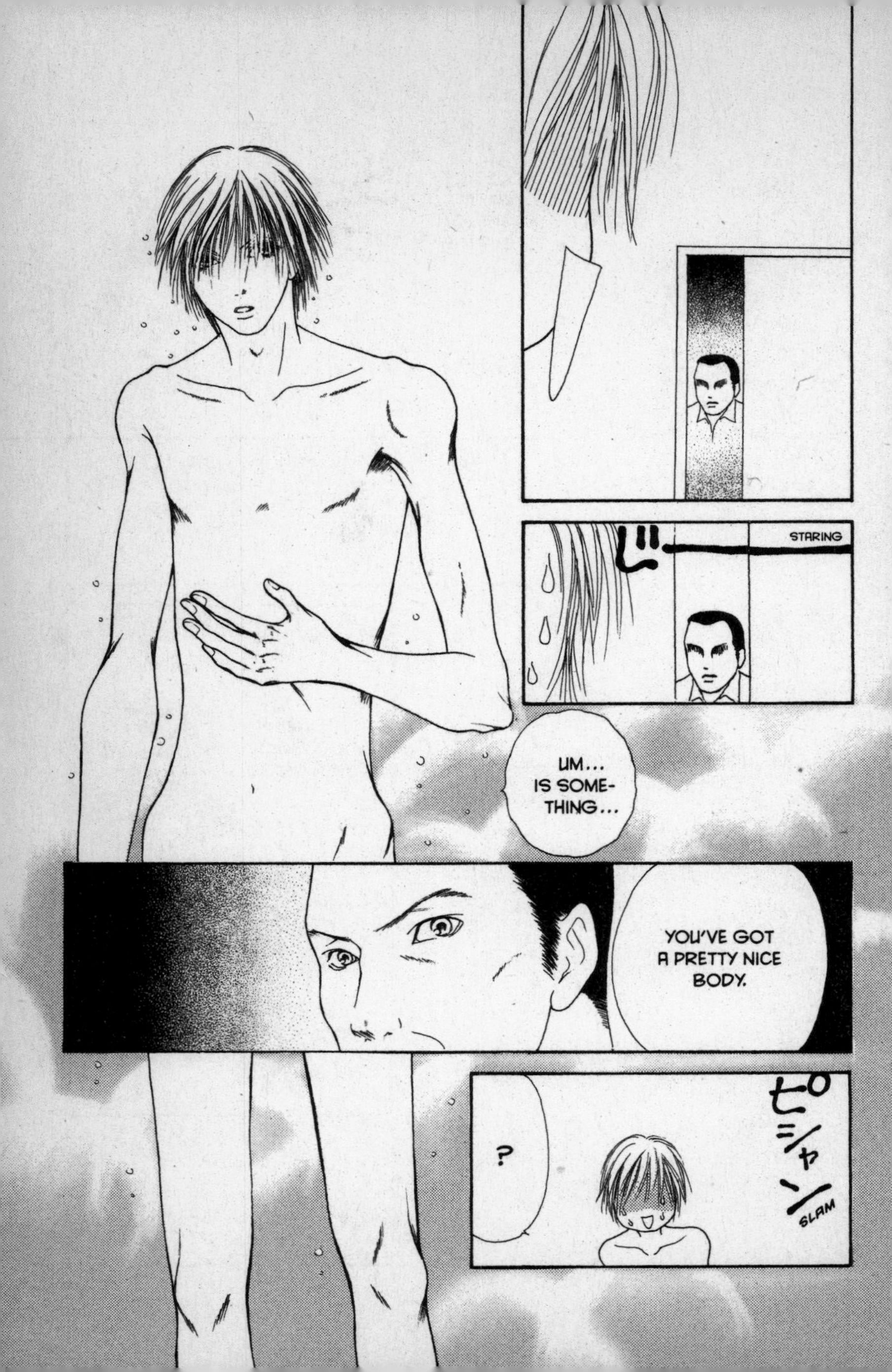

じ—
STARING
UM... IS SOME-THING...
YOU'VE GOT A PRETTY NICE BODY.
ピシャン
SLAM
?

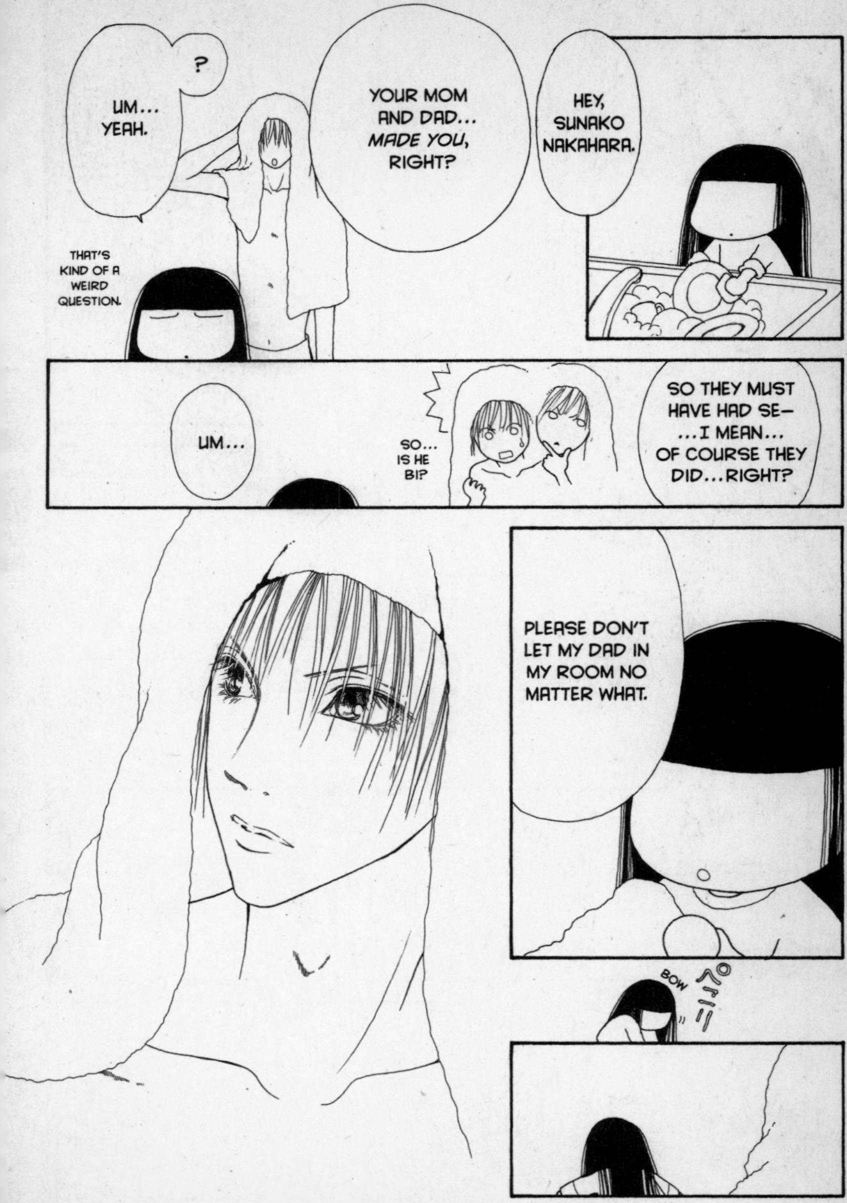
HEY, SUNAKO NAKAHARA.
YOUR MOM AND DAD... *MADE YOU*, RIGHT?
?
UM... YEAH.
THAT'S KIND OF A WEIRD QUESTION.
SO THEY MUST HAVE HAD SE— ...I MEAN... OF COURSE THEY DID...RIGHT?
SO... IS HE BI?
UM...
PLEASE DON'T LET MY DAD IN MY ROOM NO MATTER WHAT.
BOW

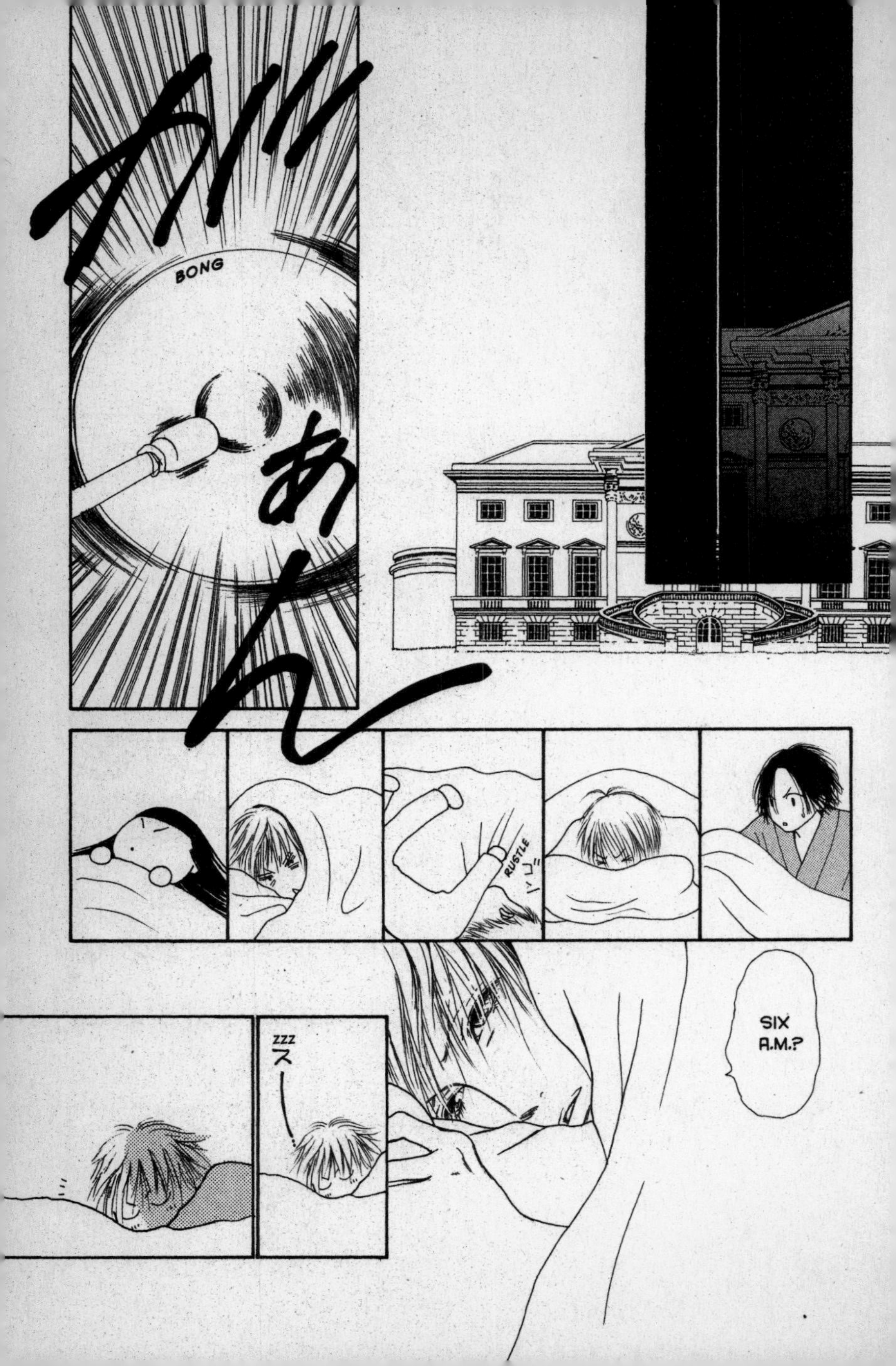

BONG
あん
RUSTLE
SIX A.M.?
ZZZ

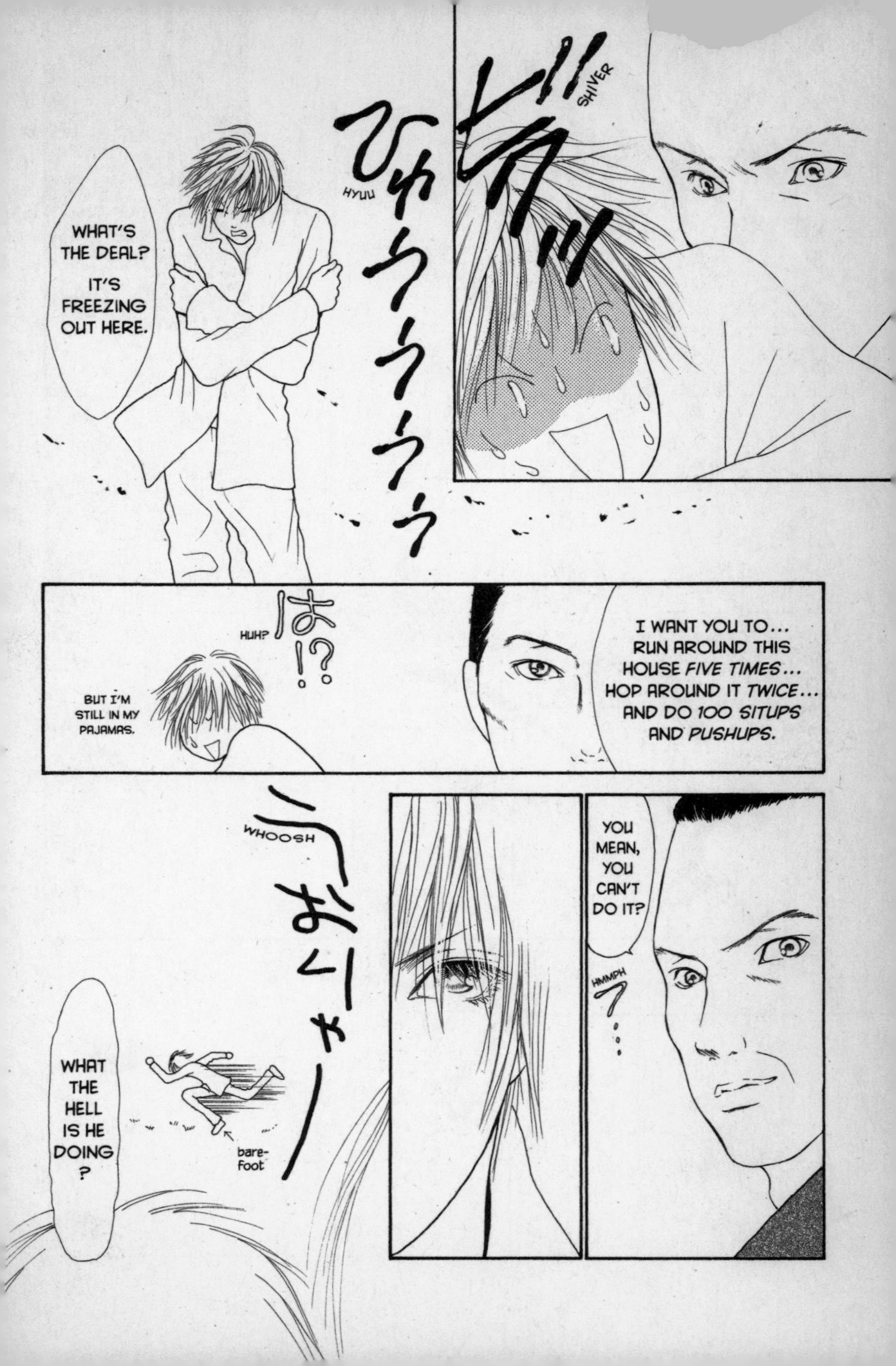
SHIVER
HYUU
WHAT'S THE DEAL? IT'S FREEZING OUT HERE.
I WANT YOU TO... RUN AROUND THIS HOUSE *FIVE TIMES*... HOP AROUND IT *TWICE*... AND DO *100 SITUPS* AND *PUSHUPS*.
HUH?
BUT I'M STILL IN MY PAJAMAS.
YOU MEAN, YOU CAN'T DO IT?
HMMPH
WHOOSH
WHAT THE HELL IS HE DOING?
bare-foot

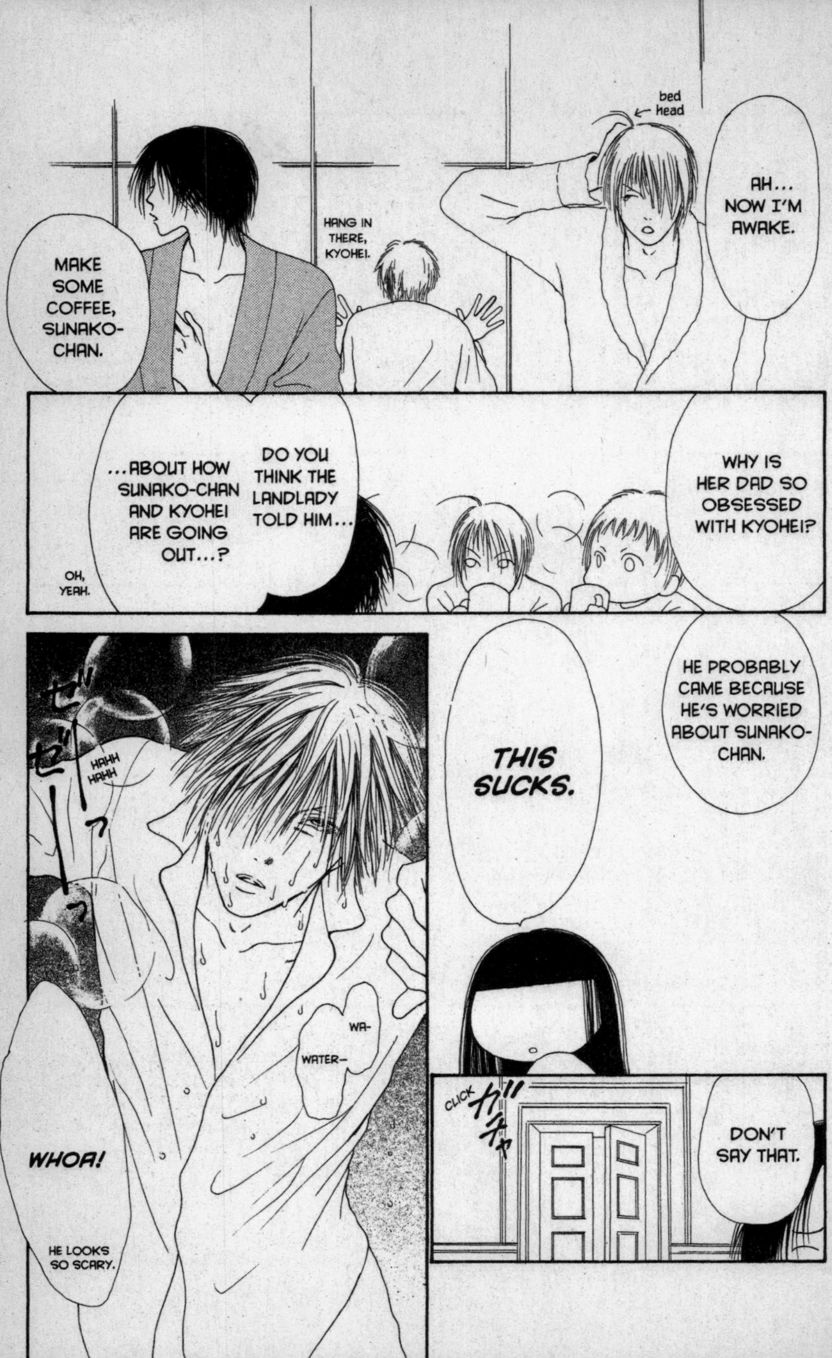
bed head
AH... NOW I'M AWAKE.
HANG IN THERE, KYOHEI.
MAKE SOME COFFEE, SUNAKO-CHAN.
WHY IS HER DAD SO OBSESSED WITH KYOHEI?
DO YOU THINK THE LANDLADY TOLD HIM...
...ABOUT HOW SUNAKO-CHAN AND KYOHEI ARE GOING OUT...?
OH, YEAH.
HE PROBABLY CAME BECAUSE HE'S WORRIED ABOUT SUNAKO-CHAN.
THIS SUCKS.
CLICK
DON'T SAY THAT.
HAHH HAHH
WA- WATER-
WHOA!
HE LOOKS SO SCARY.

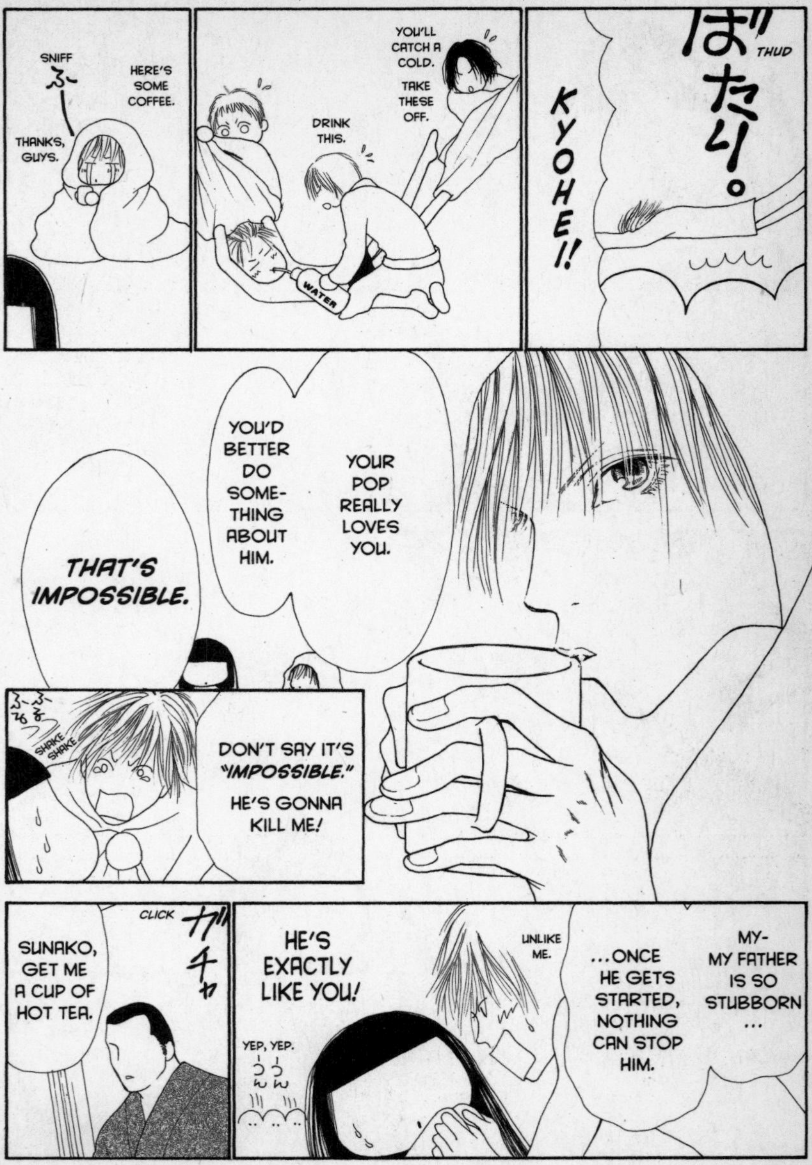
ばたり。
THUD
KYOHEI!!
YOU'LL CATCH A COLD.
TAKE THESE OFF.
DRINK THIS.
WATER
HERE'S SOME COFFEE.
ふー
SNIFF
THANKS, GUYS.
YOUR POP REALLY LOVES YOU.
YOU'D BETTER DO SOME-THING ABOUT HIM.
THAT'S IMPOSSIBLE.
ふるふる
SHAKE SHAKE
DON'T SAY IT'S "IMPOSSIBLE."
HE'S GONNA KILL ME!
MY- MY FATHER IS SO STUBBORN ...
...ONCE HE GETS STARTED, NOTHING CAN STOP HIM.
UNLIKE ME.
HE'S EXACTLY LIKE YOU!
うんうん
YEP, YEP.
ガチャ
CLICK
SUNAKO, GET ME A CUP OF HOT TEA.

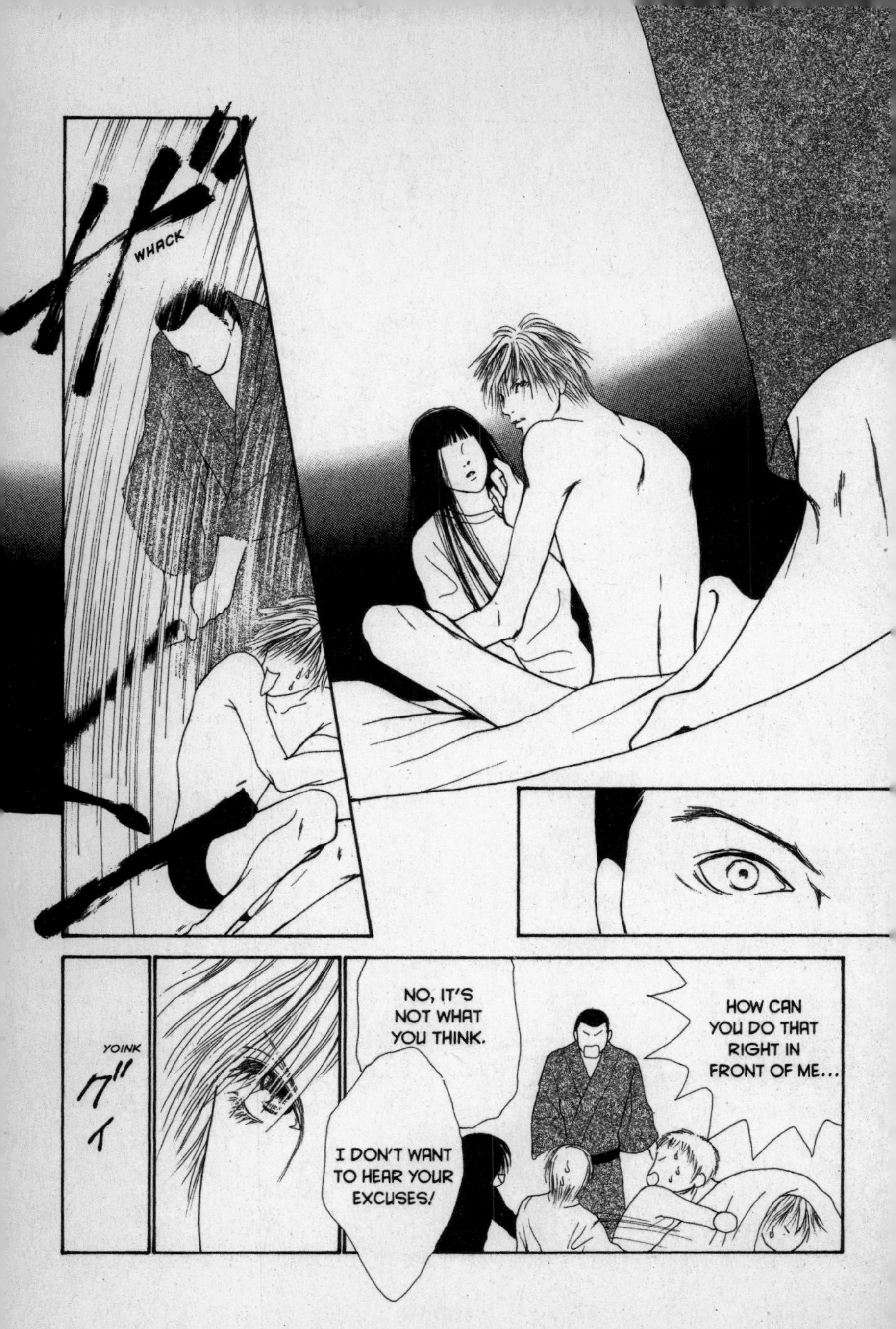
WHACK
HOW CAN YOU DO THAT RIGHT IN FRONT OF ME...
NO, IT'S NOT WHAT YOU THINK.
I DON'T WANT TO HEAR YOUR EXCUSES!
YOINK
グイ

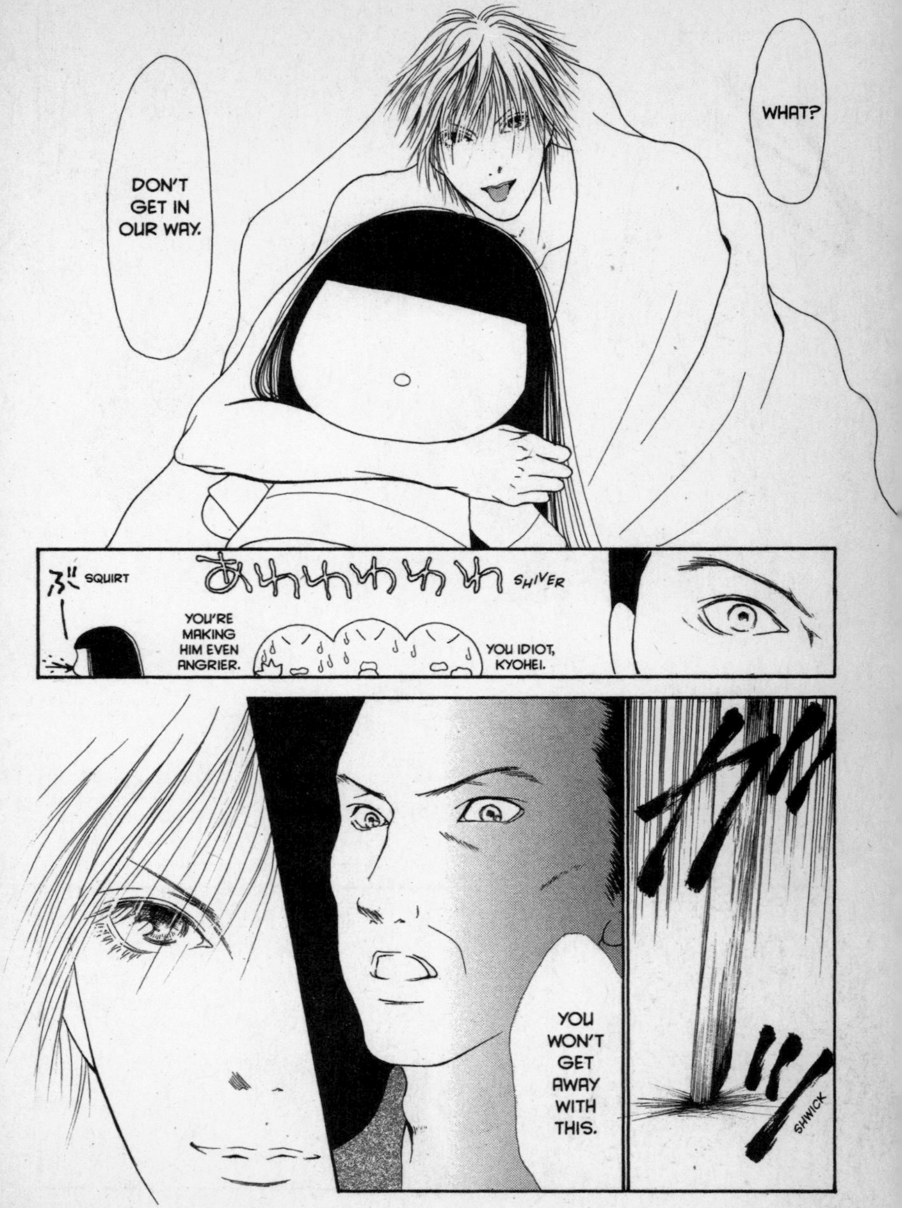
WHAT?
DON'T GET IN OUR WAY.
あわわわわわ
SHIVER
YOU IDIOT, KYOHEI.
YOU'RE MAKING HIM EVEN ANGRIER.
ぶ
SQUIRT
SHWICK
YOU WON'T GET AWAY WITH THIS.

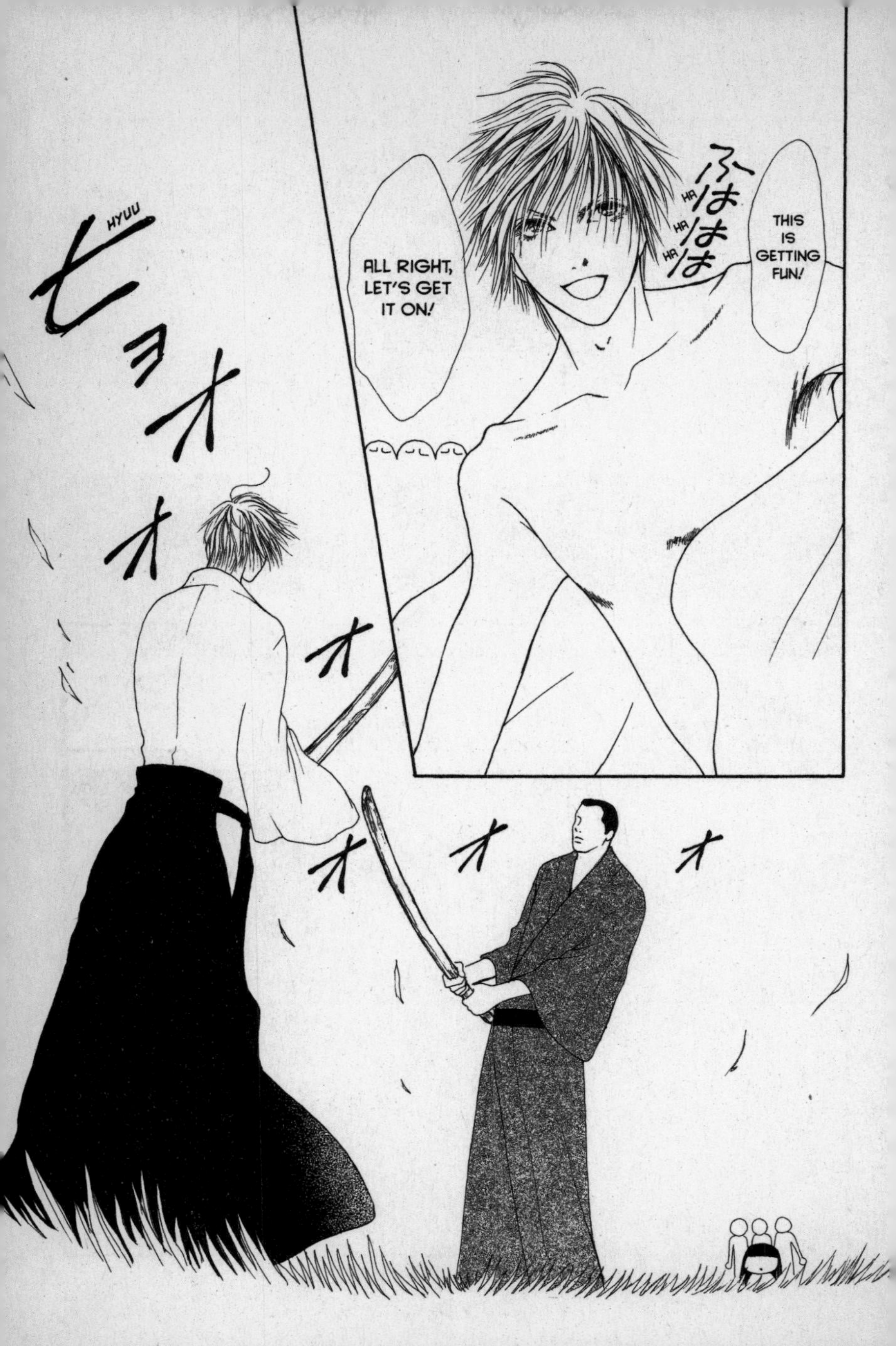
ふははは
HA HA HA
THIS IS GETTING FUN!
ALL RIGHT, LET'S GET IT ON!
ヒョオオオオオオ
HYUU

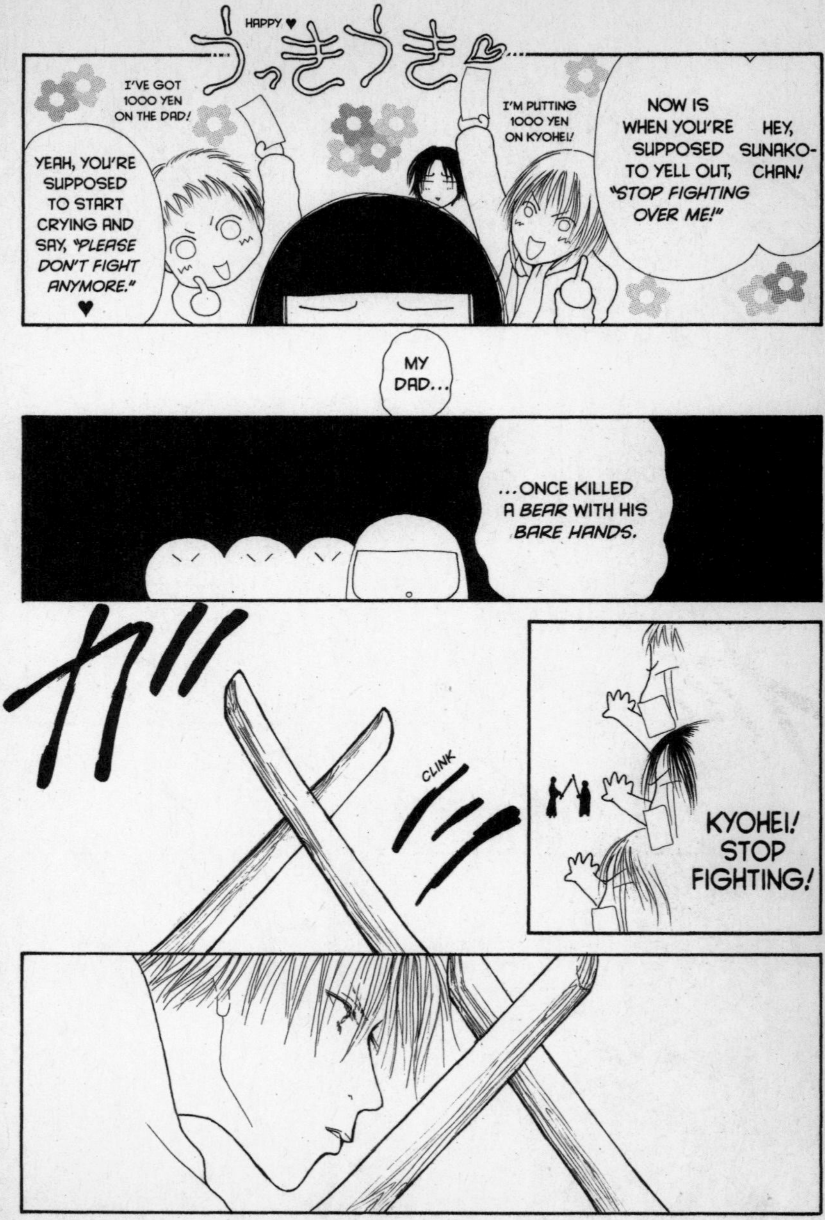
HAPPY ♥
うきうき♡
HEY, SUNAKO-CHAN!
NOW IS WHEN YOU'RE SUPPOSED TO YELL OUT, "STOP FIGHTING OVER ME!"
I'M PUTTING 1000 YEN ON KYOHEI!
I'VE GOT 1000 YEN ON THE DAD!
YEAH, YOU'RE SUPPOSED TO START CRYING AND SAY, "PLEASE DON'T FIGHT ANYMORE." ♥
MY DAD...
...ONCE KILLED A BEAR WITH HIS BARE HANDS.
KYOHEI! STOP FIGHTING!
ガ
CLINK

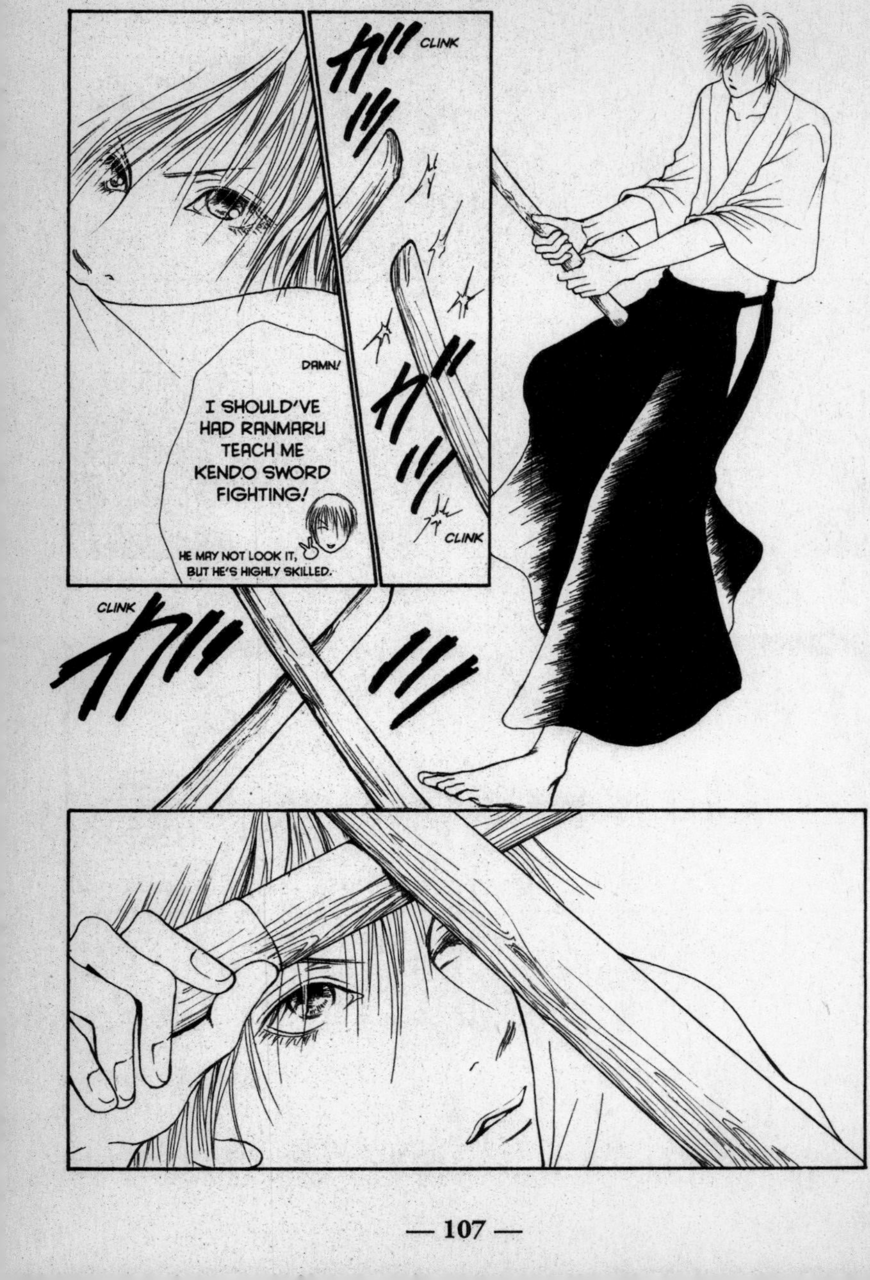
CLINK
CLINK
DAMN!
I SHOULD'VE HAD RANMARU TEACH ME KENDO SWORD FIGHTING!
HE MAY NOT LOOK IT, BUT HE'S HIGHLY SKILLED.
CLINK

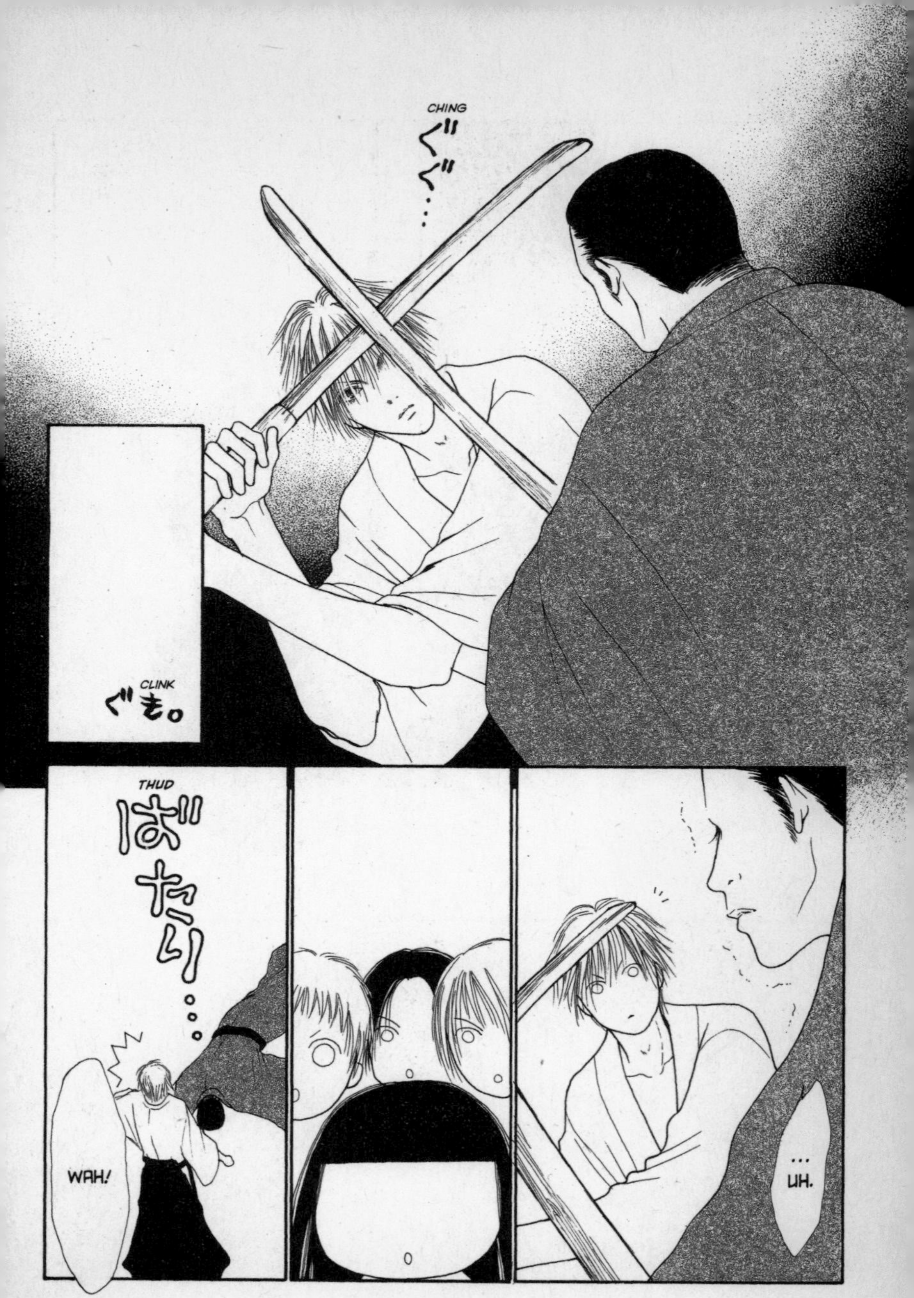
CHING
ぐぐ…
CLINK
ぐも。
... UH.
THUD
ばたり…
WAH!

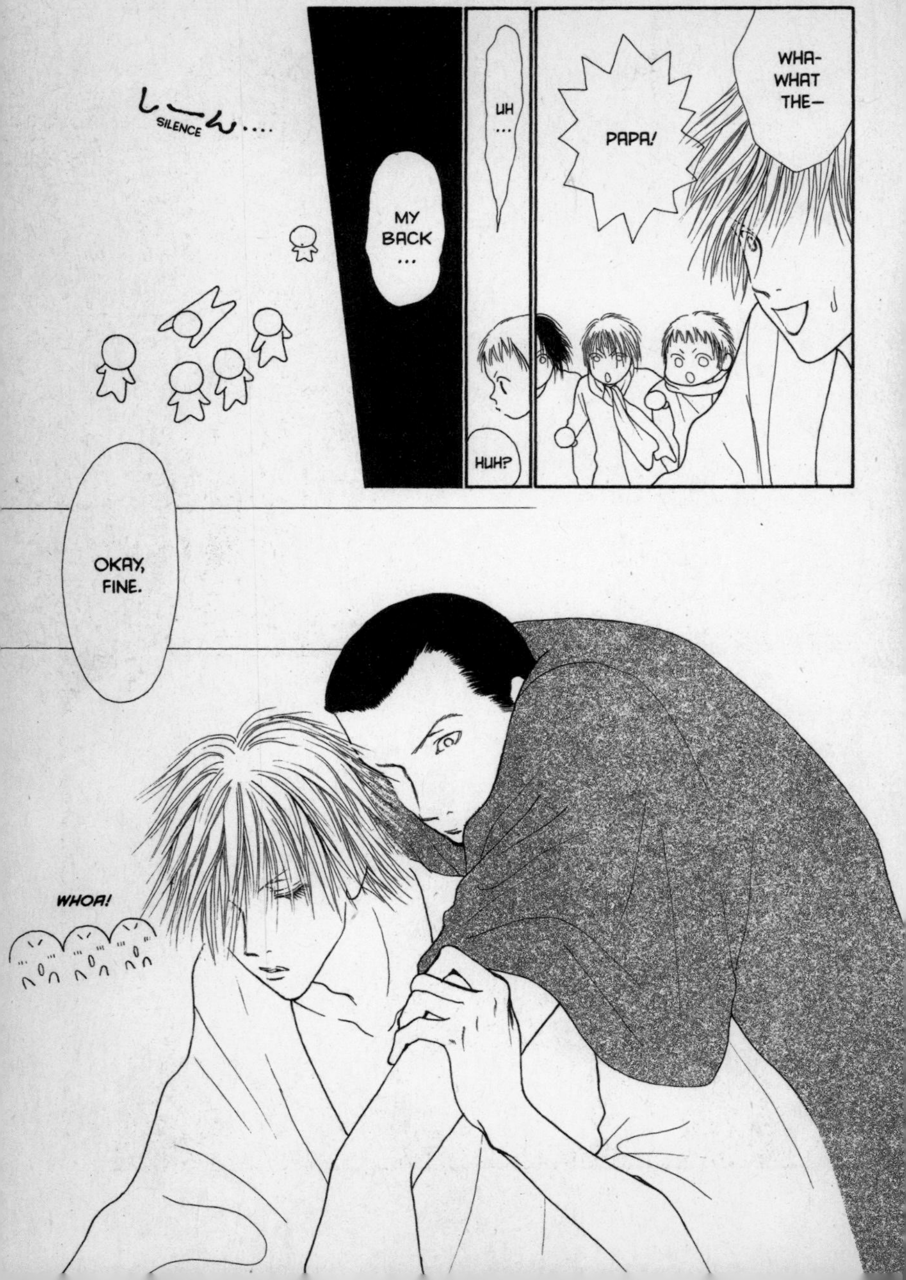

WHA- WHAT THE—
PAPA!
UH ...
HUH?
MY BACK ...
しーん SILENCE ....
OKAY, FINE.
WHOA!

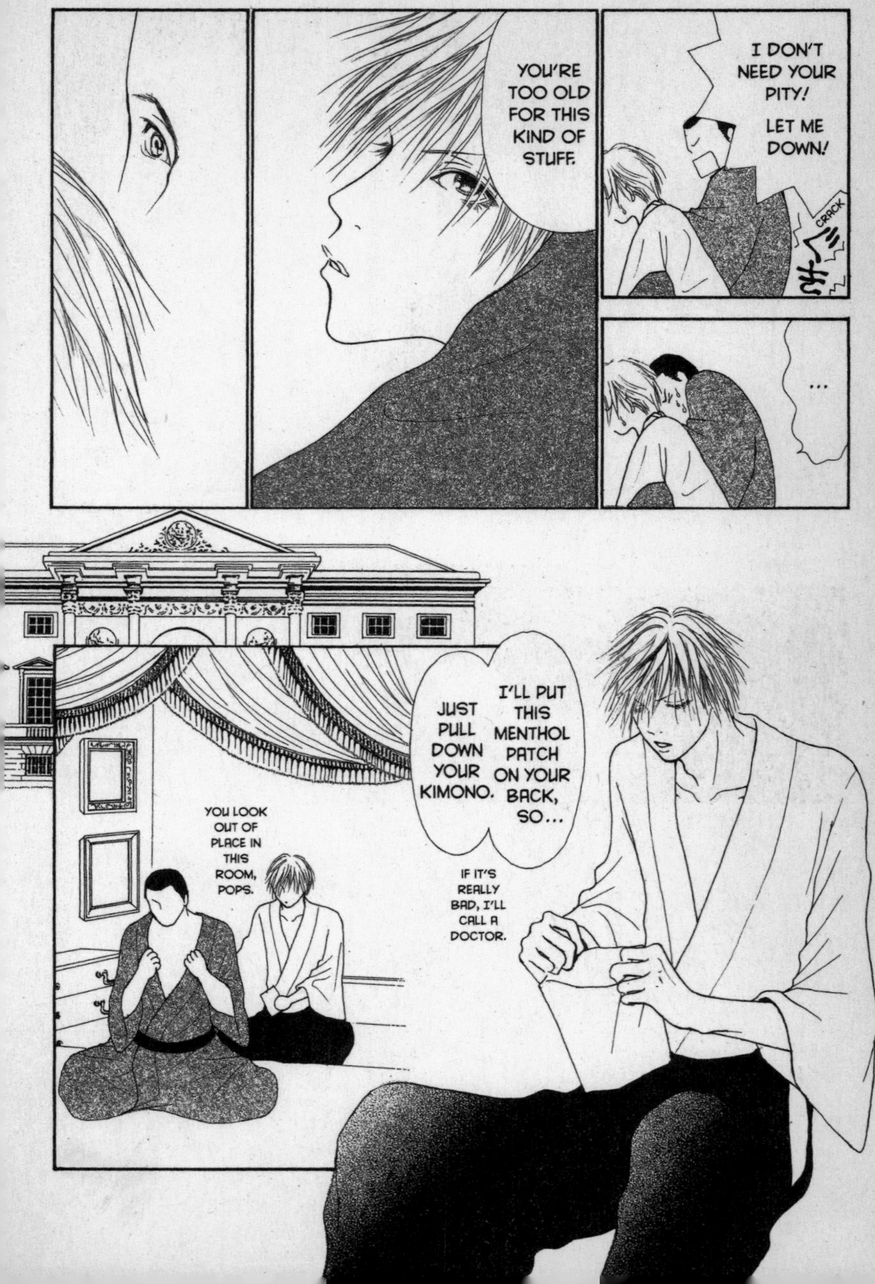
I DON'T NEED YOUR PITY!
LET ME DOWN!
CRACK
...
YOU'RE TOO OLD FOR THIS KIND OF STUFF.
I'LL PUT THIS MENTHOL PATCH ON YOUR BACK, SO...
JUST PULL DOWN YOUR KIMONO.
IF IT'S REALLY BAD, I'LL CALL A DOCTOR.
YOU LOOK OUT OF PLACE IN THIS ROOM, POPS.

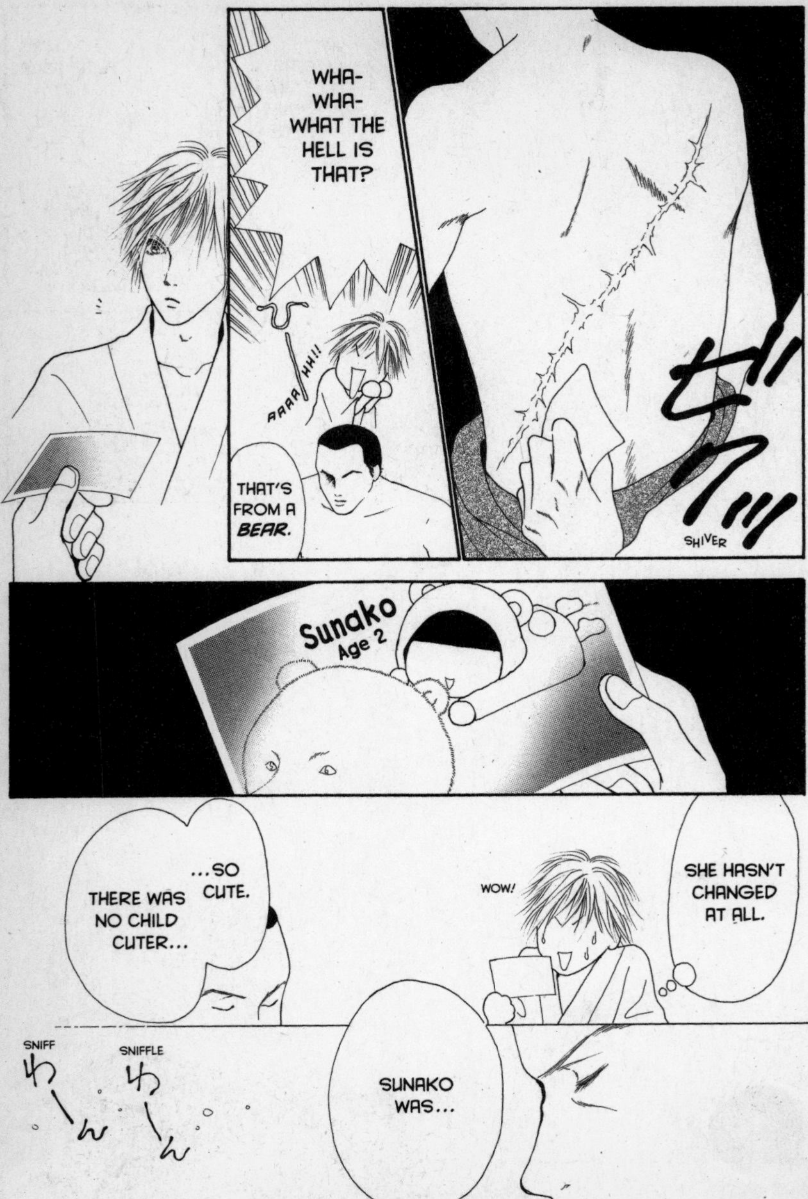

SHIVER
WHA-WHA-WHAT THE HELL IS THAT?
AAAAHH!!
THAT'S FROM A *BEAR.*
Sunako Age 2
WOW!
SHE HASN'T CHANGED AT ALL.
...SO CUTE.
THERE WAS NO CHILD CUTER...
SUNAKO WAS...
SNIFF
わーん
SNIFFLE
わーん

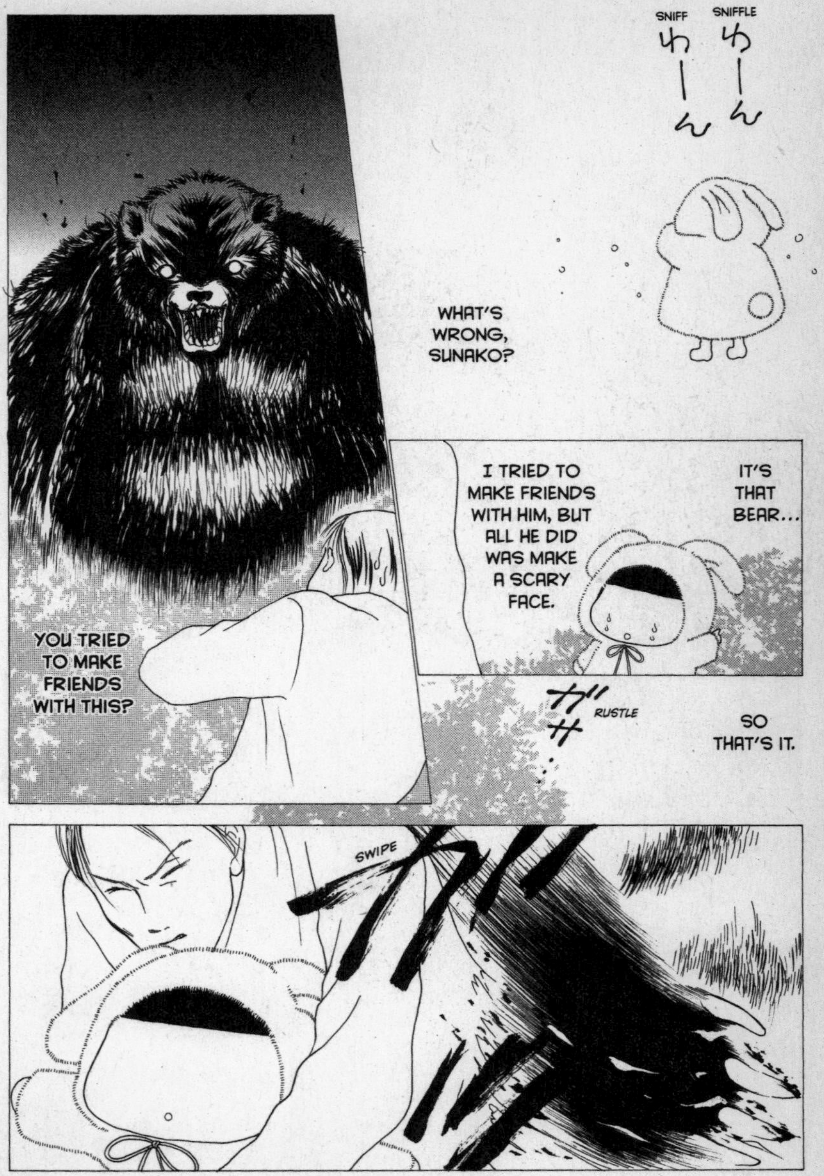
SNIFFLE
わーん
SNIFF
わーん
WHAT'S WRONG, SUNAKO?
IT'S THAT BEAR...
I TRIED TO MAKE FRIENDS WITH HIM, BUT ALL HE DID WAS MAKE A SCARY FACE.
SO THAT'S IT.
RUSTLE
YOU TRIED TO MAKE FRIENDS WITH THIS?
SWIPE

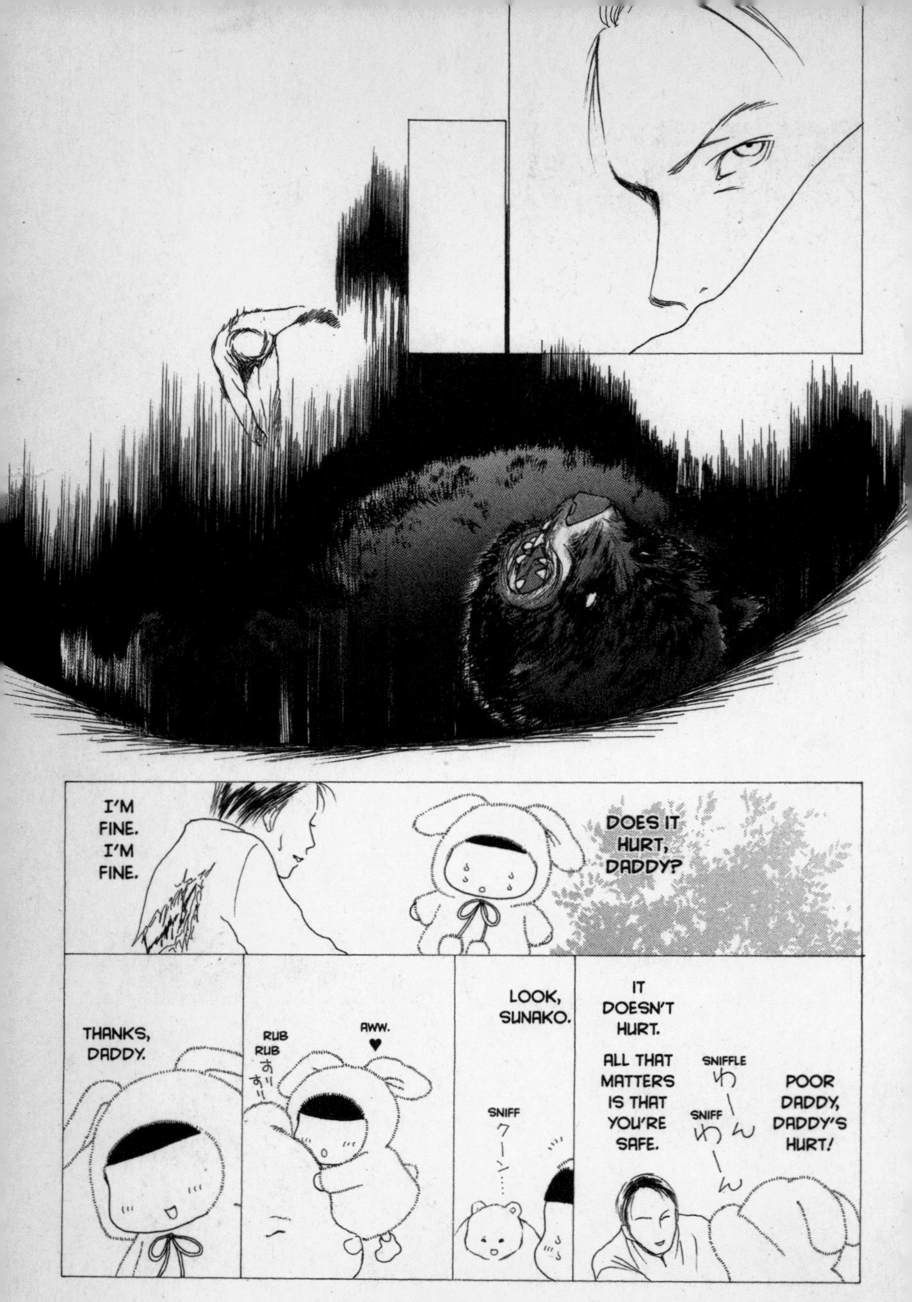
DOES IT HURT, DADDY?
I'M FINE. I'M FINE.
POOR DADDY, DADDY'S HURT!
SNIFFLE わーん
SNIFF わーん
IT DOESN'T HURT.
ALL THAT MATTERS IS THAT YOU'RE SAFE.
LOOK, SUNAKO.
SNIFF クーン……
AWW. ♥
RUB RUB すりっ
THANKS, DADDY.

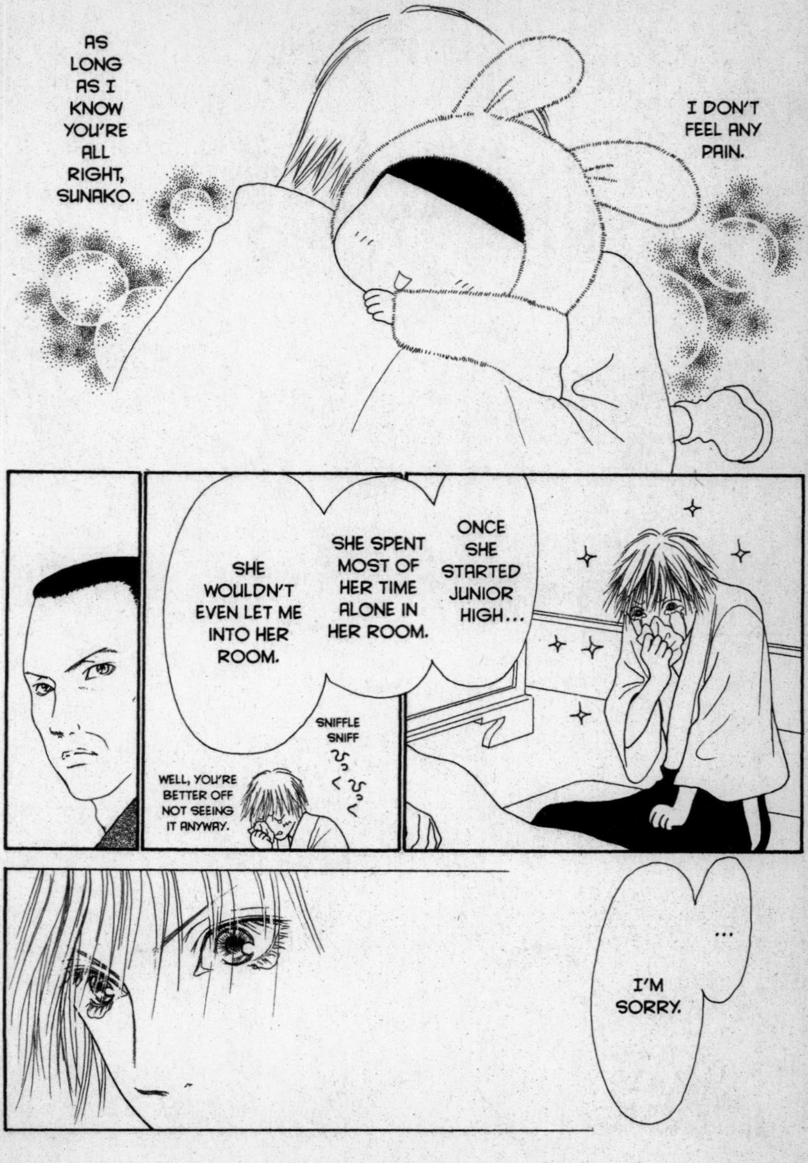
AS LONG AS I KNOW YOU'RE ALL RIGHT, SUNAKO.
I DON'T FEEL ANY PAIN.
ONCE SHE STARTED JUNIOR HIGH...
SHE SPENT MOST OF HER TIME ALONE IN HER ROOM.
SHE WOULDN'T EVEN LET ME INTO HER ROOM.
SNIFFLE SNIFF
WELL, YOU'RE BETTER OFF NOT SEEING IT ANYWAY.
...
I'M SORRY.

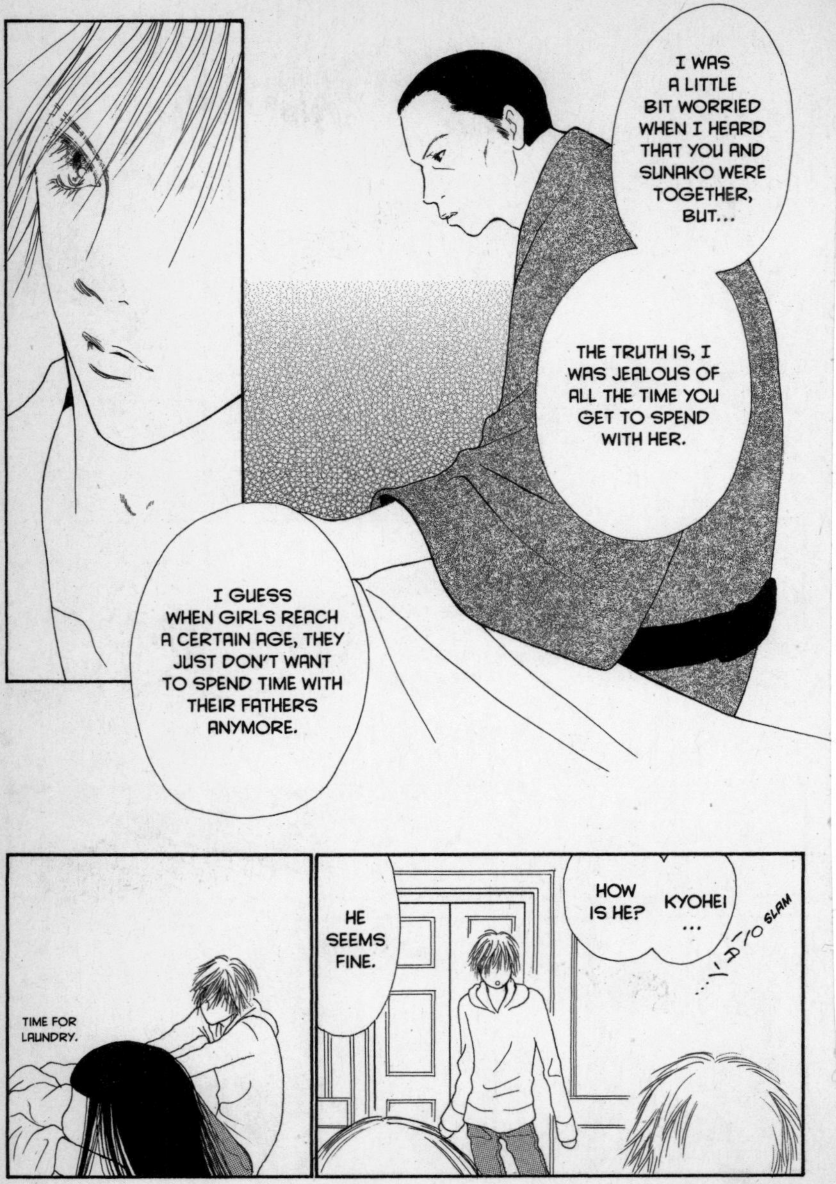
I WAS A LITTLE BIT WORRIED WHEN I HEARD THAT YOU AND SUNAKO WERE TOGETHER, BUT...
THE TRUTH IS, I WAS JEALOUS OF ALL THE TIME YOU GET TO SPEND WITH HER.
I GUESS WHEN GIRLS REACH A CERTAIN AGE, THEY JUST DON'T WANT TO SPEND TIME WITH THEIR FATHERS ANYMORE.
SLAM
KYOHEI ...
HOW IS HE?
HE SEEMS FINE.
TIME FOR LAUNDRY.

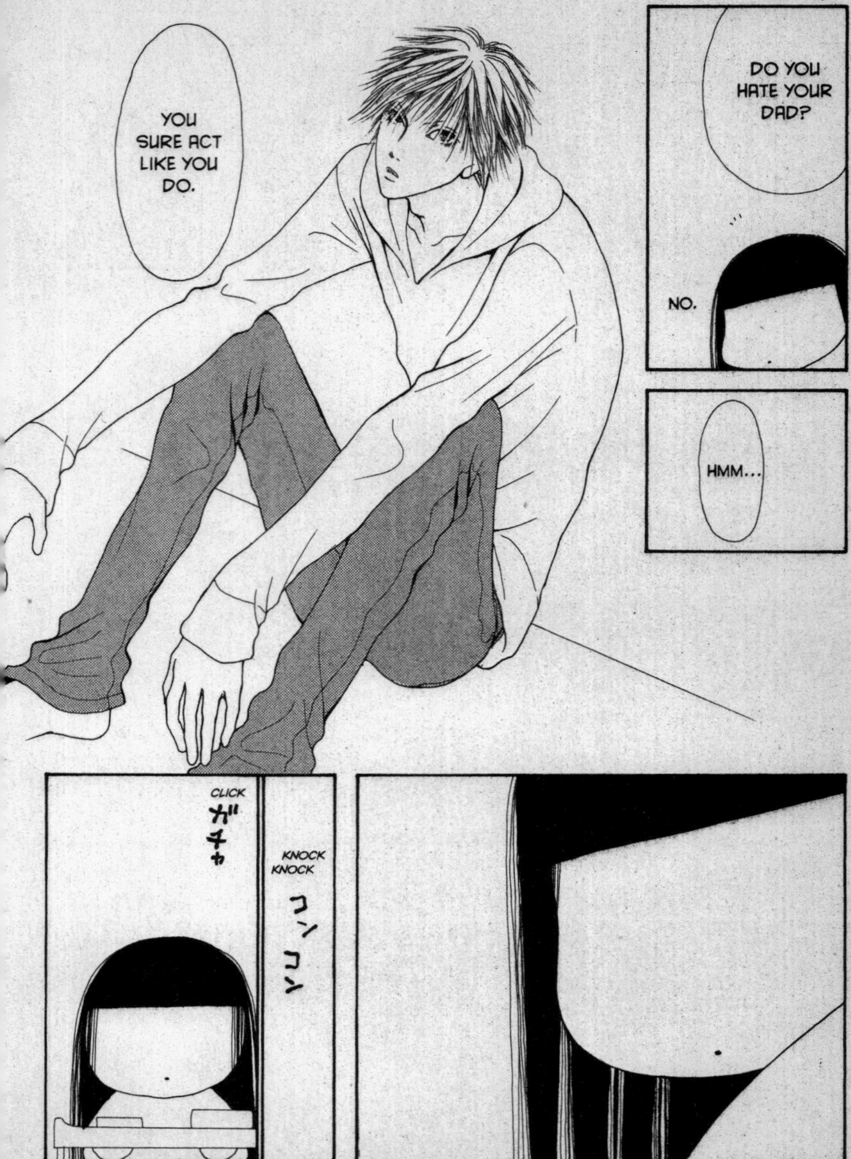
DO YOU HATE YOUR DAD?
NO.
HMM...
YOU SURE ACT LIKE YOU DO.
KNOCK KNOCK
コンコン
CLICK
ガチャ

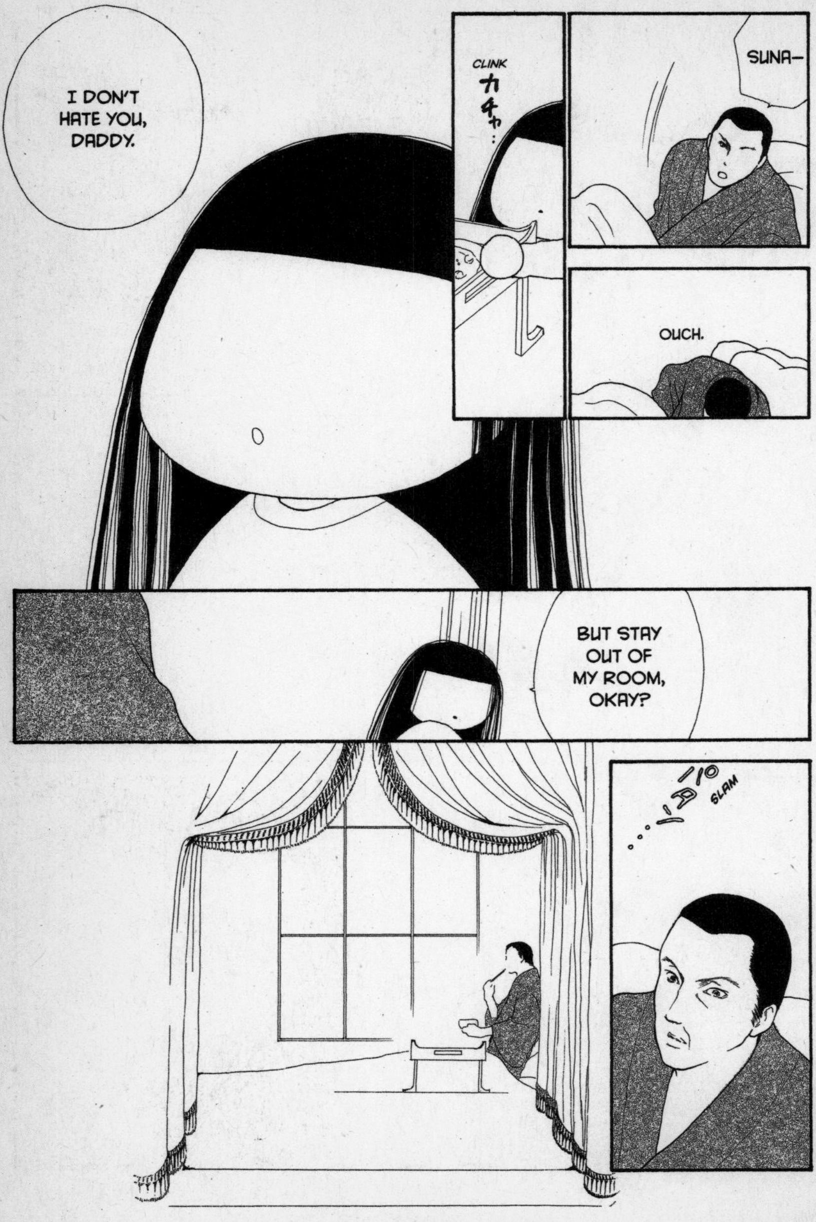
SUNA–
OUCH.
CLINK
カチャ…
I DON'T HATE YOU, DADDY.
BUT STAY OUT OF MY ROOM, OKAY?
SLAM

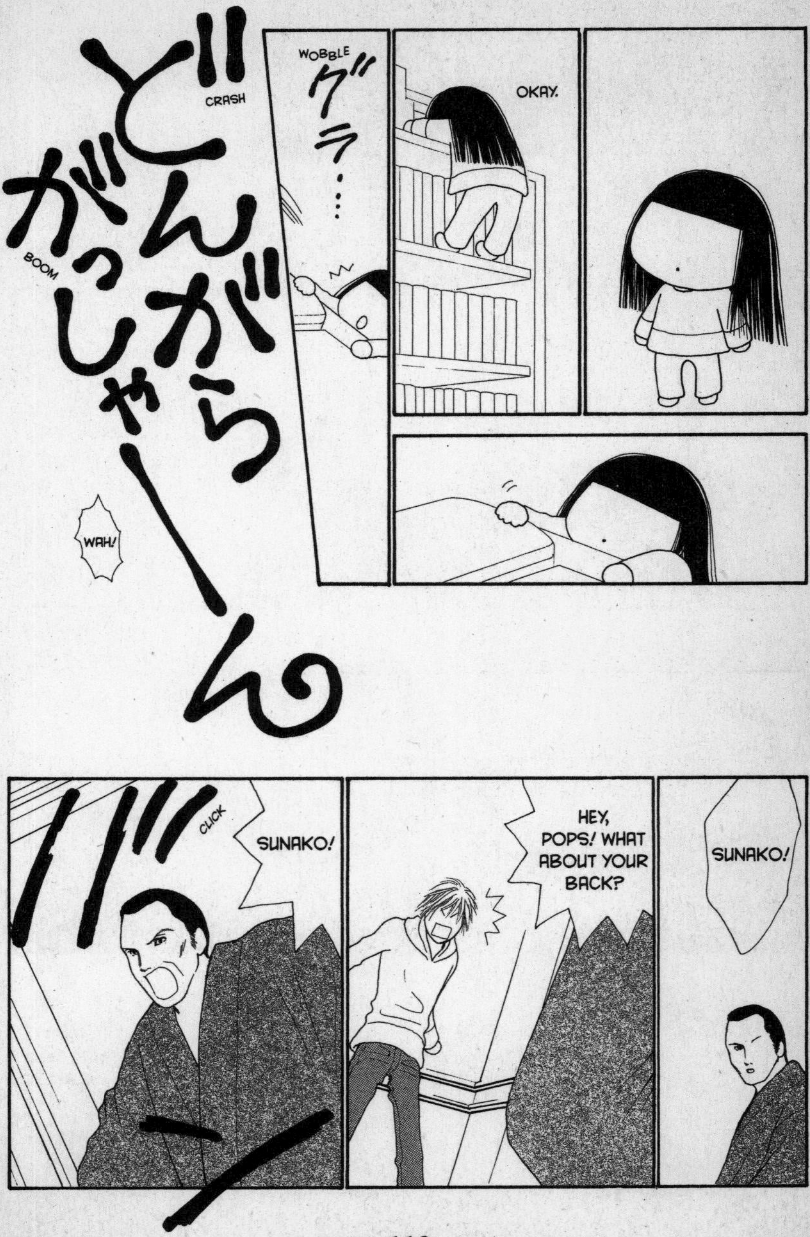
OKAY.
WOBBLE
グラ…
どんがらがっしゃーん
CRASH
BOOM
WAH!
SUNAKO!
HEY, POPS! WHAT ABOUT YOUR BACK?
CLICK
SUNAKO!

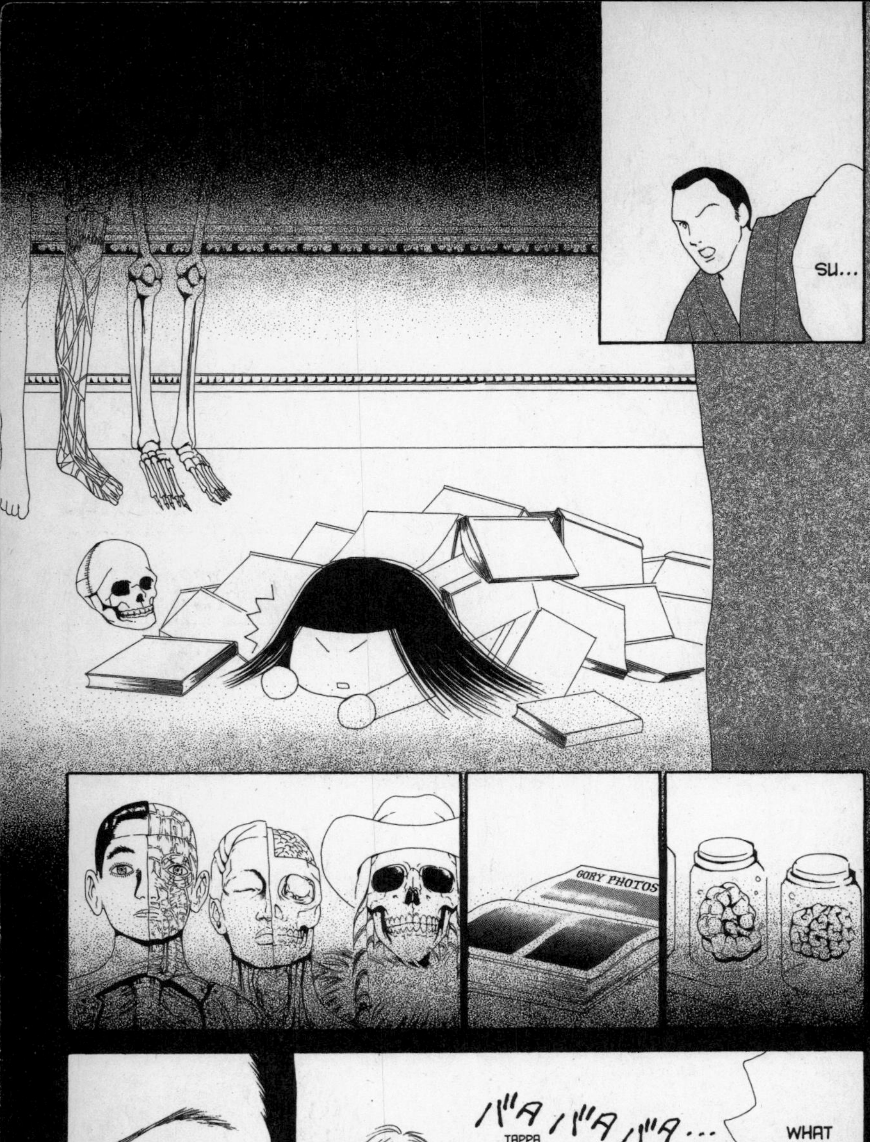
SU...
GORY PHOTOS
WHAT WAS THAT NOISE?
パタパタパタ…
TAPPA TAPPA

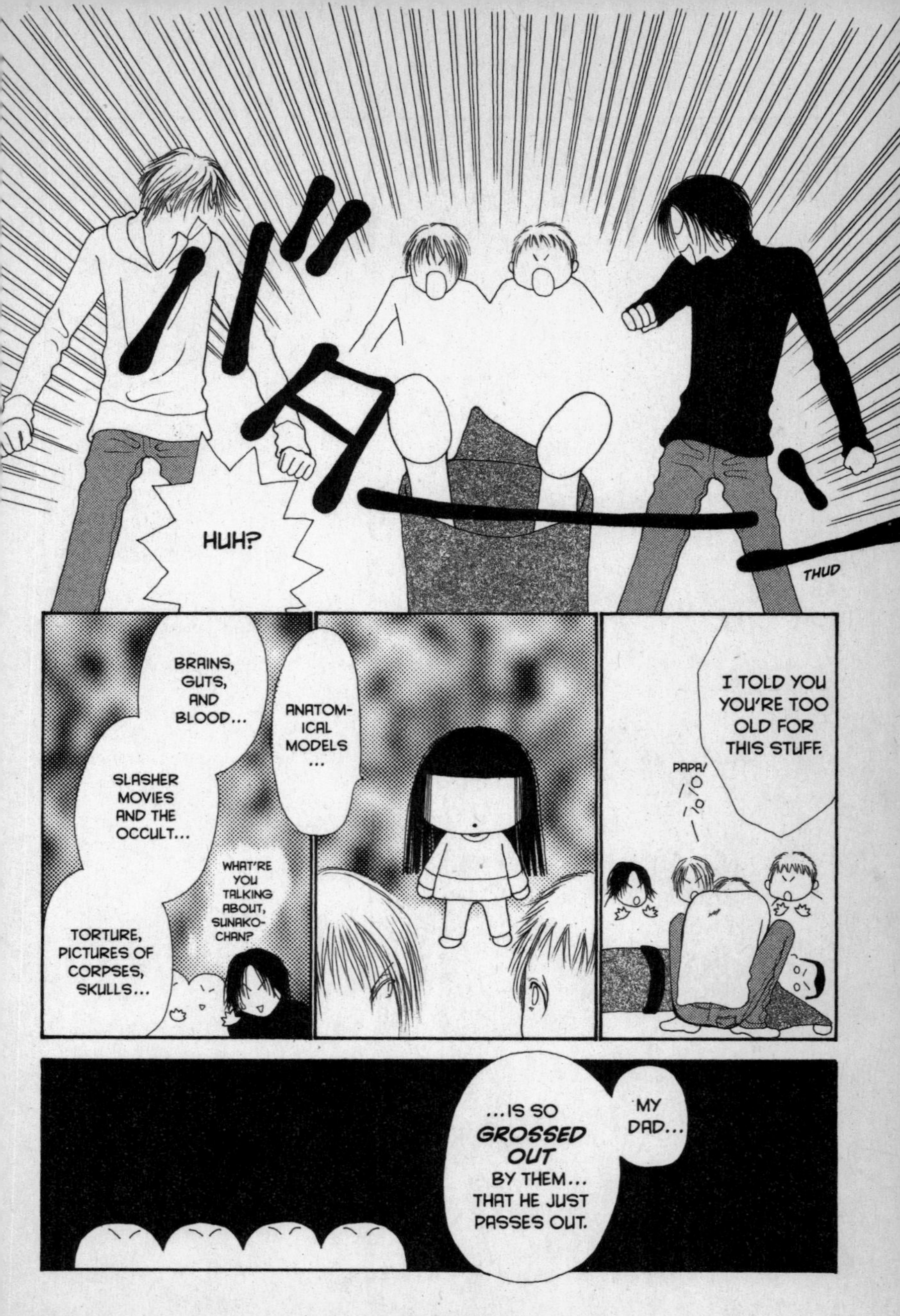

バタ
HUH?
THUD
I TOLD YOU YOU'RE TOO OLD FOR THIS STUFF.
PAPA!
ANATOM-ICAL MODELS ...
BRAINS, GUTS, AND BLOOD...
SLASHER MOVIES AND THE OCCULT...
WHAT'RE YOU TALKING ABOUT, SUNAKO-CHAN?
TORTURE, PICTURES OF CORPSES, SKULLS...
MY DAD...
...IS SO ***GROSSED OUT*** BY THEM... THAT HE JUST PASSES OUT.

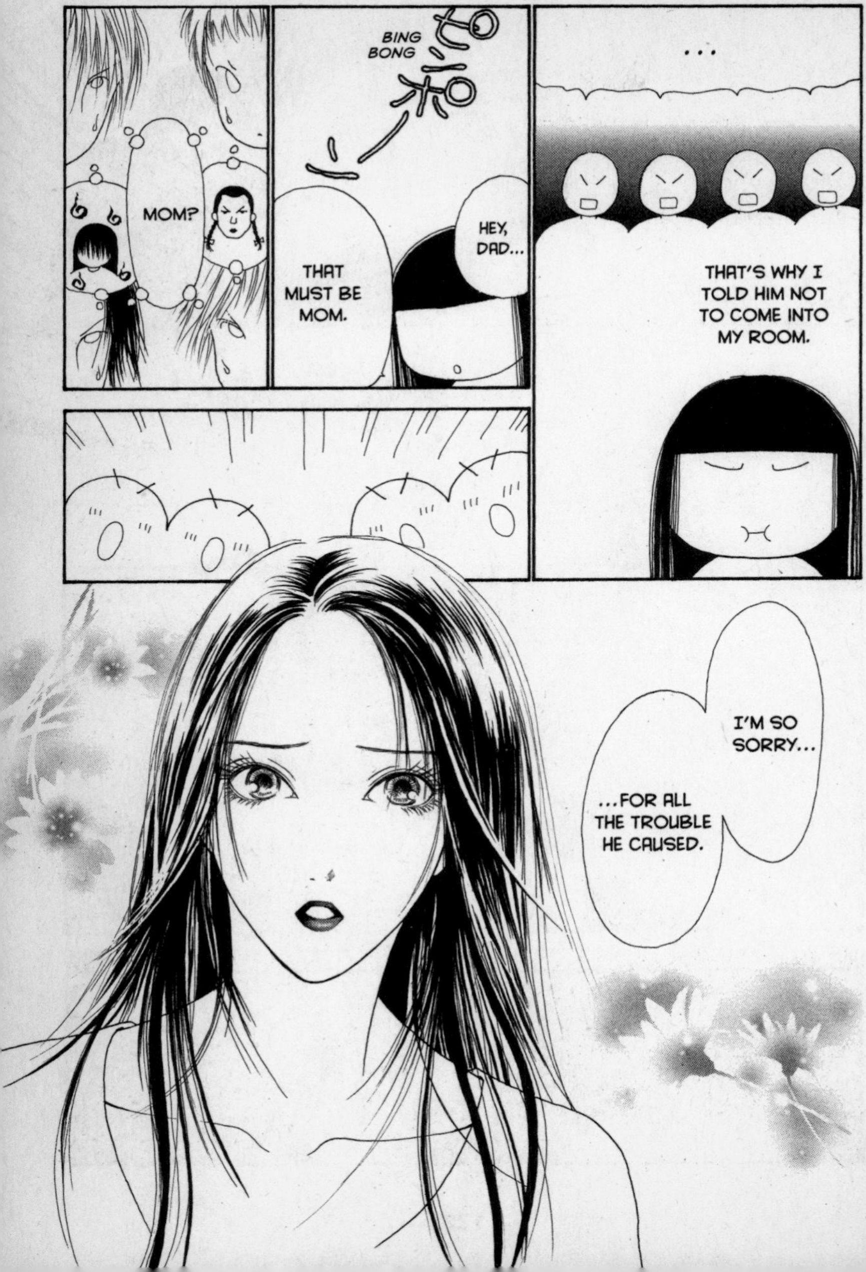
...
THAT'S WHY I TOLD HIM NOT TO COME INTO MY ROOM.
ピンポーン
BING BONG
HEY, DAD...
THAT MUST BE MOM.
MOM?
I'M SO SORRY...
...FOR ALL THE TROUBLE HE CAUSED.

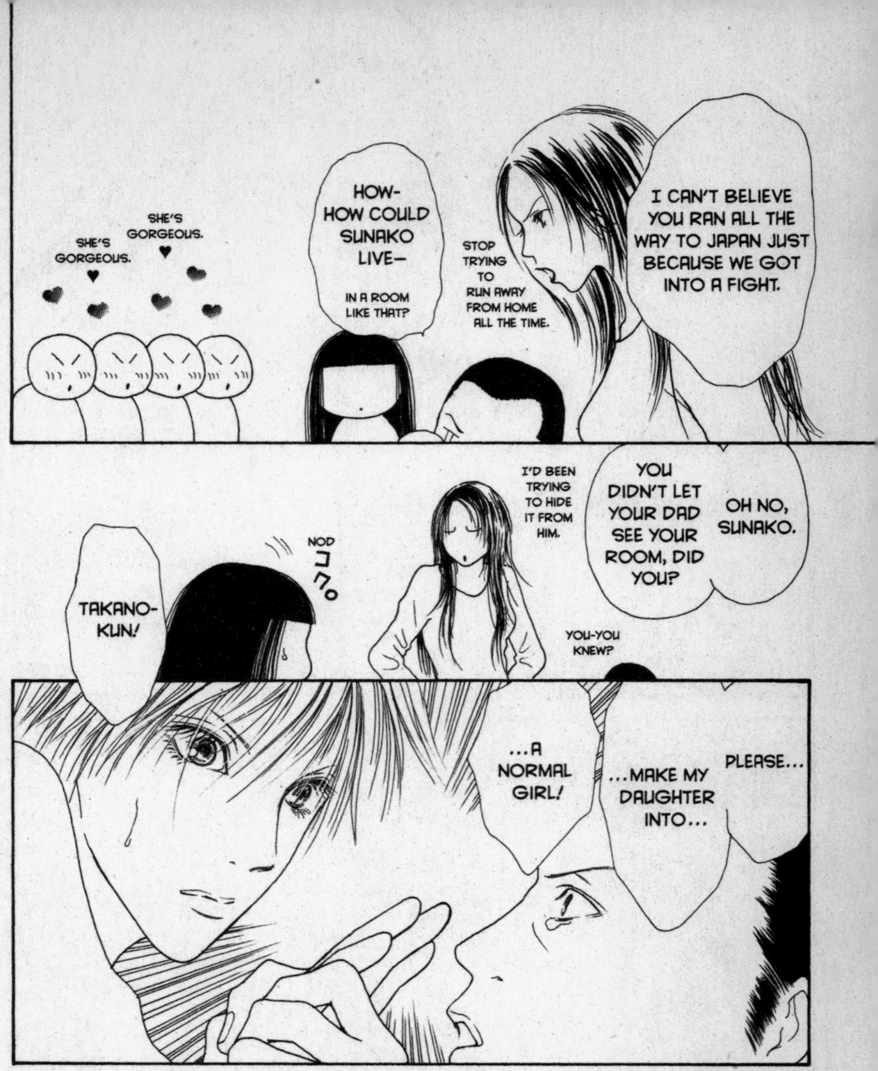
I CAN'T BELIEVE YOU RAN ALL THE WAY TO JAPAN JUST BECAUSE WE GOT INTO A FIGHT.
STOP TRYING TO RUN AWAY FROM HOME ALL THE TIME.
HOW- HOW COULD SUNAKO LIVE—
IN A ROOM LIKE THAT?
SHE'S GORGEOUS. ♥
SHE'S GORGEOUS. ♥
OH NO, SUNAKO.
YOU DIDN'T LET YOUR DAD SEE YOUR ROOM, DID YOU?
I'D BEEN TRYING TO HIDE IT FROM HIM.
YOU-YOU KNEW?
NOD
TAKANO-KUN!
PLEASE...
...MAKE MY DAUGHTER INTO...
...A NORMAL GIRL!
MIND YOUR OWN BUSINESS!
LET SUNAKO DO WHAT SHE WANTS.
NOD
NOD
BUT, BUT...

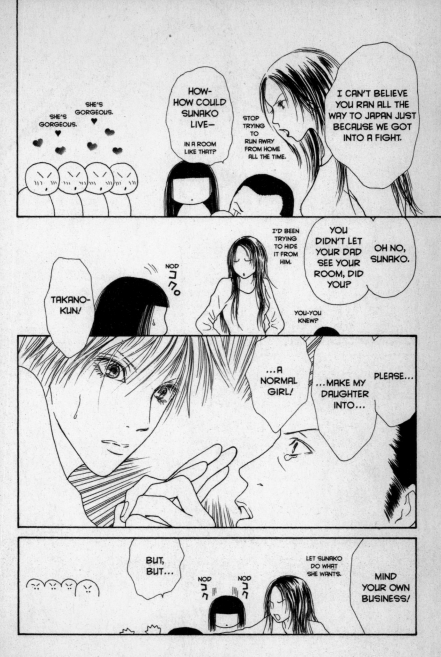

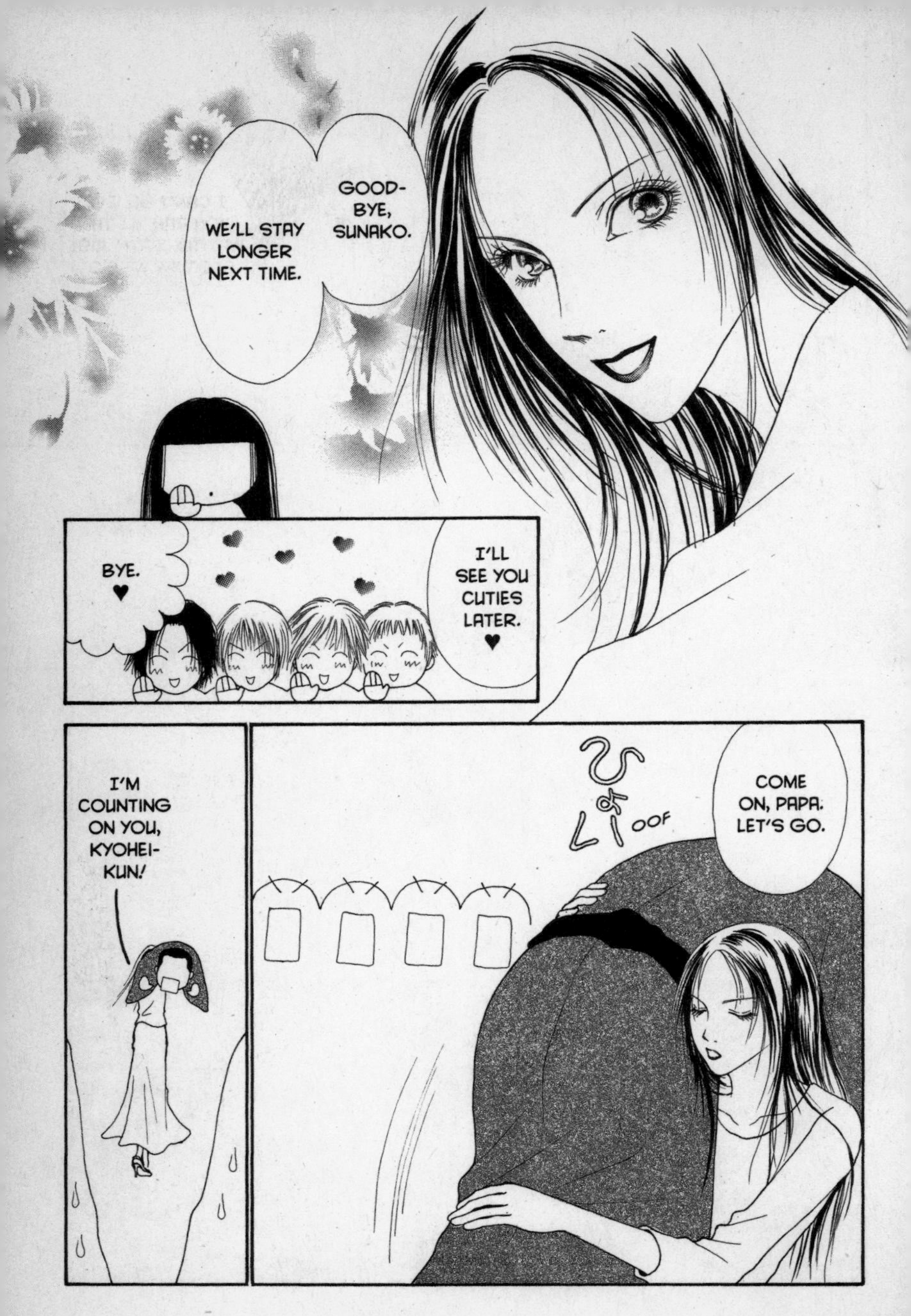
GOOD-BYE, SUNAKO.
WE'LL STAY LONGER NEXT TIME.
I'LL SEE YOU CUTIES LATER. ♥
BYE. ♥
COME ON, PAPA. LET'S GO.
OOF
I'M COUNTING ON YOU, KYOHEI-KUN!

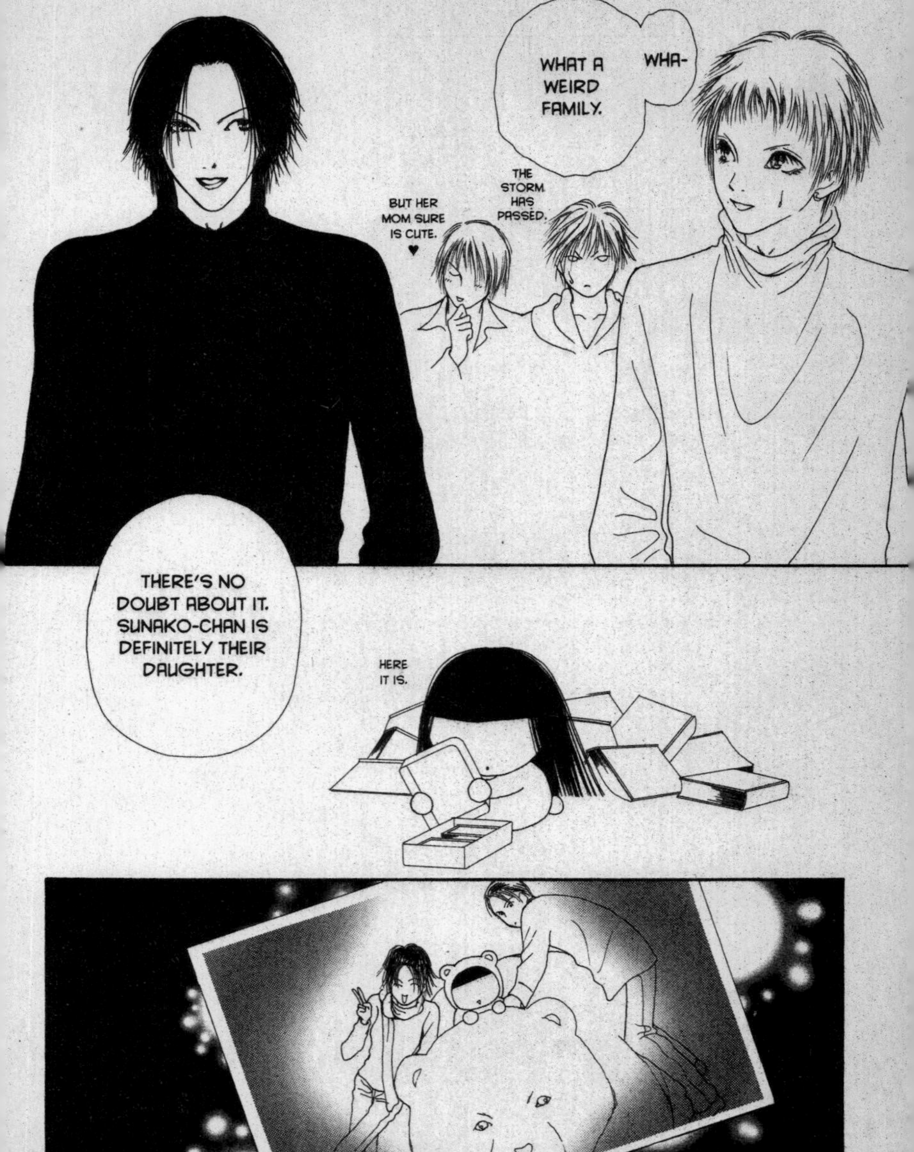
WHA-
WHAT A WEIRD FAMILY.
THE STORM HAS PASSED.
BUT HER MOM SURE IS CUTE. ♥
THERE'S NO DOUBT ABOUT IT. SUNAKO-CHAN IS DEFINITELY THEIR DAUGHTER.
HERE IT IS.

Chapter 22

Oh, My Sweet Home! (Part One)

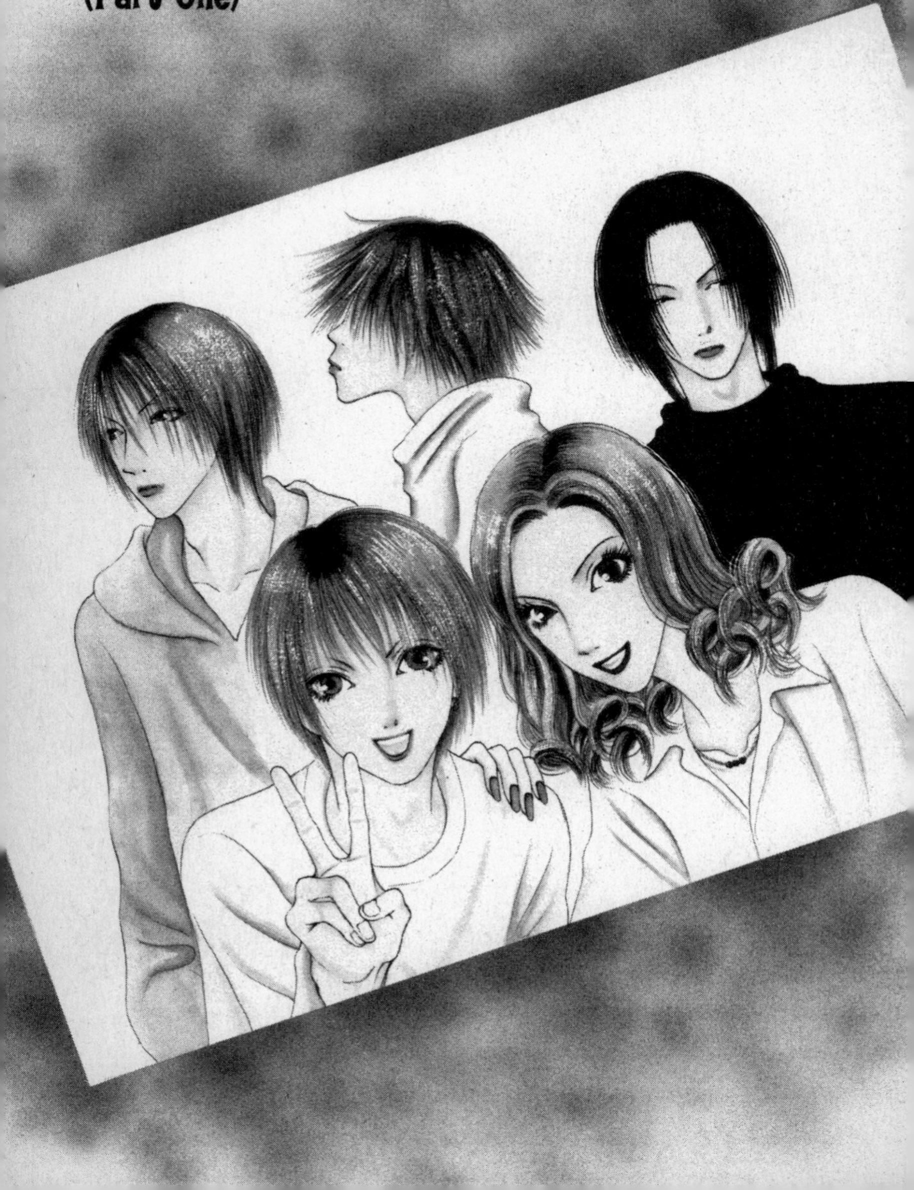

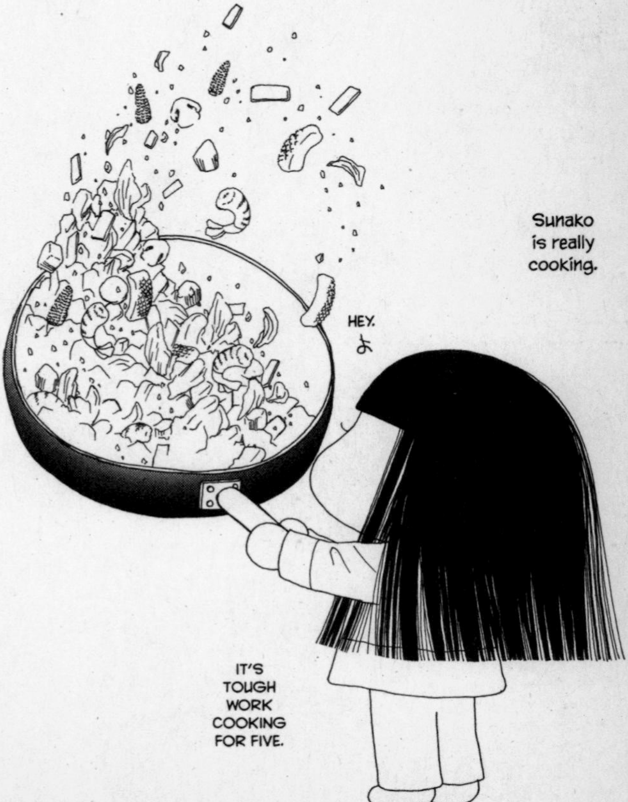
Sunako is really cooking.
HEY.
よ
IT'S TOUGH WORK COOKING FOR FIVE.

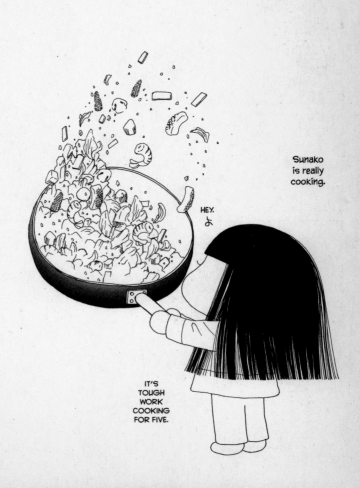

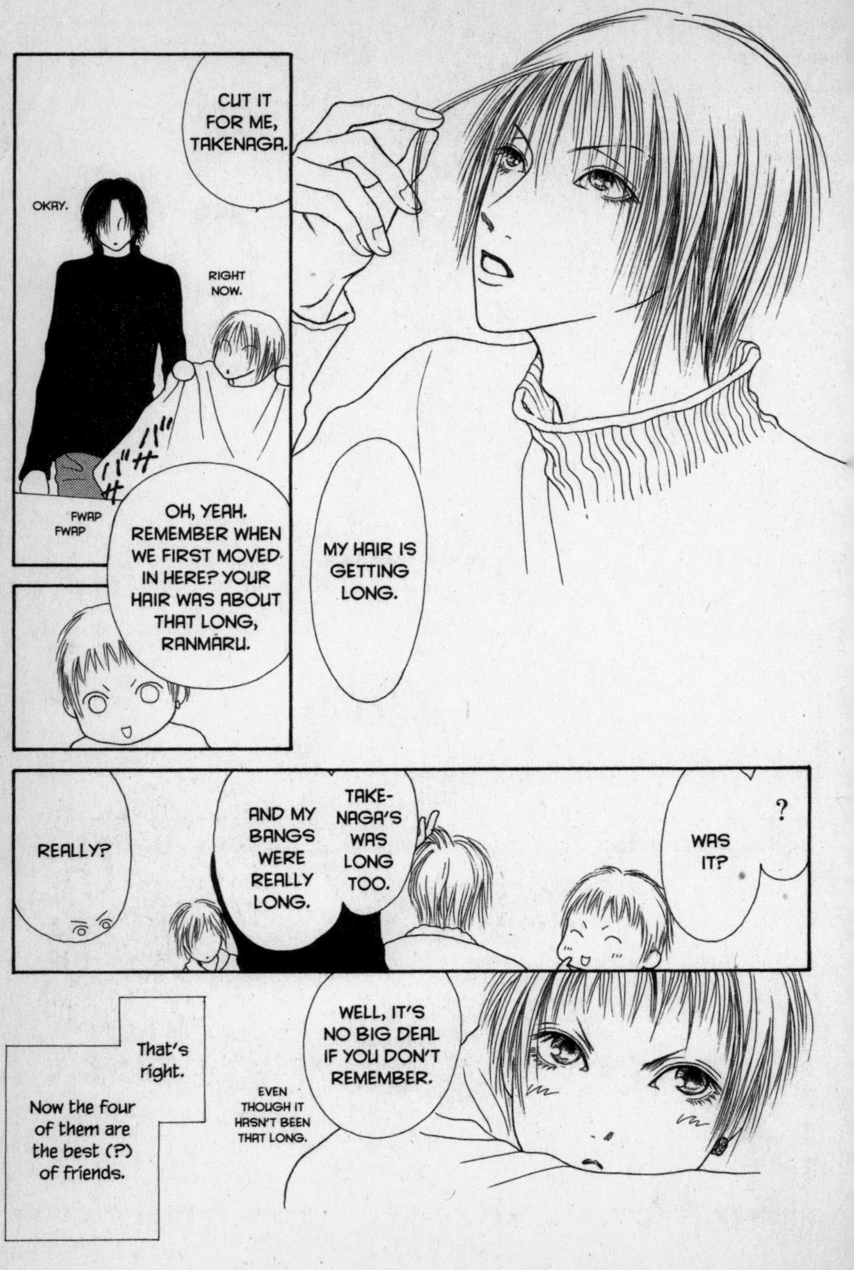
MY HAIR IS GETTING LONG.
CUT IT FOR ME, TAKENAGA.
RIGHT NOW.
OKAY.
FWAP FWAP
OH, YEAH. REMEMBER WHEN WE FIRST MOVED IN HERE? YOUR HAIR WAS ABOUT THAT LONG, RANMARU.
?
WAS IT?
TAKE-NAGA'S WAS LONG TOO.
AND MY BANGS WERE REALLY LONG.
REALLY?
WELL, IT'S NO BIG DEAL IF YOU DON'T REMEMBER.
EVEN THOUGH IT HASN'T BEEN THAT LONG.
That's right.
Now the four of them are the best (?) of friends.

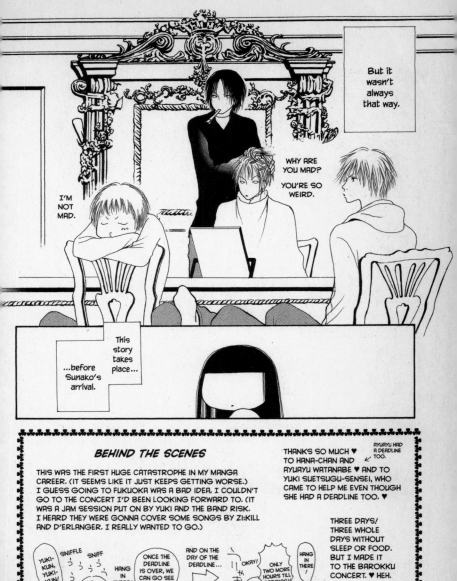

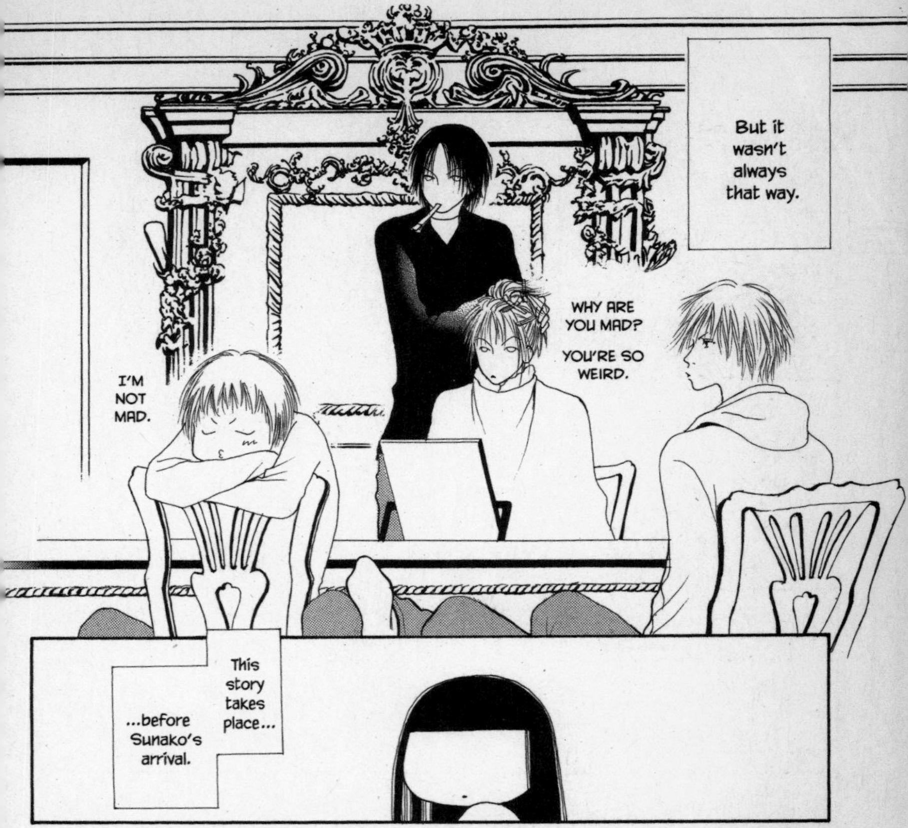
But it wasn't always that way.
WHY ARE YOU MAD?
YOU'RE SO WEIRD.
I'M NOT MAD.
This story takes place...
...before Sunako's arrival.

BEHIND THE SCENES

THIS WAS THE FIRST HUGE CATASTROPHE IN MY MANGA CAREER. (IT SEEMS LIKE IT JUST KEEPS GETTING WORSE.) I GUESS GOING TO FUKUOKA WAS A BAD IDEA. I COULDN'T GO TO THE CONCERT I'D BEEN LOOKING FORWARD TO. (IT WAS A JAM SESSION PUT ON BY YUKI AND THE BAND RISK. I HEARD THEY WERE GONNA COVER SOME SONGS BY ZI:KILL AND D'ERLANGER. I REALLY WANTED TO GO.)

THANKS SO MUCH ♥ TO HANA-CHAN AND AYUAYU WATANABE ♥ AND TO YUKI SUETSUGU-SENSEI, WHO CAME TO HELP ME EVEN THOUGH SHE HAD A DEADLINE TOO. ♥

← AYUAYU HAD A DEADLINE TOO.

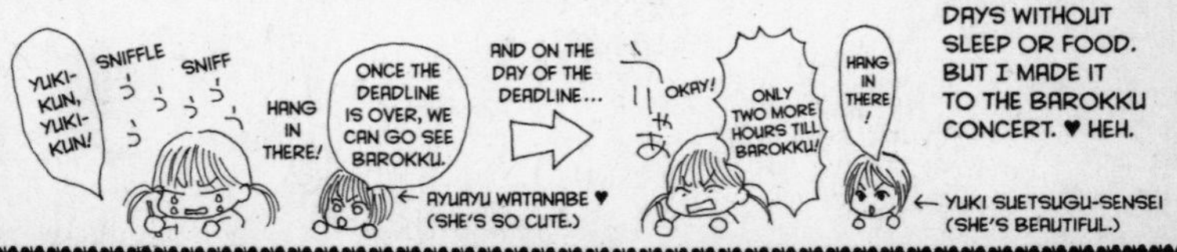
YUKI-KUN, YUKI-KUN!
SNIFFLE
SNIFF
うっうっうっ
HANG IN THERE!
ONCE THE DEADLINE IS OVER, WE CAN GO SEE BAROKKU.
← AYUAYU WATANABE ♥ (SHE'S SO CUTE.)
AND ON THE DAY OF THE DEADLINE...
OKAY!
ONLY TWO MORE HOURS TILL BAROKKU!
HANG IN THERE!
← YUKI SUETSUGU-SENSEI (SHE'S BEAUTIFUL.)

THREE DAYS! THREE WHOLE DAYS WITHOUT SLEEP OR FOOD. BUT I MADE IT TO THE BAROKKU CONCERT. ♥ HEH.

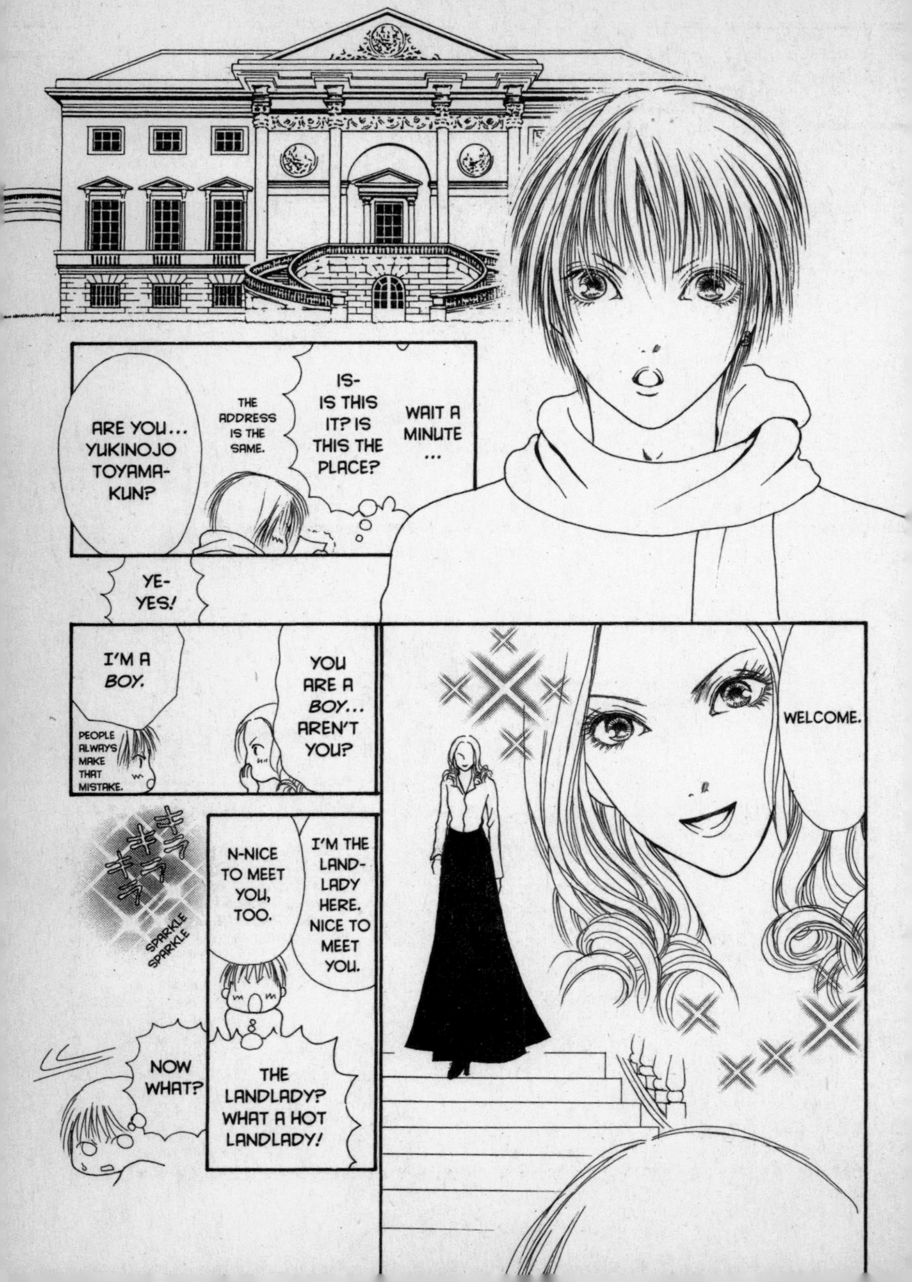
WAIT A MINUTE...
IS- IS THIS IT? IS THIS THE PLACE?
THE ADDRESS IS THE SAME.
ARE YOU... YUKINOJO TOYAMA-KUN?
YE- YES!
WELCOME.
YOU ARE A *BOY*... AREN'T YOU?
I'M A *BOY*.
PEOPLE ALWAYS MAKE THAT MISTAKE.
I'M THE LANDLADY HERE. NICE TO MEET YOU.
N-NICE TO MEET YOU, TOO.
キラ キラ
SPARKLE SPARKLE
THE LANDLADY? WHAT A HOT LANDLADY!
NOW WHAT?

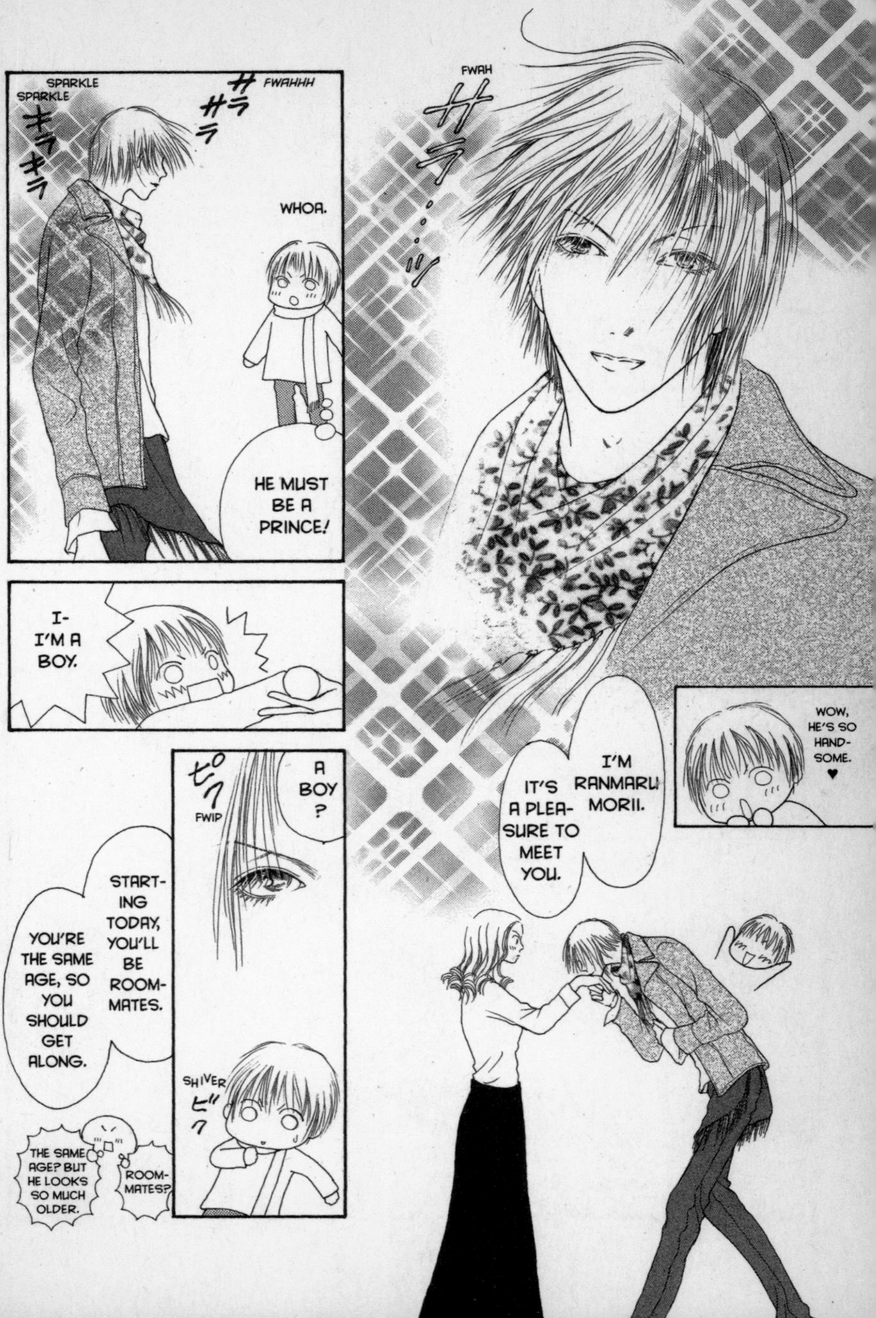
FWAH
サラ…ッ
I'M RANMARU MORII.
IT'S A PLEA-SURE TO MEET YOU.
WOW, HE'S SO HAND-SOME. ♥
SPARKLE SPARKLE
キラキラ
FWAHHH
サラサラ
WHOA.
HE MUST BE A PRINCE!
I- I'M A BOY.
A BOY?
ピク
FWIP
STARTING TODAY, YOU'LL BE ROOM-MATES.
YOU'RE THE SAME AGE, SO YOU SHOULD GET ALONG.
SHIVER
ビク
THE SAME AGE? BUT HE LOOKS SO MUCH OLDER.
ROOM-MATES?

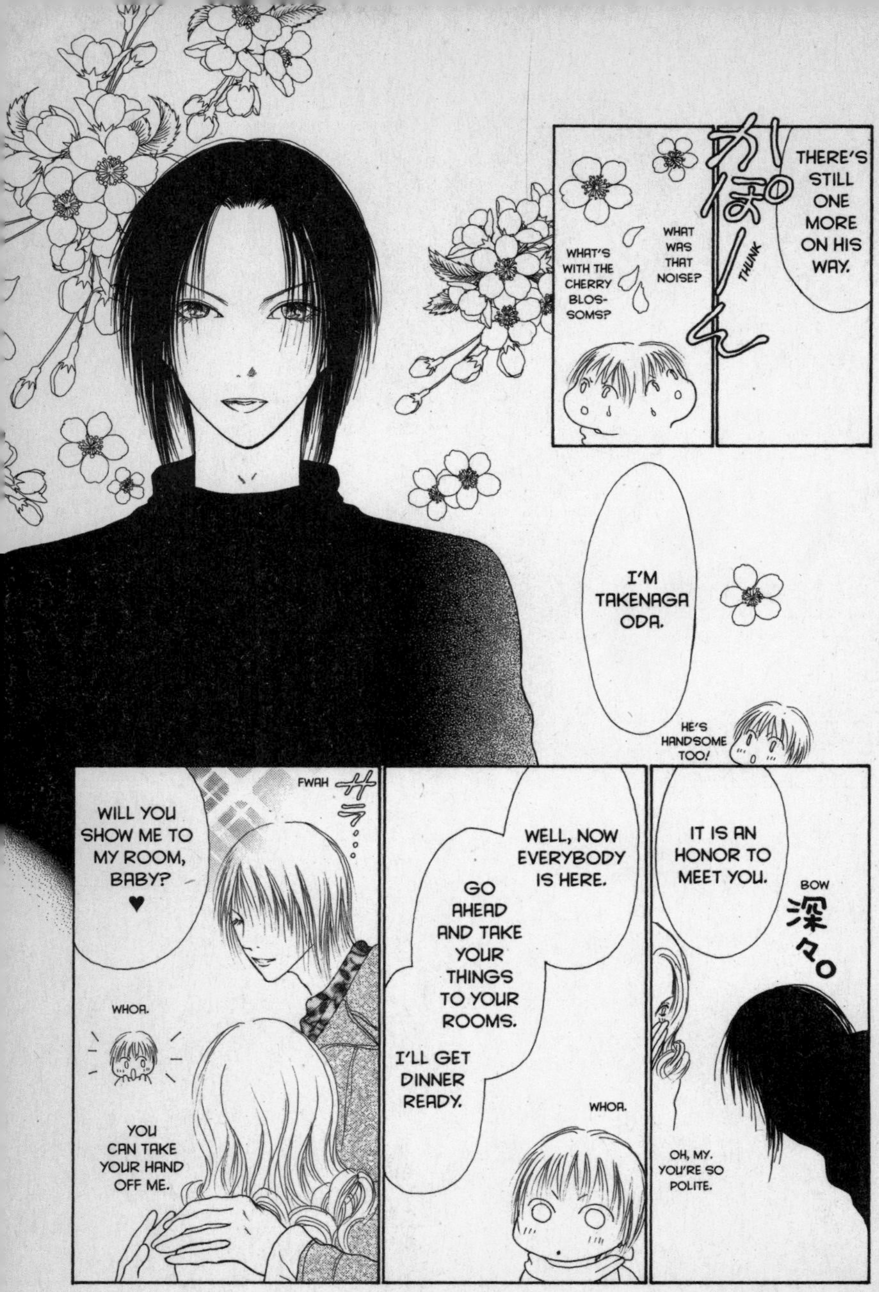
THERE'S STILL ONE MORE ON HIS WAY.
かぽーん
THUNK
WHAT WAS THAT NOISE?
WHAT'S WITH THE CHERRY BLOS-SOMS?
I'M TAKENAGA ODA.
HE'S HANDSOME TOO!
IT IS AN HONOR TO MEET YOU.
深々。
BOW
OH, MY. YOU'RE SO POLITE.
WELL, NOW EVERYBODY IS HERE.
GO AHEAD AND TAKE YOUR THINGS TO YOUR ROOMS.
I'LL GET DINNER READY.
WHOA.
サラ…
FWAH
WILL YOU SHOW ME TO MY ROOM, BABY? ♥
WHOA.
YOU CAN TAKE YOUR HAND OFF ME.

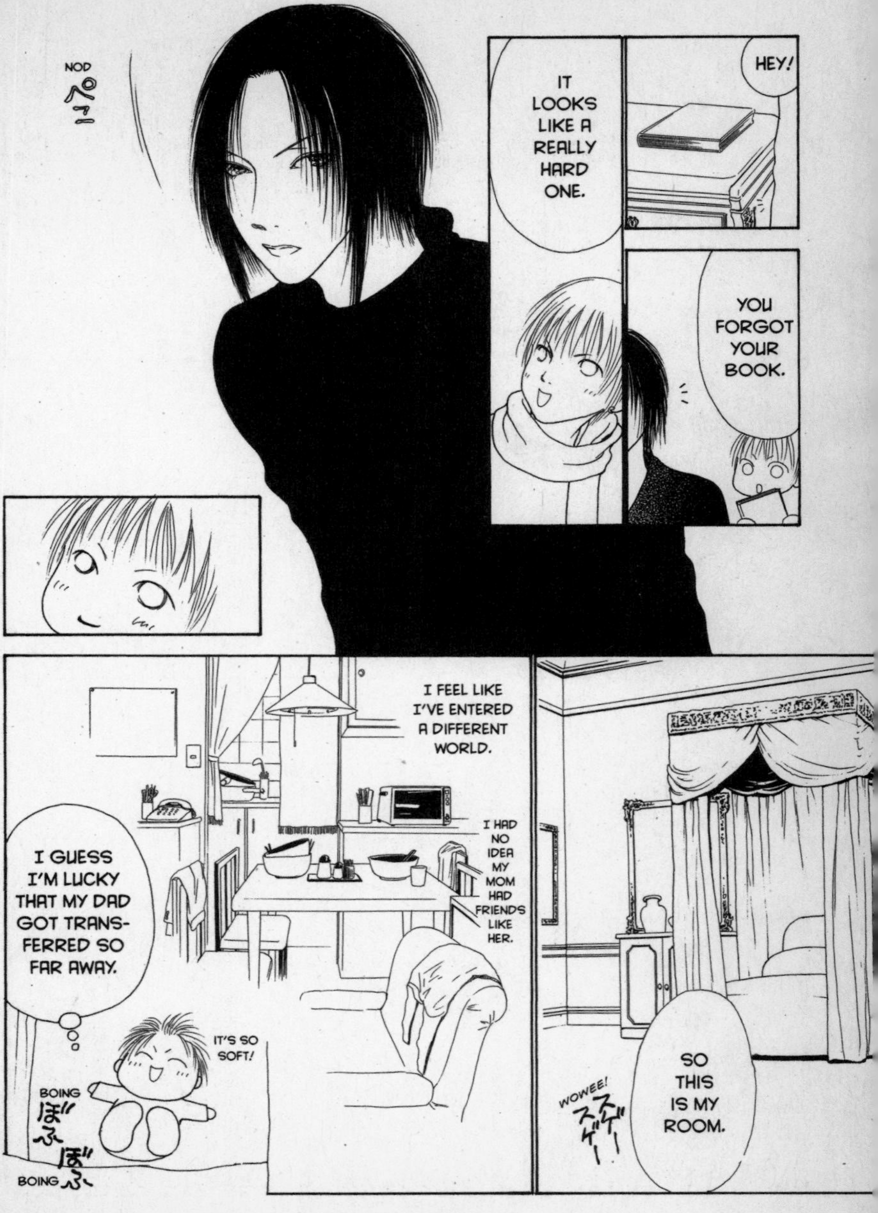
HEY!
YOU FORGOT YOUR BOOK.
IT LOOKS LIKE A REALLY HARD ONE.
NOD
ぺこ
SO THIS IS MY ROOM.
WOWEE!
スゲー
スゲー
I FEEL LIKE I'VE ENTERED A DIFFERENT WORLD.
I HAD NO IDEA MY MOM HAD FRIENDS LIKE HER.
I GUESS I'M LUCKY THAT MY DAD GOT TRANS-FERRED SO FAR AWAY.
IT'S SO SOFT!
BOING
ぼふ
ぼふ
BOING

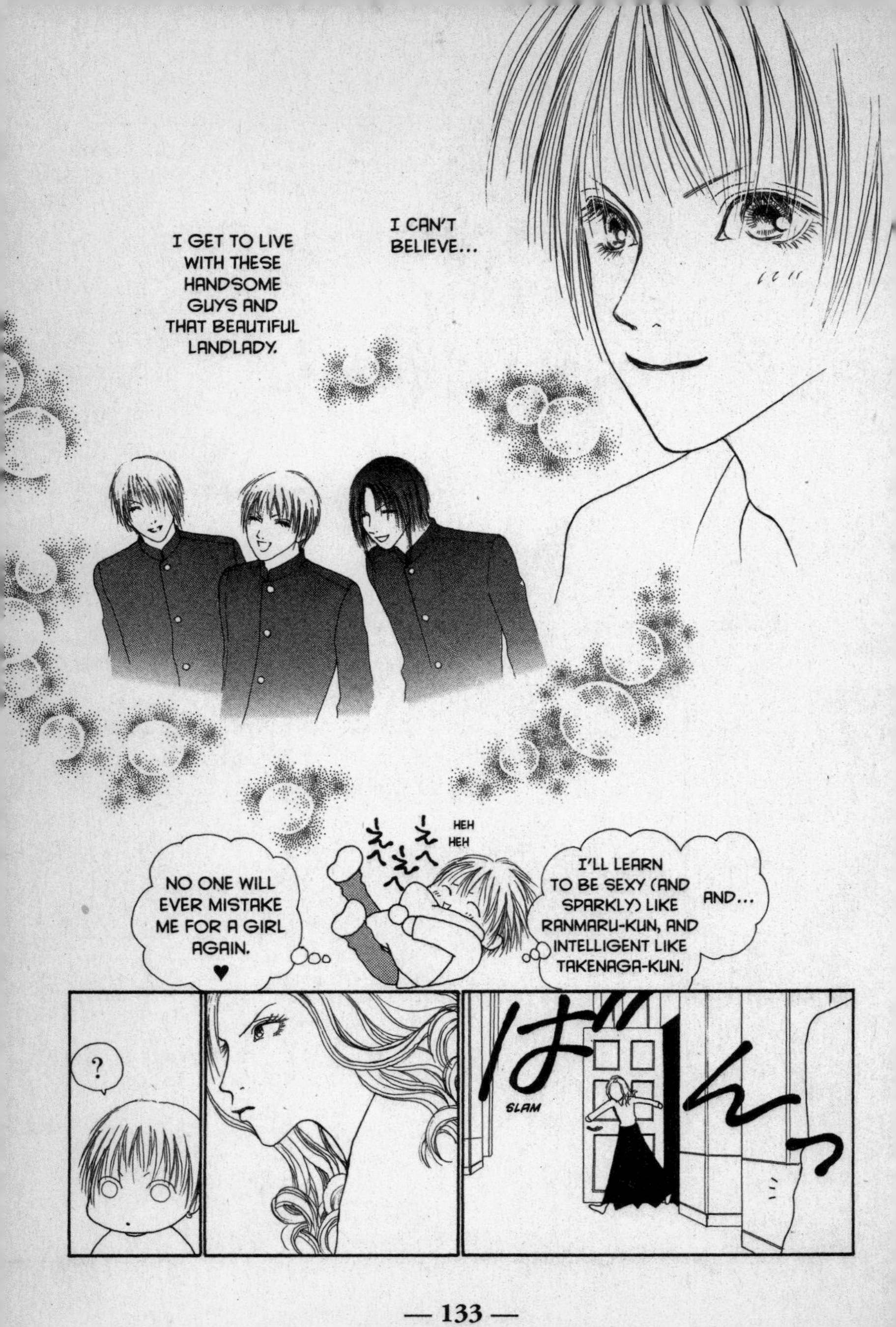
I CAN'T BELIEVE...
I GET TO LIVE WITH THESE HANDSOME GUYS AND THAT BEAUTIFUL LANDLADY.
I'LL LEARN TO BE SEXY (AND SPARKLY) LIKE RANMARU-KUN, AND INTELLIGENT LIKE TAKENAGA-KUN.
AND...
えへへ
えへへ
HEH HEH
NO ONE WILL EVER MISTAKE ME FOR A GIRL AGAIN. ♥
ばんっ
SLAM
?

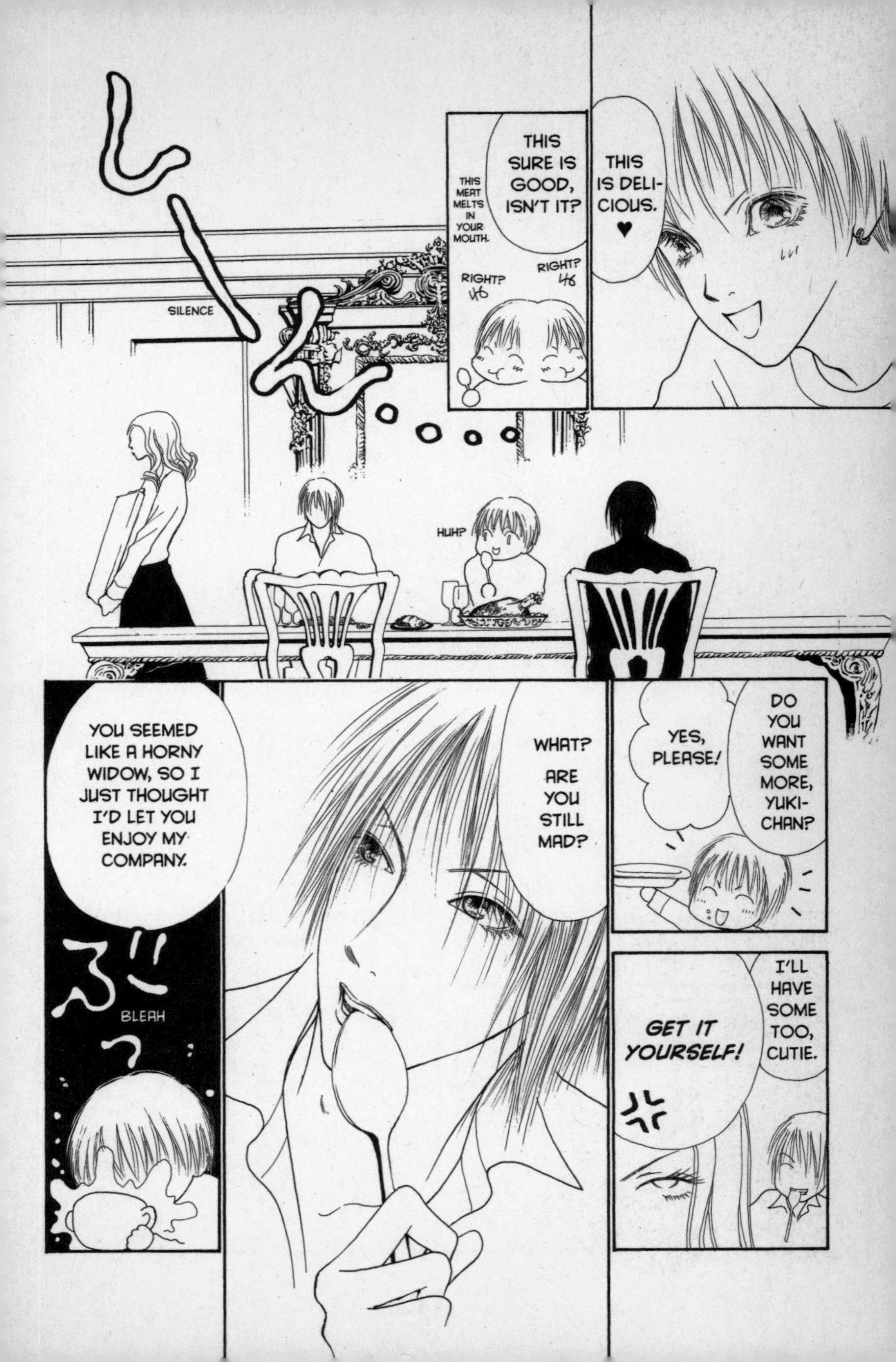
THIS IS DELICIOUS. ♥
THIS SURE IS GOOD, ISN'T IT?
THIS MEAT MELTS IN YOUR MOUTH.
RIGHT?
RIGHT?
SILENCE
HUH?
DO YOU WANT SOME MORE, YUKI-CHAN?
YES, PLEASE!
I'LL HAVE SOME TOO, CUTIE.
GET IT YOURSELF!
WHAT? ARE YOU STILL MAD?
YOU SEEMED LIKE A HORNY WIDOW, SO I JUST THOUGHT I'D LET YOU ENJOY MY COMPANY.
BLEAH

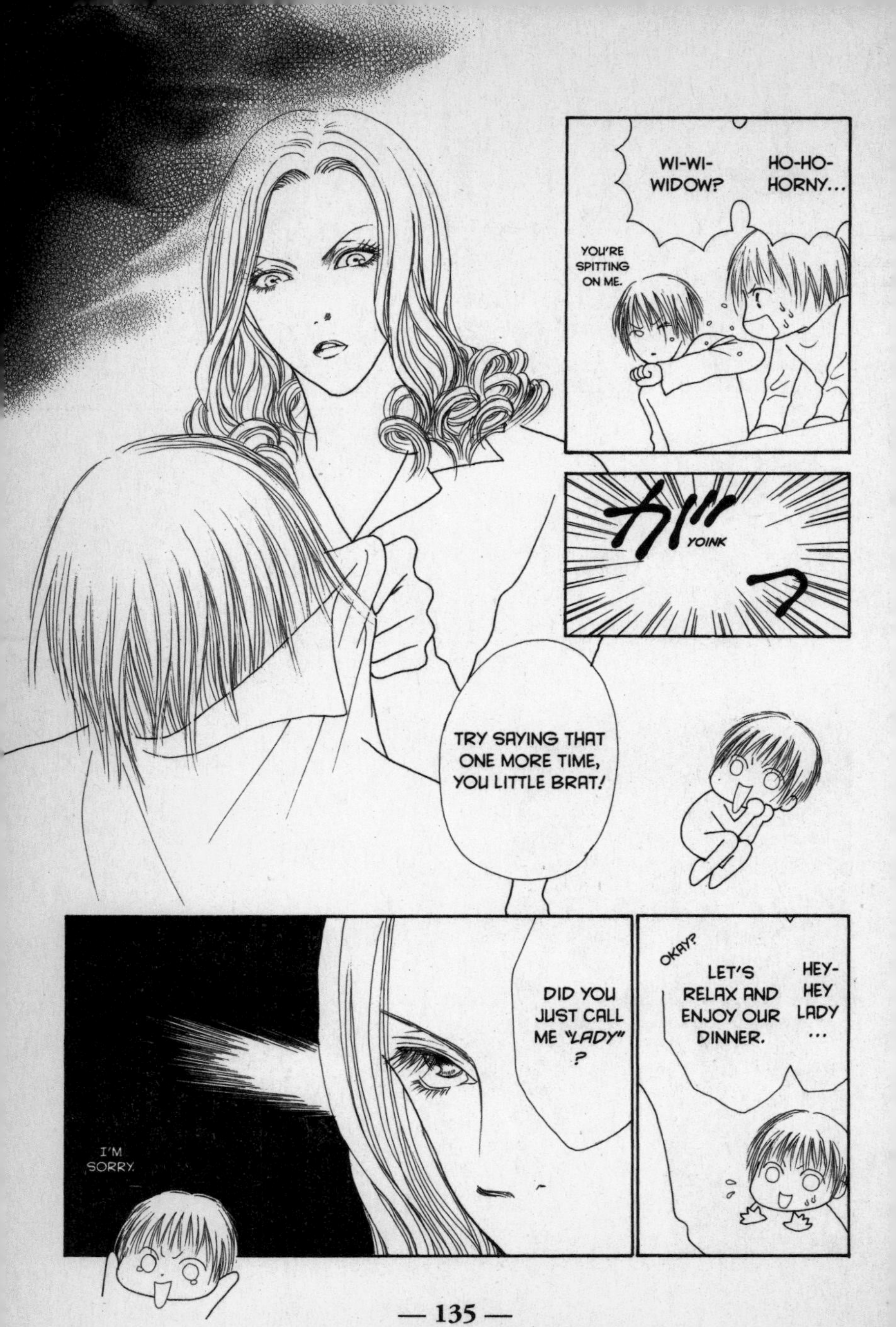
HO-HO-
HORNY...
WI-WI-
WIDOW?
YOU'RE SPITTING ON ME.
カッ
YOINK
TRY SAYING THAT ONE MORE TIME, YOU LITTLE BRAT!
HEY-HEY LADY ...
LET'S RELAX AND ENJOY OUR DINNER.
OKAY?
DID YOU JUST CALL ME "LADY" ?
I'M SORRY.

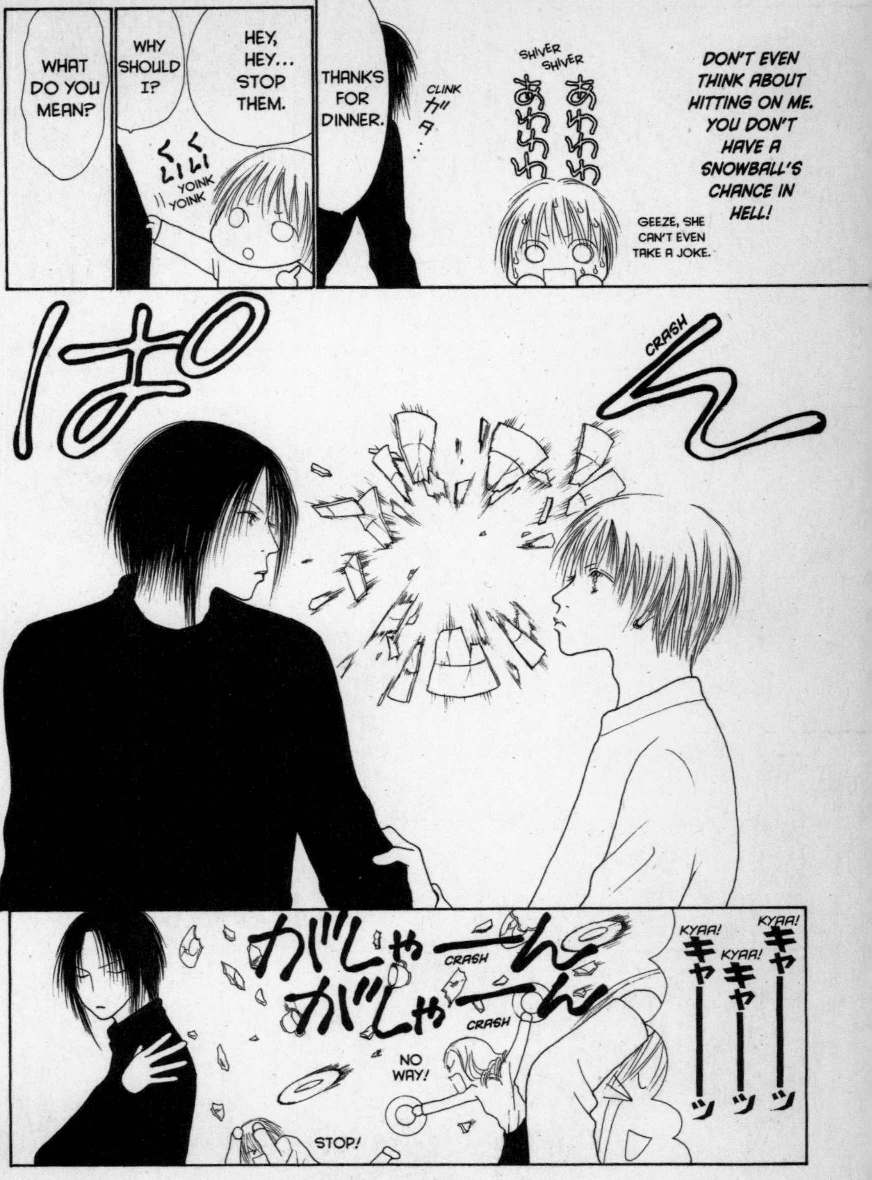
DON'T EVEN THINK ABOUT HITTING ON ME. YOU DON'T HAVE A SNOWBALL'S CHANCE IN HELL!
GEEZE, SHE CAN'T EVEN TAKE A JOKE.
SHIVER SHIVER
あわわわ あわわわ
THANKS FOR DINNER.
CLINK
ガタ…
HEY, HEY… STOP THEM.
WHY SHOULD I?
くいくい
YOINK YOINK
WHAT DO YOU MEAN?
CRASH
ぱん
KYAA! KYAA! KYAA!
キャーッ キャーッ キャーッ
がしゃーん がしゃーん
CRASH
CRASH
NO WAY!
STOP!

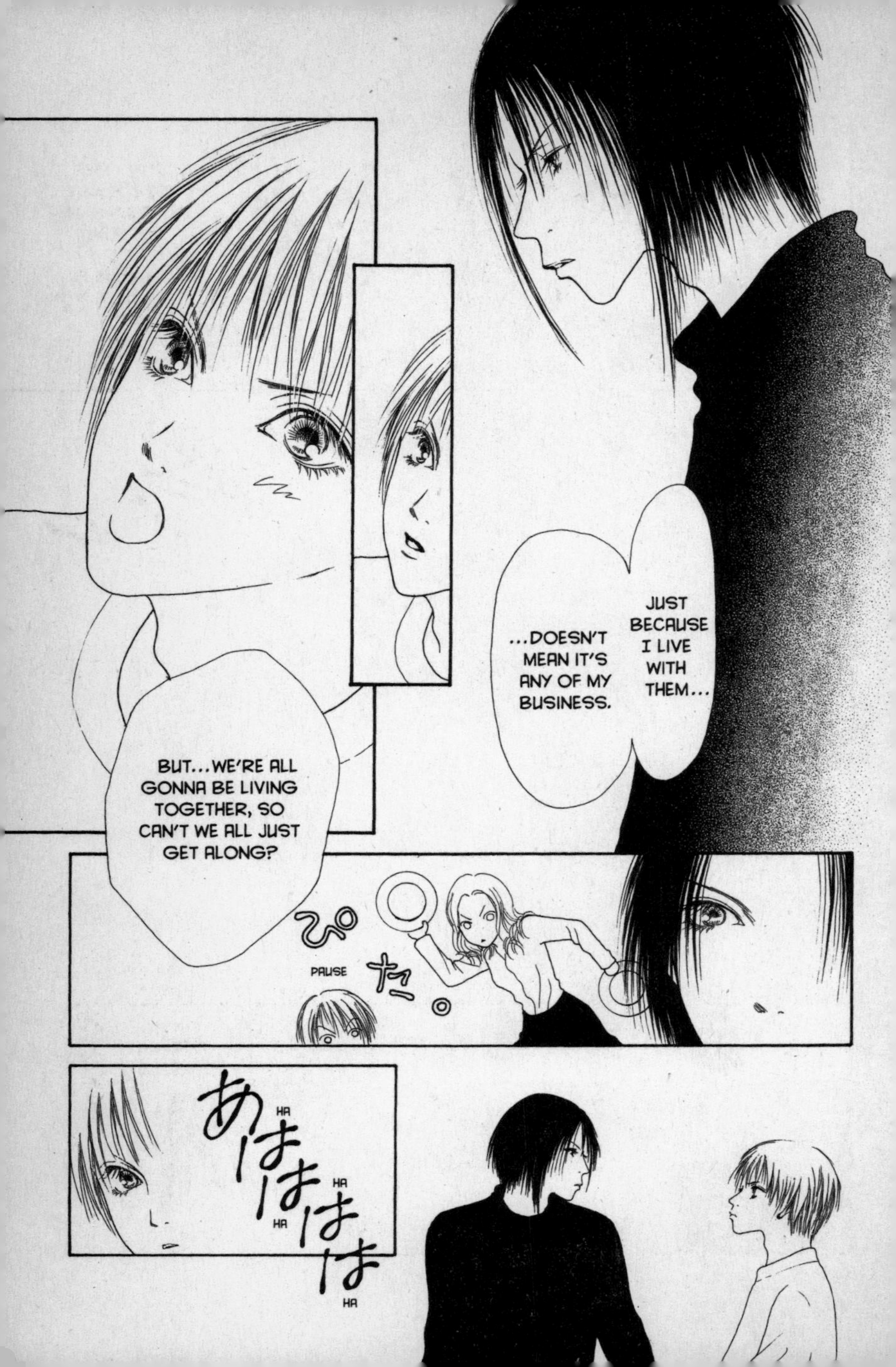
JUST BECAUSE I LIVE WITH THEM...
...DOESN'T MEAN IT'S ANY OF MY BUSINESS.
BUT...WE'RE ALL GONNA BE LIVING TOGETHER, SO CAN'T WE ALL JUST GET ALONG?
ぴたー。
PAUSE
あははは
HA HA HA HA

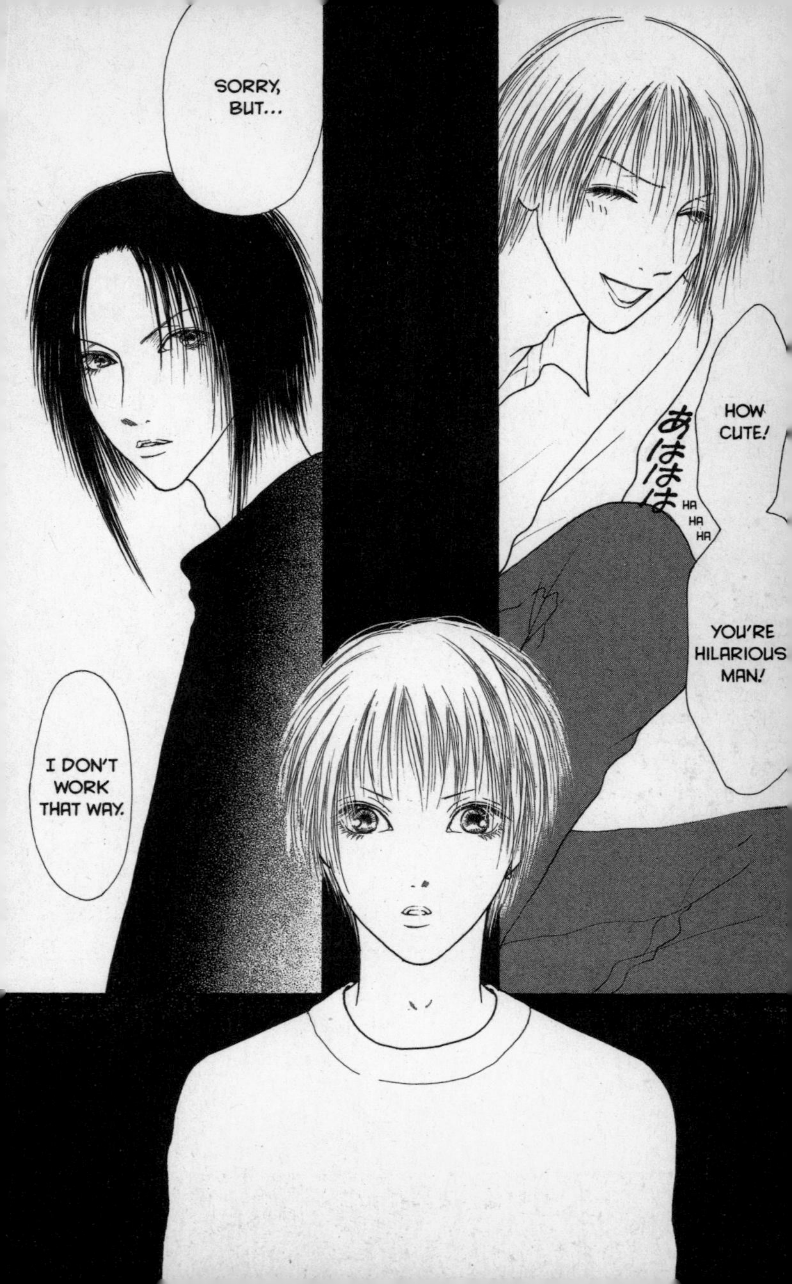

HOW CUTE!
あははは
HA HA HA
YOU'RE HILARIOUS MAN!
SORRY, BUT...
I DON'T WORK THAT WAY.

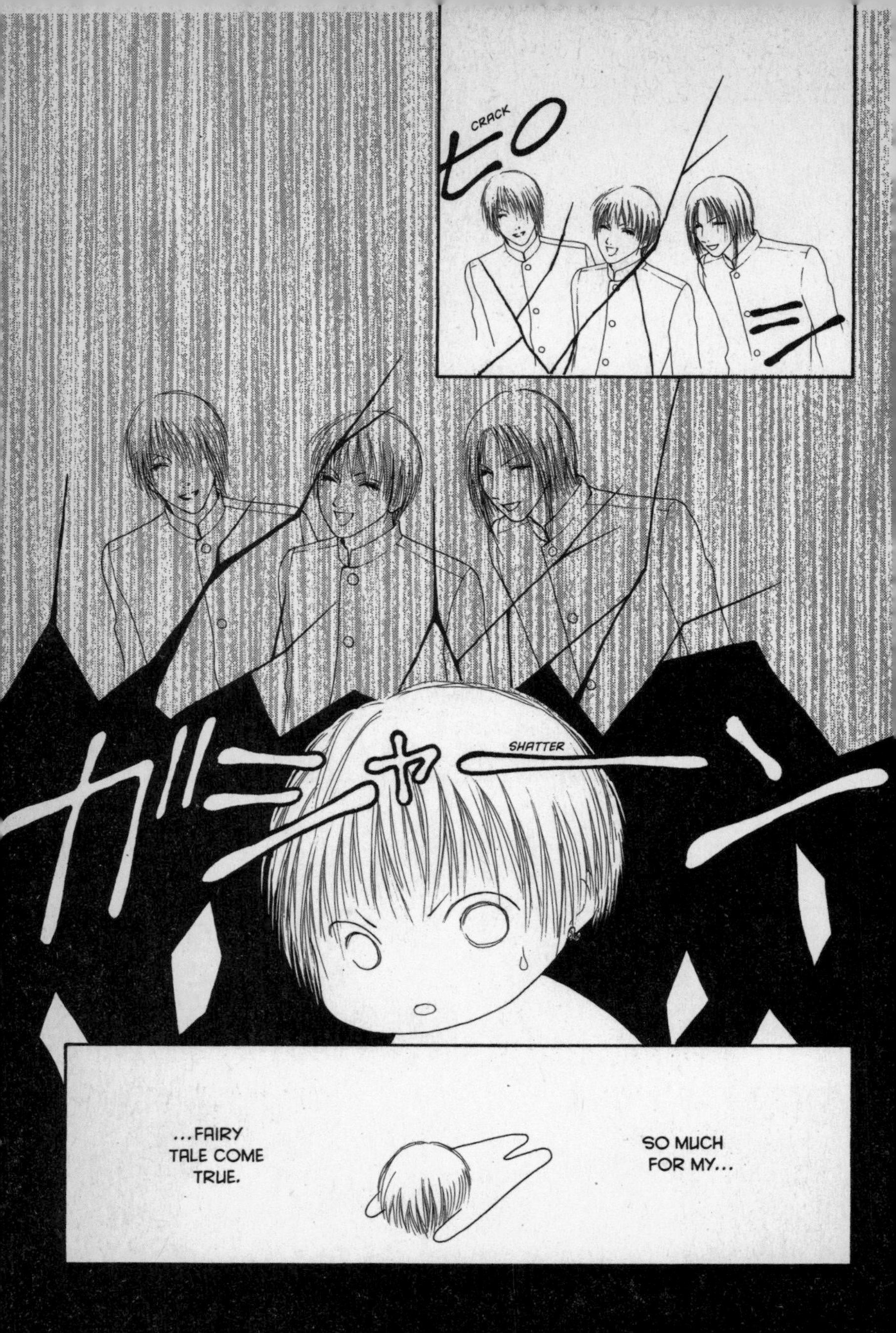
CRACK
SHATTER
SO MUCH FOR MY...
...FAIRY TALE COME TRUE.

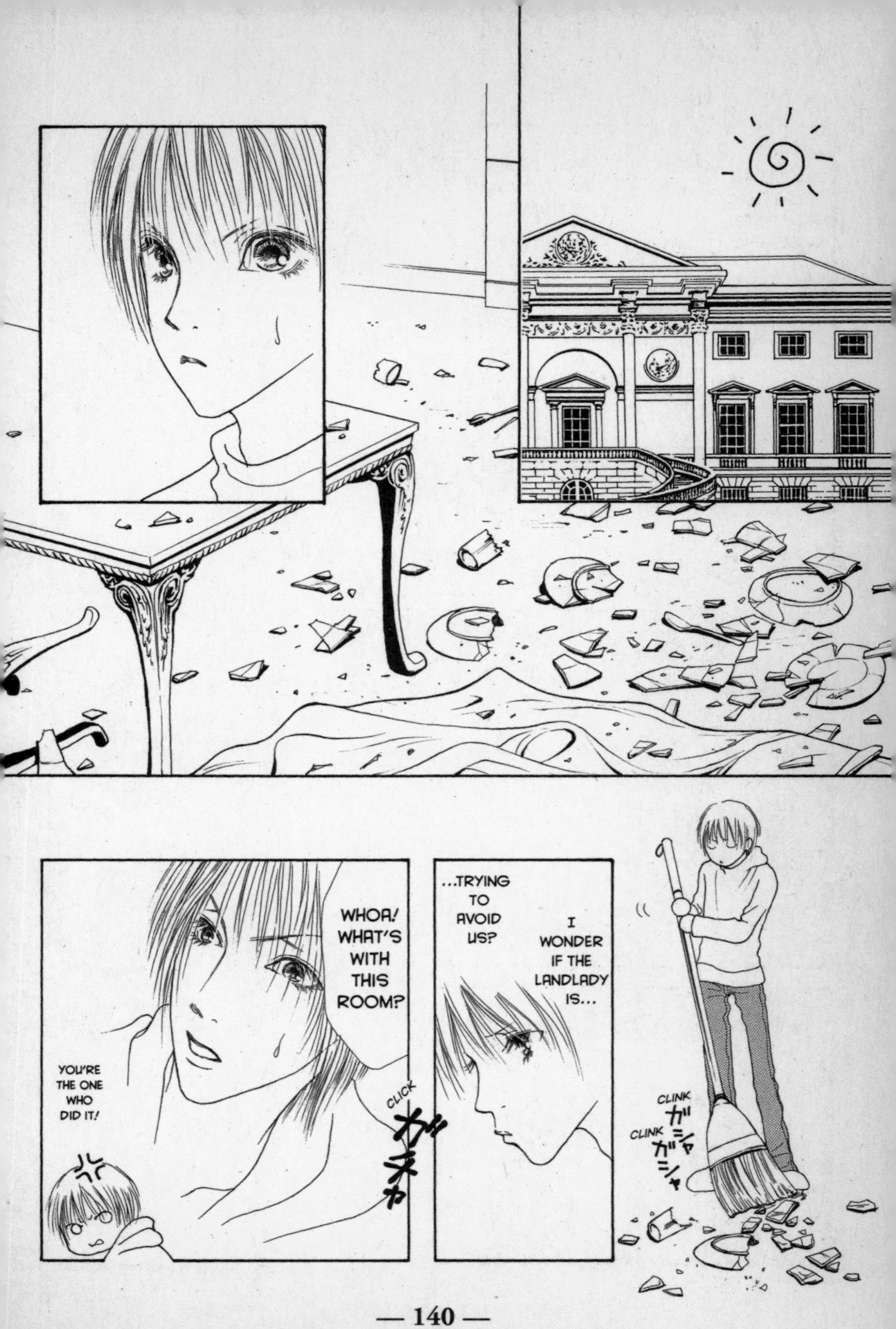
CLINK
ガシャ
CLINK
ガシャ
I WONDER IF THE LANDLADY IS...
...TRYING TO AVOID US?
WHOA! WHAT'S WITH THIS ROOM?
CLICK
ガチャ
YOU'RE THE ONE WHO DID IT!

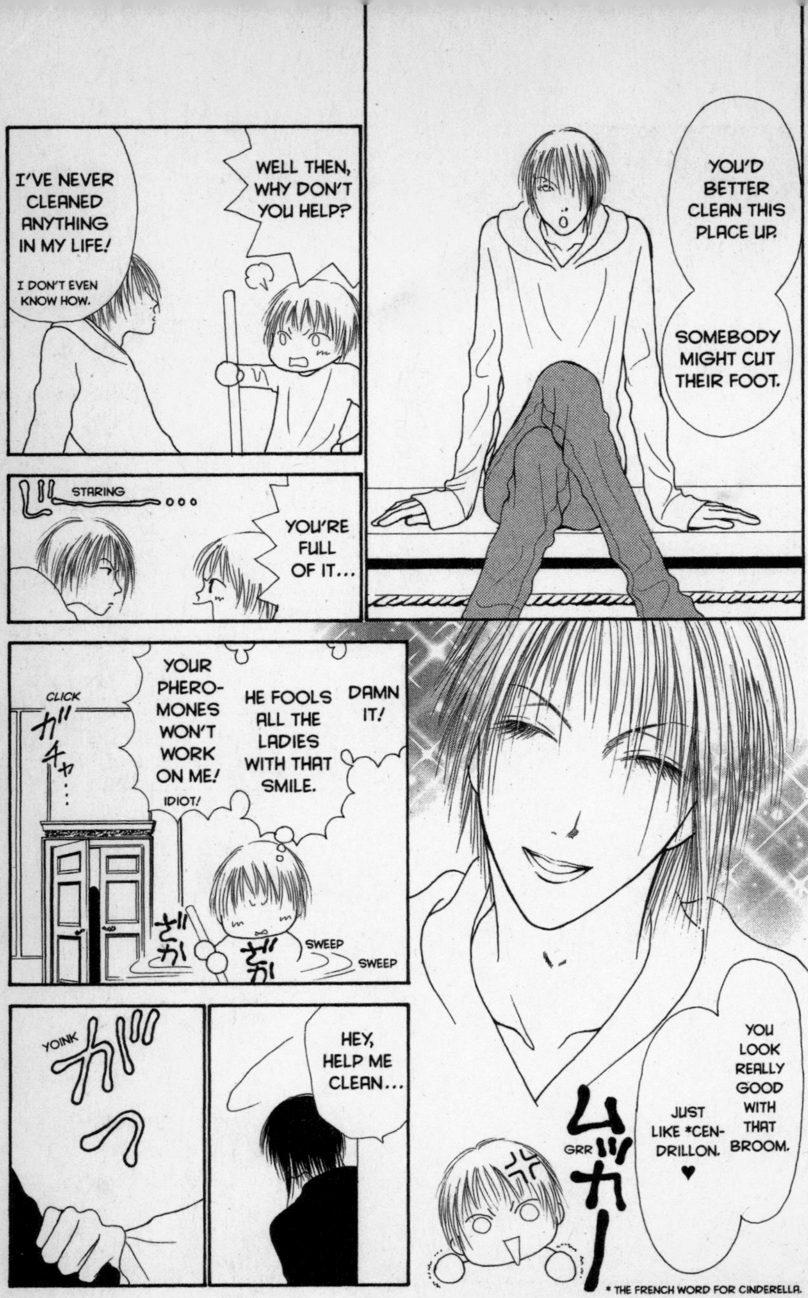
YOU'D BETTER CLEAN THIS PLACE UP.
SOMEBODY MIGHT CUT THEIR FOOT.
WELL THEN, WHY DON'T YOU HELP?
I'VE NEVER CLEANED ANYTHING IN MY LIFE!
I DON'T EVEN KNOW HOW.
STARING
YOU'RE FULL OF IT...
YOU LOOK REALLY GOOD WITH THAT BROOM.
JUST LIKE *CENDRILLON. ♥
GRR
DAMN IT!
HE FOOLS ALL THE LADIES WITH THAT SMILE.
YOUR PHEROMONES WON'T WORK ON ME!
IDIOT!
CLICK
SWEEP
SWEEP
HEY, HELP ME CLEAN...
YOINK

* THE FRENCH WORD FOR CINDERELLA.

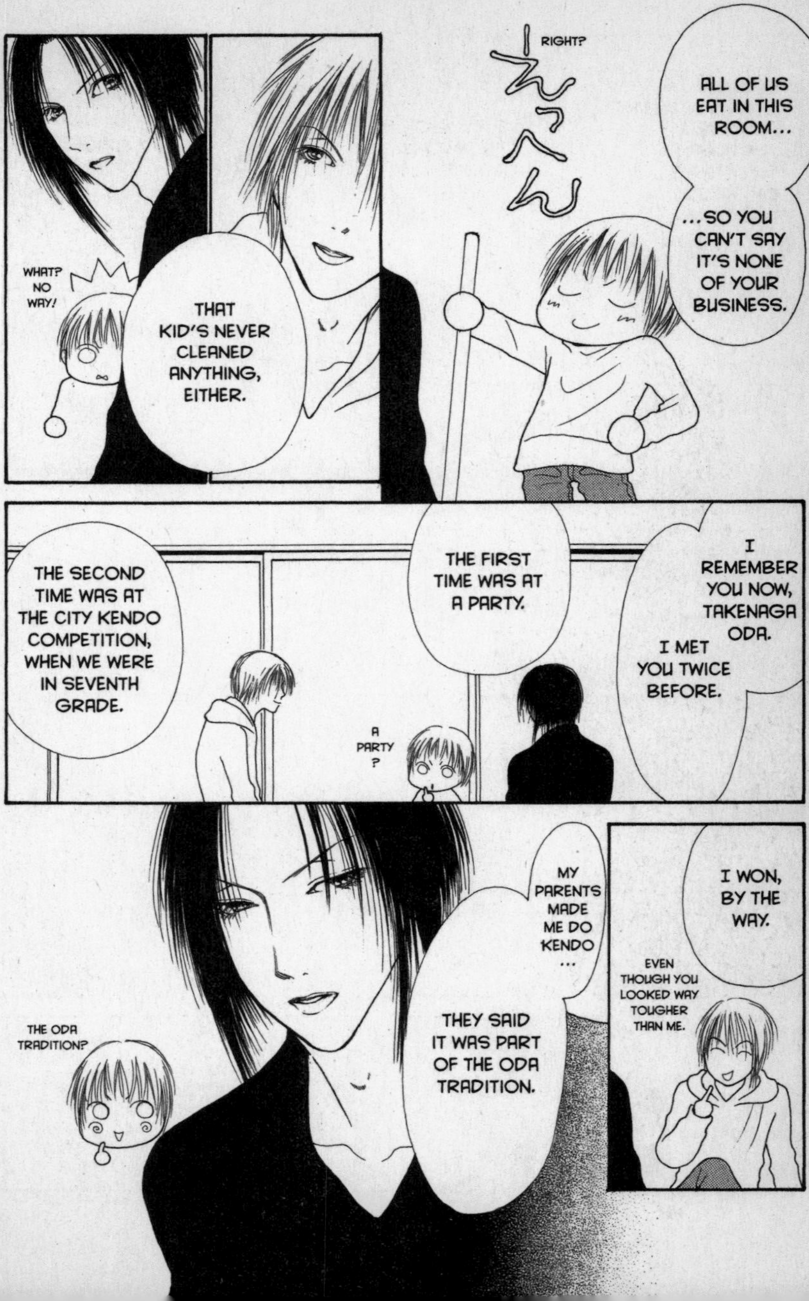
ALL OF US EAT IN THIS ROOM...
...SO YOU CAN'T SAY IT'S NONE OF YOUR BUSINESS.
RIGHT?
えっへん
THAT KID'S NEVER CLEANED ANYTHING, EITHER.
WHAT? NO WAY!
I REMEMBER YOU NOW, TAKENAGA ODA.
I MET YOU TWICE BEFORE.
THE FIRST TIME WAS AT A PARTY.
A PARTY?
THE SECOND TIME WAS AT THE CITY KENDO COMPETITION, WHEN WE WERE IN SEVENTH GRADE.
I WON, BY THE WAY.
EVEN THOUGH YOU LOOKED WAY TOUGHER THAN ME.
MY PARENTS MADE ME DO KENDO...
THEY SAID IT WAS PART OF THE ODA TRADITION.
THE ODA TRADITION?

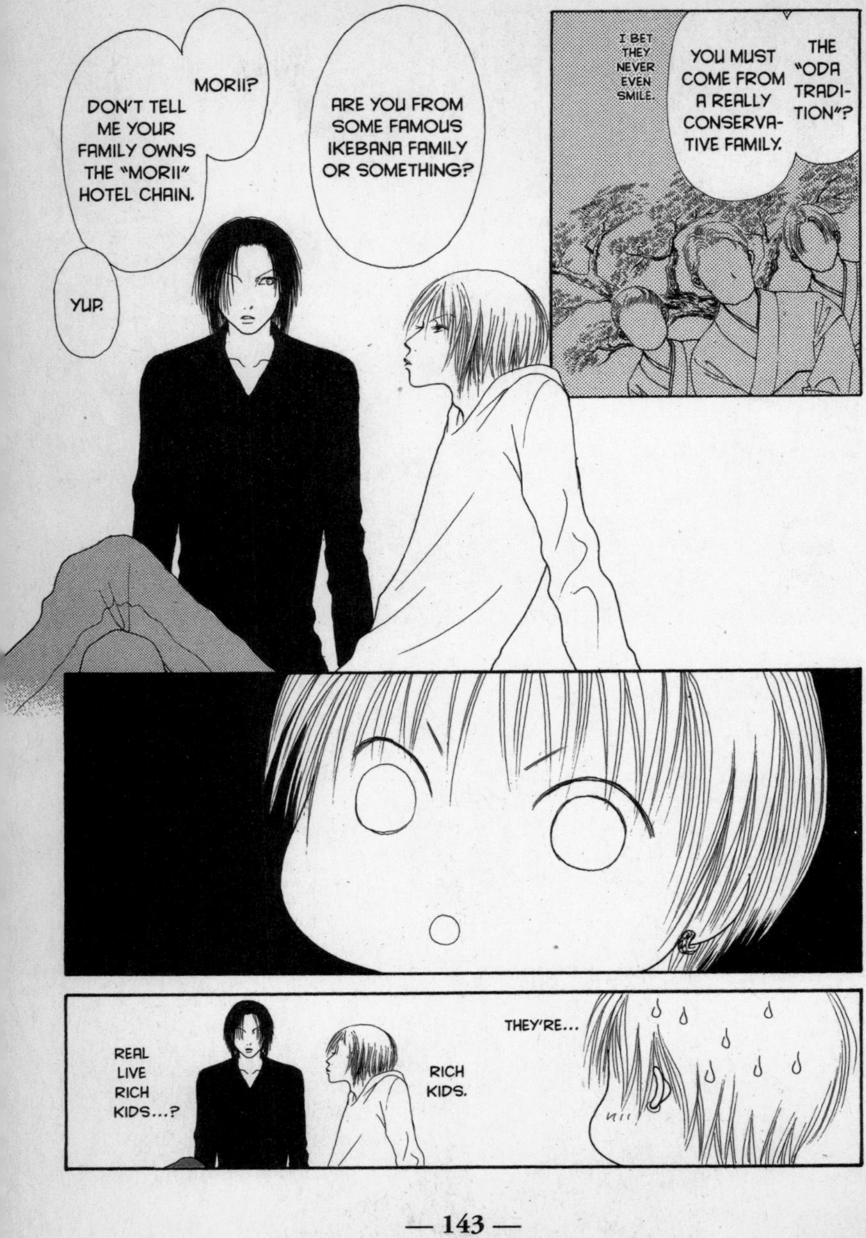
THE "ODA TRADITION"?
YOU MUST COME FROM A REALLY CONSERVATIVE FAMILY.
I BET THEY NEVER EVEN SMILE.
ARE YOU FROM SOME FAMOUS IKEBANA FAMILY OR SOMETHING?
MORII? DON'T TELL ME YOUR FAMILY OWNS THE "MORII" HOTEL CHAIN.
YUP.
THEY'RE...
RICH KIDS.
REAL LIVE RICH KIDS...?

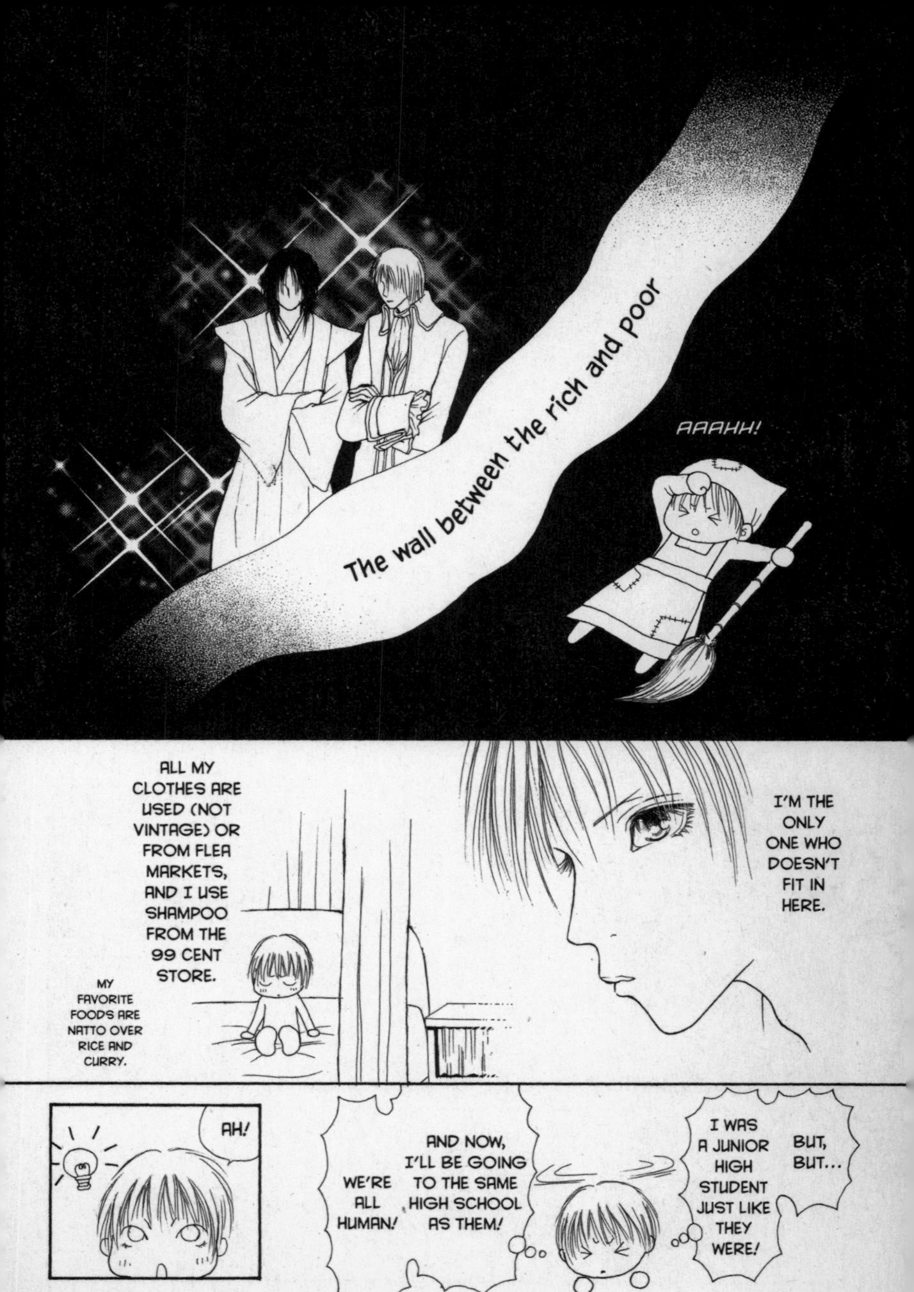
The wall between the rich and poor
AAAHH!
I'M THE ONLY ONE WHO DOESN'T FIT IN HERE.
ALL MY CLOTHES ARE USED (NOT VINTAGE) OR FROM FLEA MARKETS, AND I USE SHAMPOO FROM THE 99 CENT STORE.
MY FAVORITE FOODS ARE NATTO OVER RICE AND CURRY.
BUT, BUT...
I WAS A JUNIOR HIGH STUDENT JUST LIKE THEY WERE!
AND NOW, I'LL BE GOING TO THE SAME HIGH SCHOOL AS THEM!
WE'RE ALL HUMAN!
AH!

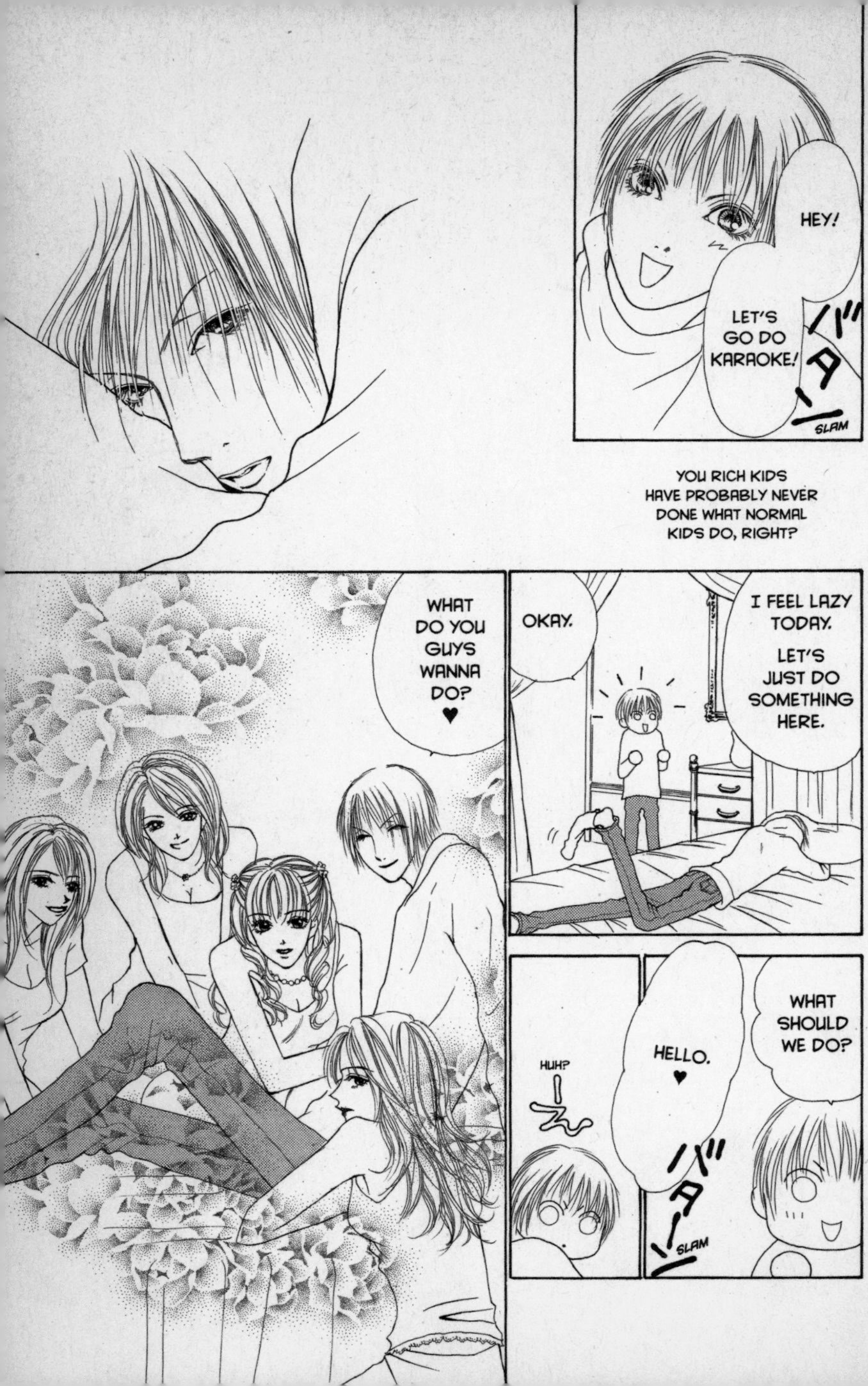
HEY!
LET'S GO DO KARAOKE!
バタン
SLAM
YOU RICH KIDS HAVE PROBABLY NEVER DONE WHAT NORMAL KIDS DO, RIGHT?
I FEEL LAZY TODAY.
LET'S JUST DO SOMETHING HERE.
OKAY.
WHAT SHOULD WE DO?
HELLO. ♥
バタン
SLAM
HUH?
WHAT DO YOU GUYS WANNA DO? ♥

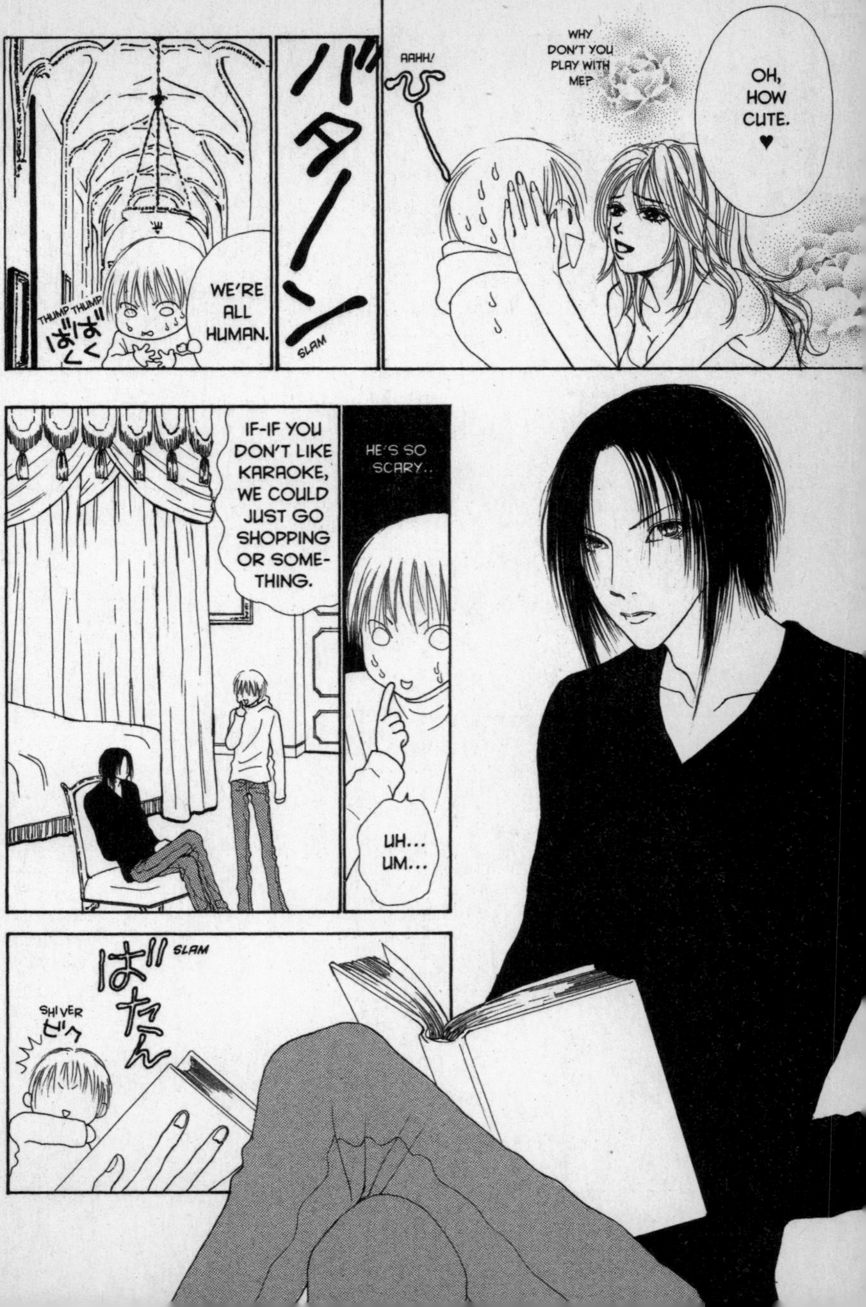
OH, HOW CUTE. ♥
WHY DON'T YOU PLAY WITH ME?
AAHH!
バターン
SLAM
WE'RE ALL HUMAN.
ばくばく
THUMP THUMP
HE'S SO SCARY..
UH... UM...
IF-IF YOU DON'T LIKE KARAOKE, WE COULD JUST GO SHOPPING OR SOME-THING.
ばたん
SLAM
ビク
SHIVER

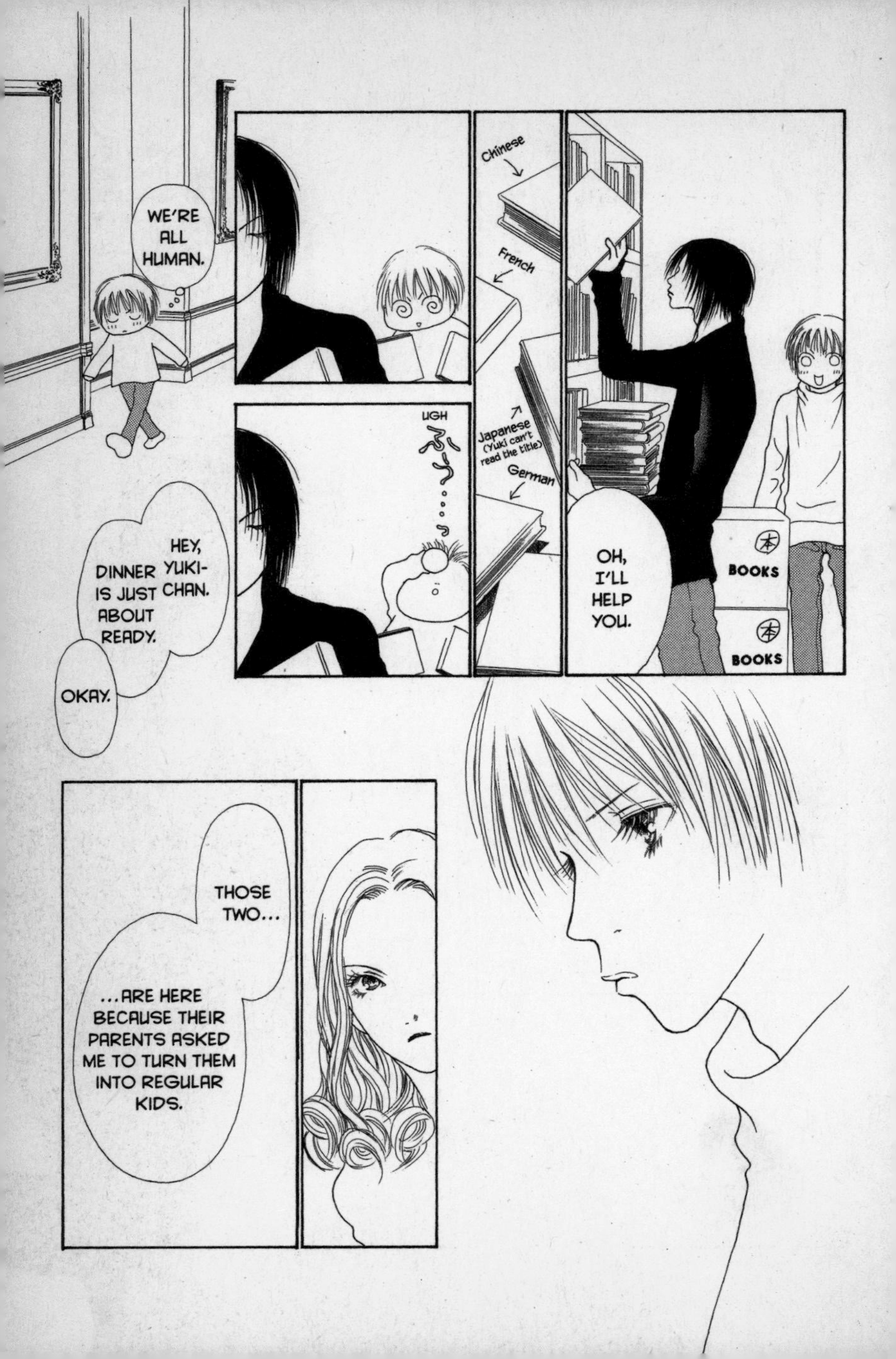
OH, I'LL HELP YOU.
Chinese
French
Japanese (Yuki can't read the title)
German
BOOKS
BOOKS
UGH
ふ～っ…
WE'RE ALL HUMAN.
HEY, YUKI-CHAN.
DINNER IS JUST ABOUT READY.
OKAY.
THOSE TWO...
...ARE HERE BECAUSE THEIR PARENTS ASKED ME TO TURN THEM INTO REGULAR KIDS.

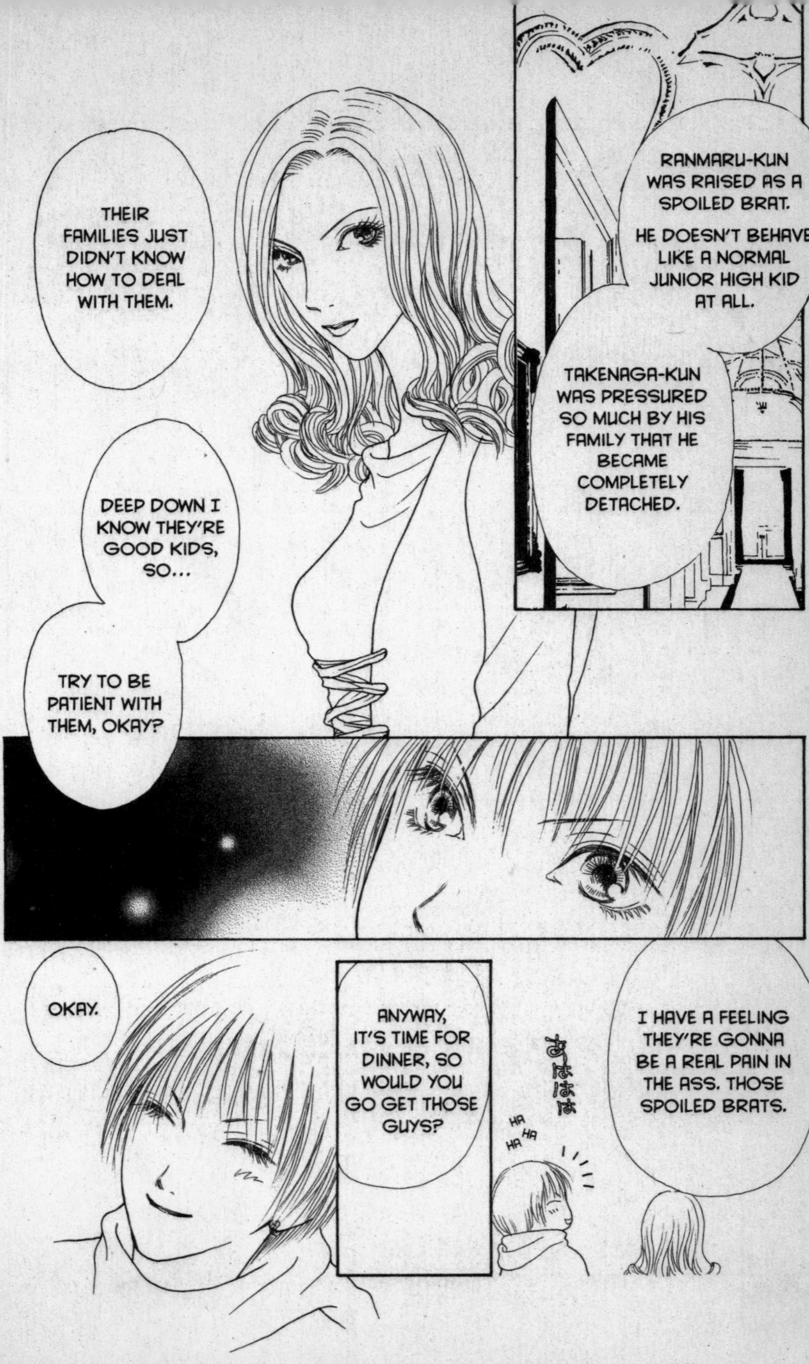

RANMARU-KUN WAS RAISED AS A SPOILED BRAT.
HE DOESN'T BEHAVE LIKE A NORMAL JUNIOR HIGH KID AT ALL.
TAKENAGA-KUN WAS PRESSURED SO MUCH BY HIS FAMILY THAT HE BECAME COMPLETELY DETACHED.
THEIR FAMILIES JUST DIDN'T KNOW HOW TO DEAL WITH THEM.
DEEP DOWN I KNOW THEY'RE GOOD KIDS, SO...
TRY TO BE PATIENT WITH THEM, OKAY?
I HAVE A FEELING THEY'RE GONNA BE A REAL PAIN IN THE ASS. THOSE SPOILED BRATS.
HA HA HA
ANYWAY, IT'S TIME FOR DINNER, SO WOULD YOU GO GET THOSE GUYS?
OKAY.

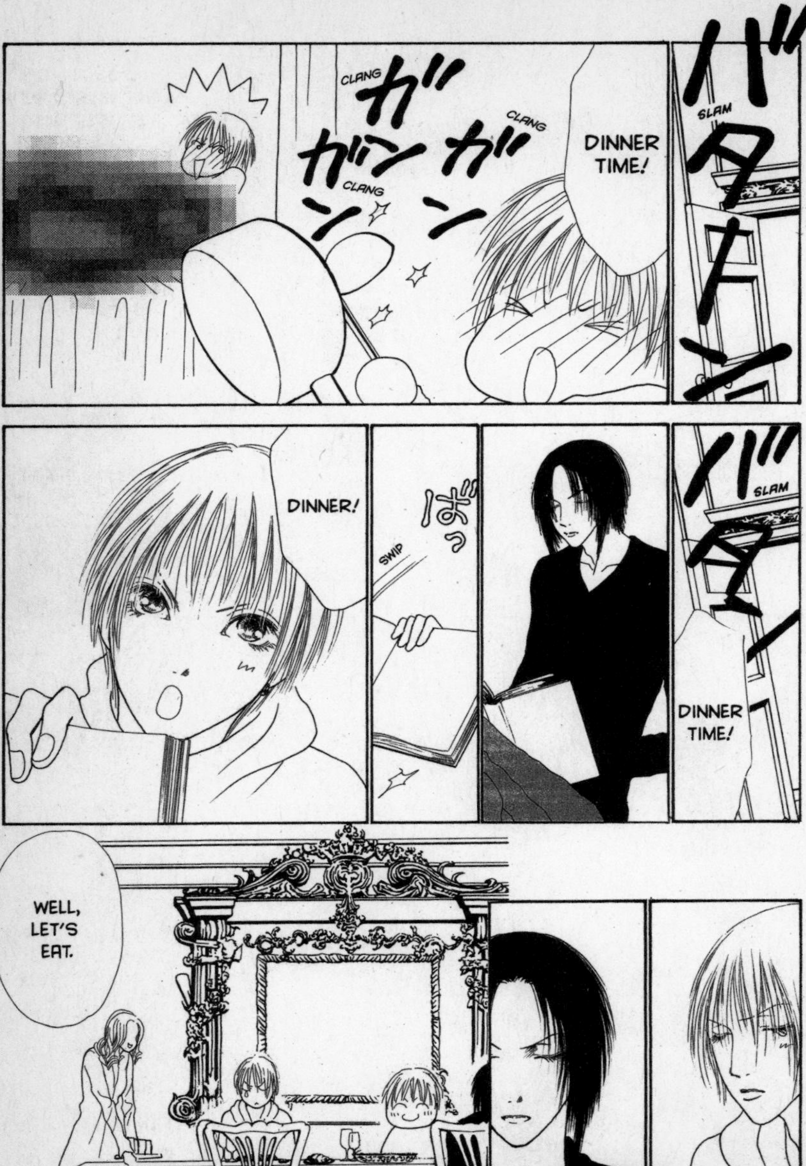
バタン
SLAM
DINNER TIME!
ガンガンガン
CLANG
CLANG
CLANG
バタン
SLAM
DINNER TIME!
ぱっ
SWIP
DINNER!
WELL, LET'S EAT.

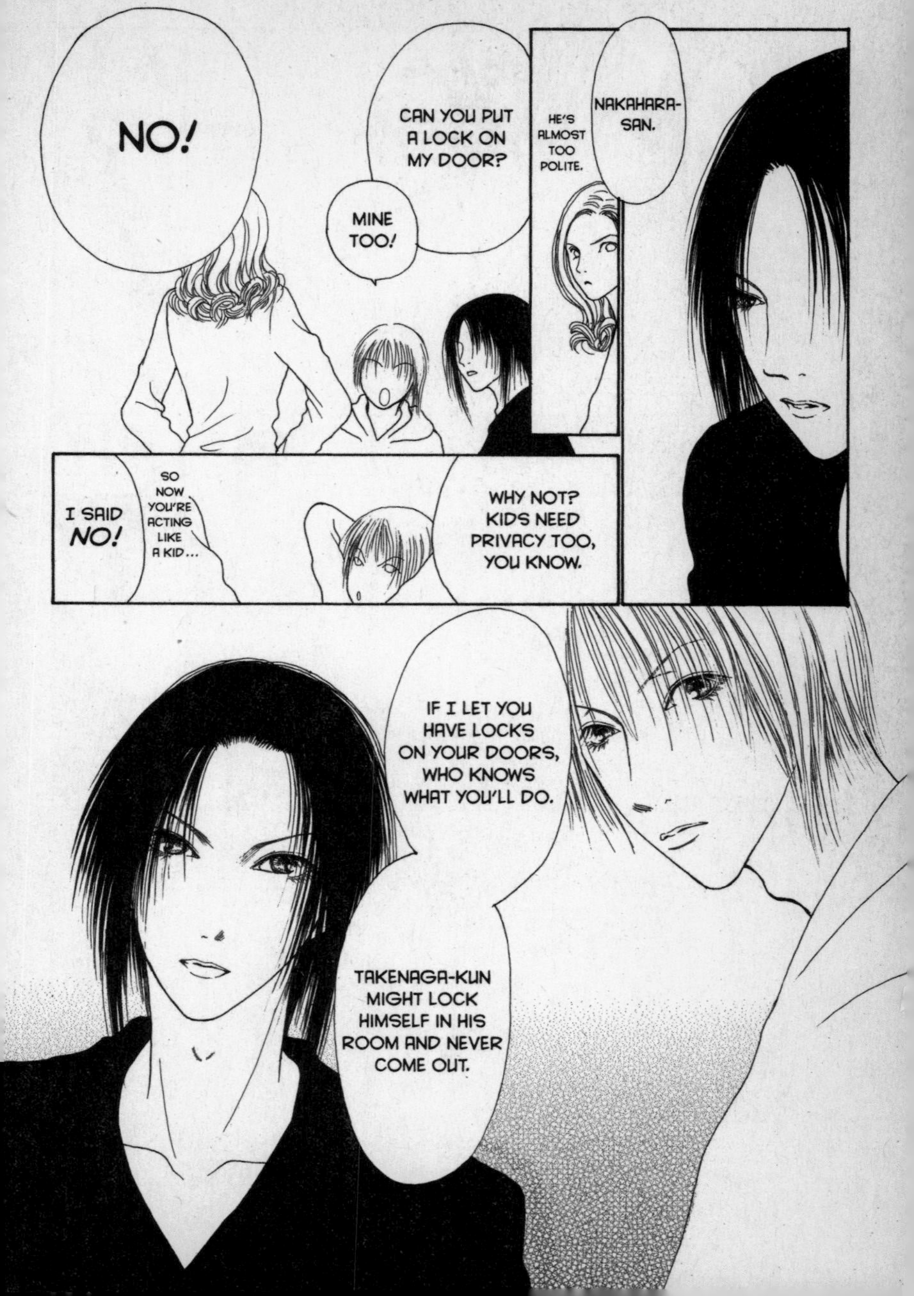
NAKAHARA-SAN.
HE'S ALMOST TOO POLITE.
CAN YOU PUT A LOCK ON MY DOOR?
MINE TOO!
NO!
WHY NOT? KIDS NEED PRIVACY TOO, YOU KNOW.
SO NOW YOU'RE ACTING LIKE A KID...
I SAID NO!
IF I LET YOU HAVE LOCKS ON YOUR DOORS, WHO KNOWS WHAT YOU'LL DO.
TAKENAGA-KUN MIGHT LOCK HIMSELF IN HIS ROOM AND NEVER COME OUT.

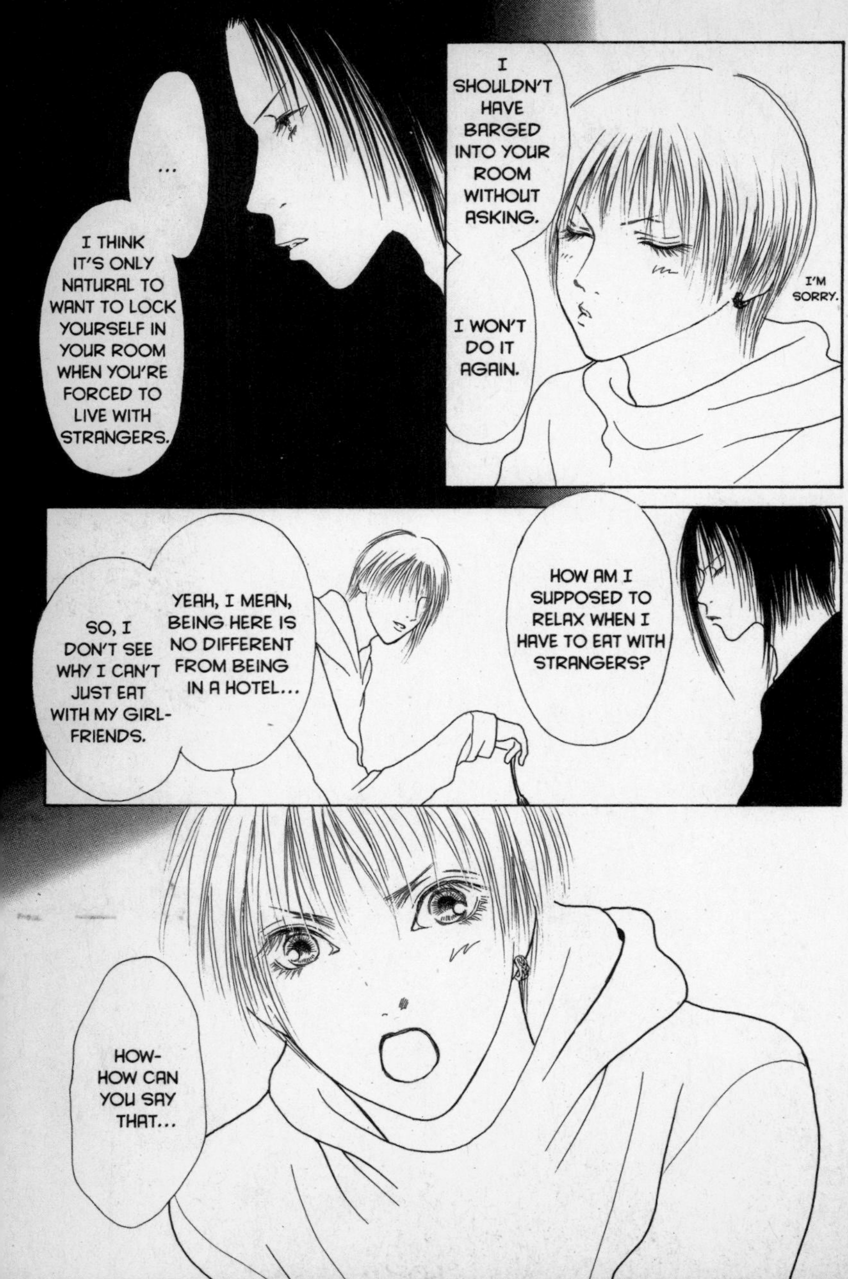
I SHOULDN'T HAVE BARGED INTO YOUR ROOM WITHOUT ASKING.
I'M SORRY.
I WON'T DO IT AGAIN.
...
I THINK IT'S ONLY NATURAL TO WANT TO LOCK YOURSELF IN YOUR ROOM WHEN YOU'RE FORCED TO LIVE WITH STRANGERS.
HOW AM I SUPPOSED TO RELAX WHEN I HAVE TO EAT WITH STRANGERS?
YEAH, I MEAN, BEING HERE IS NO DIFFERENT FROM BEING IN A HOTEL...
SO, I DON'T SEE WHY I CAN'T JUST EAT WITH MY GIRL-FRIENDS.
HOW-HOW CAN YOU SAY THAT...

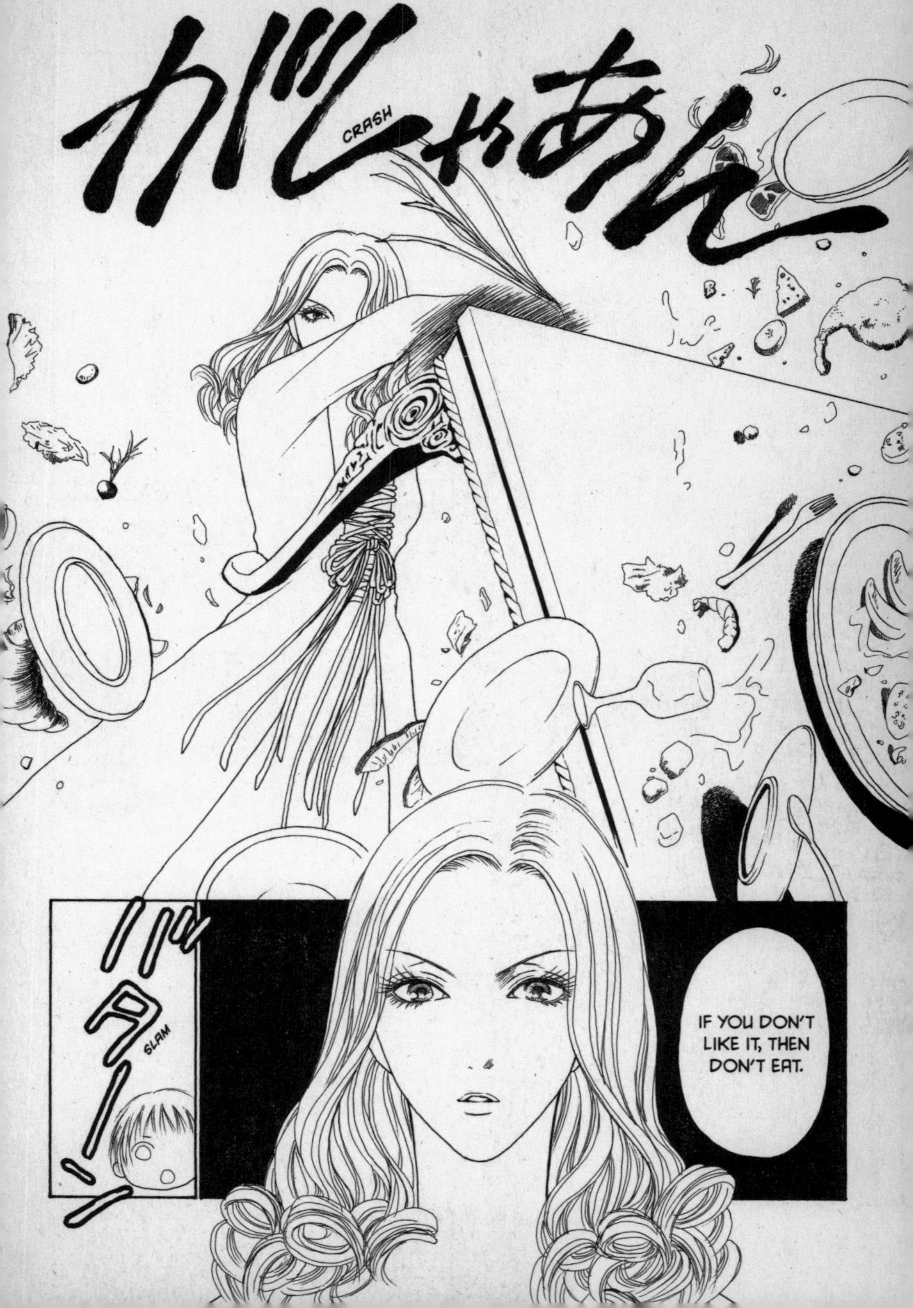
CRASH
IF YOU DON'T LIKE IT, THEN DON'T EAT.
SLAM

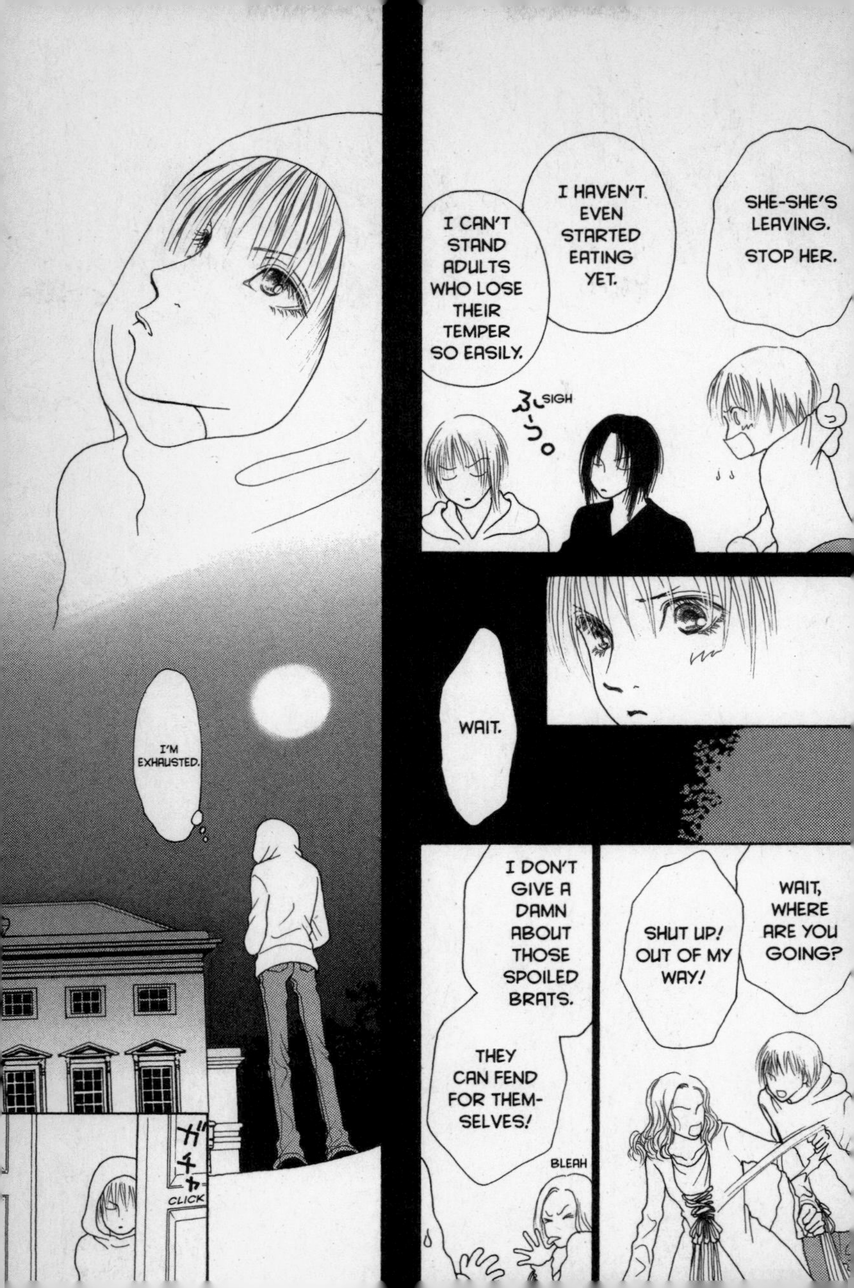
SHE-SHE'S LEAVING.
STOP HER.
I HAVEN'T EVEN STARTED EATING YET.
I CAN'T STAND ADULTS WHO LOSE THEIR TEMPER SO EASILY.
ふーっ SIGH
WAIT.
WAIT, WHERE ARE YOU GOING?
SHUT UP! OUT OF MY WAY!
I DON'T GIVE A DAMN ABOUT THOSE SPOILED BRATS.
THEY CAN FEND FOR THEM-SELVES!
BLEAH
ガチャ CLICK
I'M EXHAUSTED.

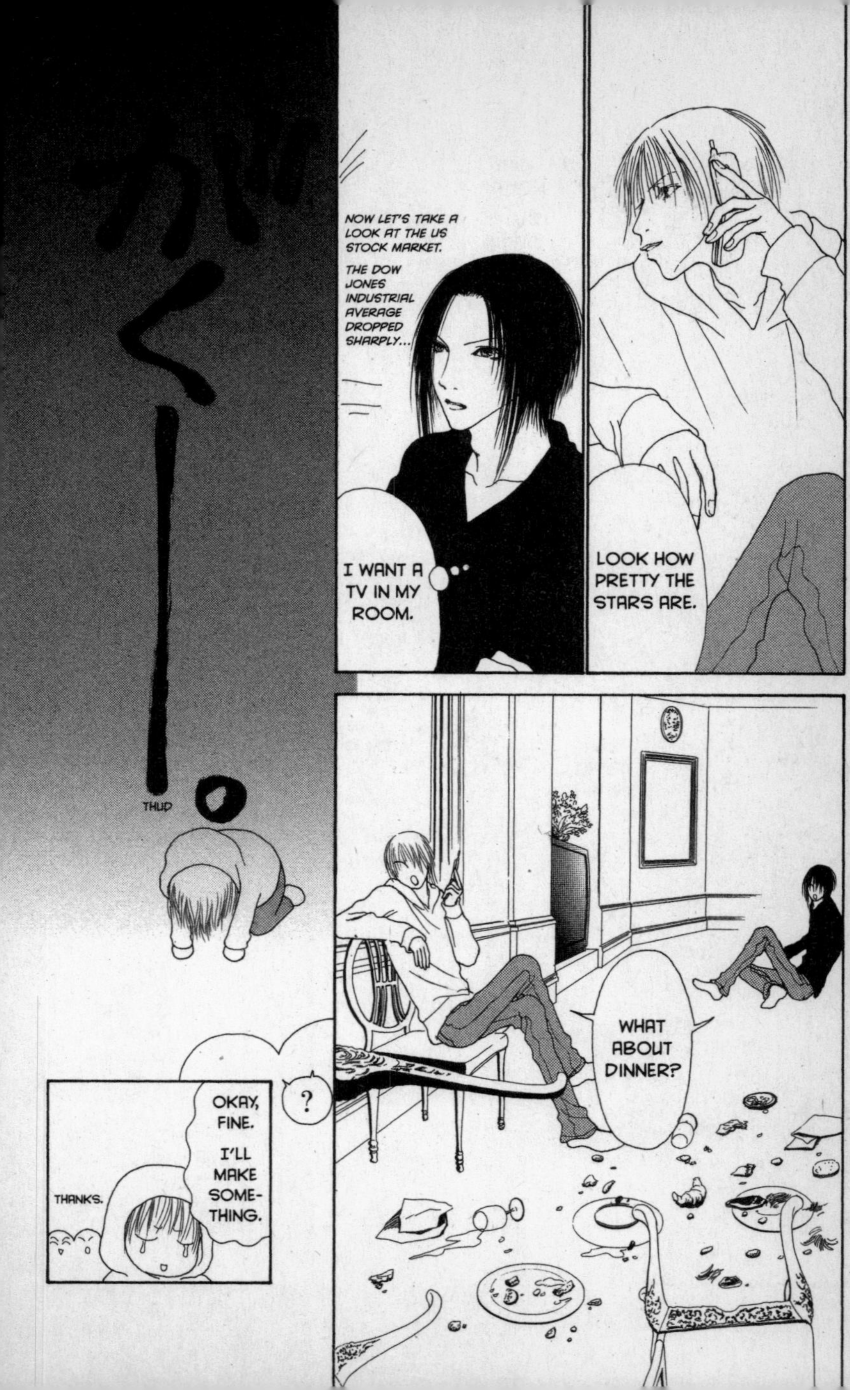
LOOK HOW PRETTY THE STARS ARE.
NOW LET'S TAKE A LOOK AT THE US STOCK MARKET.
THE DOW JONES INDUSTRIAL AVERAGE DROPPED SHARPLY...
I WANT A TV IN MY ROOM.
WHAT ABOUT DINNER?
?
THUD
OKAY, FINE.
I'LL MAKE SOMETHING.
THANKS.

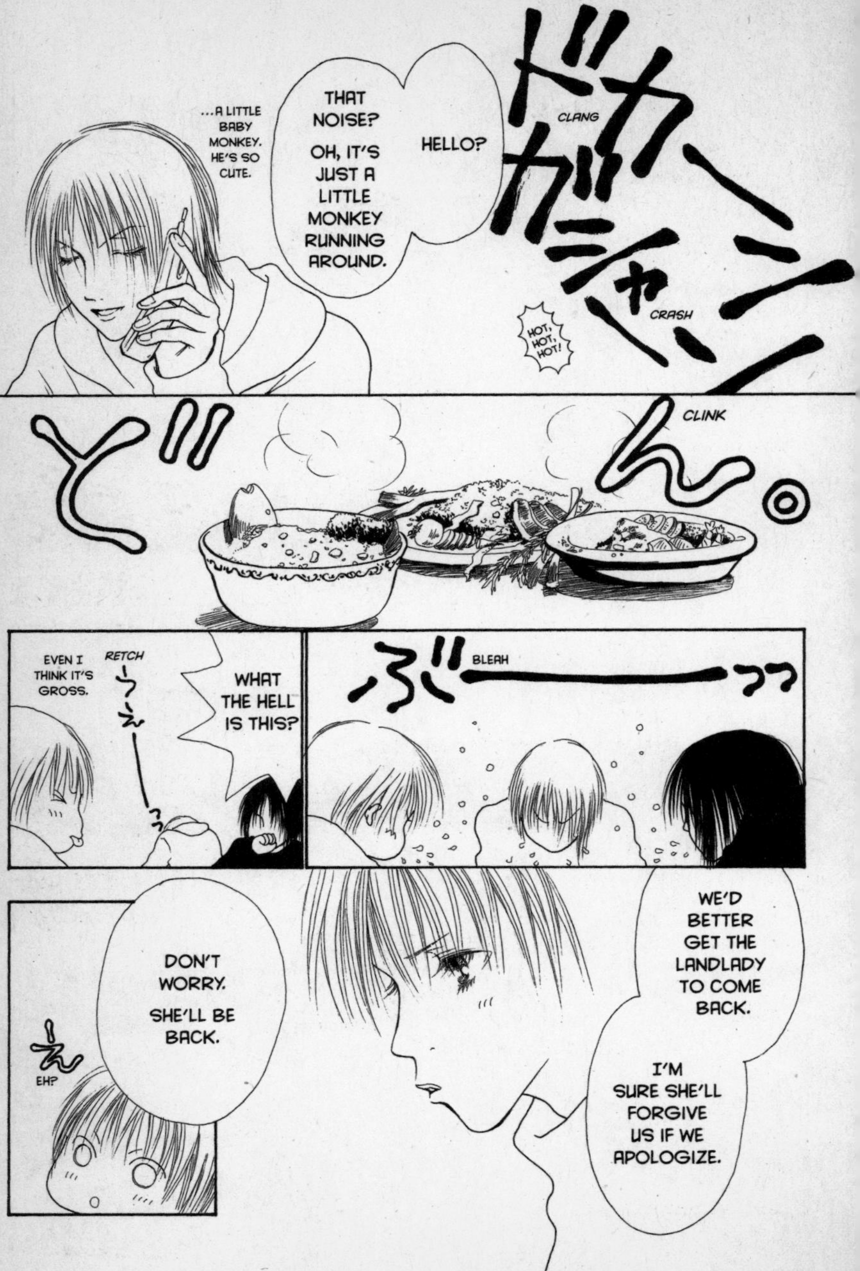

ドカーン
CLANG
ガシャーン
CRASH
HOT, HOT, HOT!
HELLO?
THAT NOISE?
OH, IT'S JUST A LITTLE MONKEY RUNNING AROUND.
...A LITTLE BABY MONKEY. HE'S SO CUTE.
どん。
CLINK
ぶーっっ
BLEAH
WHAT THE HELL IS THIS?
うぇーっ
RETCH
EVEN I THINK IT'S GROSS.
WE'D BETTER GET THE LANDLADY TO COME BACK.
I'M SURE SHE'LL FORGIVE US IF WE APOLOGIZE.
DON'T WORRY.
SHE'LL BE BACK.
え
EH?

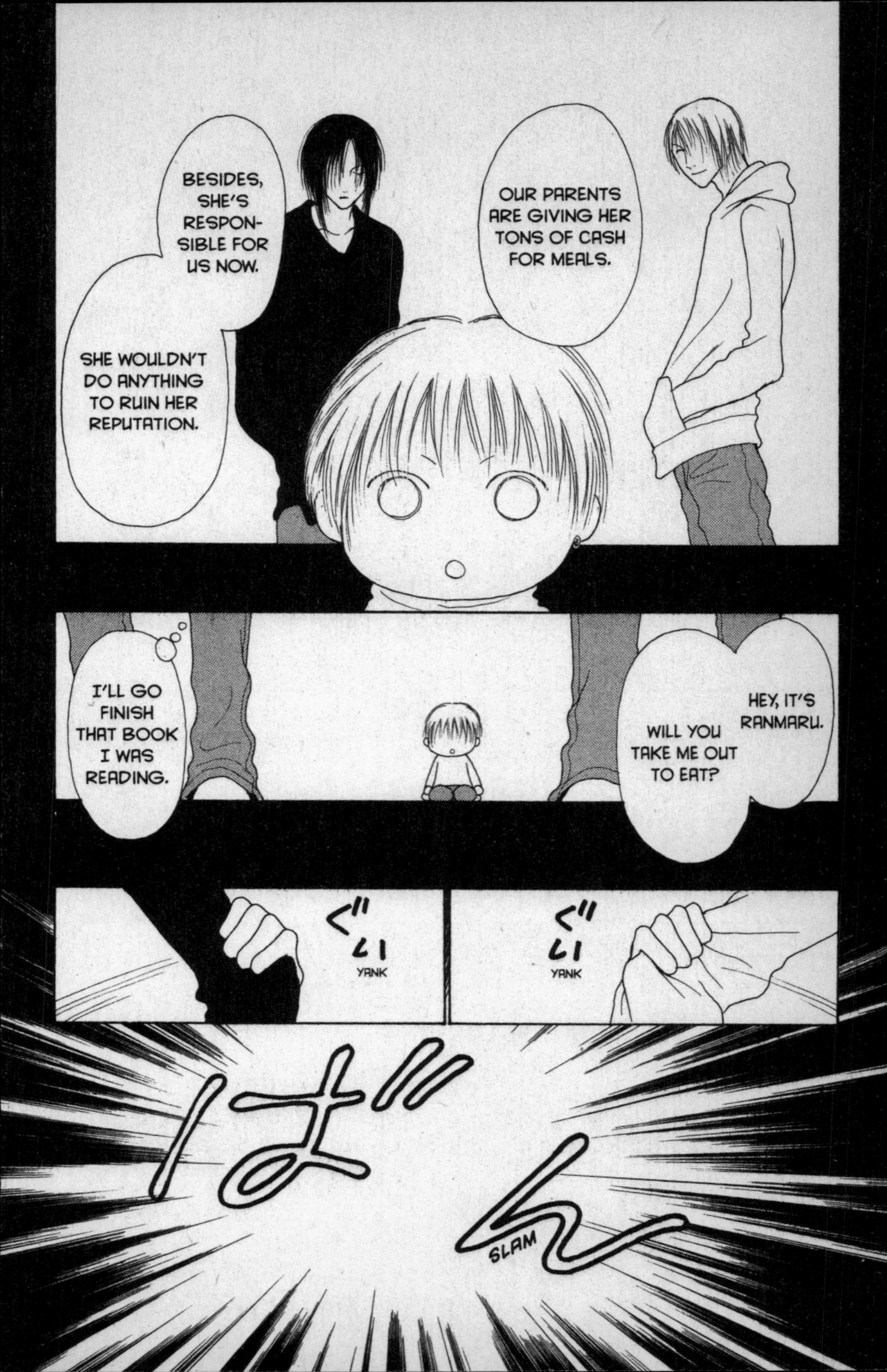
OUR PARENTS ARE GIVING HER TONS OF CASH FOR MEALS.
BESIDES, SHE'S RESPON-SIBLE FOR US NOW.
SHE WOULDN'T DO ANYTHING TO RUIN HER REPUTATION.
HEY, IT'S RANMARU.
WILL YOU TAKE ME OUT TO EAT?
I'LL GO FINISH THAT BOOK I WAS READING.
ぐい
YANK
ぐい
YANK
ばん
SLAM

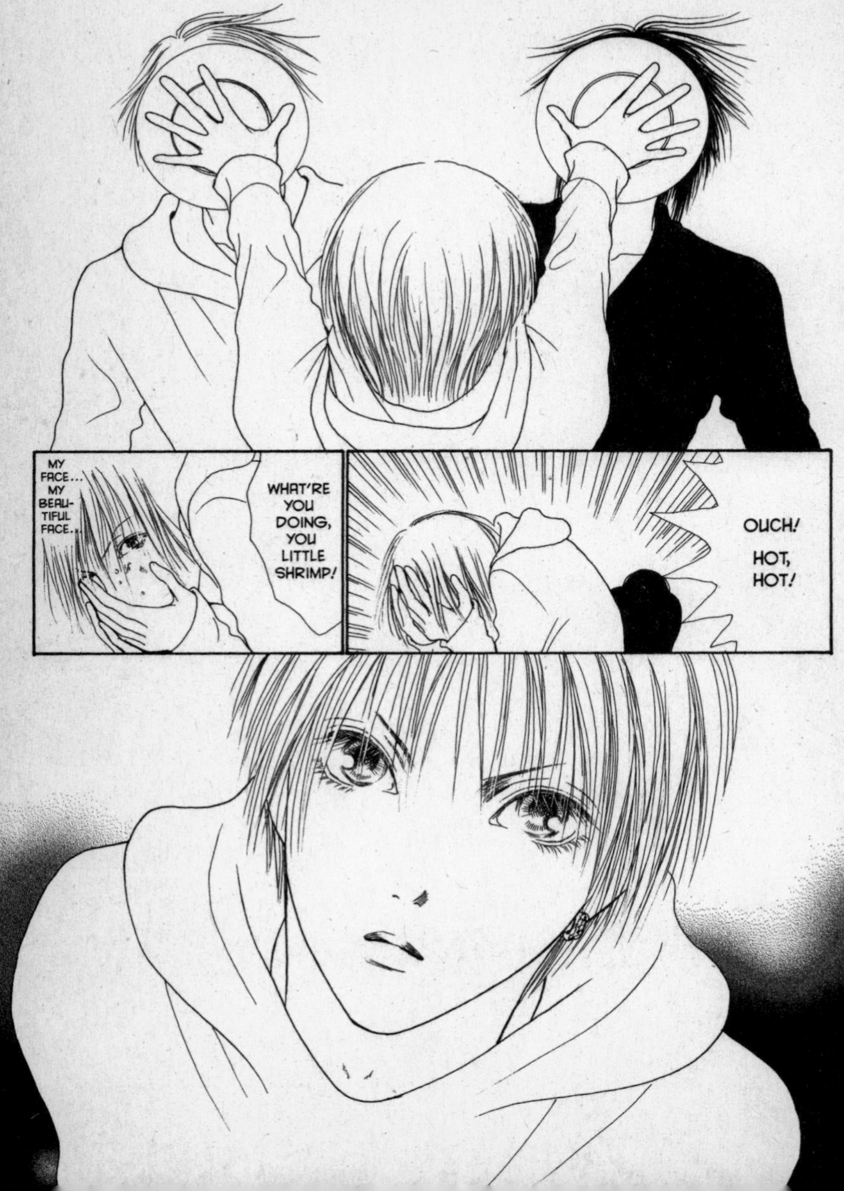
OUCH!
HOT, HOT!
WHAT'RE YOU DOING, YOU LITTLE SHRIMP!
MY FACE... MY BEAU-TIFUL FACE...

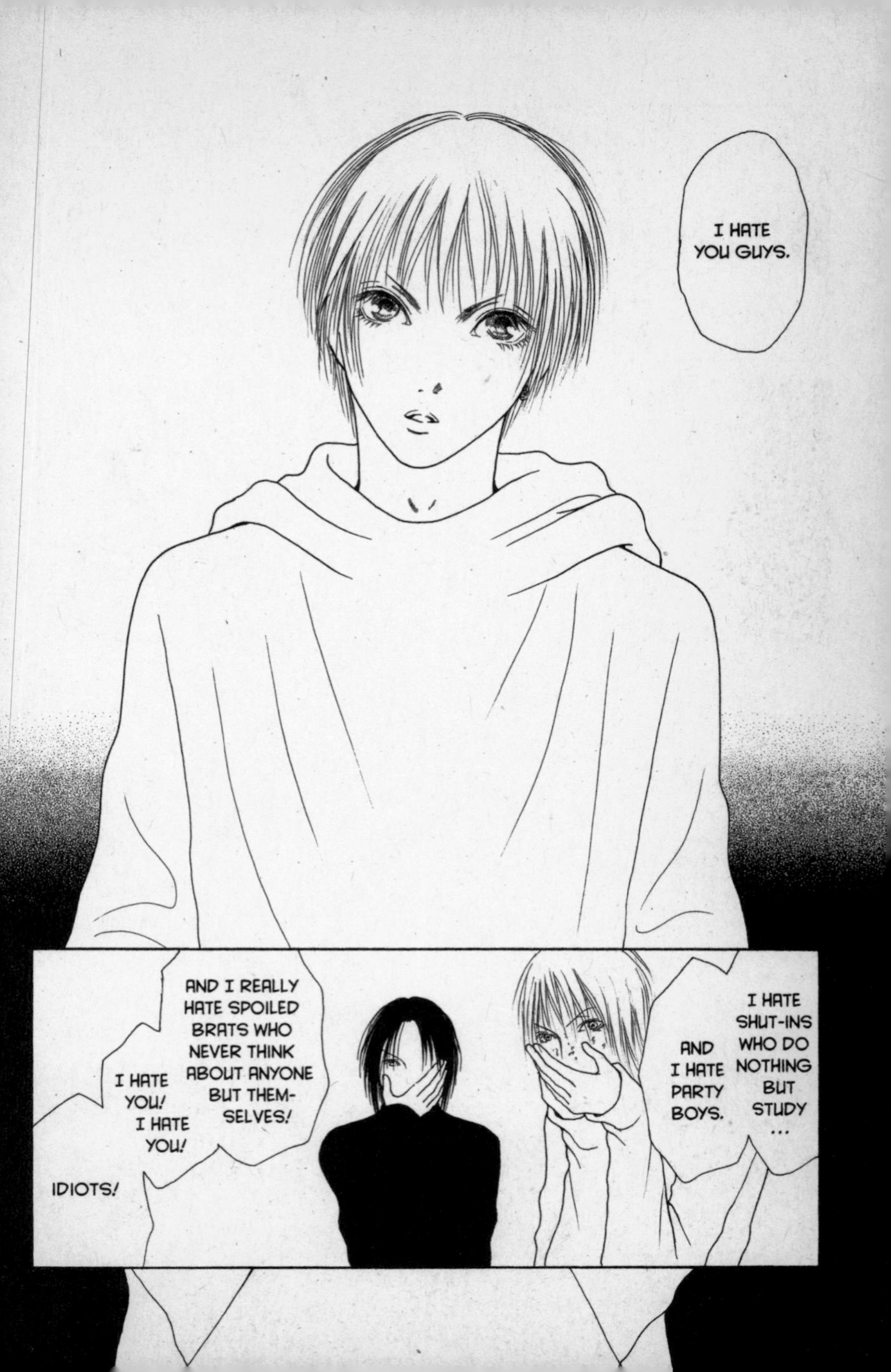
I HATE YOU GUYS.
I HATE SHUT-INS WHO DO NOTHING BUT STUDY ...
AND I HATE PARTY BOYS.
AND I REALLY HATE SPOILED BRATS WHO NEVER THINK ABOUT ANYONE BUT THEM-SELVES!
I HATE YOU! I HATE YOU!
IDIOTS!

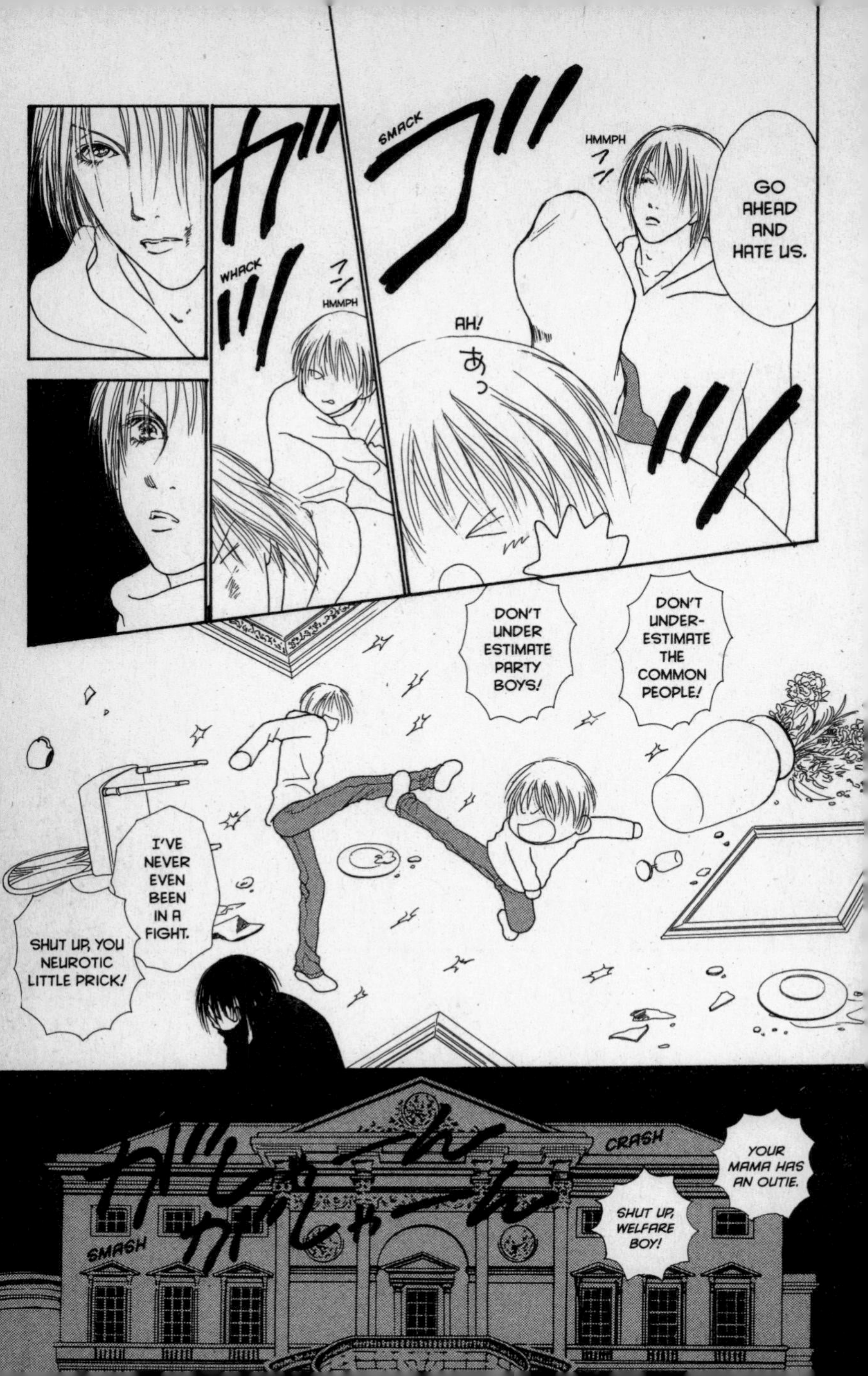
SMACK
HMMPH
GO AHEAD AND HATE US.
AH!
あっ
WHACK
HMMPH
DON'T UNDER-ESTIMATE THE COMMON PEOPLE!
DON'T UNDER ESTIMATE PARTY BOYS!
I'VE NEVER EVEN BEEN IN A FIGHT.
SHUT UP, YOU NEUROTIC LITTLE PRICK!
YOUR MAMA HAS AN OUTIE.
SHUT UP, WELFARE BOY!
CRASH
SMASH

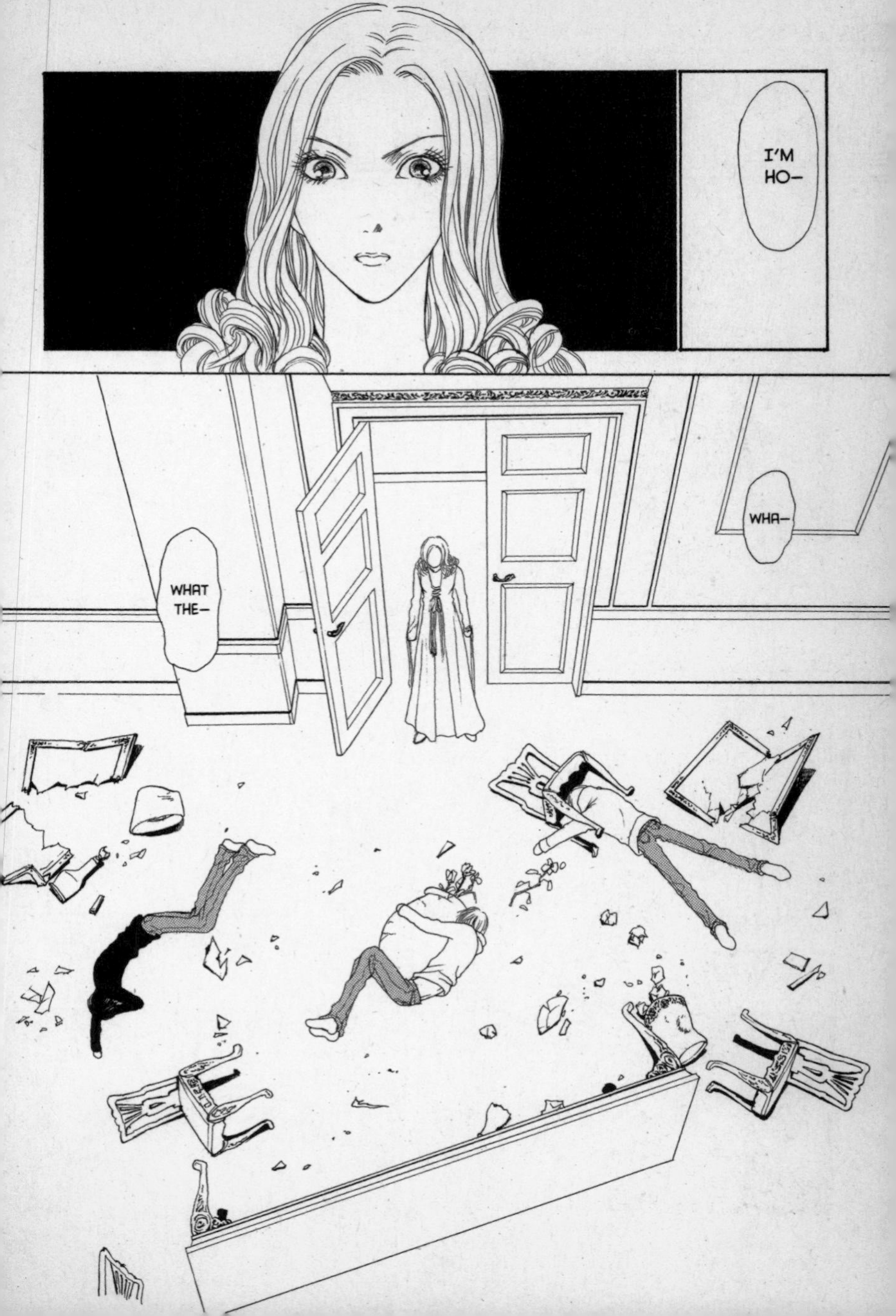
I'M HO—
WHA—
WHAT THE—

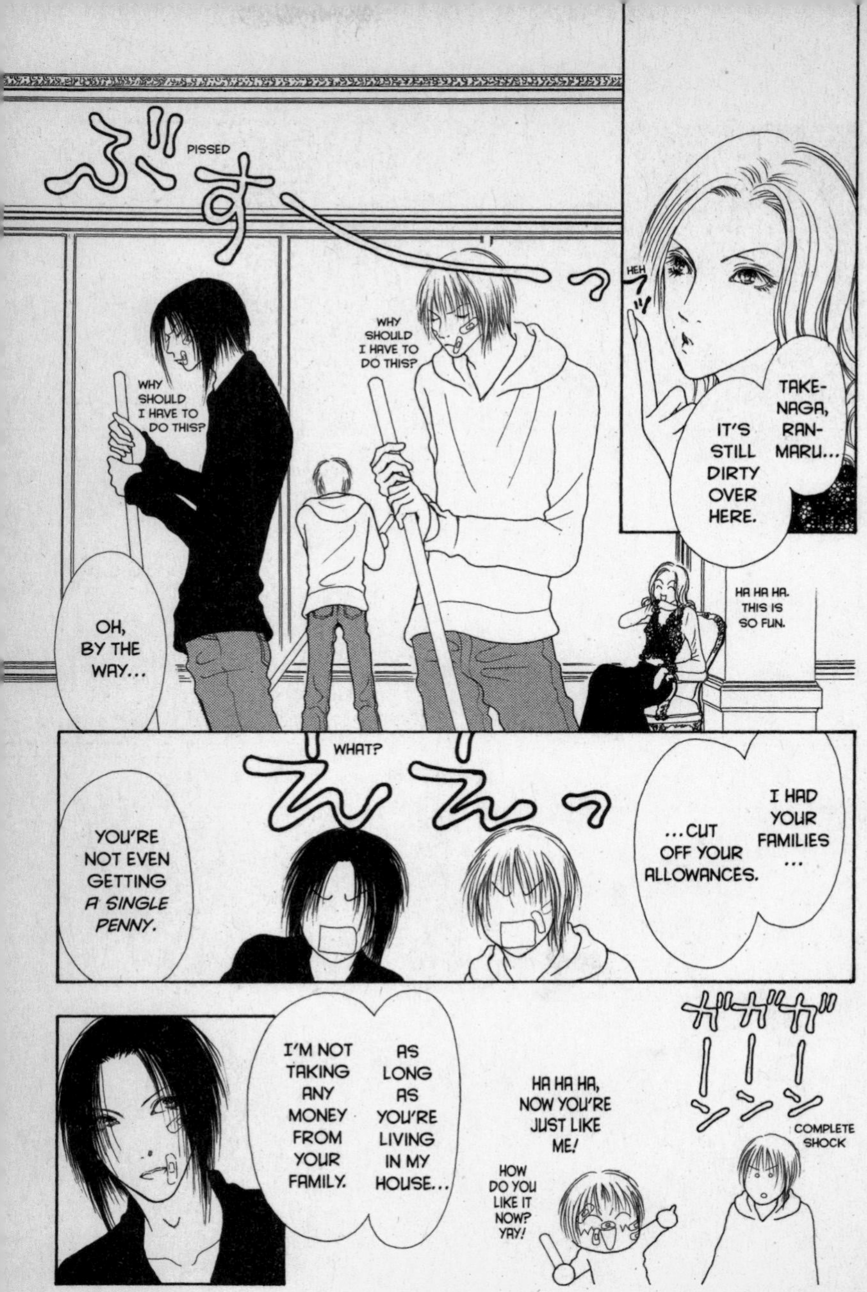
HEH
TAKE-NAGA, RAN-MARU... IT'S STILL DIRTY OVER HERE.
PISSED
WHY SHOULD I HAVE TO DO THIS?
WHY SHOULD I HAVE TO DO THIS?
HA HA HA. THIS IS SO FUN.
OH, BY THE WAY...
I HAD YOUR FAMILIES ...
...CUT OFF YOUR ALLOWANCES.
WHAT?
YOU'RE NOT EVEN GETTING A SINGLE PENNY.
COMPLETE SHOCK
HA HA HA, NOW YOU'RE JUST LIKE ME!
HOW DO YOU LIKE IT NOW? YAY!
AS LONG AS YOU'RE LIVING IN MY HOUSE...
I'M NOT TAKING ANY MONEY FROM YOUR FAMILY.

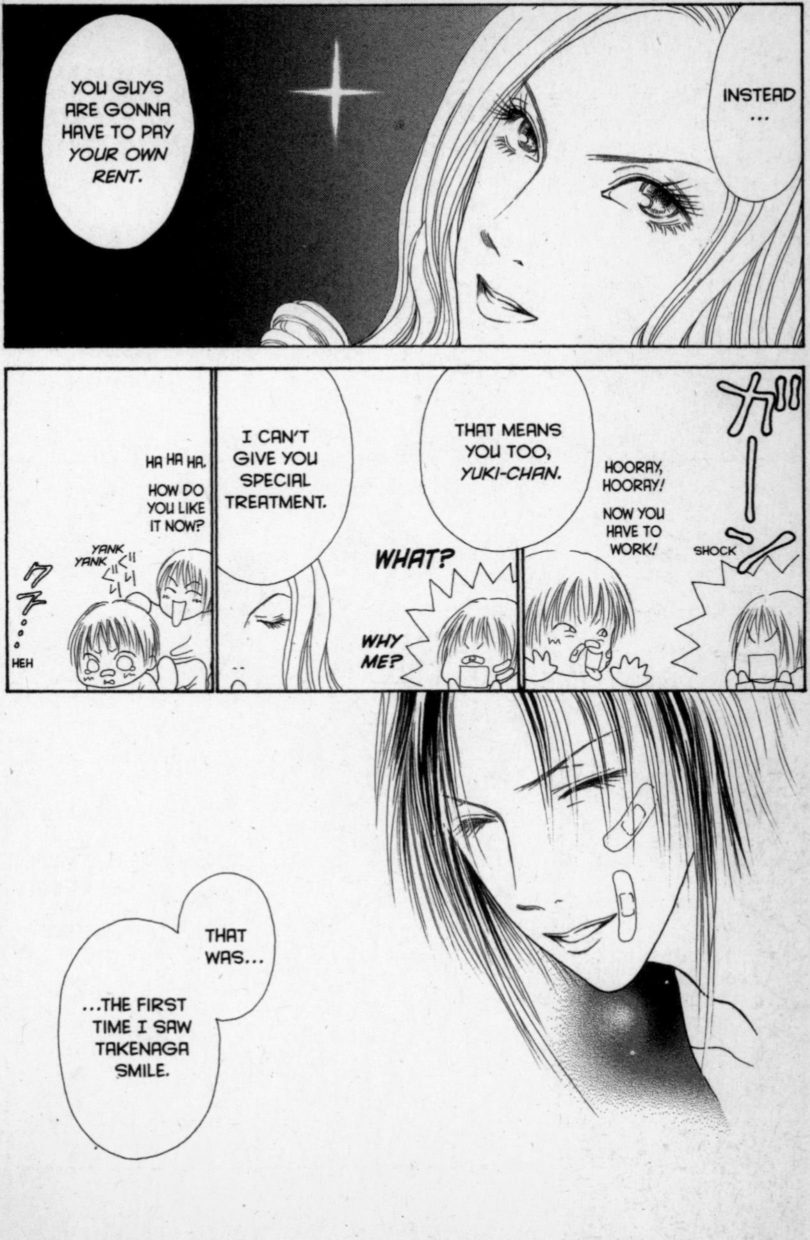
INSTEAD...
YOU GUYS ARE GONNA HAVE TO PAY *YOUR OWN* RENT.
SHOCK
HOORAY, HOORAY! NOW YOU HAVE TO WORK!
THAT MEANS YOU TOO, *YUKI-CHAN*.
WHAT?
WHY ME?
I CAN'T GIVE YOU SPECIAL TREATMENT.
HA HA HA. HOW DO YOU LIKE IT NOW?
YANK YANK
HEH
THAT WAS...
...THE FIRST TIME I SAW TAKENAGA SMILE.

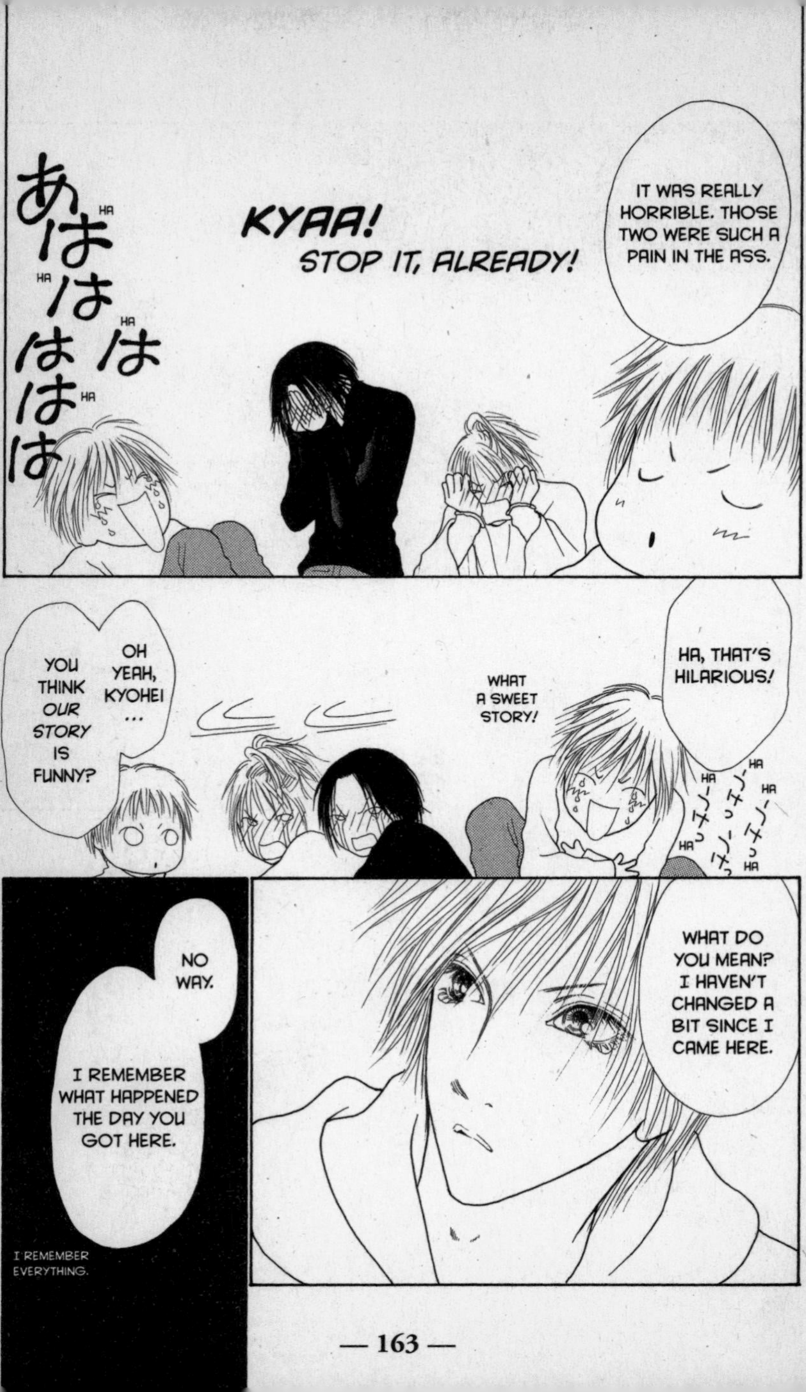
IT WAS REALLY HORRIBLE. THOSE TWO WERE SUCH A PAIN IN THE ASS.
KYAA!
STOP IT, ALREADY!
あはははは
HA HA HA HA
HA, THAT'S HILARIOUS!
HA HA HA HA
WHAT A SWEET STORY!
OH YEAH, KYOHEI...
YOU THINK OUR STORY IS FUNNY?
WHAT DO YOU MEAN? I HAVEN'T CHANGED A BIT SINCE I CAME HERE.
NO WAY.
I REMEMBER WHAT HAPPENED THE DAY YOU GOT HERE.
I REMEMBER EVERYTHING.

Originally appeared in *Bekkan Friend* issues 1-3 and 5, 2002

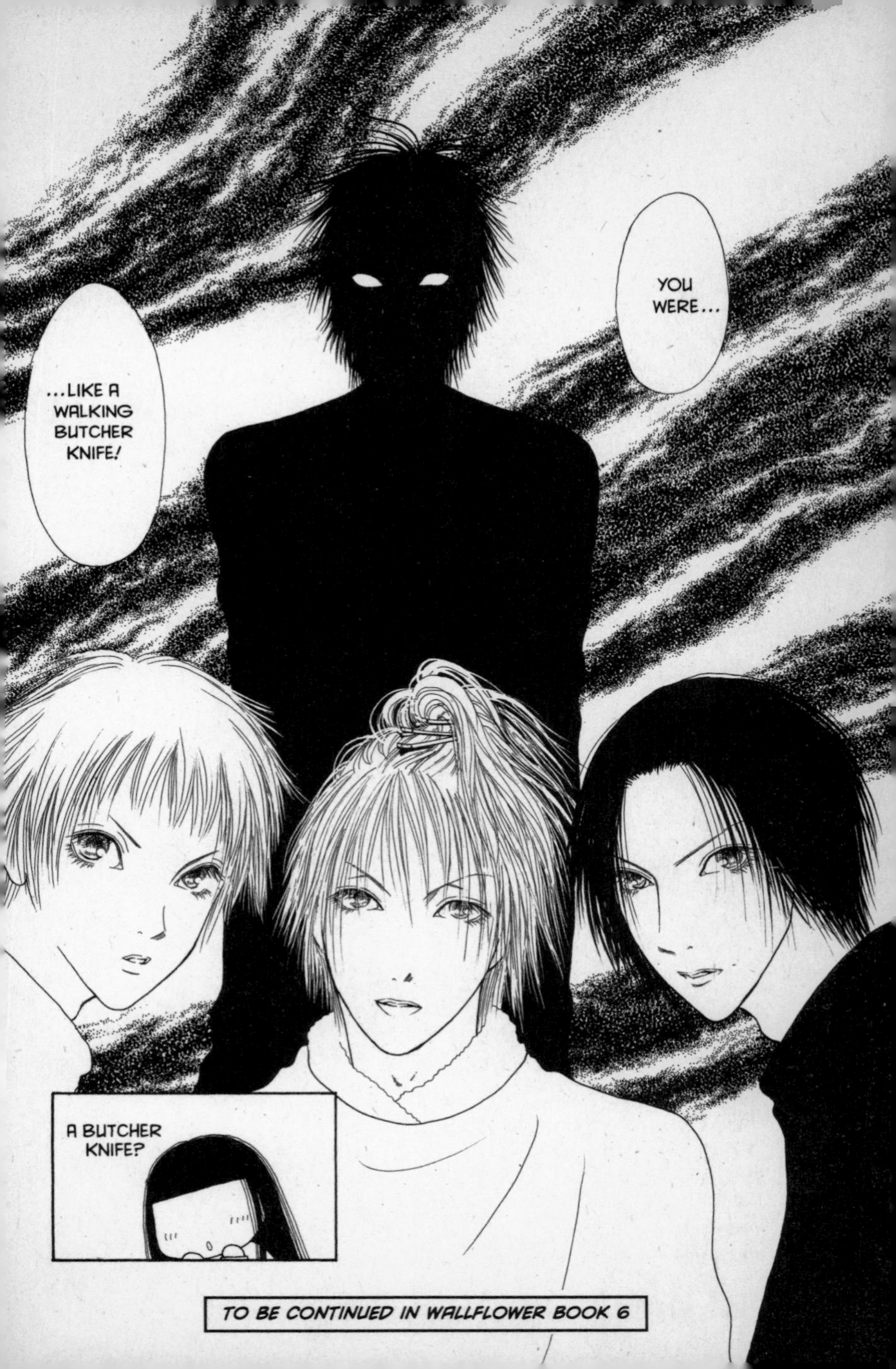
YOU WERE...
...LIKE A WALKING BUTCHER KNIFE!
A BUTCHER KNIFE?

TO BE CONTINUED IN WALLFLOWER BOOK 6

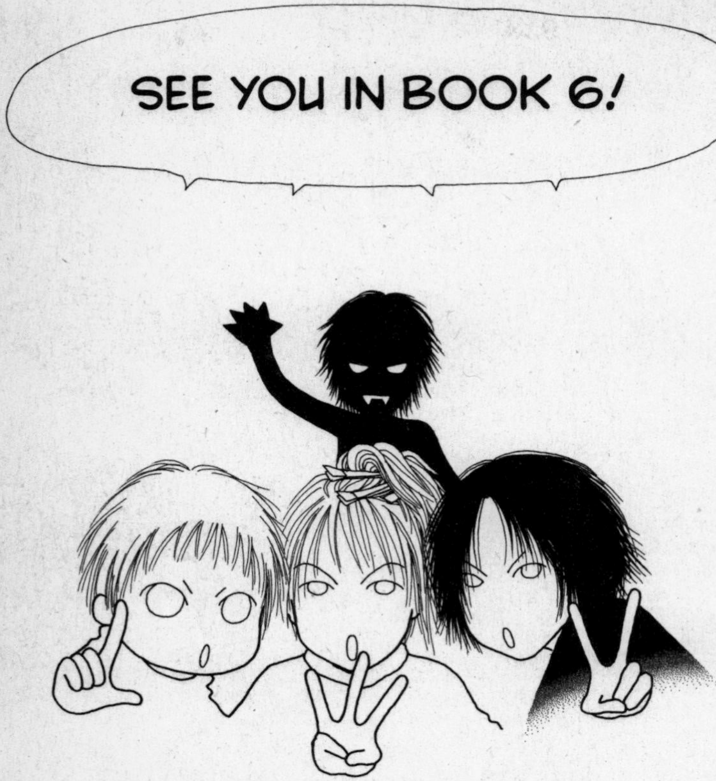
SEE YOU IN BOOK 6!

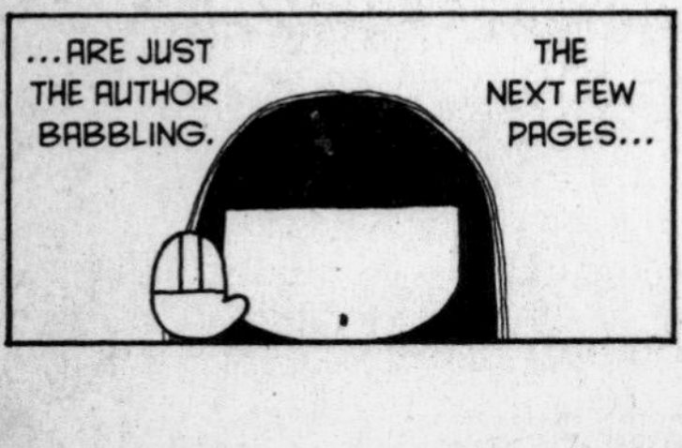
THE NEXT FEW PAGES...
...ARE JUST THE AUTHOR BABBLING.

HELLO. I'M TOMOKO HAYAKAWA.

THANK YOU FOR BUYING KODANSHA COMICS.

THANK YOU SO MUCH.

I HAVEN'T EVEN HAD AN INTERNET CONNECTION FOR THE LAST SIX MONTHS...HOW EMBARRASSING...

I DON'T HAVE A WEBSITE, AND I DON'T HAVE ENOUGH TIME TO RESPOND TO FAN LETTERS, SO THIS IS ALMOST THE ONLY TIME I GET TO MAKE CONTACT WITH YOU GUYS.

I'M SO SORRY. PLEASE BE PATIENT...

FORGIVE ME IF I WRITE TOO MUCH PERSONAL STUFF.

I AM STILL A HUGE FAN OF KIYOHARU FROM THE BAND SADS AND BANSAKU FROM THE BAND BARROKU.

I'M STILL GOING TO CONCERTS TO SEE THESE TWO BANDS, ALONG WITH RISK, SHOCKING LEMON AND MY FRIEND'S BAND.

RECENTLY, THEY CHANGED THEIR NAME TO "WRISK."

I WENT TO THEIR "FAN PARTY." HEH HEH. LEMON-SAN IS SO FUNNY!

OH, YEAH, I'M ALSO A FAN OF YUKI FROM THE BAND RISK. ♥ I WAS LOOKING AT AN OLD KIYOHARU POSTER, AND I ALMOST THOUGHT HE WAS YUKI-KUN.

OCCASIONALLY, I WILL GO CHECK OUT NEW BANDS AND OLD BANDS I USED TO LIKE... ← I WILL TELL YOU MORE ABOUT THIS LATER.

...BY THE WAY, I HARDLY EVER GO OUT UNLESS THERE'S A CONCERT TO GO TO! KYAA! WHAT'S UP WITH THAT?

I'VE GAINED SO MUCH WEIGHT THAT I'M TOO EMBARRASSED TO SEE ANYONE, SO I'M ON A DIET? ← I PUT A "?" THERE FOR A REASON...I'M IN SO MUCH TROUBLE. GYAA!

I WON'T BE ABLE TO FIT INTO ANY CLOTHES DESIGNED BY GAULTIER ANYMORE... OH, NO! (I OFTEN GO SHOPPING IN OMOTESANDO.) THANKS, HIGASHIZAWA-SAN. ♥

...SIGH. IT'S NO GOOD TO STAY INSIDE ALL THE TIME...NOW I'M GONNA GO TO KOMAZAWA PARK FOR A WALK...

CLIPPINGS OF KIYOHARU

THANKS SO MUCH FOR SENDING ME CLIPPINGS. ♥♥♥ I'VE SAID THIS BEFORE, BUT PLEASE DON'T FEEL TOO MUCH PRESSURE TO SEND CLIPPINGS. I'M HAPPY JUST GETTING YOUR LETTERS.

CLIPPINGS OF BAROKKU

THANKS FOR SENDING ME THEIR CLIPPINGS TOO. ♥ ♥ ♥ I LOVE GETTING THEM EVEN IF THEY'RE JUST COLOR COPIES. THANKS. ♥ ALSO, THANKS FOR THE FLYERS ♥ AND OLD CLIPPINGS OF AFTER EFFECT. ♥ I'M GLAD THAT BAROKKU HAS BECOME MORE POPULAR. ♥ THANKS FOR ALL THE CLIPPINGS OF VARIOUS CELEBRITIES. ♥ JOHNNIES JR, MANA-SAMA ♥ ETC.

I GET A LOT OF LETTERS FROM FANS OF THE BAND DIE EN GREY AND PIERROT. I'LL CHECK THEM OUT SOMETIME. THEY ARE SO POPULAR. I WAS LOOKING AT A MAGAZINE THE OTHER DAY, AND I SAW A PHOTO OF DIR-SAN WITHOUT ANY MAKE UP. THE GUY WITH RED HAIR IS CUTE. ♥ THE DRUMMER HAS A NICE BODY... SORRY, I DON'T KNOW THEIR NAMES.

SEEMS LIKE GACKT-SAN IS GETTING MORE FANS THESE DAYS. MY FRIEND IS A HUGE FAN OF HIS, SO I WENT TO SEE HIM IN CONCERT A FEW TIMES. I SAW EBI PLAYING DRUMS WITH HIM ON A VIDEO, SO I WAS LOOKING FORWARD TO SEEING HIM, BUT EBI WASN'T THERE . . . GRR . . . MASA-KUN IS SO CUTE. ♥ HE'S TOTALLY MY TYPE. WELL, GACKT IS CUTE TOO.

I'VE BEEN WATCHING "DOUMOTO KYODAI" ON TV ALL THE TIME BECAUSE RANMARU IS ON THAT SHOW. ♥ (MY FRIEND IS A HUGE FAN OF HIS.) I WAS SURPRISED TO HEAR HIM BEING CALLED "TSUCHII."

*THIS RANMARU HAS NOTHING TO DO WITH MY CHARACTER "RANMARU." REFER TO BOOK 1. ⟵ SHAMELESS SELF PROMOTION?

PEOPLE ASK ME ALL THE TIME, "WHICH CHARACTER IS YOUR FAVORITE?" SO HERE'S MY ANSWER. IT'S THE SMALL VERSION OF SUNAKO! BECAUSE SHE'S EASY TO DRAW! MY SECOND FAVORITE IS THE SMALL VERSION OF YUKI. HE'S EASY TO DRAW TOO ... SORRY FOR HAVING SUCH A STUPID REASON ...

PEOPLE ALSO ASK ME, "WHY DO YOU ALWAYS MAKE SUNAKO LOOK SO SMALL?" HERE'S MY ANSWER.

IT'S BECAUSE ...

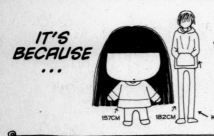

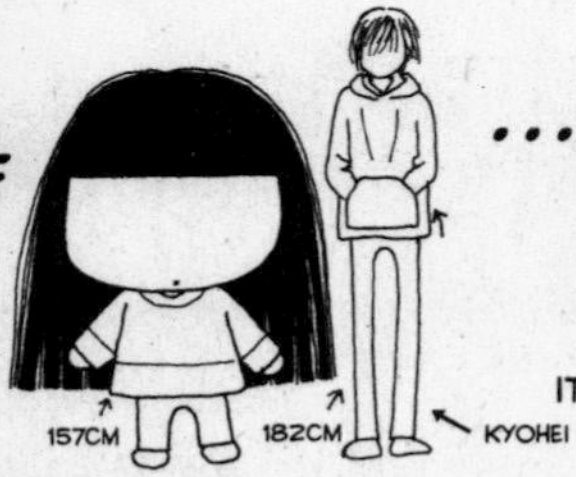
157CM
182CM
KYOHEI

... IF I DREW HER TO SCALE, SHE WOULD LOOK REALLY SCARY.

IT'S A BIG HEADED MONSTER! KYAA!

WELL ... I DIDN'T GET TO ANSWER MANY QUESTIONS AFTER ALL. I'LL TRY HARDER IN BOOK 6. (I HOPE I'LL GET MORE PAGES.)

IF YOU HAVE ANY CELEBRITIES YOU'D LIKE TO RECOMMEND (ACTORS OR MUSICIANS ETC.), PLEASE LET ME KNOW.

OH, I ALREADY CHECKED OUT TAKERU KOBAYASHI-KUN IN "FOOD FIGHTER" ♥ AND ALSO YOSUKE KUBOZUKA-KUN AND TOMOHISA YAMASHITA-KUN. (DID I GET THEIR NAMES RIGHT?) THEY ARE SO CUTE.... LOTS OF PEOPLE HAVE TOLD ME ABOUT THEM.

THANKS TO ALL THOSE WHO SENT ME MDS OF THEIR FAVORITE BANDS. ♥ I ALWAYS LISTEN TO THEM. I DON'T LISTEN EXCLUSIVELY TO GLAM BANDS. REALLY. I LISTEN TO ALL KINDS OF MUSIC. ♥ I LIKE ROCK AND 70'S POP MUSIC. I HATE RAP. VISUALLY, I LIKE GUYS WHO ARE GORGEOUS, MASCULINE AND A LITTLE BIT DANGEROUS. ⟵ THEY ACTUALLY DO EXIST IF YOU LOOK IN THE RIGHT PLACE! HIROTO KOUMOTO IS MY DREAM GUY. WHERE CAN I FIND SOMEONE WHO LOOKS LIKE HIM ...? ♥

I GET SO MANY REQUESTS FROM PEOPLE SAYING, "I WANT TO SEE THE FOUR GUYS PLAYING IN A BAND!" I DON'T THINK THAT'LL HAPPEN IN THE STORY, SO I WILL TAKE THIS OPPORTUNITY TO MAKE YOUR DREAM COME TRUE.

⟵ I HOPE YOU LIKE IT.

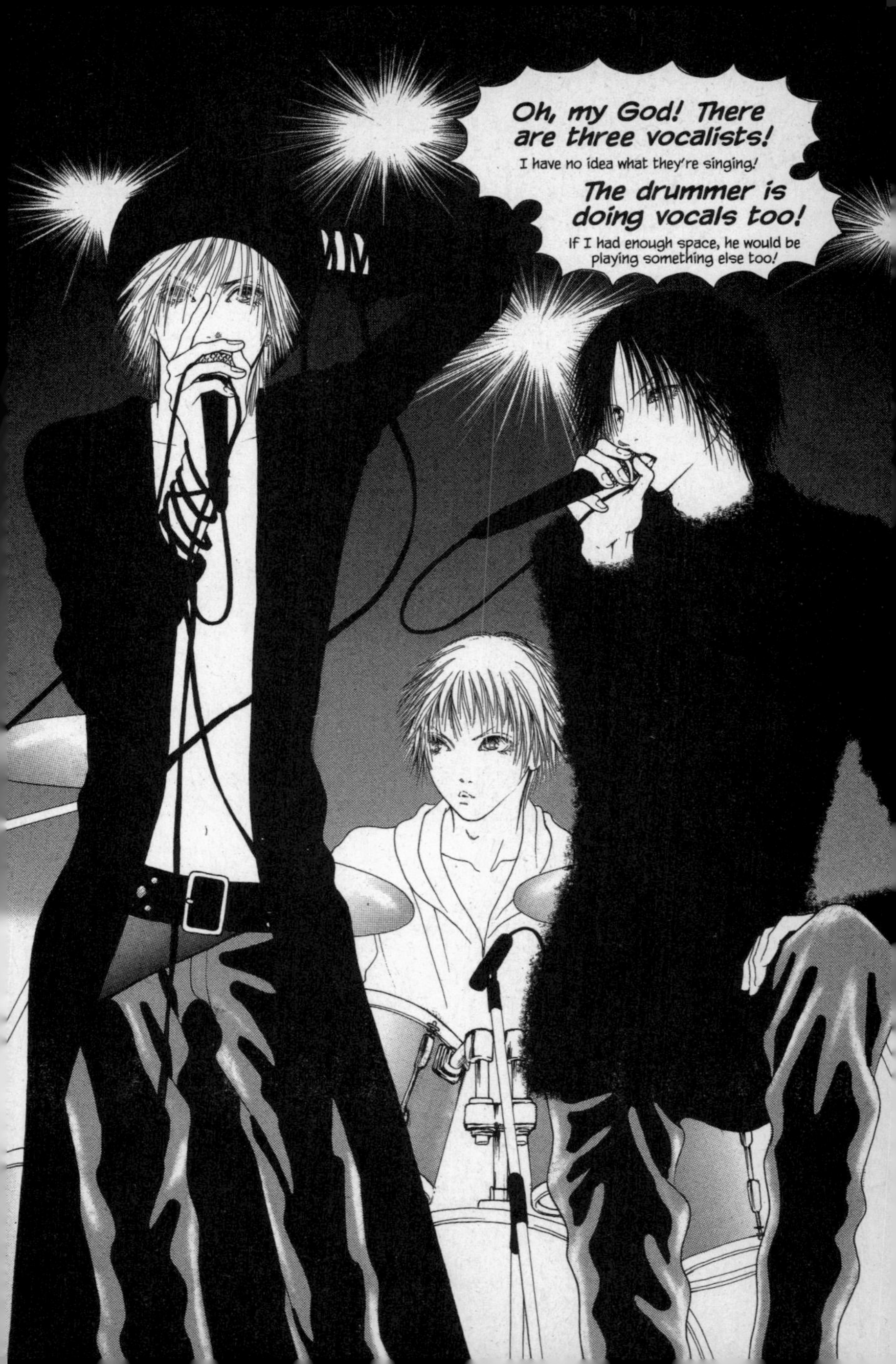
Oh, my God! There are three vocalists!
I have no idea what they're singing!
The drummer is doing vocals too!
If I had enough space, he would be playing something else too!

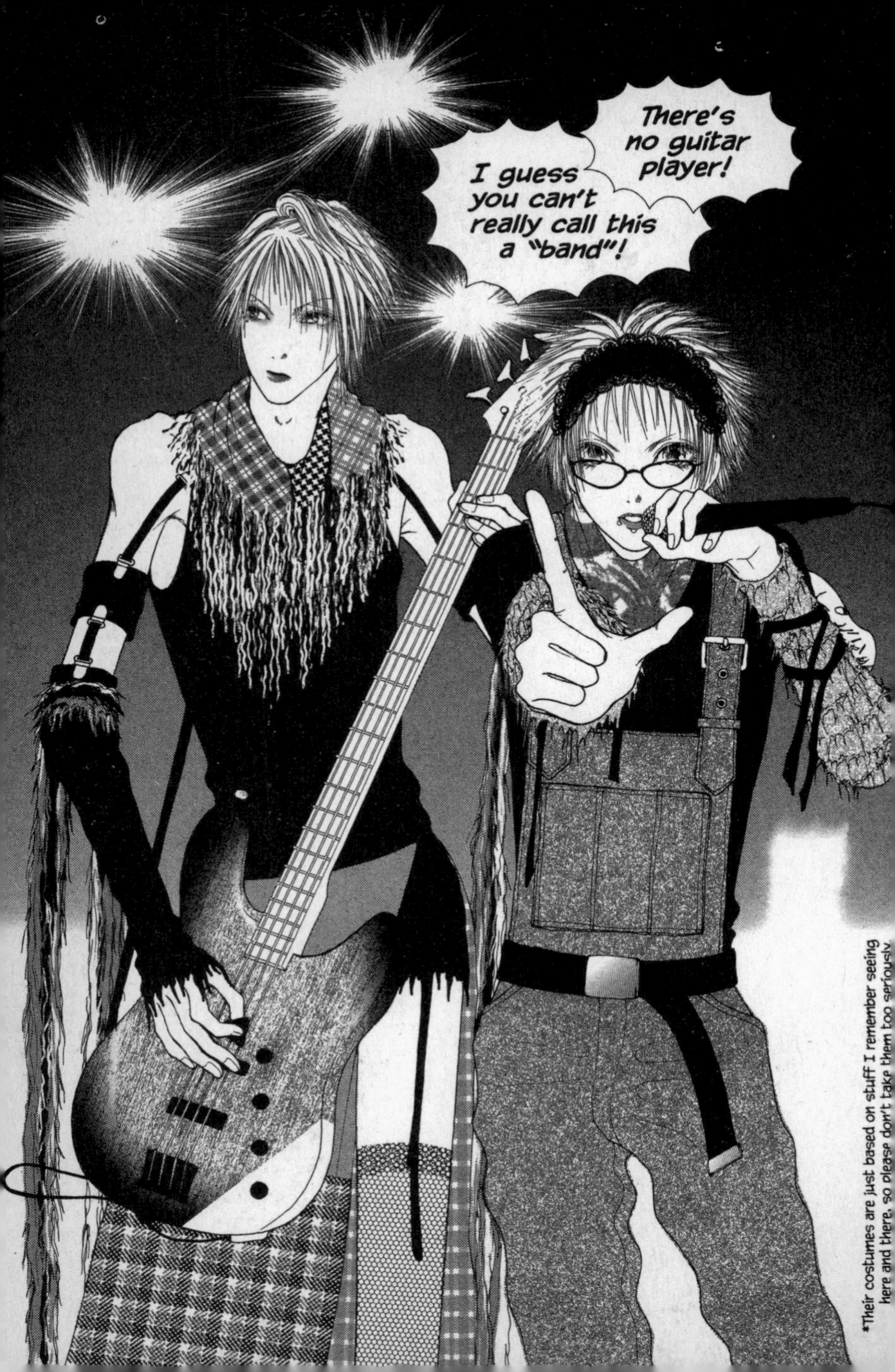
There's no guitar player!
I guess you can't really call this a "band"!
*Their costumes are just based on stuff I remember seeing here and there, so please don't take them too seriously.

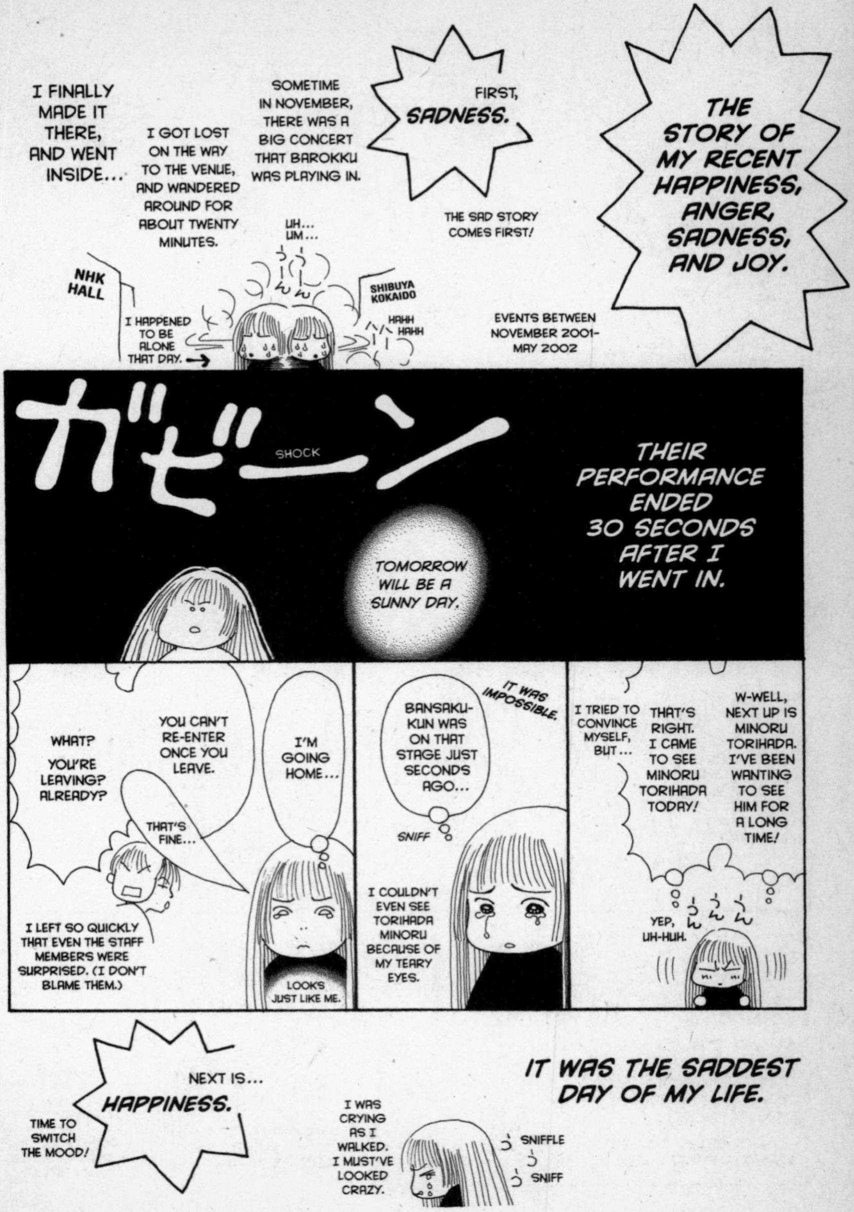
THE STORY OF MY RECENT HAPPINESS, ANGER, SADNESS, AND JOY.
EVENTS BETWEEN NOVEMBER 2001-MAY 2002
FIRST, SADNESS.
THE SAD STORY COMES FIRST!
SOMETIME IN NOVEMBER, THERE WAS A BIG CONCERT THAT BAROKKU WAS PLAYING IN.
UH... UM...
SHIBUYA KOKAIDO
HAHH HAHH
I GOT LOST ON THE WAY TO THE VENUE, AND WANDERED AROUND FOR ABOUT TWENTY MINUTES.
I FINALLY MADE IT THERE, AND WENT INSIDE...
NHK HALL
I HAPPENED TO BE ALONE THAT DAY.
THEIR PERFORMANCE ENDED 30 SECONDS AFTER I WENT IN.
ガビーン
SHOCK
TOMORROW WILL BE A SUNNY DAY.
W-WELL, NEXT UP IS MINORU TORIHADA. I'VE BEEN WANTING TO SEE HIM FOR A LONG TIME!
THAT'S RIGHT. I CAME TO SEE MINORU TORIHADA TODAY!
I TRIED TO CONVINCE MYSELF, BUT...
YEP, UH-HUH.
IT WAS IMPOSSIBLE.
BANSAKU-KUN WAS ON THAT STAGE JUST SECONDS AGO...
SNIFF
I COULDN'T EVEN SEE TORIHADA MINORU BECAUSE OF MY TEARY EYES.
I'M GOING HOME...
YOU CAN'T RE-ENTER ONCE YOU LEAVE.
WHAT? YOU'RE LEAVING? ALREADY?
THAT'S FINE...
LOOKS JUST LIKE ME.
I LEFT SO QUICKLY THAT EVEN THE STAFF MEMBERS WERE SURPRISED. (I DON'T BLAME THEM.)
IT WAS THE SADDEST DAY OF MY LIFE.
SNIFFLE
SNIFF
I WAS CRYING AS I WALKED. I MUST'VE LOOKED CRAZY.
NEXT IS... HAPPINESS.
TIME TO SWITCH THE MOOD!

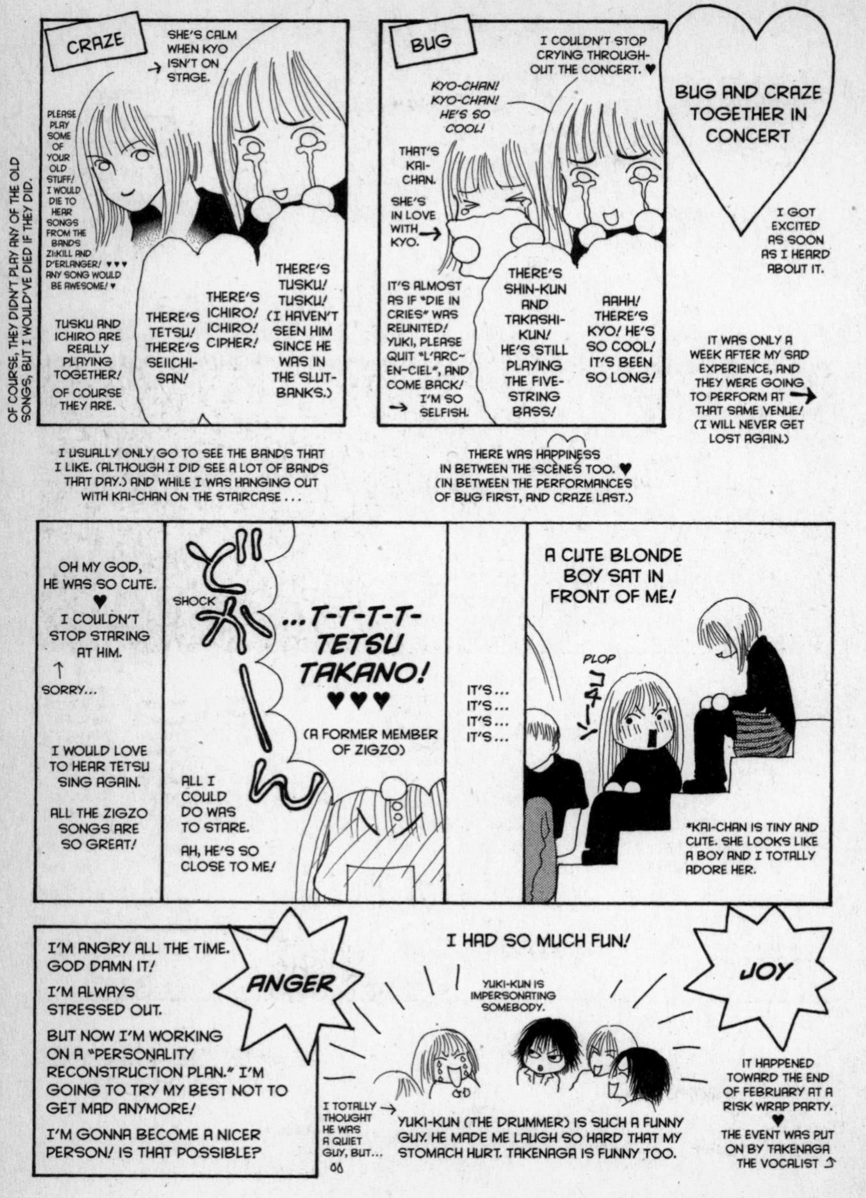

BUG AND CRAZE TOGETHER IN CONCERT
I GOT EXCITED AS SOON AS I HEARD ABOUT IT.
IT WAS ONLY A WEEK AFTER MY SAD EXPERIENCE, AND THEY WERE GOING TO PERFORM AT THAT SAME VENUE! (I WILL NEVER GET LOST AGAIN.)
BUG
I COULDN'T STOP CRYING THROUGHOUT THE CONCERT. ♥
KYO-CHAN! KYO-CHAN! HE'S SO COOL!
THAT'S KAI-CHAN.
SHE'S IN LOVE WITH KYO.
AAHH! THERE'S KYO! HE'S SO COOL! IT'S BEEN SO LONG!
THERE'S SHIN-KUN AND TAKASHI-KUN! HE'S STILL PLAYING THE FIVE-STRING BASS!
IT'S ALMOST AS IF "DIE IN CRIES" WAS REUNITED! YUKI, PLEASE QUIT "L'ARC~EN~CIEL", AND COME BACK!
I'M SO SELFISH.
CRAZE
SHE'S CALM WHEN KYO ISN'T ON STAGE.
THERE'S TUSKU! TUSKU! (I HAVEN'T SEEN HIM SINCE HE WAS IN THE SLUT-BANKS.)
THERE'S ICHIRO! ICHIRO! CIPHER!
THERE'S TETSU! THERE'S SEIICHI-SAN!
PLEASE PLAY SOME OF YOUR OLD STUFF! I WOULD DIE TO HEAR SONGS FROM THE BANDS ZI:KILL AND D'ERLANGER! ♥♥♥ ANY SONG WOULD BE AWESOME! ♥
TUSKU AND ICHIRO ARE REALLY PLAYING TOGETHER!
OF COURSE THEY ARE.
OF COURSE, THEY DIDN'T PLAY ANY OF THE OLD SONGS, BUT I WOULD'VE DIED IF THEY DID.
THERE WAS HAPPINESS IN BETWEEN THE SCENES TOO. ♥ (IN BETWEEN THE PERFORMANCES OF BUG FIRST, AND CRAZE LAST.)
I USUALLY ONLY GO TO SEE THE BANDS THAT I LIKE. (ALTHOUGH I DID SEE A LOT OF BANDS THAT DAY.) AND WHILE I WAS HANGING OUT WITH KAI-CHAN ON THE STAIRCASE . . .
A CUTE BLONDE BOY SAT IN FRONT OF ME!
PLOP
*KAI-CHAN IS TINY AND CUTE. SHE LOOKS LIKE A BOY AND I TOTALLY ADORE HER.
IT'S... IT'S... IT'S... IT'S...
SHOCK
...T-T-T-T-TETSU TAKANO! ♥♥♥
(A FORMER MEMBER OF ZIGZO)
ALL I COULD DO WAS TO STARE.
AH, HE'S SO CLOSE TO ME!
OH MY GOD, HE WAS SO CUTE. ♥
I COULDN'T STOP STARING AT HIM.
SORRY...
I WOULD LOVE TO HEAR TETSU SING AGAIN.
ALL THE ZIGZO SONGS ARE SO GREAT!
JOY
IT HAPPENED TOWARD THE END OF FEBRUARY AT A RISK WRAP PARTY. ♥
THE EVENT WAS PUT ON BY TAKENAGA THE VOCALIST
I HAD SO MUCH FUN!
YUKI-KUN IS IMPERSONATING SOMEBODY.
YUKI-KUN (THE DRUMMER) IS SUCH A FUNNY GUY. HE MADE ME LAUGH SO HARD THAT MY STOMACH HURT. TAKENAGA IS FUNNY TOO.
I TOTALLY THOUGHT HE WAS A QUIET GUY, BUT...
ANGER
I'M ANGRY ALL THE TIME. GOD DAMN IT!
I'M ALWAYS STRESSED OUT.
BUT NOW I'M WORKING ON A "PERSONALITY RECONSTRUCTION PLAN." I'M GOING TO TRY MY BEST NOT TO GET MAD ANYMORE!
I'M GONNA BECOME A NICER PERSON! IS THAT POSSIBLE?

THANK YOU SO MUCH FOR READING ALL OF THIS. ♥

SPECIAL THANKS TO:

YUKI SUETSUGU-SAMA,

SHO HIROSE-SAMA,

AYUAYU WATANABE-SAMA,

ATSUKO NANBA-SAMA,

YUKIO IKEDA-SAMA,

HANA-CHAN,

IYU KOZAKURA-SAMA,

AKIRA YUUKI-SAMA,

MACHIKO SAKURAI-SAMA

MINE-SAMA,

SHIOZAWA-SAMA,

INO-SAMA,

EVERYBODY IN THE EDITING DEPARTMENT,

EVERYBODY WHO'S READING THIS BOOK, AND EVERYBODY WHO SENT ME LETTERS.

I'M SUPPORTED BY SO MANY WONDERFUL PEOPLE. (IN OTHER WORDS, I'M A PAIN IN THE ASS.) WITHOUT YOU GUYS, THIS BOOK WOULD NOT EXIST.

ALL THE MANGA ARTISTS WHO HELPED ME, EVERYBODY IN THE EDITING DEPARTMENT, FANS WHO SENT ME LETTERS, VETERAN MANGA ARTISTS, MY FAMILY, RELATIVES AND MY PRECIOUS FRIENDS ... THANK YOU ALL FOR YOUR SUPPORT.

NOW I HAVE SO MUCH MORE APPRECIATION FOR "HUMAN KINDNESS." YOU GUYS WERE ALWAYS THERE FOR ME, BUT I WAS SO CAUGHT UP WITH THINGS THAT I TOOK YOU ALL FOR GRANTED. I DIDN'T EVEN NOTICE HOW FORTUNATE I WAS TO JUST HAVE YOU ALL IN MY LIFE. I CAUSED YOU ALL SO MUCH TROUBLE, ESPECIALLY MY CLOSE FRIENDS (BOTH MALE AND FEMALE) AND MY FAMILY. . . . I WISH I COULD INCLUDE ALL OF YOUR NAMES HERE. YOUR KINDNESS MEANS SO MUCH TO ME, ESPECIALLY WHEN I'M FEELING A BIT DEPRESSED.

THANK YOU SO MUCH, EVERYBODY! I LOVE YOU ALL! ♥♥♥

HOPE YOU'LL STICK AROUND. ♥

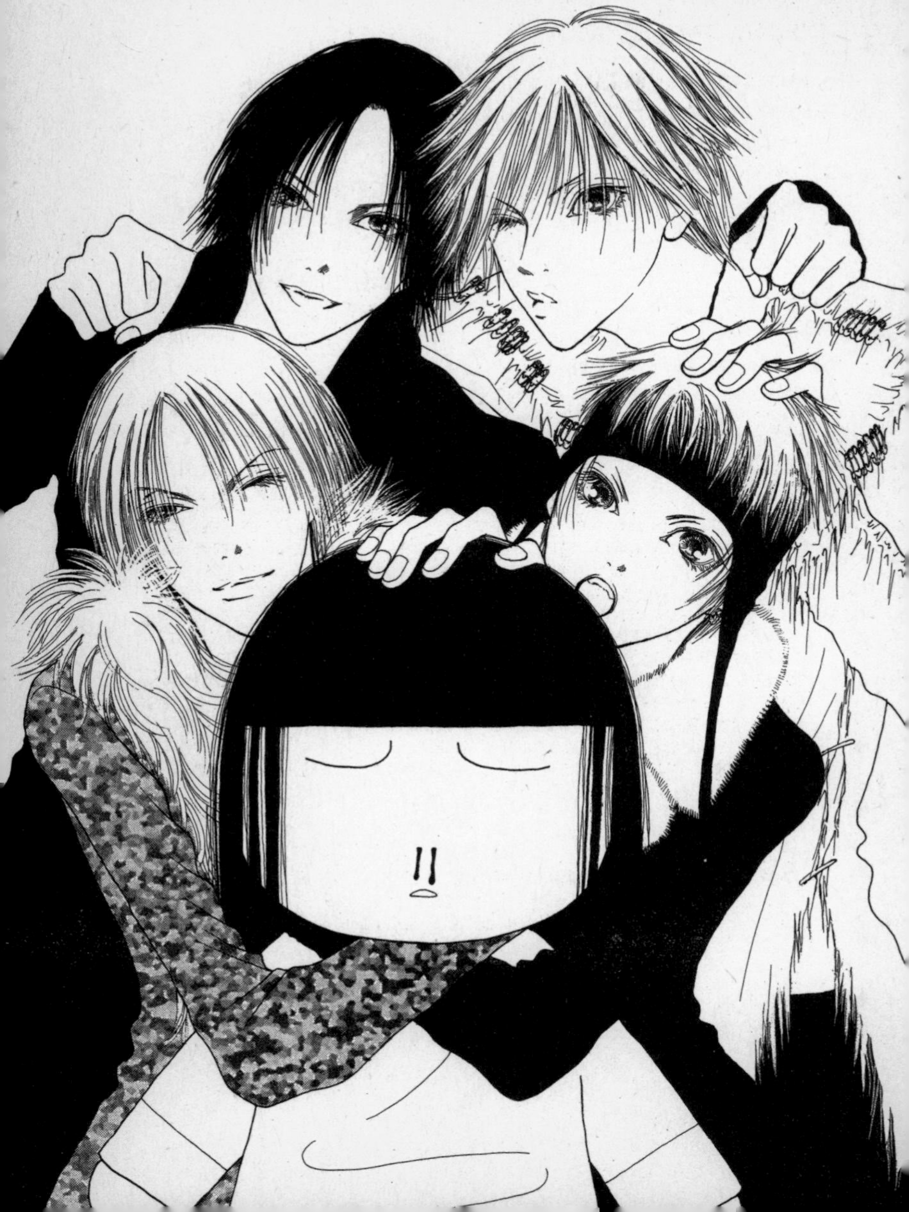

About the Creator

Tomoko Hayakawa was born on March 4.

   Since her debut as a manga creator, Tomoko Hayakawa has
worked on many shojo titles with the theme of romantic love—only
to realize that she could write about other subjects as well. She
decided to pack her newest story with the things she likes most,
which led to her current, enormously popular series, *The Wallflower*.
   Her favorite things are: Tim Burton's *The Nightmare Before
Christmas*, Jean-Paul Gaultier, and samurai dramas on TV. Her
hobbies are collecting items with skull designs and watching
bishonen (beautiful boys). Her dream is to build a mansion like the
one that the Addams family lives in. Her favorite pastime is to lie
around at home with her cat, Ten (whose full name is Tennosuke).

   Her zodiac sign is Pisces, and her blood group is AB.

Honorifics

Throughout the Del Rey Manga books, you will find Japanese honorifics left intact in the translations. For those not familiar with how the Japanese use honorifics, and more important, how they differ from American honorifics, we present this brief overview.

Politeness has always been a critical facet of Japanese culture. Ever since the feudal era, when Japan was a highly stratified society, use of honorifics—which can be defined as polite speech that indicates relationship or status—has played an essential role in the Japanese language. When addressing someone in Japanese, an honorific usually takes the form of a suffix attached to one's name (example: "Asuna-san"), or as a title at the end of one's name or in place of the name itself (example: "Negi-sensei," or simply "Sensei!").

Honorifics can be expressions of respect or endearment. In the context of manga and anime, honorifics give insight into the nature of the relationship between characters. Many translations into English leave out these important honorifics, and therefore distort the "feel" of the original Japanese. Because Japanese honorifics contain nuances that English honorifics lack, it is our policy at Del Rey not to translate them. Here, instead, is a guide to some of the honorifics you may encounter in Del Rey Manga.

-san: This is the most common honorific, and is equivalent to Mr., Miss, Ms., Mrs., etc. It is the all-purpose honorific and can be used in any situation where politeness is required.

-sama: This is one level higher than "-san" and it is used to confer great respect.

-dono: This comes from the word "tono," which means "lord." It is an even higher level than "-sama," and confers utmost respect.

-kun: This suffix is used at the end of boys' names to express familiarity or endearment. It is also sometimes used by men among friends, or when addressing someone younger or of a lower station.

-chan: This is used to express endearment, mostly toward girls. It is also used for little boys, pets, and even among lovers. It gives a sense of childish cuteness.

Bozu: This is an informal way to refer to a boy, similar to the English term "kid" or "squirt."

Sempai/Senpai: This title suggests that the addressee is one's "senior" in a group or organization. It is most often used in a school setting, where underclassmen refer to their upperclassmen as "sempai." It can also be used in the workplace, such as when a newer employee addresses an employee who has seniority in the company.

Kohai: This is the opposite of "sempai," and is used toward underclassmen in school or newcomers in the workplace. It connotes that the addressee is of lower station.

Sensei: Literally meaning "one who has come before," this title is used for teachers, doctors, or masters of any profession or art.

[blank]: Usually forgotten in these lists, but perhaps the most significant difference between Japanese and English. The lack of honorific means that the speaker has permission to address the person in a very intimate way. Usually, only family, spouses, or very close friends have this kind of permission. Known as *yobisute,* it can be gratifying when someone who has earned the intimacy starts to call one by one's name without an honorific. But when that intimacy hasn't been earned, it can be very insulting.

Translation Notes

Japanese is a tricky language for most Westerners, and translation is often more art than science. For your edification and reading pleasure, here are notes on some of the places where we could have gone in a different direction in our translation of the work, or where a Japanese cultural reference is used.

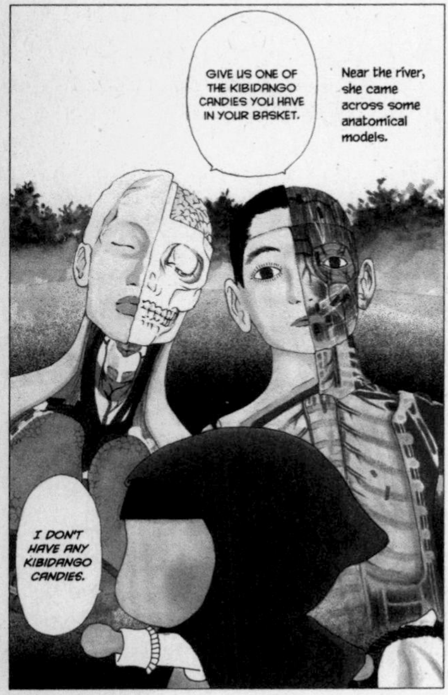
Near the river, she came across some anatomical models.
GIVE US ONE OF THE KIBIDANGO CANDIES YOU HAVE IN YOUR BASKET.
I DON'T HAVE ANY KIBIDANGO CANDIES.

Kibidango candy (page 4)

Kibidango is a type of Japanese sweet made from rice. This is a reference to the Japanese fairy tale "Momotaroo," in which a young boy named Momotaroo offers Kibidango to some animals in exchange for their help.

Lolita (page 16)

The term "Lolita" comes from Nabokov's novel *Lolita* about an older man who is obsessed with a young girl. In Japan this kind of behavior is referred to as a "Lolita complex." "Lolita" girls are girls who dress in clothes that make them look like children, i.e., bonnets and ribbons.

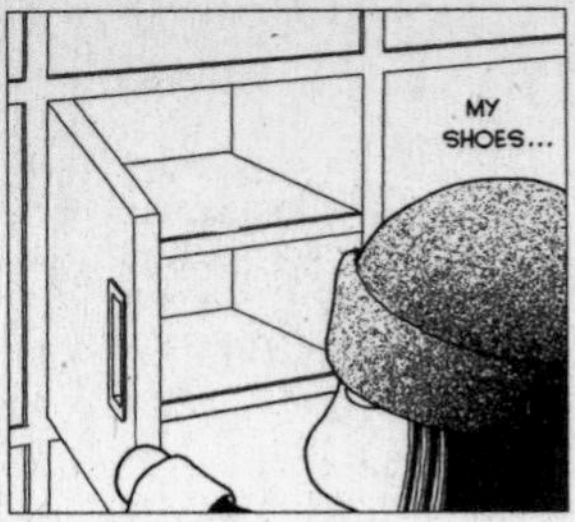
MY SHOES...

Shoe lockers (page 24)

Sunako is looking into her shoe locker. Schools in Japan have shoe lockers because students wear special indoor shoes in the classroom. Stealing a person's shoes is a common type of schoolyard mischief.

Show your love for him on Valentine's Day (page 50)

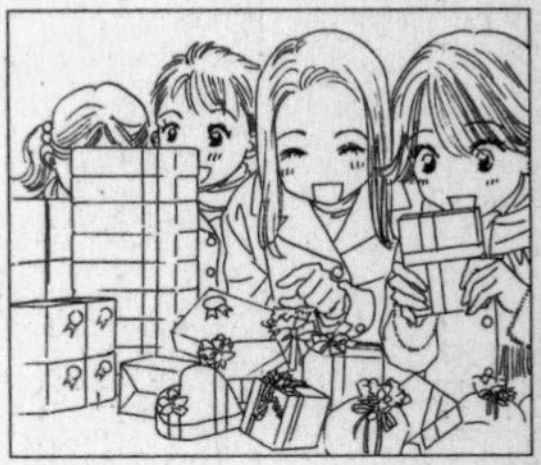

In Japan, Valentine's Day is a day when girls give boys presents. There is another holiday, called White Day, when boys give presents to the girls.

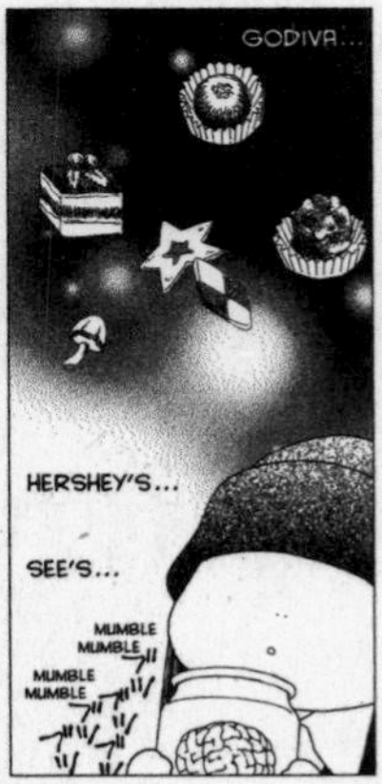
GODIVA...
HERSHEY'S...
SEE'S...
MUMBLE MUMBLE
MUMBLE MUMBLE

Chocolate makers (page 66)

Sunako actually says Godiva, Meiji, Morinaga. Meiji and Morinaga are two popular Japanese chocolate makers.

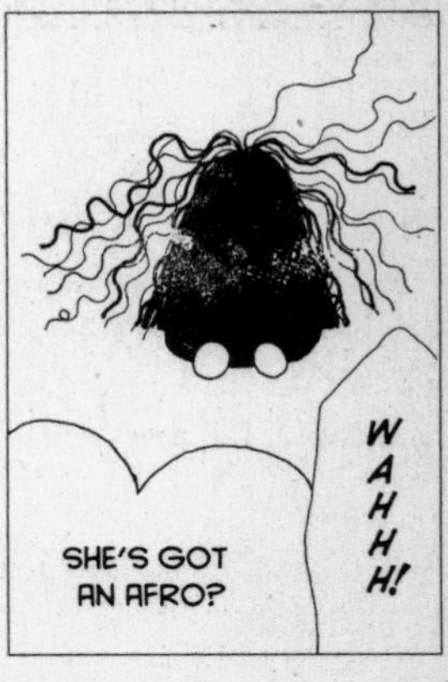
WAHHH!
SHE'S GOT AN AFRO?

Dorifu Comedy group (page 72)

The girls are actually saying "Dorifu." Dorifu is a comedy group known for a gag in which they appear in afro wigs. Apparently, Sunako looks like she's wearing an afro wig.

Akihiro Miwa (page 89)

Akihiro Miwa is a famous Japanese singer and actor.

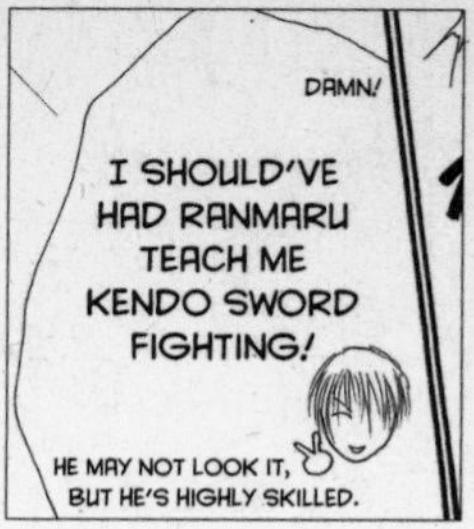
DAMN!
I SHOULD'VE HAD RANMARU TEACH ME KENDO SWORD FIGHTING!
HE MAY NOT LOOK IT, BUT HE'S HIGHLY SKILLED.

Kendo fighting (page 107)

Kendo is a style of Japanese sword play that is commonly taught in high school and college.

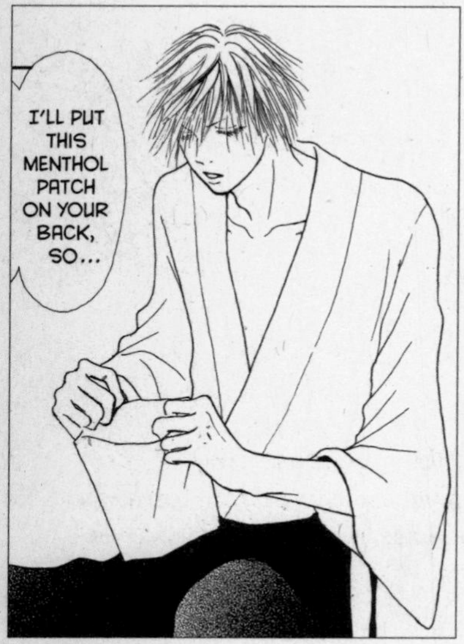
I'LL PUT THIS MENTHOL PATCH ON YOUR BACK, SO...

Shippu (page 110)

Kyohei is using a "shippu." A shippu is a stick-on bandage coated with menthol and camphor that is used to help relieve sore muscles.

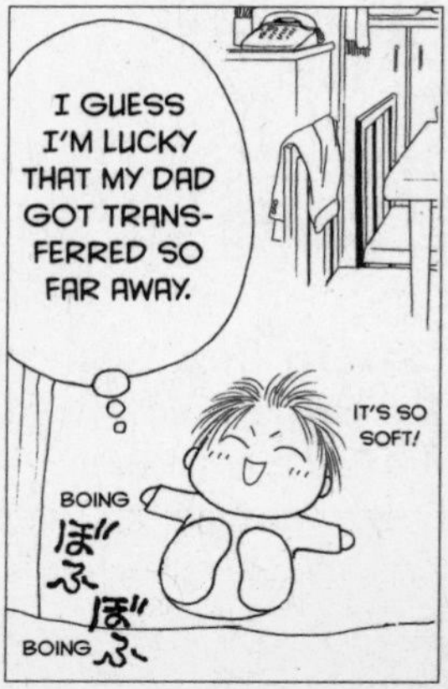
I GUESS I'M LUCKY THAT MY DAD GOT TRANS-FERRED SO FAR AWAY.
IT'S SO SOFT!
BOING ぼふ
BOING ぼふ

Work relocation (page 132)

It is common for Japanese company workers to be transferred to distant locations. Male workers are sometimes relocated far away from their families.

Ikebana (page 143)

Ikebana is the Japanese art of flower arranging.

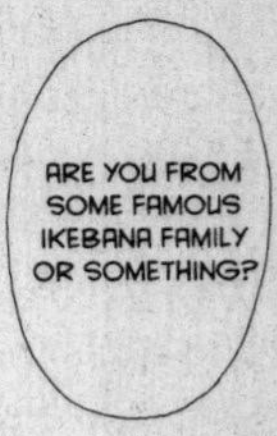
ARE YOU FROM SOME FAMOUS IKEBANA FAMILY OR SOMETHING?

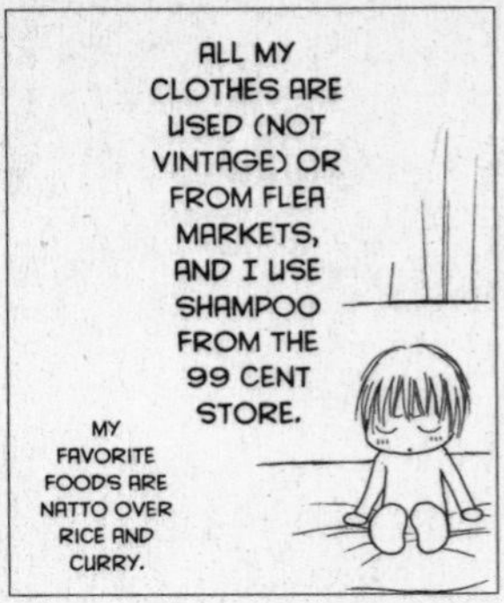
ALL MY CLOTHES ARE USED (NOT VINTAGE) OR FROM FLEA MARKETS, AND I USE SHAMPOO FROM THE 99 CENT STORE.
MY FAVORITE FOODS ARE NATTO OVER RICE AND CURRY.

Natto (page 144)

"Natto" is fermented soybeans. It is a very cheap and popular food that is famous for its strong smell and sticky, gooey consistency.

Kanji characters (page 147)

This Japanese book's title is written in Japanese kanji. There are thousands of kanji characters used in Japanese. Apparently this kanji is too difficult for Yuki to read.

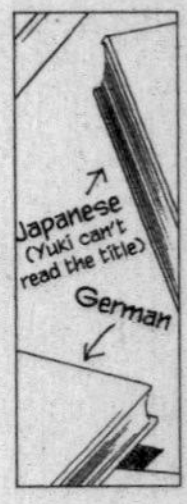
Japanese (Yuki can't read the title)
German

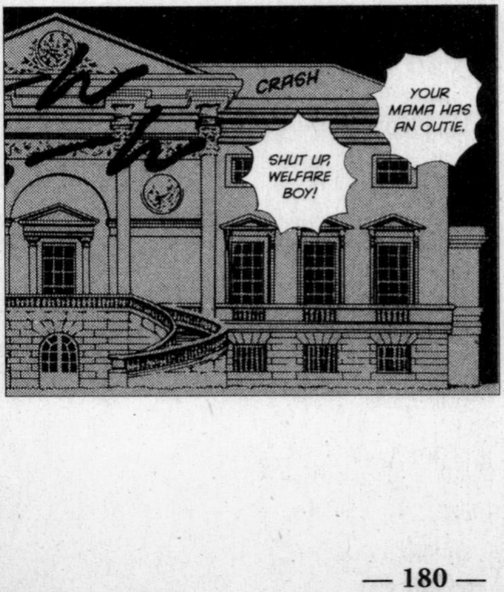
YOUR MAMA HAS AN OUTIE.
CRASH
SHUT UP, WELFARE BOY!

Outie (page 159)

This is a common insult in Japan, outie meaning "outie" belly button.

Preview of Volume 6

We're pleased to present you a preview from Volume 6. This volume will be available in English on December 28, 2005, but for now you'll have to make do with Japanese!

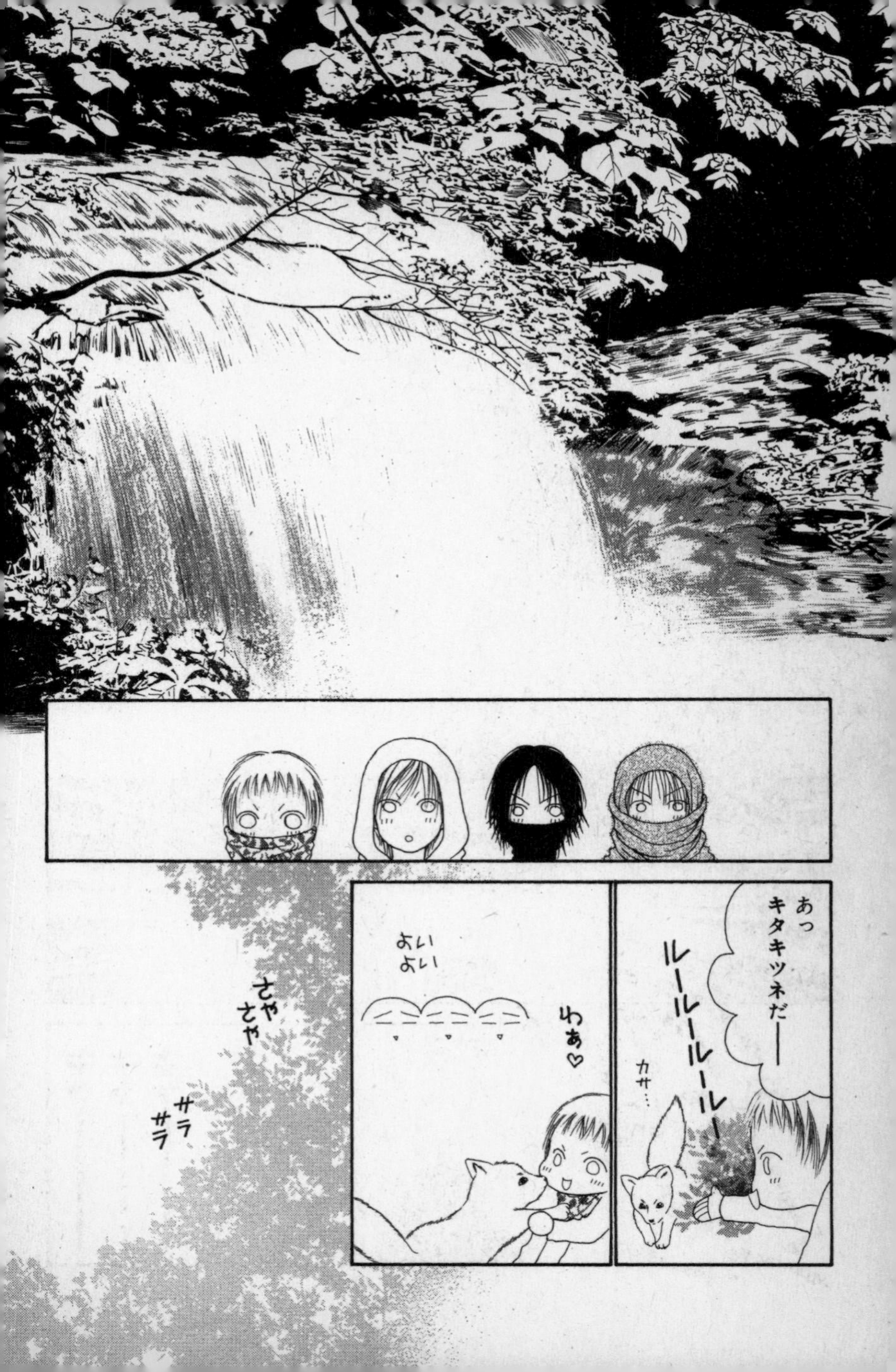
あっ
キタキツネだ——
ルールールールー
カサ…
わぁ♡
よいよい
さやさや
サラサラ

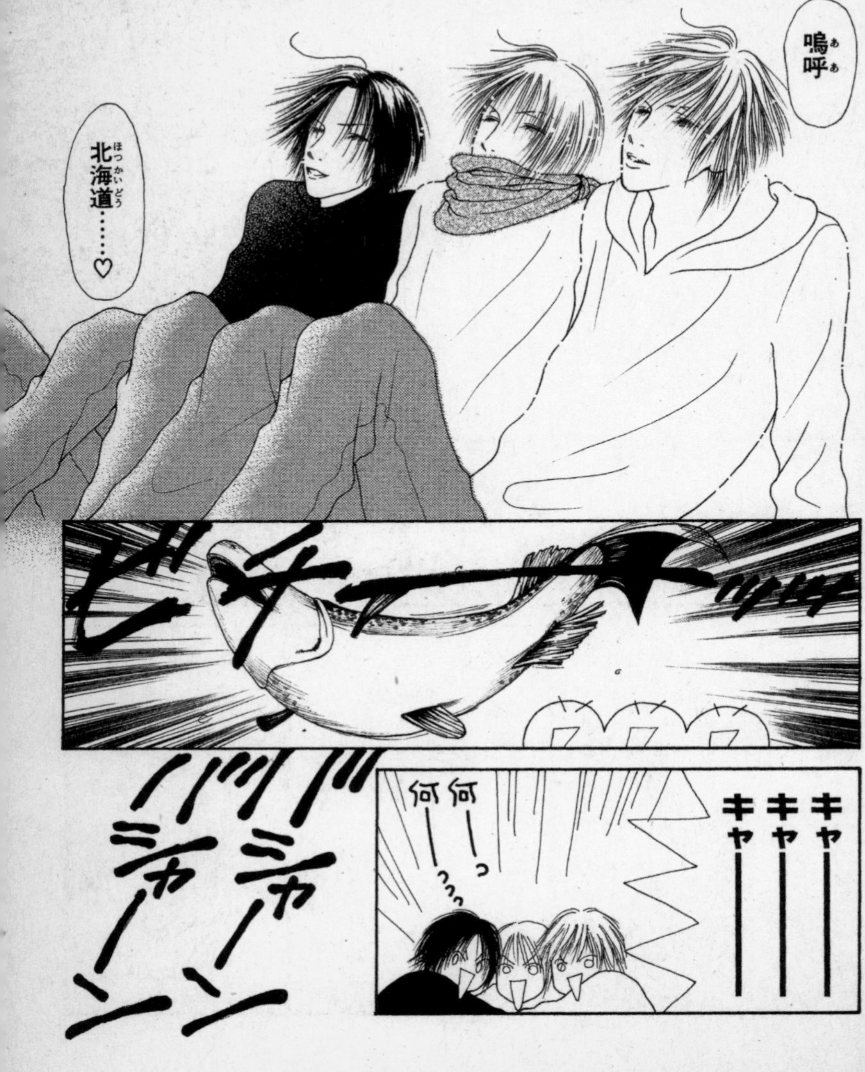
嗚呼(ああ)
北海道(ほっかいどう)……♡
ビチーーッッ
キャーー
キャーー
キャーー
何ーーっ
何ーーっっっ
バシャーン
バシャーン

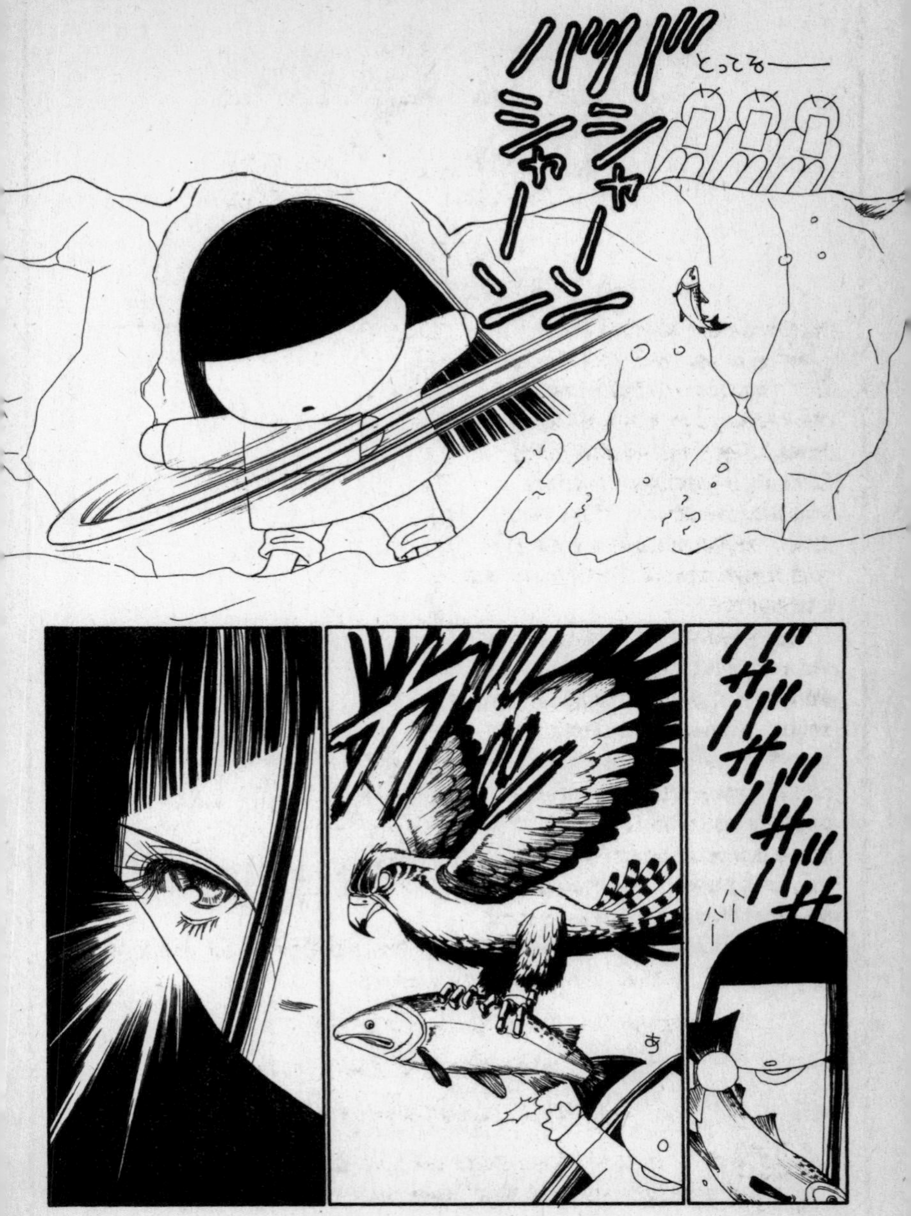

バッバ
シャーン
シャーン
とってるー
バサバサバサバサ
ハー
ハー
ガッ
あ

Guru Guru Pon-Chan

VOLUME 2
BY SATOMI IKEZAWA

Ponta is a normal Labrador Pretriever puppy, the Koizumi family's pet. Full of energy, she is always up to some kind of trouble. However, when Grandpa Koizumi, a passionate amateur inventor, creates the "Guru Guru Bone," which empowers animals with human speech, Ponta turns into a human girl!

Surprised but undaunted, Ponta ventures out of the house and meets Mirai Iwaki, the most popular boy at school. Saved by Mirai from a speeding car, Ponta reverts to her normal puppy self. Yet much has changed for Ponta during her short adventure as a human. Her heart throbs and her face flushes as she thinks of Mirai now. She is in love!

Ages 13+

Using the power of the "Guru Guru Bone," Ponta switches back and forth from dog to human, but can she win Mirai's love?

WINNER OF THE KODANSHA MANGA OF THE YEAR AWARD!

Includes special extras after the story!

VOLUME 2: On sale October 25, 2005

For more information and to sign up for Del Rey's manga e-newsletter, visit www.delreymanga.com

Othello

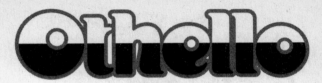

VOLUME 5

BY SATOMI IKEZAWA

TAKING MATTERS TO NEW HEIGHTS

5
Othello
satomi ikezawa

Ages: 16+

Master manipulator Megumi Hano—Hano-chan—is enraged by her failure to bring down timid Yaya Higuchi and her alter ego, the confident and boisterous Nana. So Hano-chan decides to take the ultimate revenge. Using the singing contract that Yaya desperately wishes to null and void as a means to her mean-spirited ends, Hano-chan makes her an offer. She will rip it up . . . if Yaya agrees to play a little game with her. If Yaya can catch Hano-chan and steal the contract, Hano will cancel the agreement and return the application fee. Sounds simple, yes? But there's a little hitch. Yaya must chase Hano while skydiving!

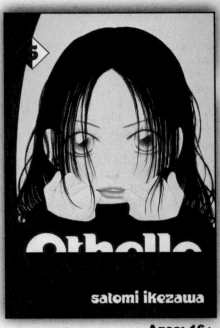

Includes special extras after the story!

VOLUME 5: On sale September 27, 2005

DEL REY

For more information and to sign up for Del Rey's manga e-newsletter, visit www.delreymanga.com

Nodame Cantabile

VOLUME 3
BY TOMOKO NINOMIYA

MUSICAL DISSONANCE

Student prodigy Shinichi Chiaki just can't shake Nodame, no matter how hard he tries. Now he is forced to tutor her and Mine all night. So much for music being comforting!

Then Shinichi gets a golden opportunity: the chance to temporarily fill in for Maestro Stresemann as conductor for the S orchestra. But after an unfortunate mishap, the maestro defects to the A orchestra and challenges Shinichi to a public-performance duel. With only weeks to prepare, can members of the inexperienced S orchestra pull themselves together to rival the confidence of the A orchestra? It's going to take a lot of hard work—and inspiration from a certain free-spirited girl with a crush. The battle Shinichi can't afford to lose has begun!

3

Nodame Cantabile
TOMOKO NINOMIYA
Winner of the Kodansha Manga of the Year Award

Ages: 16 +

Includes special extras after the story!

VOLUME 3: On sale November 29, 2005!

For more information and to sign up for Del Rey's manga e-newsletter, visit www.delreymanga.com

TOMARE!

止まれ
[STOP!]

You're going the wrong way!

Manga is a completely different type of reading experience.

To start at the *beginning*, go to the *end*!

That's right! Authentic manga is read the traditional Japanese way—from right to left. Exactly the *opposite* of how American books are read. It's easy to follow: Just go to the other end of the book, and read each page—and each panel—from right side to left side, starting at the top right. Now you're experiencing manga as it was meant to be!